MW00785152

HARRY H. WOODRING

HARRY H. WOODRING

A Political Biography of FDR's Controversial Secretary of War

by

KEITH D. McFARLAND

Handwritten annotations:

BECAME HEAD OF DEPT. OF HISTORY
GRADUATE DEAN
PRESIDENT OF TEXAS A & M
FOR 10 YEARS.

CONSIDERED THE WEAKEST MEMBER OF FDR'S CABINET. MISSY RAILED AGAINST HIM & FDR FINALLY FORCED HIM OUT.

THE UNIVERSITY PRESS OF KANSAS
Lawrence / Manhattan / Wichita

ALSO WROTE: LOUIS JOHNSON

Library of Congress Cataloging in Publication Data

McFarland, Keith D   1940-
Harry H. Woodring : a political biography of FDR's
controversial Secretary of War.

Bibliography: p.
1.   Woodring, Harry Hines, 1887-1967.
E748.W79M32   353.6'092'4 [B]   75-2336
ISBN 0-7006-0130-9

To Nancy

Preface

Few American Presidents have been more respected, admired, and loved than Franklin D. Roosevelt. In the eyes of many he was, and still is, looked upon as a man who could do no wrong. Thus, there has been a tendency to disregard, ignore, or ridicule those administrative officials who disagreed with his policies and did what they could to change them. The numerous accounts of United States foreign and military policy from 1937 through 1940 have been limited primarily to the activities of those members of the Roosevelt administration who, along with the President, worked to aid the Allies. There were, nevertheless, a few men in the War Department and in Congress who opposed sending military aid to Britain and France as long as the United States Army was so ill equipped. The men who opposed the President's military-aid policy were not ignorant or disloyal; they were intelligent, patriotic Americans who believed that such a program was endangering the national security. This is the story of one of those men.

Any person familiar with the administration of President Franklin D. Roosevelt is undoubtedly aware of many of the key figures who surrounded that well-known Chief Executive. The names of such cabinet members as Cordell Hull, Henry Morgenthau, Jr., Harry Hopkins, Harold Ickes, Frances Perkins, Henry Wallace, James Farley, Dan Roper, Claude Swanson, and Henry Stimson are all well known. There is, however, a colleague of those individuals who is virtually unheard of. That person is Harry H. Woodring, who served as Secretary of War from 1936 to mid 1940.

It is indeed surprising that Woodring should be the forgotten man of the Roosevelt administration. In terms of length of service he was by no means a short-timer, for he served on FDR's "team" for more than seven years —three as Assistant Secretary of War and four as Secretary of War. Consequently, his anonymity does not stem from a short period of public exposure. Neither should the position that he filled have contributed to his obscurity. Although the activities of the Secretary of War and the War Department are generally ignored in peacetime, such was not the case in the 1930s. With the breakdown of world peace, the matter of national defense became a major concern, and the United States military establishment became increasingly important. With the expanding influence of the Army came considerable publicity; before long, most Americans knew at least a little about Secretary of War Woodring and his activities as head of the War Department. Nor should he be forgotten and ignored because he was less significant or less interesting than other figures in the administration. His dealings with Roosevelt were extensive, and on many key issues his influence was considerable. Furthermore, it is doubtful that the story of any of Roosevelt's cabinet members is more interesting than that of Woodring. He was one of the most controversial persons of the period, having the dubious distinction of being the only man that Roosevelt ever removed from his cabinet.

A primary reason that Woodring is an "unknown" is that virtually nothing has been written of his service as Secretary of War. Many members of the Roosevelt administration who were far less important than Woodring have either written, or have collaborated on writing, accounts of their activities in that period. Woodring, however, was one of the few individuals closely associated with Roosevelt who did not write an autobiography, memoirs, or some other personal account of what took place during those years. His reasons for never attempting to explain or justify his actions are not entirely clear, but in the years immediately following his removal, Woodring did not wish to offend or embarrass President Roosevelt. Several years after the latter's death, Woodring started to work on an autobiography, but numerous business ventures, along with his policital activities, kept him from getting beyond his childhood years.

Woodring's lack of notoriety on the national scene is hardly surprising when one discovers that he is scarcely known within the confines of his home state. Even the residents of Elk City, the village from which he came, and Neodesha, the town that he considered home, seem to be unaware of, or at least unwilling to acknowledge, the fact that one of their own became Governor and later went on to influence national policy as Secretary of War.

After Woodring's removal from the cabinet in June of 1940, Duke Shoop of the *Kansas City Star* wrote: "Some day, when the next chapter of the career of Harry Woodring is written, the letters, reports, and records of the present day international intrigue—all of it centering on the issue of how far we should go in helping the Allies—will make interesting reading." It is the purpose of this study not only to write the chapter that Mr. Shoop envisioned, but also to examine, for the first time, Woodring's entire political career. Very few individuals, including historians, know who Harry Woodring was, what he attempted to do, and what he accomplished. This study will attempt to answer those questions. Perhaps, with a better understanding of the man, his problems, and his actions, it will be possible to place him in proper historical perspective.

Little did I realize when I originally undertook this study that it would ultimately involve so many people. I wish to acknowledge the help of all those who assisted me in some way, because without their help this book could never have been written. Special thanks must go to Cooper C. Woodring, of Plandome, New York, who permitted me to be the first person to examine his father's personal papers. Not only did he give me complete access to those papers, but he placed no restrictions on my use of them; his only request was that I be objective. For his cooperation plus the fine hospitality that he and his wife, Sue, showed me during the period I was going through the papers, I will be forever grateful. Thanks must also go to Melissa Woodring Jager for granting me permission to utilize her father's papers.

A number of friends and colleagues were of great help in this undertaking. I would especially like to express my appreciation to: Harry L. Coles of Ohio State University, who guided this study in its initial phase; to George H. Lobdell of Ohio University and Jack B. Gray of East Texas State University for their suggestions on ways to improve the content and style; to Debra Taylor Crawford, my typist, who somehow deciphered my handwriting and turned it into meaningful drafts and ultimately into a final manuscript; to Virginia Seaver and John H. Langley of the University Press of Kansas for their assistance and understanding in the editing and publishing of this book; to Dr. H. M. Lafferty and the Faculty Research Committee of East Texas State University for the confidence they expressed in me by the awarding of two research grants to assist in the preparation of this study. Special thanks go to my East Texas State University colleague Nancy R. Lenoir, who put her editorial pen to this work and greatly enhanced its value.

Many people took time out from their busy schedules to share with me their recollections of Harry Woodring or some aspect of his career; to all of those people, whose names appear on pages 320–22, I express my deepest gratitude. Special thanks must go to Helen Coolidge Woodring, who gave me so much time and answered so many questions on three different occasions.

Many librarians and archivists went above and beyond the call of duty to assist me in securing the materials needed. Unfortunately, not all of those who helped me can be cited here, but a few deserve special mention: Edgar Nixon and Joseph Marshall of the Franklin D. Roosevelt Library; John Taylor and Thomas Hohmann of the Modern Military Records Division of the National Archives; Philip P. Brower of the Bureau of Archives of the MacArthur Memorial; Joseph G. Gambone of the Kansas State Historical Society; and Diane Saucier of the East Texas State University Library.

Finally, most credit must go to my wife, Nancy, and to our three children, Mark, Carolyn, and Dianna, for without their encouragement, support, and understanding this book could never have been completed.

Commerce, Texas   Keith McFarland
28 April 1975

Contents

List of Illustrations

1

From Boyhood to Banker

"Is this true?" shouted Missouri Senator Bennett Clark on the floor of the Senate.[1] Many found the first reports hard to believe, but word of the cabinet shake-up soon spread throughout the capital and across the nation. Secretary of War Harry Woodring had been fired. Washington was stunned. It was early on that spring afternoon that President Franklin D. Roosevelt made the startling announcement that he had asked for and received the resignation of his controversial Secretary of War. On that day—20 June 1940— Harry H. Woodring achieved the dubious distinction of being the only man ever booted out of the Roosevelt cabinet.[2]

Throughout his tempestuous tenure in Washington, Woodring had become embroiled in numerous feuds with Roosevelt, and the President had always attempted to accommodate his contentious War Department head. When, however, the question of aid to the Allies arose, Roosevelt determined that he could no longer tolerate Woodring's divergent views. Roosevelt was a strong advocate of providing that aid, but Woodring, whose position on the issue had wavered in the past, had become a strong opponent of that course. The President could no longer accept obstructionism in his War Department. Secretary Woodring had to go.

The action created a furor in Congress, but such a response had frequently followed Harry Woodring. A number of congressmen called for an investigation into the dismissal of this patriotic American; others condemned his isolationism and the controversy within his department. Amid this at-

1

mosphere of confusion, Harry Woodring and his family quietly bid a short and pleasant farewell to Roosevelt at the White House, then headed back to Kansas in the family station wagon. Thus ended his Washington career, a major chapter in the colorful and controversial life that had begun fifty-three years before in Elk City, Kansas.

A warm spring rain was gently sponging the lush green countryside of southeast Kansas as the first light of day appeared in the eastern sky. Most of the twelve hundred residents of the small, thriving town of Elk City were not yet stirring, but in a small pink frame house on Montgomery Avenue the excited Hines Woodring was anxiously awaiting the opportunity to broadcast news of his good fortune to his many friends around town.[3] On the previous night, 30 May 1887, the fifty-one-year-old grain dealer had become a father for the sixth time. The birth of this child, however, was something special: it was the first boy.[4] This new addition to the family was like a dream come true for Hines Woodring and his thirty-eight-year-old wife, Melissa, who, after more than twenty years of marriage and five daughters, had practically given up hope of ever having a son. The proud parents first named the new child Jacob Cleveland, but after several days they had second thoughts and decided to call him Harry Hines instead.[5]

To Hines Woodring the birth of his son was quite gratifying, because it meant that he now had a male heir to carry on the family name as well as its traditions. These factors meant a great deal to the new father, who was very proud of his family heritage, even though it was not an especially distinguished one. The Woodrings pointed with pride to their lineage, which could be traced back to the Vautrin family which lived in the Lorraine section of France about the time of the Protestant Reformation. Some members of the family had become Huguenots, and when religious persecution of protestants began in 1572, they fled to Kirrberg, in Alsace. In the years that followed, the family became moderately successful farmers, soon winning a respected position in the community. It was in Kirrberg that the German influence caused the name to be changed from Vautrin to Wotring.

All went well in Alsace until the early eighteenth century, when increased persecution of Huguenots, plus continual warfare along the French-German border, forced many inhabitants to flee. One of those choosing to leave was John Daniel Wotring, who, in the summer of 1739, loaded his family on the ship *Robert and Alice* and headed for America. Arriving in Philadelphia, the family remained there for two years before moving first to York County, Pennsylvania, and then to a Moravian colony at Graceland, Maryland. From Graceland the family, whose name gradually changed to

2

Woodring, spread north into New Jersey, south into Virigina, and west to Kentucky.[6]

One of John Daniel Wotring's grandsons, John Wotring, took his new bride, Christina Wolf, to Hardin County, Kentucky, in the spring of 1796. A year later the first of their twelve children, Jacob, was born. Jacob was quite satisfied to scratch out a living on his small farm; thus, he grew to manhood, married Mary Hahn in 1822, raised six children, and died without ever leaving the hills of central Kentucky.[7] Although Jacob was content to spend his entire life in one place, such was not to be the case with his fourth child, Hines, who was born near Elizabethtown, Kentucky, on 28 January 1836. Growing up on a backwoods farm in the 1840s and 1850s was difficult, for it was no easy task raising livestock, clearing land, and harvesting crops. Since the financial returns from farming were rather limited, Hines Woodring supplemented his income by buying and selling grain and by painting houses and barns. Although such a life had its drawbacks, it also had its compensations, for it instilled in Hines Woodring a fondness for hunting, horse racing, and out-of-door living.[8]

When the Civil War came in 1861, Hines Woodring, like so many other young Kentuckians, was unsure about which side he should cast his lot with. While his sentiments were with the Union, he had reservations about joining its cause, because all four of his brothers had joined the Confederate Army. A reluctance to fight against his own kin, coupled with an unwillingness to join them, led to several years of indecision for Hines. Consequently, he remained on his farm until March of 1865.

At that time he traveled north to Lafayette, Indiana, where he enlisted in Company B, 154th Indiana Volunteer Infantry. It was less than two weeks later that General Lee surrendered to General Grant, thus ending the long and bitter war; however, because he had just entered the Army, Private Hines Woodring was not immediately mustered out. Instead he was promoted to corporal and sent to Stevenson Station, Virginia, where he guarded commissary supplies until his discharge in August 1865.[9]

Feeling that his family would not accept a "Yankee," Hines Woodring decided not to return to Kentucky. Instead he traveled to Boone County, Indiana, where he took up farming. It was here that he met, fell in love with, and, on 30 September 1866, married Melissa Jane Cooper, the daughter of Burnside and Eliza Bennett Cooper of Thorntown. The following year the first of five daughters, Mary Lou ("Effa"), was born. During the next four years Hines Woodring struggled to eke out a living on his small farm, but as the westward movement gained momentum, he longed to become a part of it. Stories of rich, cheap land in the west, along with encouraging letters from his younger brother, Dr. William Woodring, who was living in

3

Montgomery County, Kansas, convinced him that it was time to move on. So, in the early spring of 1871, he sold everything he had and headed for the "promised land."

With nothing more than the clothes on their backs and a few dollars from the sale of their farm, Hines and Melissa Woodring and four-year-old Effa set out for Kansas. Although he had come west to farm, Hines Woodring changed his mind when he arrived at the Territorial land office at Humbolt and learned that, as an inducement to settlers, free lots were available at Elk City, forty-five miles to the southwest. To obtain a lot, one simply had to build and settle on it. Never one to pass up a bargain, the Civil War veteran accepted the offer and moved to the new town, where he built a home and established a butcher shop. This new business venture failed to prosper; consequently, seven months later the Woodrings moved to a farm seven miles to the northwest. For the next six years "Hi" Woodring, as he was now called, made a living by growing corn, wheat, and sorghum on the rich farmland of Montgomery County.[10] It was during this period that three more daughters, Dolly, who died at age three, Claudine, and Lida were born. These were difficult years, for living in a flimsy, drafty house in which one froze in winter and sweltered in summer was not conducive to good health. Furthermore, Hi and his family faced the problems of contaminated water, outlaws, dust storms, drought, prairie fires, flash floods, and grasshoppers. In spite of such obstacles, farming was generally profitable for families that had several males. But for a household with only one male, it was too burdensome; thus, in 1878 Hines Woodring moved back to Elk City and entered the grain business. Upon returning to the village, which now numbered nearly four hundred, the family moved into the small pink house north of Duck Creek, where Grace was born in 1882 and Harry in 1887.[11]

From the time of his arrival in Elk City in 1871, Hines Woodring began to take an active role in local affairs. In the following years he served, at various times, as School-Board Clerk, City Clerk, City Treasurer, Councilman, and Mayor.[12] Although not active in state or national politics, Hi—except during the 1890s, when he became a Populist—openly proclaimed his allegiance to the Democratic party and voiced support for its candidates.[13] Busy as he was with his business and political pursuits, the jovial, outgoing grain dealer still found enough time for social and religious activities. He was a founder and one of the most active members of the local chapter of the Grand Army of the Republic (G.A.R), as well as a leading member of the Masons. Religion also played an important role in his life: he was for many years a deacon and Sunday School teacher in the First Christian Church. Of the many activities enjoyed by Hines Woodring, none provided

4

him with more satisfaction than horses and horse racing. This love, which he had developed as a child growing up in Kentucky, always stayed with him; and limited though the family finances were, he nearly always owned at least one race horse, which he would send around the county-fair circuit. This love of horses was one of the few things that Hines passed on to his son.[14]

Elk City was an ideal place to be raising a family in the 1880s and 1890s. Thanks in large part to two railroads—the Atchison, Topeka and Santa Fe and the Missouri Pacific—the town was quite prosperous; its grain elevators, flour mill, sorghum mill, bedspring plant, brickyard, and many lesser establishments provided employment for anyone who wanted work and was willing to do it. Discovery of both oil and gas in this area in the late nineties added to the prosperity. By the turn of the century the outlook for Elk City was indeed bright, and predictions were being made that the population would soon climb to two thousand. The economic prosperity of the town also accounted for other material assets, such as gas street lights, broad sidewalks, a good telephone system, and fine schools. Large trees and attractive homes lining the wide streets made the village on the banks of the Elk River a beautiful place in which to live. Added to this were the river and several creeks for fishing and swimming, and rolling hills for running and hiking —all of which made a first-rate place for a boy to grow to manhood.[15]

But the many merits of growing up in a town like Elk City were of little consequence to Harry Woodring. While other boys were swimming, wrestling, playing marbles and baseball, he was unable to engage in such activities. Two factors served to deny young Harry a typical childhood. The first of these was his being dominated by four overprotective sisters; the second was the increasingly difficult economic plight of his family.

Because of his numerous business, civic, and social activities, Hines Woodring did not spend much time at home. As a result, the task of rearing Harry fell upon his mother and his four older sisters. Since the sisters were between five and twenty years older than Harry, their relationship to him was more like that of mother to son instead of sister to brother. Not wanting to see their little brother get injured in any way, the sisters made sure that he was rarely out of their sight. Because they kept "Son," as they always called him, with them all the time, he never had the opportunity to engage in the activities usually enjoyed by boys of his age. Instead of playing baseball, exploring, or engaging in a good mud fight, Harry grew up keeping spotlessly clean, playing house or dolls, or doing needlework. His being surrounded by women and having little contact with his father affected Harry's dress, speech, and mannerisms. These effeminate characteristics were amusing to other boys, and after first calling him "Sissy," they settled on "Daughter," a name that plagued him until he was in high school.[16] There were some positive aspects to being raised by his sisters, the most notable being an appreciation for and a basic love of reading; thus, from an early age, Harry was surrounded by books. As he grew older, he read more and more in the area of history, politics, and current events. These reading habits were never lost; consequently, he was always aware of what was happening on the state, national, and international scenes.[17]

As influential upon "Son" Woodring's early development as the domination of his four sisters was his family's financial situation. The income of a small grain dealer in a Kansas farm town was never very large, and it was all that Hines Woodring could do to provide his wife and children with food, clothing, and the other necessities of life. The family got by well enough until 1893, when Hines, while working at the mill, fell and broke his hip. Because medical treatment was inadequate at that time, the injury failed to heal properly, and thereafter Hi Woodring could walk only with great difficulty. As a consequence of this injury he was no longer able to perform the physical tasks generally required in operating a mill. He was able to do some light work and to serve in an advisory capacity at a larger mill, but such jobs were intermittent. Since the family breadwinner was no longer able to work steadily and since no other member of the household was capable of taking up the slack, the economic condition of the Woodring family became extremely difficult. In the lean years that followed, young Harry came to know, understand, and appreciate the true meaning of poverty. It was not extreme poverty, for the members of the family never went hungry or wore rags, but neither did they experience the standard of living enjoyed by most other residents of Elk City.[18]

The economic plight of the Woodring family forced Harry out into the "cruel world" at the age of nine. A desire to help carry a share of the financial load led him to embark on his first business venture—selling popcorn. Each day after school the ambitious fourth grader would run home to pick up the corn just popped by his mother or sisters and would go from door to door, selling his product for five cents a bag. This humble beginning was never forgotten by the boy from Elk City, who, years later, was to say on numerous occasions, "I made enough money peddling popcorn from house to house to buy my own clothes, and I enjoyed it."[19]

With the rise of Populism in Kansas in the early 1890s, Hines Woodring temporarily turned his political allegiance from the Democratic to the Populist party, campaigning locally for its candidates. Such efforts paid dividends in 1897, when Hi was rewarded for his campaign activity by the newly elected Populist Governor, John W. Leedy, who appointed him a Deputy State Grain Inspector, at a salary of $75 a month.[20] The new position, which

6

required that the family move to Parsons, alleviated financial pressures. This proved to be only a temporary boon, however, because Hines lost his job when the Republicans regained control of the Statehouse in 1899. Shortly thereafter the Woodrings returned to Elk City and moved into an attractive two-story house on Maple Street.[21]

Again, hard times returned. Although the two eldest daughters, Mary Lou and Claudine, had married and moved away, there was still a house to be paid for and five mouths to feed on the irregular income and the small pension of a sixty-four-year-old Civil War veteran. To help pay the family's expenses, Harry, who was just entering his teens, began taking any job that would add a few pennies to the family coffers. The young lad was no longer afraid of getting dirty or engaging in work; thus, while other boys his age were seeking to avoid work, "Daughter" Woodring was trying to find it.[22]

The financial needs of the family, along with considerable teasing by other students, made the thought of quitting school rather appealing to Harry, but his sisters, especially Claudine, who had been a teacher before her marriage, convinced him to remain in school. Attending Elk City Grade and High School through the tenth grade, Harry always proved to be an excellent student, especially in math, government, and history.[23] Going hand in hand with his interests in the last two subjects was an interest in politics. Although he was not exactly certain what the designation meant, Harry, from the time he was a very young boy, proclaimed that he, like his father, was a Democrat. The youngster soon discovered that such claims were hazardous to one's health in a Republican state like Kansas, for on a number of occasions he was snowballed and beaten up because of his political affiliation.[24]

When the Woodrings moved into the house on Maple Street in 1899, their new neighbor was O. T. Hayward, president of the First National Bank of Elk City. During the next several years the bank president had many opportunities to observe the honesty, reliability, and perseverance of the boy next door; therefore it was not surprising that he offered the sixteen-year-old high-school student a job as janitor and errand boy at the bank. In his new position Harry made the fires, swept the floors, washed the windows, cleaned the spittoons, and ran errands; for all this he received five dollars a month.[25] No one ever started any lower in the banking profession than Woodring.

During this period he was maturing rapidly, and the youngster who had been teased and ignored by his peers became increasingly popular with members of both sexes.[26] After the first semester of his junior year at Elk City High School, Harry decided to change schools. This was a difficult decision, because he had a job and numerous friends and he was doing well

7

in school; however, he believed that the county high school, with its broader curriculum, would offer him more. His mind made up, the boy from Elk City, in January 1904, enrolled in the Montgomery County High School, at nearby Independence, Kansas. Upon Harry's departure, the editor of the *Elk City Enterprise* noted that one of the town's "rising young men" was changing schools.[27]

Although Harry did well at his new school, he was not satisfied with the type of education that he was receiving. By this time he had developed more than a casual interest in the operations of O. T. Hayward's bank, and he hoped to find permanent employment there when he completed his education. The high-school courses he was taking would be adequate, but he desired something with a more utilitarian value—courses that would help him in the bank. A business-school education was what he really wanted, but that seemed to be out of the question. While such schools could be found in Kansas City, the tuition and the cost of living there were more than the family could afford.

Never one to be defeated easily, Harry searched for and finally found a solution to his problem. Living in Lebanon, Indiana, were Louisa and Samuel Cason, an aunt and uncle. A business school—the Lebanon Business University—had recently opened in that town. What a set up!—he could live with Aunt Louisa and Uncle Samuel and attend the "University." When Harry convinced his mother to write her sister to see what she thought of the idea, the response was just what the boy had hoped for: the Casons would love to have Harry come to live with them; after all, they had no children of their own, and he could be their "son" for a while. Arrangements were made, and in June of 1904 the boy from Elk City traveled to Lebanon, where he was to spend ten enjoyable months at the beautiful home on South Meridian Street.[28]

Shortly after his arrival, Harry enrolled at the "University," which was a less-than-reputable commercial operation offering courses in bookkeeping, typewriting, commercial law, banking, correspondence, and office practice. Fortunately, the school's manager-teacher, Henry F. Raber, was a better teacher than he was a businessman, and Harry learned well the subjects and skills that were taught. This education was to be of considerable value to him in the years that followed.[29] Having completed all the courses that he felt were necessary for his future success, the young man returned home in the spring of 1905, his formal education ended.[30] Although he came close, he never did earn a high-school diploma.

Upon his return to Elk City, Harry was given a job as a bookkeeper at the First National Bank. The same good work habits, the care, and the conscientiousness that had always characterized him continued, and two years later he was rewarded by promotion to assistant cashier. These were happy but not carefree years for the young bank employee. Since his father was no longer able to do any work, the burden of caring for his parents and his sister Lida was now squarely on his shoulders. This responsibility to his family caused the young banker to question seriously his future in Elk City. He had a steady job, but it did not pay especially well; furthermore, his future in the bank did not appear bright, because the once thriving village was now in a state of decline. The oil and gas finds of the 1890s were playing out; hundreds of Elk City citizens were leaving for new fields; and it was evident that the village had already reached its peak and was now on the way down. Such a community is unattractive to any businessman, but it is especially discouraging to someone in the field of banking. Under these circumstances Harry Woodring began to look for greener pastures.[31]

An opportunity to move came early in 1909, when Harry was offered a job, which he accepted, as an assistant cashier at the First National Bank of Neodesha.[32] Neodesha, a thriving town of three thousand, which lay twenty miles northeast of Elk City, was, at that time, the center of the Mid-Continent Oil Field. The rapidly expanding gas and oil industries provided the basis for the economic expansion of the town.[33] Since new people were arriving daily, new businesses were being established, and land values were going up. Neodesha was definitely a town with a bright future, and Harry Woodring was glad to be a part of it. The twenty-two-year-old assistant bank cashier worked hard at his new job, and within a few months he was promoted to cashier. Feeling more financially secure than at any time in his life, he purchased a home on North Eighth Street and brought his parents and his sister Lida to live with him.[34]

The move to Neodesha in 1909 ushered in what proved to be the nine most uneventful years in the life of Harry Woodring. The routine was nearly always the same: five days a week he would walk to work, put in the short work day that made a bank employee the envy of his neighbors, walk home, work in his garden, and spend the evening reading and looking after his parents. Because of a deep sense of obligation to his parents, he insisted on remaining at home and helping Lida look after them; consequently, he engaged in few outside activities, and he had few friends.[35] Occasionally he would go to a movie, play tennis, or have a date with Helen McDonald, whose father, J. C. McDonald, was President of Standard Oil of Kansas. One was more likely, however, to find him spending a quiet evening at home.[36] Sunday would find Harry at the First Christian Church, where he was one of the most faithful and hard-working members. Although his interest in state and national politics was increasing in these years, he did not engage in any political activities.

9

At the time that the United States entered World War I in the spring of 1917, it is highly unlikely that anyone, including those closest to him, would have predicted a bright future for the thirty-year-old introvert, who appeared to be destined to spend the rest of his life as a cashier in a small-town bank. When the newly enacted Selective Service System went into effect, it did not call Harry Woodring; and because his mother, father, and sister were dependent upon him, he was not inclined to join. For a time it appeared that the war would pass him by, but when his mother suffered a stroke and passed away in January 1918, Harry felt that a major burden had been taken off his shoulders; he was then free to leave his family and join the Army. He agreed to remain at home until the spring thaw permitted burial of his mother's body.[37] Interment came on 5 May 1918, and later that afternoon Harry was on his way to Washington, D.C., to enlist in the United States Army.[38] On his own initiative he was giving up the secure life of a banker for the uncertain but, in all likelihood, more exciting life of a soldier.

The nation's capital was a beehive of activity when Woodring arrived in May of 1918. Everywhere he went, people were busy doing their share to help win the war that would "make the world safe for democracy." The young man from Neodesha would have liked to spend several days touring the city, but he had more pressing matters to take care of. Since he was not one to take a major decision lightly, the choice of which branch of the military to serve in was of great importance. In order to be sure that he got both sides of the story, he visited both the War Department and the Navy Department to discuss the opportunities that each offered. On his return to the War Department, he encountered a young lieutenant in the Tank Corps, who told him of the advantages and opportunities in this new branch of the Army. Convinced that the tank was the weapon of the future and that the Tank Corps was the branch most likely to offer opportunity for promotion, he moved in that direction. He enlisted on May 8, and three days later Private Harry Woodring was on his way to the Tank Training Center at Camp Colt, near Gettysburg, Pennsylvania.[39]

The training of Tank Corps personnel that took place at Camp Colt consisted of both basic military training and specialized training in tank tactics and equipment. The camp was under the command of a bright, aggressive young officer, Maj. Dwight D. Eisenhower, who had more than his share of problems—the biggest being the lack of tanks. Although the weapon of the future was on the drawing board, America had not yet started to produce them; therefore, Eisenhower had only one tank, a French Re-

10

nault, with which to train the ten thousand officers and men stationed at Colt. Under such circumstances, training was limited primarily to that of a basic nature.[40]

Upon his arrival at Camp Colt, Woodring, because of his clerical background, was immediately sent to the personnel section of Casual Company Number 1 (the camp's administrative company), where a typist was needed. For the next three months Private Woodring lived a rather leisurely and pleasant life, processing records of new recruits and making up pay records.[41] His job frequently necessitated working late or arising at two or three o'clock in the morning to help process the records of incoming personnel. Although such a position meant irregular working hours, it also meant extended periods of free time. On some days it meant no work at all; consequently, there was considerable opportunity for sleeping, playing tennis and baseball, and writing letters home. Under such circumstances, securing a pass was no problem, and Woodring and his buddies frequently went into Gettysburg for supper, church, a dance, or a movie.[42]

Although the nature of his duties exempted Harry from some facets of military life, such as reveille and K.P., he did receive training in close order drill, radio and telegraph operation, riflery, and the care and operation of machine guns and light artillery. Except for a violent reaction to his typhoid shots, several instances of food poisoning, and dysentery, Woodring was quite pleased with army life. His satisfaction certainly had to stem from other than monetary reasons, because the deduction of a $15 allotment to his father left him only $8 a month.[43]

From the time that Woodring arrived at Camp Colt he expressed a desire to become an officer, but it soon became apparent that competition for entrance into Officer's Training School was very stiff. His first attempt to gain entrance into the school was unsuccessful, but in August he tried again and succeeded.[44] His joy was short lived when he realized that he had won only half the battle; the mark of success was in finishing the school rather than in getting into it.[45] The purpose of the schooling and of its difficulty was best described by the Camp Commander, then Lieutenant Colonel Eisenhower, who stated that it "was intended primarily as a place of elimination of unfit candidates for commission, and . . . it was purposely made as intensive as possible, in order to quickly eliminate the unfit."[46]

On 25 August 1918 Woodring, along with five hundred other enlisted men, entered the Tank Corps Officers Training School, thus beginning five grueling weeks of training. The physical demands were great, for the days were long and hard, with vigorous physical training, close order drill, rifle-range firing, and cross-country hiking requiring a physical stamina that Woodring did not know he possessed. Just as strenuous were the mental

11

demands that resulted from classroom instruction and follow-up examinations in such subjects as communications, tank operations and tactics, reconnaissance, artillery principles, and administrative affairs. Predictably, the "wash out" rate was high, and Woodring himself frequently felt that he would not make it. On September 9, less than three weeks into the program, he wrote in his diary: "Hanging on to school by a thin thread." On the following day, after three interviews with evaluating officers, he sheepishly wrote: "Bobbing up and down but still here." A week later he was almost ready to give up, because he was convinced that there was "little hope for me."[47] Still, he carried on, working as hard as he could. When the original 500 students dropped to 300 and then to 250, he still remained; then on 24 September he survived the final cut, thus making him one of the 150 members of his class to earn a commission. On 6 October, in what he described as "one of the greatest satisfactions of my life," Woodring was commissioned a second lieutenant in the Army Tank Corps.[48] Two days later he received his new assignment: he was to return to Casual Company as its Personnel Officer. He was pleased to return to Casual, because he had many friends there, and he understood the operations of the Personnel Section. As the new lieutenant settled into his first assignment, the war in Europe was rapidly coming to a close. Several weeks later the Armistice was signed, and one week after that, Camp Colt was abandoned, and most of its personnel, including Woodring, were sent to Fort Dix, New Jersey, for mustering out. At Dix he continued to function as a personnel officer until his discharge on 15 December 1918.[49]

Woodring's encounter with the Army during the war was both pleasing and gratifying. Because of the nature of his duties, the winning of a commission, and the many fine acquaintances that he had made, he left the military with a positive attitude towards it and its leaders. Perhaps one of the most satisfying aspects of his "Army days" was the start of many friendships that were to last a lifetime, including those with Dwight D. Eisenhower and Floyd L. Parks (later a lieutenant general of World War II fame).[50] But even more important to Woodring was the change that the Army made in his personality. The new way of life brought about a metamorphosis in him; the introvert of Neodesha emerged as an extrovert at Camp Colt, and before long he had a large circle of close friends.[51] The man leaving Fort Dix in December 1918 was also quite different in that he had a confidence in himself that theretofore had been lacking. The bumps and bruises of army life had also done much to dull and eliminate some of his effeminate traits. As one close relative said, "Harry was a different man when he came out of the army—he was a man—it took the sissyness out of him."[52] There was no question that the Army had been beneficial for Harry Woodring.

After being discharged from the Army, Woodring returned to Neodesha, uncertain about his future plans. His old job was awaiting him at the First National Bank, but because he felt that there was little opportunity for advancement in that position, he decided to look elsewhere. One thing was certain: he wanted to remain in banking. Thus, after failing to obtain a job as a state bank examiner, he accepted a job as assistant cashier at the Mid-West National Bank in Kansas City, Missouri.[53] For the next three years he lived a quiet life, working in Kansas City during the week and returning home on the weekends to visit his father and sister or to take out Helen McDonald, whom he had continued to date intermittently for a number of years. One of the things that Harry liked most about dating Helen was that when he went to pick her up he had an opportunity to visit with her father, J. C. McDonald. Every time the two men got together the talk inevitably turned to banking and finance, for in addition to being President of Standard Oil of Kansas, McDonald was President of the First National Bank of Neodesha. McDonald was quite impressed with Woodring's knowledge of banking, and as time passed, he became increasingly fond of him.[54] This relationship was to pay big dividends to Woodring in March 1922, when a major reorganization of the bank was undertaken, and McDonald asked him to become its managing director.[55] The thirty-five-year-old assistant cashier jumped at the opportunity, returning home to undertake his new job.

For the next seven years Woodring ran the bank in an efficient and businesslike manner. With common sense and a good eye for property values, he succeeded in creating one of the strongest banks in southeast Kansas.[56] Woodring's business acumen not only made money for the bank's stockholders; it also resulted in some handsome returns for himself. By making some wise investments, both locally and in a bullish stock market, he accumulated enough funds to purchase a controlling interest in the bank and make himself vice-president. His success soon won for him the respect and admiration of local civic and business leaders, as well as the community at large. Word of his effectiveness soon spread to others in his profession, and they honored him with a term as Vice-President of the Kansas Bankers Association.[57]

Being a small-town banker brought with it a number of community responsibilities, and soon Woodring found himself thrust into a number of business, civic, and fraternal activities. The cordiality that had emerged at Camp Colt now became a major asset, and the personable, yet soft-spoken, bachelor gained an increasingly wide circle of friends and acquaintances. As the 1920s rolled on, Woodring emerged as one of the major "work horses" of the community.

Much of his time was spent in promoting the economic well-being of Wilson County and the surrounding area, for the success of his bank was dependent on the prosperity of the entire section. Because agriculture was of primary importance to the area, Woodring worked hard to promote programs that would aid farmers and increase their production. As an active member of the Grange and the Farm Bureau, he came to gain a deeper understanding of the many problems facing the farmer. The desire to help the tiller of the soil increase production led him to play a major role in creating Southeast Kansas Incorporated and the Wilson County Banker-Farmer Lime and Legume Project. In the latter program, Woodring, who believed that bankers should serve as liaison between agricultural specialists and farmers, gained state and national prominence by establishing a program whereby county bankers brought farmers together with county farm agents and state agricultural experts to set up test areas in order to demonstrate the value of certain methods of fertilization. The results were so successful that other farmers, after witnessing the increased yields, quickly adopted the new methods. In May 1926 even Governor Ben S. Paulen came to Wilson County to observe the project and to talk with the man responsible for it, Harry Woodring. The Governor came away quite impressed with the program and its coordinator.[58]

In 1927 Woodring joined with a dozen other prominent leaders from a nine-county area to form Southeast Kansas Incorporated, a regional organization designed to promote the agricultural, industrial, and commercial development of the area. For several years the Neodesha banker served as chairman of the group's Agricultural Committee.[59] While serving in that capacity, he became increasingly concerned over the damage that annual flooding inflicted on the rich Kansas farmlands. In the spring of 1927 devastating floods hit the valleys of the Ohio and Mississippi rivers, and because of his knowledge in this matter, Woodring was sent as a delegate to the Mississippi Flood Control Conference, which was held in Chicago in June. Coming away from the session with the firm belief that flood control was a government responsibility, both at the state and the federal level, he called on Governor Paulen to take action that would help alleviate the problem of flooding.[60] The Governor responded favorably to the proposal by calling a statewide Flood Control Conference in September, and subsequently he appointed Woodring to serve as a member and Secretary of the ad hoc Flood Control and Water Conservation Commission, the body that was largely responsible for the drafting of the Kansas Conservatory Act of 1929. The

14

Sunflower State was now headed toward effective flood control, and the man from Neodesha had done much to start it on its way.[61]

Although he was busy working at the bank and promoting areawide economic development, Woodring still found time for many other activities. It was in these years that he became an avid bridge player, and he and his sister Lida frequently had another couple over to their house for an evening of cards. Home gardening activity also began to increase in 1926, when he bought a large two-story house set on a four-acre plot at the corner of First and Wisconsin streets. Harry and his elderly father spent considerable time outside, working on the grounds and maintaining the large vegetable garden that graced the east side of the home.[62] As in the past, he continued to be one of the most active members of the First Christian Church, where he taught Sunday School, sponsored the Christian Endeavor group, and served as a deacon.[63] Although he spent considerable time working at his home, church, and bank, he increasingly engaged in activities outside their purview. He was now going out more than ever: afternoons were spent on the tennis courts; evenings at the movies; and Saturday nights at nearby Independence, watching the fights.[64] Membership in the Masons, who had numerous activities, also added to his social life.

Of all the activities, both business and social, that he engaged in during the 1920s, none offered Woodring more enjoyment and satisfaction or meant more to his subsequent career than did his membership in the American Legion. In June of 1919 the Tank Corps veteran had become a charter member of Neodesha's Seward-Ayers Post of the American Legion.[65] During the next three years in Kansas City he maintained his membership in that organization, even though he was not active in its affairs. Then in 1922, upon his return to Neodesha, he plunged into the post's activities with unbounded enthusiasm.[66] His superior cooking ability, which he had gained from his sisters, was a major asset to Woodring and the local group, for he was able to turn their picnics, fish frys, and stag dinners into first-class feasts. His culinary magic, along with his pleasing personality and tremendous enthusiasm, soon made him one of the most popular and respected members of the group. When, in 1925, Harry's fellow Legionnaires elected him to the first of two consecutive terms as Post Commander, they had no idea that the election would start Woodring down a road that would lead to the Statehouse and the highest echelons of the federal government.[67]

Under Woodring the Seward-Ayers Post became one of the largest and most active in the state. His success in acquiring new members soon caught the attention of state Legion officials, and in 1927 he was made Chairman of the State Membership Committee. Although the national membership of the Legion was increasing, the fortunes of the Kansas group were sagging, for it had lost nearly 1,800 members during the preceding year. Woodring met the challenge of declining numbers with his usual zeal and enthusiasm, and in the following year the state organization added more than 1,000 men to its rolls, increasing its membership from 17,924 to 19,009.[68]

As State Membership Chairman, Woodring had the opportunity to visit posts throughout the state. Before long he was known by Legion officials all over Kansas as one of the most dedicated and hard-working members of the Kansas Department. His labors were rewarded in September 1928, when, at the state convention held in Pittsburg, he was elected State Commander.[69]

Heading one of the most active Legion departments in the country was practically a full-time job, requiring the expenditure of considerable amounts of time on business and administrative matters and even more time attending and promoting local Legion activities. Each week found Commander Woodring visiting two, three, or four local posts in order to participate in or observe one of their activities. Believing that one of his major responsibilities was to make the public aware of the programs and activities of the American Legion, Woodring used every possible opportunity to appear before local civic and service groups to tell about his organization. Wherever he went, he used his position and influence to meet local politicians and businessmen and to speak to the Lions Club, the Rotary Club, and other civic groups. Before long he was known to thousands of people from one end of Kansas to the other.[70] As State Commander, Harry Woodring began to experience a new way of life, which included attending conferences and conventions, making speeches, traveling, meeting people, and being wined and dined. While it was a new and busy style of life, it was also exciting, and the man from Neodesha loved every minute of it.

As Woodring became more deeply involved in the activities of the Legion, his interest in the bank declined. At the same time that his enthusiasm for business started on the downswing, he began to toy with the idea of entering politics. This new interest, which had long manifested itself in a keen awareness of state and national affairs, was stimulated by the growing awareness of his oratorical skill as well as by the sense of influence and power that he experienced while serving as a spokesman for twenty thousand Legionnaires. Because he had the glitter of politics in his eyes, the prospect of spending the rest of his life as a small-town banker became less and less appealing.[71] Furthermore, Woodring had always liked a challenge, and banking no longer seemed to be able to provide that challenge. Since he had risen from janitor to vice-president and majority stockholder of a successful bank, there did not seem to be much more to achieve in that profession.

Early in 1929, shortly after the death of his father, Woodring began seriously to consider selling his interest in the First National Bank. In March, when he heard that some directors were trying to "sell out from under him," he beat them to the punch by selling out first. Two weeks later he severed all relations with the bank and announced that his plans for the future were uncertain. Thus, the moderately wealthy bachelor had, at the age of forty-one, retired from the occupation that had been so good to him.[72] His retirement from banking came at a most fortunate time for Woodring, because seven months later came the great stock-market crash and a subsequent rash of bank failures. In leaving his profession of nearly twenty-five years, Woodring brought one career to an end, but he was about to embark on a new and more exciting one.

2

Venture into Politics

When forty-one-year-old Harry Woodring left the banking business in the spring of 1929, it was not with the intention of retiring, but with the idea of striking out in a new direction. Although he announced that his future plans were "indefinite," he had, during the previous twelve months, been formulating plans to pursue a career in politics.[1]

Woodring's decision to become a politician was not really surprising in light of his lifelong interest in history, government, and contemporary affairs and his love of displaying oratorical skill. While the decision to enter the rough-and-tumble world of politics can be understood in view of his deep interest, it is difficult to comprehend when one considers his slim chances of achieving success in such an endeavor. In entering the Kansas political arena—particularly at that time—Woodring had two major handicaps. First, because he had had no political experience and had not been active in party affairs, he was not only politically naïve, he also lacked the close personal acquaintances and associations so essential in gaining party support. His second, and most important, handicap was his political affiliation: he was a Democrat, and for a member of that party to seek political office in "Republican" Kansas was almost tantamount to political suicide.[2]

While Woodring's desire to enter politics may have gone back to the early 1920s, he did not express such an idea until 1928. Early in that year Woodring indicated to several leading Democrats in his section of the state that he wished to seek political office—preferably a seat in the United States

18

House of Representatives.[3] Such expressions were well received by the officials of the Democratic party, who were always on the lookout for promising candidates, especially ones like Woodring who could go a long way in financing their own campaigns. With the encouragement and support of Carl V. Rice, a Parsons attorney who was chairman of the Third Congressional District Committee, Woodring set out to build up his candidacy. To make his name and face familiar to people throughout his congressional district, Woodring made numerous nonpartisan speeches on such things as the Lime and Legume Project, flood control, and current affairs. He also used his position as State Chairman of the American Legion Membership Committee to visit and talk to every Legion post in the district.[4]

Although he made a good impression and was well received by the dozens of groups before which he appeared that spring, his enthusiasm for seeking a congressional seat waned as the tide of "Coolidge Prosperity" increasingly convinced him that 1928 would be an unusually bad year for Kansas Democrats. Feeling that this would not be the time to try to unseat the Republican incumbent, Congressman W. H. Sproul, Woodring decided instead to seek election as State Commander of the American Legion.[5] While his support of and loyalty to the Legion were genuine, there can be little doubt that he was constantly aware of the opportunity for public exposure that the position afforded.[6]

As previously noted. Woodring not only won the state commandership, he also used that position to make his name and face familiar to thousands of people throughout Kansas. It was in late 1929 that Woodring, who still had his eye on the Third Congressional District seat, attended a Legion meeting in Parsons, Kansas, at which Harold McGugin, a Coffeyville attorney and a Republican member of the state legislature, spoke. In a private conversation after the meeting, McGugin, a good friend of Woodring's who had been instrumental in getting him elected State Commander of the Legion, revealed that he was going to try to unseat Congressman Sproul in the upcoming primary. This revelation was quite upsetting to Woodring, who believed that McGugin had a good chance to win the Republican nomination; should this occur, it meant that he and McGugin would be facing each other in the general election. Unwilling to face the prospect of a political battle with a good friend, Woodring, in December 1929, decided to give up his idea of trying to go to Congress.[7]

The decision to abandon the congressional race did not mean that the former banker from Wilson County was forsaking politics: it merely meant that he was looking in another political direction. He turned his sights from Washington to Topeka and the governorship of Kansas. This idea seemed rather foolhardy to everyone except Woodring himself, for the gubernatorial prospects of a Democrat who was a political novice were not very promising. Nevertheless, the fact that the state of Kansas had elected only three Democratic Governors in its seventy-six-year history did not discourage him. He felt that his statewide acquaintances, along with difficulties in the state Republican organization and a possible nationwide reaction against the country's growing economic ills, could pave the way for victory.[8]

Initially, many of the Democratic leaders in the state were not very enthusiastic about Woodring's candidacy. This coolness stemmed from two basic factors. First, they resented having a political upstart—a man who had done nothing for the party in the past—seek the nomination for such a high post. Because it had long been the accepted practice in Kansas Democratic circles to give nominations for key posts to loyal party members as a reward for years of faithful service, they felt that Woodring was attempting to cut in on some Democrat who was more deserving. The second major reason for the party's coolness toward his candidacy was the fear that the young, ambitious Woodring might wage a vigorous—and expensive—campaign. Believing that the Republican Governor, Clyde M. Reed, would be unbeatable in 1930, a number of Democrats were opposed to spending the party's limited campaign funds on a hopeless race.

Woodring's first major break in attaining the governorship came in late December 1929, when Carl Rice, who was still chairman of the Third District Democratic Committee, agreed to support his candidacy. Although Rice seemed to doubt that his friend could go all the way, he felt that the publicity gained in the campaign would help set him up for a subsequent campaign for the governorship or a congressional seat.

Woodring's venture into politics officially got underway at Pittsburg, Kansas, on 9 January 1930, when the Third District caucus—with Rice and his influential wife, Ruth, wielding their influence—endorsed him as the party's nominee for Governor.[9] Two weeks later, on 24 January, the candidate announced that his "hat was in the ring." At that time he called for lower taxes and set the major theme of his campaign by citing the state's "due need of a business administration," which he could provide. Just what such a business administration would entail was left conveniently vague.[10] The former banker had thus taken the plunge into politics and had done so virtually alone. He had the verbal support of a few Democrats from southeast Kansas, but that was about all. When Woodring opened his primary-campaign headquarters in the Jayhawk Hotel in Topeka in early April, he had no organization and no funds except his own, which were not extensive. His campaign started out as near to a one-man show as was possible.[11]

If securing the support of Carl Rice had been Woodring's first major break, his second came in early April, when he succeeded in getting John W.

Wells, the chairman of the Democratic State Committee, to manage his primary campaign. Convincing the politically experienced Wells, who had numerous contacts in the party, to cast his lot with him was a tremendous coup for Woodring; it gave his campaign a big boost. Wells's astuteness was immediately displayed by the manner in which he resigned his chairmanship of the state party. Instead of stepping down in a quiet manner, he tendered his resignation with considerable fanfare, indicating that he was leaving his important post in order to manage Woodring's campaign. In this fashion the new manager succeeded in gaining considerable statewide publicity for himself, his party, and his candidate.[12]

Facing Woodring in the primary was Noah L. Bowman, a seventy-year-old lawyer from Garnett. Bowman, who had announced his candidacy in February, was a refined old gentleman who had served in both houses of the legislature and was currently a member of the House. Nearly four decades of legal and political activity—some as a Populist, but most as a Democrat—had put him in good stead with many old party leaders, including the former Democratic Governor Jonathan M. Davis.[13]

Woodring's strategy in the primary campaign was to win the nomination by appealing to the younger members of the party without incurring the wrath of the old-line members; thus, throughout the contest he carefully sought to avoid attacking the elderly Bowman, his ideas, or his supporters. Party unity was the name of the game, and in order to maintain that unity and still win the nomination, Woodring had to attack the corrupt Republicans and convince the majority of Democrats that he was the best man to cope with the state's problems. Throughout the contest, Woodring divided his time between telling what was wrong with the Republicans and what was right about Harry Woodring. Highlighting nearly every speech were references to Governor Reed and the Republican machine that controlled the state legislature through the use of patronage, a call for an end to the "present intolerable situation," and a claim that the "only hope of the people" was the election of a good, qualified Democratic Governor—namely himself.[14] Both his campaign literature and his speeches emphasized that he was the type of man who could best provide the business administration that Kansas so drastically needed. Frequent mention was also made of his Legion and business activities, especially his outstanding banking career, the implication being that since he had succeeded in those endeavors, he could certainly do the same in the business of running the state.[15] Although he promised to provide efficiency, economy, and tax reductions, Woodring never explained how he would do so. After all, he was trying to sell himself, not a program; that would come in the general election.

During this campaign, Woodring capitalized on three of his major assets: oratorical skill, boundless energy, and age. Those Kansans who came to hear the short, balding candidate give a speech were rarely disappointed. His forceful delivery and the ability to express his thoughts and ideas clearly, along with a rather folksy approach, enabled him to get and hold the attention of practically any audience. While his poor command of grammar alarmed some individuals, his overall effectiveness as a public speaker generally caused them to overlook that fault.[16] In fact, his poor English was probably an asset rather than a liability while he was campaigning in rural Kansas. Woodring benefited not only from the quality of his speeches, but from the quantity of them as well. Because he was a very vigorous man, he was able to pursue a hectic and demanding schedule. As one newspaper noted during the course of the campaign, he "appears here, there and everywhere that two or three people gather together."[17] He traveled continually, frequently giving three or four speeches daily. In the hot, dusty days of June and July 1930, he traveled to 94 of the state's 105 counties in quest of votes, and his pace was so lively that even the staff of his own headquarters had difficulty keeping up with him.[18]

Age was another asset utilized by Woodring. He emphasized his relative youth and the need for young blood in the governorship; and when the press continually reported that he was forty years old, he did nothing to let it know that he was actually forty-three. It was not long before he was recognized as the candidate of the younger crowd in his party, and the fact that the contest was essentially a young-old feud was openly acknowledged. The young, or Woodring, faction had the support of Jouett Shouse—former national committeeman from Argonia, who was serving as chairman of the Democratic National Executive Committee—and national committeeman Dudley Doolittle of Strong City. This group was aligned against the old, conservative Jonathan Davis–Noah Bowman wing of the party.

Bowman, in spite of his age, carried on a rather spirited campaign, making hundreds of appearances and claiming that he would cut taxes considerably.[19] The financial advantage of the old-crowd candidate over his opponent enabled him to spend considerably more on campaign literature and advertising. Since Woodring's funds were rather limited, his newspaper advertising was practically nil; however, John Wells came up with several innovations that were quite successful in getting maximum publicity for the campaign dollar.[20] By occasionally using an airplane to fly into a rural community to make a speech, Woodring received more attention than a dozen ads would have brought, because large crowds came out to see the landing and the takeoff in a nearby pasture, and local newspapers gave considerable publicity to such events.[21] Movietone advertising—a two-minute film pitch by Woodring—was used at several large theaters, and a number of radio

22

speeches were made in the week before the election.[22] The bulk of the campaigning was on a much more economical scale: generally Woodring, accompanied by a friend, drove from town to town, where they set up a public-address system on the square, and the candidate made a speech. Winning the vote of the gentler sex was likewise done at minimum cost, with female members of local "Woodring for Governor" clubs sponsoring "Woodring Bridge Parties," which provided an afternoon of bridge, cookies, and ice cream.[23] Such innovations enabled the political newcomer from Neodesha to run his campaign on a shoestring.

When the primary campaign came to a close on 4 August, a tired Harry Woodring was confident that he would win the nomination, because, as he said, "The Democrats of this state have come to the conclusion that the nomination of a businessman, rather than a politician, would prove more beneficial to the common people."[24] This optimism was apparently warranted, because on the following day Kansas Democrats went to the polls and cast 37,888 votes for Woodring and only 26,321 for Bowman.[25] The younger crowd was now in control. Although pleased by his victory, Woodring was not inclined to celebrate. He realized that the real challenge was just beginning. Getting the nomination was the easy part of the journey to the governor's mansion; the difficult road lay ahead. Exhausted by months of traveling, speaking, and shaking hands, the newly chosen Democratic nominee decided to spend several weeks resting for the vigorous campaign that lay ahead. As he relaxed and reflected on the primary, he was gratified that the contest "was conducted in a clean, constructive manner and resulted in no personal animosity or bitterness" among the state's Democrats.[26] Fortunately for Woodring, Kansas Republicans could not make the same claim.

Whereas the Democratic primary had been a gentlemanly, refined, and rather dull contest which had ended with party unity still intact, the Republican contest had been an exciting knock-down-drag-out affair which ended with the defeat of the incumbent Governor and with the party split wide open. This was nothing new, for factionalism had rocked the Republican party in Kansas throughout the 1920s as the old-guard conservatives and the progressives fought to gain the upper hand.[27] In 1928 the progressives had succeeded in putting their man, newspaper publisher Clyde M. Reed, into the governorship. Reed proved to be an able and effective state executive; but his less-than-winsome personality, the deteriorating economic picture, and the determination of the party conservatives to unseat him—all spelled trouble. In the 1930 primary the old guard selected a young candidate, Frank ("Chief") Haucke of Council Grove, to face Reed, and there followed one of the most bitterly fought primaries ever witnessed by Kansans. Although the candidates avoided attacking each other, the members of their respective factions maligned and abused one another viciously. The contest between the youthful Haucke and the elderly Reed was similar to that of the Democrats in that it was a battle of young versus old; however, in this unusual case, the younger crowd represented the conservatives, and the older crowd represented the progressives. Although Haucke's followers represented the younger crowd, they were being led by old-time politicians who were out to defeat Reed in any way they could. "Give the young men a chance" became the slogan of the anti-Reed people, and Kansas Republicans did just that as they gave Haucke 158,113 votes to the Governor's 131,988.[28] The lines were now drawn for the November general election, with the candidates of the younger crowd, Frank Haucke and Harry Woodring, set to do battle.[29]

Frank ("Chief") Haucke, a soft-spoken farmer from Morris County, possessed personal attributes that made him a nearly perfect candidate—he was good-looking, modest, clean-living, and personable. After graduating from high school, the tall, muscular man, who was of German ancestry and had exceptional athletic ability, went first to Kansas State Agricultural College and then to Cornell, where he starred on the football team. During World War I he joined the Army and was sent to France, where he received two wounds in the battle of Chateau Thierry. After the war he returned to his father's 1,500-acre farm outside Council Grove. Before long he was engaging in American Legion activities and was elected State Commander in 1924. It was about this time that he met and became friends with another active Legionnaire, Harry Woodring. In 1926 he entered politics, being elected to the first of two terms as a state representative. The nickname Chief was first given to him by his friends because of his large collection of Indian relics, which he had gathered since he was a boy; then, in the mid 1920s, when the Kaw Indian tribe "adopted him" and called him Chief as an expression of its appreciation for an Indian monument that he constructed, the name came into general use. Candidate Haucke's personal life was above reproach, and his supporters always made much of the fact that he was an honest, hard-working young man who did not smoke, drink, or "run around."[30]

During the course of the campaign, newspapermen frequently pointed out the similarities between the two candidates, "Honest Frank" and "Handsome Harry." Such comparisons were not surprising, because both men were bachelors, shy, young, veterans, and past State Commanders of the American Legion who neither smoked nor drank. Physically, however, the two presented an interesting study in contrasts: stretching up more than six feet, the tall, muscular Haucke towered over his short, plump rival, who barely hit the five-and-one-half-foot mark. Other than size, the most noticeably

24

different characteristic was their hair. While the brown-eyed Chief had a "good head of hair," the blue-eyed former banker had thin hair and frontal baldness, which made his eyebrows seem high and his ears appear larger than they really were. Although Haucke was probably the better looking of the two, it was Woodring who picked up the nickname "Handsome." The reason for this was that the term was used to refer not to physical attributes but to his manner of dress, and it was in this respect that the stylish, immaculately dressed Woodring outdistanced his rival and consequently became "Handsome Harry."[31]

The day after the primary election, Woodring indicated that his campaign for the general election would be "no pink tea affair" but a vigorous, hard-fought battle "for the interests and welfare of the average citizen" and against "interests unfriendly to the masses."[32] After making this public statement, he spent several weeks resting and mapping out his campaign strategy. The first major problem he faced was the appointment of the Chairman of the State Democratic Committee. Traditionally it was the prerogative of the Democratic gubernatorial nominee to name the State Chairman, a post that the candidate generally filled with his campaign manager.[33] Had this precedent been followed, Woodring would have appointed John Wells to the high post; however, that appointment was never made. There was no doubt that Wells possessed considerable political skill and ability, but an increasing tendency on Wells's part to indulge in alcohol and to engage in promiscuous activities caused Woodring to feel that such actions could possibly be used by the opposition to discredit his candidacy. While Woodring was grateful for Wells's contribution to his success, he felt that he had no alternative but to let him go.[34] To avoid embarrassment to everyone concerned, it was announced that Wells would be unable to assume the state chairmanship because of poor health.[35]

The dismissal of Wells, which at the time appeared to be a blow to Woodring's campaign, actually turned out to be a blessing in disguise, because he was replaced by Guy T. Helvering, described by one historian as perhaps "the best practical politician yet developed in Kansas."[36] The Ohio-born Helvering grew up in the Sunflower State and graduated from the University of Kansas before securing his law degree from the University of Michigan. Hanging out his shingle at Marysville, Kansas, he soon gained a reputation as a topnotch lawyer. In 1912, following a successful stint as prosecuting attorney of Marshall County, the thirty-four-year-old Democrat was elected to the first of three consecutive terms as Congressman from the Fifth Congressional District. Six years in Congress gave him a good insight into and understanding of the world of politics. After being swept from office in the Republican landslide of 1920, Helvering went to Salina, Kansas, where he acquired milling, land, and banking interests, becoming in time the head of the city's largest bank. Shortly thereafter he expressed his satisfaction with banking and vowed that he would never again become involved in "big politics."[37] He kept that promise until June of 1930, when Woodring visited him at his Salina bank and asked for his political support. Helvering was so impressed with the enthusiasm, apparent ability, and personality of the young candidate that he agreed to help him.[38] During the primary the former Congressman used his wide acquaintance with local party leaders to drum up support for his candidate. He was also involved in the formulation of party strategy, but most of his work was behind the scenes. After the primary and the decision to let Wells go, Woodring asked Helvering to serve both as his campaign manager and as chairman of the State Democratic Committee. The split in the Republican party, along with pressure from Woodring and other party leaders, led the "retired" politician to accept the offer.[39] Although the politically astute Helvering was the campaign manager, this did not mean that he told Woodring what to do. He gave advice and he gave it freely, and his candidate frequently followed it; but there was never any question that Woodring would, and in fact did, run his own campaign.[40]

That the Democrats were going to take the initiative and wage an aggressive campaign became evident when the party leaders gathered in Topeka during the last week of August to plan their strategy and draw up a platform. They immediately broke the Democratic tradition of waiting for the Republican platform to appear before deciding on their positions. On Sunday, 24 August, Woodring and a group of his advisers, which included Helvering, Carl Rice, Mrs. Carl Rice (who was acting chairman of the state party), and Dudley Doolittle, met, hammered out, and released to the press a tentative platform, which they hoped would be approved first by the Resolutions Committee and subsequently by the Party Council. Acceptance by those two groups would make it the official party platform.[41] The proposed platform included the usual pledges to uphold the law, improve education, lower taxes, and provide efficiency and economy; but it also promised continuance of the "splendid" highway-construction program of the Reed administration, supported a presidential primary, favored the establishment of a separate state Labor Department, pledged itself to nonpolitical reapportionment, and promised more equitable distribution of taxes by adjusting property valuations. On only one issue, the state income tax amendment, did the proposed document fail to take a position. Instead of taking a stand on this controversial subject, which was to appear on the November ballot, the platform took no stand, indicating instead that the party would be con-

26

tent to "let the will of the people prevail."[42] This position came close to shattering party harmony.

Although Woodring personally favored passage of the income tax amendment, he and his advisers were afraid that party endorsement of the hotly disputed measure might antagonize a large number of voters and provide an issue that the Republicans could effectively attack. For these reasons they favored a middle-of-the-road policy that would alienate neither the supporters nor the opponents of the tax. When the Resolutions Committee met on Tuesday, 26 August, to consider the proposed platform, all went well until the plank on the income tax came up. At that time State Senator A. L. Scott, after reminding the committee that over the years the party had supported the idea of a state income tax, introduced an amendment calling for endorsement of it. Scott was joined by several others—including former Governor Jonathan M. Davis, the party's candidate for the United States Senate—who indicated that they were convinced that the party should take a firm stand for the amendment. Guy Helvering also sided with the Scott-Davis forces, but the defenders of the original plank stood firm. With neither side willing to back down, a deadlock appeared to be imminent. At this point Edgar Bennett of Marysville, after acknowledging the dangers of a party split if a compromise were not reached, suggested that Woodring, since he would be carrying the heaviest burden in the election, should be permitted to write the plank as he saw fit. This met with the approval of everyone except Davis. With the party on the verge of a factional fight that could seriously hinder its upcoming chances for success. Woodring rose and proposed that the plank read: "We believe in the principle of the income tax, however, we believe the adoption of the amendment is not a partisan issue. . . ." This change, which endorsed the principle of the tax without committing the party to the amendment, was quite acceptable to both factions and thus became a part of the official platform.[43] When the State Democratic Council adjourned on that August 26, candidate Woodring had won approval of his platform and had still maintained the party unity that he knew was so essential if he were to achieve victory in November.

The 1930 gubernatorial campaign opened on a friendly note on September 1, when Woodring joined his friend and political rival Frank Haucke at the State American Legion Convention at Emporia. The cordiality that prevailed was warm and sincere as the two former State Commanders chatted, lunched together, and rode in the same car in the parade.[44] Although neither candidate made a speech or mentioned the election, there was no question that the quest for votes, especially among Legionnaires, had begun. When

Woodring left the convention on 2 September, his opening campaign speech was still a week and a half away, but he and his staff were not idle during that period. State headquarters were opened at the Jayhawk Hotel in Topeka, itineraries were arranged, position papers were drawn up, campaign literature was secured, funds were solicited, and behind-the-scenes efforts were made to get the covert, if not the overt, support of disgruntled Republicans, including Governor Reed.[45]

On Friday, 12 September, more than three hundred people jammed into the Franklin County courtroom in Ottawa, Kansas, to hear Woodring give the speech that launched his campaign for the governorship. It was no secret that his only hope for success was to hold the votes of his own party and to attract the votes of those Reed Republicans who were still bitter over their candidate's defeat in the primary. His pursuit of this strategy led Woodring to do the bulk of his campaigning in the areas that Reed had carried and, while in those areas, to praise the Governor and his programs. This appeal was evident in his keynote address, as he lashed out at the "machine crowd of politicians—the Shawnee county dynasty," headed by Republican State Chairman John D. M. Hamilton, which had repudiated the Reed administration because it "could not be controlled." Woodring expressed his contempt for such "gang rule," and he assured his audience that he was "not the pawn of any faction or group of hungry or disgruntled politicians." He then turned briefly to the tax question. While stating that this would be "the dominant issue in the campaign," he carefully skirted the subject by declaring only that the tax burden must be distributed in a more equitable fashion. He closed by pledging to carry forward the Reed road-building program, and he promised to administer efficiently the business of Kansas.[46] In attacking "reactionary machine rule" and pledging to run the state in a businesslike fashion, Woodring set forth the two issues that he was to dwell on for the duration of the contest.

When Woodring opened his campaign in September, he was a decided underdog, even though the Republican party was still split. One major newspaper set his odds at 1,000-to-1, and political observers throughout the state gave him little chance of defeating Haucke.[47] Nevertheless, the Democratic candidate carried his campaign to the people, speaking before gatherings large and small and telling them that a vote for him would not be wasted, because he could win.[48] One reason for his optimism, but a reason that he never mentioned publicly, was the depression. As the problems of unemployment, deflation, and hunger hit more and more Kansas homes, Woodring stood to benefit politically, because he would gain support from the disappointed voters who would react against the party in power. He was counting heavily on the "discontent vote."[49] Throughout September the campaign remained a one-sided affair, because the Republicans had decided to delay the start of their earnest campaigning until October, by which time they hoped that "the enthusiastic young Mr. Woodring will have talked himself out."[50] There was another gubernatorial candidate, Socialist J. B. Shields of Lost Springs, but no one, including Shields himself, seemed to take his candidacy seriously.[51] As the days of September faded, the race for Governor gave little evidence of being anything other than a routine campaign. Little did Kansans realize that they were about to witness "the most astonishing, dramatic, and colorful race in Kansas history."[52]

The series of events that was to breathe new life and excitement into the race was set in motion on September 19, when Dr. John R. Brinkley of Milford announced that he was an independent candidate for governor. With this announcement, one of the most unusual and controversial figures ever to grace the Kansas political stage became part of the campaign struggle.[53] Brinkley, who had "graduated" from several medical schools of questionable repute, had come to Kansas in 1918 and had set up a practice in Milford, a small village seventy miles west of Topeka. The next few years brought nothing but success to the likable country doctor as his medical practice grew and he opened his own drugstore. In 1922 he received some notoriety when he established the first radio station in Kansas, KFKB, a powerful station whose signal could reach most of the state.

What started the red-haired, goateed medico on the way to fame were his "goat gland" transplants, which supposedly restored masculine virility. This idea had, in all likelihood, come from rejuvenation experiments involving the sex glands of chimpanzees, which were being undertaken in Europe at that time. "Doc" Brinkley started performing his rejuvenation operations, which consisted of implanting the glands of a goat into the center of a man's testicles, for a modest fee of fifty dollars. A number of individuals were more than pleased with the doctor's work, and the testimonials of childless couples who subsequently became parents and of impotent men who were now enjoying an active and satisfying sex life began to spread Brinkley's name far and wide. When the patients started to roll into Milford, the cost of the operation was raised to $750, but still they came. It was soon necessary to build and equip a hospital large enough to handle the nearly two hundred patients who underwent surgery every week. Brinkley increasingly used his radio station to tell Kansans about the "new life" that they could enjoy after a short stay at the Milford clinic; and for those who could not make the trip, the next best thing was to take his "four phase compound," which could be purchased at drugstores throughout the state. About this time, late 1927, he began to receive letters from listeners, who inquired about their various ailments. In response, the "Doctor" began to

29

dispense his medical advice via the air waves, and before long he was receiving thousands of letters each week for his "Medical Question Box of the Air." The pride of Milford was a well known, wealthy man—just how wealthy no one knew, but he was able to build a beautiful home, open his own bank, enlarge his clinic, and purchase several airplanes.[54] The "goat gland" specialist was on top of the world.

Then in 1928 things went sour. Brinkley's troubles started when the crusading *Kansas City Star* accused him of being a "quack" who was fraudulently taking advantage of a gullible public, and this exposé soon led the State Medical Board to investigate the activities of the Milford physician. During lengthy hearings, the board heard from many witnesses, both professional and nonprofessional, including a large number who came to Brinkley's defense by attesting to the success of the operation. In the end, however, his license was revoked. This did not put an end to his troubles, because the *Star* continued to mount pressure to have his radio license revoked.[55] Frustrated by what he considered to be a campaign of persecution against him, "Doc" decided to do something about it; thus, in mid September 1930, half in anger, half in jest, he announced that he would be a write-in candidate for Governor.[56]

Brinkley's announcement attracted practically no attention, because no one, including the party leaders and candidates, took him seriously or gave him the slightest chance of succeeding. It would be difficult for an independent to do well even if he were on the ballot; but Brinkley was not, and could not be put on it, because Kansas law required that independents file for candidacy forty days prior to the primary—a deadline that was already past.[57] Even if that law were successfully challenged in the courts, there would be another problem, because the ballots had already been printed. That Woodring and Haucke were not initially concerned over Brinkley's activities seems evident from the fact that on 2 October, the day after Haucke's keynote address at Manhattan, they boarded a train and headed for Boston, Massachusetts, and the national convention of the American Legion.[58] For the next ten days the two friends, who were both delegates-at-large, forgot their political differences as they roomed together and worked successfully for the election of another Kansan, Ralph T. O'Neil, to the office of National Commander.[59] To see the two candidates enjoying themselves at the convention, one would never have thought that in less than a month they would be facing each other in an election. This enjoyable and leisurely interlude came to an end on 11 October, just a little more than three weeks before election day.

When the two candidates arrived back in the Sunflower State, they were surprised and somewhat alarmed at the rapid turn of events that had taken place in their absence. While they had been vacationing, Brinkley had been working overtime. Utilizing his radio station to the fullest possible advantage, the aspiring candidate was gaining a rather substantial following by playing on the increasing discontent brought on by the depression, and by promising to provide Kansas with good roads, free clinics, free schoolbooks, fair taxes, and honest government. Thousands of Kansans who had previously looked to Brinkley to cure their physical ills now turned to him to cure the state's political ills.[60] Although both major party candidates were becoming increasingly alarmed over Brinkley's growing strength, Woodring was especially concerned, because that strength was coming primarily from the discontented voters, a source of support on which he was counting heavily.[61]

After returning from Boston, candidate Woodring met with chairman Helvering to consider how they should handle the strange turn of events. In the end they decided to follow their original strategy of attacking the Republican "machine," praising the administration of rejected Governor Reed, and letting the electorate know that Woodring was the best man to give the state a business administration.[62] This decision to continue making Haucke, not Brinkley, the main target was based primarily on the belief that it was the former who was the major threat. Furthermore, there was uncertainty over the reaction of the voters to a verbal assault on Brinkley, and that was the only way to attack him, since he had no party or political record to condemn. Woodring was apparently convinced that a name-calling contest between himself and the "Doctor" would seriously divide the discontent vote and thus give Haucke an easy victory. In this dilemma, Woodring pushed vigorously ahead, as originally planned, virtually ignoring the man from Milford.

Although "Chief" Haucke was out scouring the countryside for votes, he never really went on the warpath. Because the Republican candidate realized that if he were to be victorious, he had to unite his badly split party, his strategy was primarily that of peacemaker. He continually appealed to Republican Kansas to stay in the fold of the party that had served it so well in the past.[63] Almost as important as party unity was the emphasis on his personal attributes. Haucke and his supporters frequently reminded the voters that he was an honorable, honest, clean, and forthright young man —just the kind of person that would make a good Governor.[64] He also espoused a rather conservative legislative program, which called for good roads, better schools, lower property taxes, economy, and all those other wonderful things that no one could oppose. Promises to enforce prohibition, as well as opposition to large corporation farming, also found their way into many speeches.[65] Predictably, Haucke took an occasional swat at Woodring

31

or Brinkley, just as they did at him and at each other, but this was always done in a dignified way. Mudslinging did not find its way into this contest.

As the campaign entered its last two hectic weeks, the speeches, programs, and campaign styles of Woodring and Haucke were quite similar; but not Brinkley's. In addition to the hours spent on the radio, the Milford medicineman was now making personal appearances before crowds numbering in the thousands. These gatherings would generally open with a few songs by the Western singing star Roy Faulkner, after which Brinkley would appear and give an emotion-packed speech interlaced with quotations from the Bible, appeals for votes, and an explanation of where and how to write his name on the ballot.[66] With his almost limitless funds, he was also able to flood the state with "J. R. Brinkley" pencils and bumper stickers.[67] The large crowds he was now attracting, along with his strong showing in a number of straw votes, indicated that Brinkley was a serious contender who might well step into the governor's mansion.[68] As one seasoned political observer wrote just one week before the election, "Republican and Democratic candidates and campaign speakers are talking issues—depression, prohibition, party loyalty, party platforms, records and the usual line. But to be quite frank about it, the voters are talking Brinkley."[69]

During the last week of the campaign, Woodring centered most of his time on two new issues—prohibition and personal loyalty. Prior to this time the prohibition question had been unimportant, because both candidates had pledged themselves to strict enforcement. Then, on 25 October, the Republican State Chairman, John Hamilton, issued a statement calling the voters' attention to the fact that Woodring "was lined up with the same crowd which is trying to make the Democratic party wet." When Woodring indicated that he would not back a wet for President, the Republicans pointed out that he had supported Al Smith, a wet candidate, in the 1928 presidential election. Woodring, realizing the importance of the liquor issue in dry Kansas, struck back by noting that, as a State Representative, Frank Haucke had originally opposed a $40,000 appropriation for the enforcement of prohibition. Both candidates continued to question each other's stand on the enforcement of prohibition right up to election day.[70]

The big issue that Woodring was forced to deal with on the eve of the election was one that he had never anticipated and one that the opposition had not planned: the question of his personal loyalty. The issue arose at a Republican rally that was held at the National Military Home in Leavenworth on 30 October. At this gathering of fifteen hundred former servicemen, William D. Reilly, a Leavenworth attorney who was active in the American Legion, started out by lauding Frank Haucke, who was sitting on the platform. He then told his audience that during the recent National

Legion Convention in Boston, Woodring had deserted the cause of Kansan Ralph T. O'Neil, who was seeking the commandership, and had returned home to campaign, while Haucke had continued to work for O'Neil. This incident, according to Reilly, showed "the difference between the two men."[71] Woodring initially ignored the statement, apparently feeling that responsible reporters would verify the story, see that there was no truth to it, and learn that he was in fact in Boston at the time that he was allegedly campaigning in Kansas. The reporters, however, reported only what Reilly had said, and on the following day, papers throughout Kansas carried stories with the caption "Woodring Accused of 'Running Out on Ralph T. O'Neil.'" Feeling that the record had to be set straight, Woodring spent election eve, 3 November, in Leavenworth, denying the "running out" charge. He quoted statements from O'Neil thanking him for his support in Boston, and he closed by saying that he would "rather not be elected governor than run out on a friend."[72] That night a tired Harry Woodring returned to Neodesha to vote and await the decision of the voters.

As the campaign came to an end, Woodring, Haucke, and Brinkley all expressed confidence that they would win. But if they had no doubts as to the outcome, the seasoned observers of Kansas politics did. There were simply too many unanswered questions for an intelligent forecast to be made. Would the disgruntled Reed supporters vote the party line or switch their votes to one of the other candidates? Would the bulk of the discontent vote go to Woodring or to Brinkley? How many votes intended for Brinkley would be thrown out on technicalities? These and many other questions could be answered only by the electorate. If there was one thing that observers agreed on more than anything else, it was that "Brinkley's campaign has just about destroyed whatever chance Woodring, the Democratic nominee, had of defeating Haucke."[73] This belief was based on the assumption that the discontent vote would be badly split. Although one could find newspapermen who picked Haucke, some who gave Brinkley the nod, and a few who picked Woodring, their predictions were so couched with "ifs" and "maybes" as to give them little credence. If ever an election was a tossup, this was it.

It was perhaps appropriate that one of the most unusual political campaigns in Kansas history should have had a most unusual ending. When the residents of the Jayhawk State went to the polls on November 4, they assumed that by that night or early the next morning they would know who their new Governor would be. Such was not to be the case, however. In fact, more than ten days were to elapse before the results of the contest were known. The earliest returns made it clear that in spite of a very strong showing by Brinkley, the contest was going to result in a battle between the

33

two party regulars. In the days that followed, the lead changed hands so many times that the two men were said to be taking turns being Governor.[74] As Woodring later recalled, "perhaps no man was governor as many times as I was for eleven days—I was governor in the morning, and in the evening I wasn't governor."[75]

The election was so close that it was not until all the absentee votes were counted on 14 November that it was fairly certain that Woodring was the winner. Final tabulations showed Woodring gathering 217,171 votes to Haucke's 216,920 and Brinkley's 183,278.[76] With more than 617,000 votes cast, Woodring squeezed out a victory by a mere 251 votes. Considerable controversy developed over the election results, primarily because of the large number of ballots cast for Brinkley that were allegedly thrown out because they were not marked properly. Consequently, controversy raged and continued to rage over this so-called short count election.[77] Charges of irregularities, fraud, and conspiracy filled the air, but for reasons still not entirely clear, neither Haucke nor Brinkley asked for a recount, and on 26 November, Woodring was officially declared the winner.[78] Ten months before, they had said it could not be done; but as a result of hard work, the Depression, and a split in the Republican party, Harry Woodring had been elected Governor of Kansas.

In early December, after several weeks of much-needed rest at his home in Neodesha, the Governor-elect took up temporary residence in the Jayhawk Hotel in Topeka. During the following month he met almost continually with Guy Helvering and other key advisers, considering appointments, formulating programs and policies, and working on his message to the legislature. Since Kansas Democrats rarely got a chance to share the spoils of office, they were not about to let the opportunity slip by when it arose. During this period, Woodring was besieged by hundreds of loyal Democrats, who were anxious to share in the political plums that they felt were rightfully theirs. While the Governor-to-be saw some of the office seekers, most were dealt with by Chairman Helvering.[79]

Not all of Woodring's visitors, however, were unsolicited. He invited leading businessmen throughout the state to confer with him on such matters as roads, welfare, unemployment, and taxation. He was especially concerned about the last, because the election that had brought him victory had brought defeat not only to all the other Democratic candidates for statewide office but also to the income tax amendment, which he had considered so vital.[80] One thing that he wished to avoid during this period was prematurely committing himself to particular plans, programs, or policies that might later prove difficult, if not impossible, to implement. As a result he refused to discuss his programs publicly until they had been formulated and presented to the state legislature.[81] The only exception to this was his announcement that he would urge resubmission of the income tax amendment to the voters.[82] While the Governor-elect buried himself in political matters, his unmarried sister, Lida, who was to serve as the state's "First Lady" for her bachelor brother, was busy preparing for their move into the executive mansion.[83] In early January 1931 Woodring put the final touches on his message to the legislature, appointed Leslie E. Wallace, editor of a Democratic paper in Larned, as his private secretary, and prepared for his January inauguration on 12 January.[84]

3

Governor of Kansas

The cold north wind swept across the Kansas plains and into the streets of the capital city of Topeka. The temperature was hovering near the freezing mark as most of the city's sixty-five thousand residents huddled together with thousands of out-of-town visitors to view the inaugural parade of Governor Harry Woodring. About eleven o'clock on the morning of that cloudy 12 January 1931, the Governor-elect and the outgoing Governor, Clyde M. Reed, walked out of the Statehouse and stepped into the open automobile that was to serve as their parade vehicle. Then, with nearly a dozen bands, half a dozen National Guard units, and hundreds of marchers from a score of patriotic organizations leading the way, the procession wove its way through the business district toward the city auditorium, where the inauguration ceremony was to take place.

The auditorium was overflowing as hundreds of Woodring's friends and acquaintances joined an array of state and local officials, newsmen, and curiosity seekers to witness the proceedings. Outside the building, hundreds more stood in the freezing weather to hear the program over a public-address system which could be heard not only in the immediate area, but throughout the downtown business district. When the platform party entered the assembly hall and headed toward the stage, the crowd lost its composure and began to shout and cheer, much as it would have at a University of Kansas football game. After the noisy throng finally quieted down, Guy Helvering, who was presiding, introduced Governor Reed, who gave a short farewell address in which he recapped the accomplishments of his administration. At the end of the speech, Reed, in "an unusual and gracious proceeding for an outgoing governor," introduced his successor and "close personal friend" in a most laudatory fashion. After wishing him good luck and adding that he would need it, Reed turned the platform over to Woodring, who then stepped to the podium and gave one of the shortest inaugural addresses in the history of the state.

Speaking both to a statewide radio audience and to those assembled, Woodring began by describing the conflicting emotions that he was experiencing as he embarked upon his new task. On the one hand, he claimed, he was honored by having been chosen Governor, but his joy was tempered by the sobering realization that he had an obligation to provide the kind of leadership that Kansas citizens expected. Next he expressed his utmost confidence in representative government and urged Kansans to take a greater interest and a more active role in the affairs of the state. He then announced that although he believed that "government is an agency of welfare," he did not intend to flood the state with a large number of programs designed to meet the "temporary" ills facing Kansas and its citizens: "It is not my intention to be swept off my feet by an instant demand to meet certain conditions that I consider are only passing. I shall stand firm for a safe, sound business administration." He did not, however, spell out the programs of his administration—he was saving that for the message to the legislature.[1]

Upon the completion of his speech, Woodring turned to William A. Johnston, the Chief Justice of the Kansas Supreme Court, and took the oath that made him Governor. With a National Guard artillery unit booming out a seventeen-gun salute to the new Chief Executive, the ceremony ended. That night, Governor Woodring, accompanied by his sister Lida, performed his first official function—hosting the inaugural reception.[2] For that event, lights, flags, and flowers were used to turn the staid old Statehouse into a large, attractive ballroom. Beautifully gowned women, tuxedoed politicians, and uniformed officers talked, laughed, and danced until the wee hours of the morning on that happy, festive occasion.[3]

But beneath the joy and gaiety of the moment lay the realization of those present that their state, like nearly every other state in the union, was in serious trouble. Although many people tried to ignore it, the impact of the Depression was becoming more apparent with each passing day. The deteriorating situation was especially evident in agriculture, which was the basis of Kansas economy. The record crops attested to the fact that 1930 had been a good year weather-wise. Kansas not only maintained its rank as the nation's leading wheat-growing state, but it did so by producing a record-breaking 186 million bushels. Production of the state's other leading staple crop—corn—also rose to a record high. But while production was rising, prices were falling as an already saturated market became flooded. Wheat prices, which stood at ninety-nine cents a bushel in 1929, dropped to sixty-three cents in 1930 and were to decline to thirty-three cents during Woodring's first year in office. Corn prices had likewise begun to plummet, going from nearly a dollar a bushel in 1929 to sixty-two cents in 1930. Overall, Kansas saw the value of its agricultural products drop from $548 million in 1929 to $441 million the following year, a loss of more than $100 million. The problems of overproduction and deflation were playing havoc with the incomes of thousands of Kansas farmers and were resulting in declining land prices, delinquent taxes, mortgages, and foreclosures. Two of the state's main industries—meatpacking and milling—were also suffering serious setbacks. Overproduction, high shipping costs, and the decreasing ability of Americans to buy meat served to put a damper on the economically important packing industry. In flour production Kansas retained its number two ranking, but declining exports and reduced consumption of bread resulted in an overall decrease in production and a subsequent increase in unemployment in the milling industry.[4]

The impact of the growing economic crisis did not limit itself to agriculture. Banks, too, felt the impact of hard times as dozens went broke and countless others were forced to absorb huge losses. The oil industry, which had long been a major producer of wealth in the state, was also in serious trouble. Not only had the bottom fallen completely out of the market, but one of the state's largest purchasers, Prairie Oil and Gas Company, had stopped purchasing Kansas oil eleven days before Woodring's inauguration. The very survival of the state's oil industry was very much in doubt. The coal industry also saw a significant increase in unemployment as lower demands and mechanization took their toll. Throughout the state there was a growing disillusionment as citizens witnessed and experienced declining farm prices, increasing unemployment, and growing tax burdens.[5] All was not well in Kansas in January 1931 as Harry Woodring assumed the governorship.

The official responsibilities of a Governor fall into three general categories: ceremonial, administrative, and legislative. Although the first two consume the bulk of his time, it is generally upon the latter that an evaluation of his success is based. Woodring realized this, and he was determined to achieve legislative success. He knew that by doing so he would not only benefit his state and its citizens, he would also enhance his chances for reelection. There were, however, several obstacles. With a biennial session, which would fall in the first two months of his term, there would be no time to get his feet wet before dealing with the legislature. His legislative

38

record, whether good or bad, would be made in those first crucial eight weeks in office—there would be no second chance. To complicate matters further, the Governor faced a legislature that was dominated by the opposition party.[6] Realizing the difficulties facing him, Woodring had attempted to prepare for them by using the period between the election and the inauguration to formulate, with great care and thought, his program. He had made numerous public statements indicating his strong desire to cooperate and get along with the Republican legislature.[7]

On 14 January, just two days after his inauguration, Woodring appeared before a joint session of the Kansas legislature to give the most important speech he had ever made. He started his "state of the state" message by reminding those assembled that he could only make recommendations, that they were the ones with the authority to accept or reject the measures. He asked only that they approach his proposals, as he had, in a nonpartisan fashion.[8] Woodring made such an appeal because he knew that the success or failure of his program lay in the hands of Republicans, who held 37 of 40 seats in the senate and 76 of 125 in the house.[9] Having made his plea for bipartisan support, he then set forth the cures that he proposed for the state's ills. First and foremost he turned to taxes—"the paramount problem that confronts this legislature and the problem that should have prior consideration." As he saw it, immediate tax relief and reform were absolutely essential. Immediate relief could be provided by reducing state expenditures, tightening the methods of assessment, and tapping certain additional sources of revenue. Reform, he maintained, was necessary in order to bring about a shift in the tax burden from real estate and tangible property, upon which the tax had become practically confiscatory, to all forms of wealth. To bring this redistribution about, he asked that the income tax amendment be resubmitted to the voters for approval. He also urged that steps be taken to assure that governmental units would follow a "pay as you go" plan in financing public improvements and would "not over-mortgage the public income of future generations" by excessive purchase of long-term bonds.

The idea of ultimately easing the financial burden of the average Kansas family, whose income was dropping rapidly, motivated both his tax program and his proposal that adequate funds be made available to the Public Service Commission so that it could undertake action to bring about reduction in gas, electric, and telephone rates. Turning to education, he accused the State Textbook Commission of making "needless and expensive changes" in textbooks, and he called for a complete investigation of that body. Highways and automobiles received attention as he vowed to continue the highway program of former Governor Reed, urged the licensing of motor-vehicle drivers, and asked that commercial vehicles be forced to pay a greater share of road-maintenance costs. Other major recommendations included creation of a crippled children's commission, a state program to support the crippled and handicapped, the tightening of laws to protect purchasers of corporate securities, and the establishment of a separate Labor Department. In closing his lengthy message, the Governor once more reiterated his willingness to cooperate with the legislature in order to see his proposals enacted.[10]

The Governor's message was very well received, and the favorable impression it made on legislators, newspapermen, and citizens in general did much to win the confidence of many Kansans who had questioned this young man's ability to be Governor. Even a staunch Republican like William Allen White wrote an editorial praising the speech, calling it "an intelligent discussion of state affairs [which] was straightforward, well-advised and well-spoken." Concerning the impresson made by Woodring, White said: "One couldn't ask more from a governor in his first inaugural. Kansas will mark up her estimate of the young governor appreciably."[11] White's evaluation of the new Democratic Governor and his proposed program was not atypical.[12] Even the pro-Republican *Topeka Daily Capital* carried an editorial praising Woodring's message.[13]

In the weeks following his address, Woodring busied himself with the state's oil crisis and other administrative matters as he anxiously waited to see what action would be taken on his legislative proposals. One, two, and then three weeks passed, and except for a resolution establishing the Textbook Commission and a few minor bills raising various fees, little was done. Since the early weeks of a session normally found bills being hammered out in committee, it was not unusual that so few had received consideration after three weeks. But what bothered Woodring was that it seemed doubtful that much was going to be done.[14] The legislature appeared to be dragging its feet, and around the Statehouse, talk was spreading that, in light of the unsettled conditions throughout the state, "the wisest course was for the legislature to pass the appropriation bills, local measures and just enough tax legislation to appease Mr. John Taxpayer, then adjourn and go home."[15] Up to this time Governor Woodring had trod softly, because he did not wish to pressure or antagonize the members of the legislature; however, with three weeks of an eight-week session gone, he felt that the time had come to exert some leadership and to attempt to push through some legislation, especially on the tax issue.

Early in February the Governor let it be known that if the legislature failed to pass some major laws to help ease and equalize the tax burden, he would call it back into special session for that purpose. The threat of a special session sent shivers up the backs of many legislators, who feared a violent reaction from disenchanted voters if they were forced to return to Topeka to

40

do something that should have been done in the regular session. The impact of Woodring's warning was soon evident as various committees began to reexamine his message and to review tax bills previously submitted. When several committees began sending delegations to quiz the Governor on tax matters and his proposals, it became evident that the major obstacle to tax reform was the lack of leadership rather than the lack of interest. Woodring therefore concluded that the best way to lead a body that was now looking for assistance was to go before it with an even more detailed tax plan than the one included in his "state of the state" address.[16]

On 16 February, Governor Woodring appeared before a joint session of the Kansas legislature to deliver a special message dealing solely with taxation. He minced no words as he told of the need "to lift a part of the load now borne by real and tangible personal property, and so far as possible to distribute it to other forms of wealth which hitherto either in whole or in part have escaped the tax burden." He then set forth, in considerable detail, recommendations calling for resubmission of the income tax amendment, submission of a tax-limitation amendment that would limit the general property tax to 2 percent of the assessed valuation, creation of county assessment boards, assessment of all banks and public utilities by the State Tax Commission instead of by local assessors, taxing of bank assets, a tax on insurance premiums, tightening of the cigarette tax law, and fee increases for services performed by nine different state agencies. While he was reluctant to accept the principle of the proposed intangibles tax law, he indicated his willingness to accept it if it were the will of the legislature. The Governor closed with a plea for economy and a pledge to institute drastic reductions in departments and agencies that were under his control.[17]

The Governor's special message seemed to cajole a dallying legislature into action, and during the next four weeks the solons forged a record that they could be proud of. In an effort to establish a more equitable basis for future taxation, it was decided to submit the income tax and tax limitation amendments to the voters in the 1932 election. In order to improve present conditions, an intangibles tax, providing for a rate of fifty cents per one hundred dollars, was reenacted; the gasoline tax was raised from two cents per gallon to three in order to carry on the road-building program; new bus and truck mileage taxes were instituted; a bank tax law providing for the taxing of the assets of banks and building and loan companies was passed, in order to end a situation whereby those institutions were paying taxes only on their real estate and tangible property; and teeth were put into the cigarette tax law. Another act that was not a tax measure per se but that was closely related was a budget law that required all taxing districts to hold open budget hearings. It provided that budgets had to be published and

41

made available before a hearing took place.[18] Governor Woodring was indeed pleased with the tax measures passed during the 1931 session, because he had advocated and worked for each of them except the intangibles tax, and he had failed only in his effort to get the assessment laws strengthened.[19]

In addition to seeing his tax recommendations enacted, the Governor saw the legislature act favorably on nearly every other request made in his initial message. The continual pleas for economy apparently had some impact, for the legislators cut biennium appropriations nearly $1 million below those of the previous session. Although Woodring was disappointed when the legislature refused his recommendation that utility companies be forced to pay the full cost of the Public Service Commission's actions to establish fair utility rates, he was pleased when it appropriated $100,000 for that purpose. The Blue Sky Commission received additional powers to police the sale of stocks, thus giving Kansas, according to the commission's chairman, "the best securities law in the United States."[20] Probably no legislation made the Governor happier than that establishing a permanent Crippled Children's Commission and providing a program of state and county care and support for crippled children and for individuals who were otherwise handicapped. Upon leaving the office of Governor, Woodring was to say that, as far as a permanent program was concerned, this was "the outstanding accomplishment of my administration."[21] Congressional reapportionment, a law requiring the licensing of all drivers of motor vehicles, and the creation of a separate Labor Department—all of which Woodring had advocated—were also provided for. In addition, favorable responses were made to the Governor's requests to set up a commission to study the textbook question and a commission to examine conditions at state penal and charitable institutions and make recommendations for upgrading them.

Besides enacting measures that the Governor championed, the legislature also passed a number of other statutes of great importance. These included laws that placed holding companies under the supervision of the Public Service Commission (P.S.C.), gave the P.S.C. the right to supervise oil proration, outlawed corporation farming, prohibited utilities from engaging in merchandising, created a state aircraft board, and gave county commissioners the power to levy a tax to care for the poor.[22] In terms of the number of bills passed, the 1931 session was not prolific, for it passed only about 329 measures, of which a mere 46 had statewide application; but, as can be seen, the quality of them was impressive.[23]

Of the several hundred measures sent to Governor Woodring for his signature, all except two were approved; however, his veto of those two—a resolution creating a committee to investigate the State Highway Commission, and a capital punishment bill—was to cause quite a stir. As the road-building program of Governor Clyde M. Reed gained momentum in 1929 and 1930, the Highway Department, which was under the control of a six-man State Highway Commission, became the state's largest agency both in terms of the number of its employees and the funds that it spent. Before long the air was filled with rumors of graft and corruption in the letting of contracts and with charges of employees being forced to make political contributions.[24] With such reports circulating, it was not surprising that Republican Senator Claude Bradney of Columbus, at the beginning of the 1931 session, introduced a resolution creating a committee to investigate the activities of the Highway Commission. Both parties supported the measure, which passed by large majorities in both houses.

Although Governor Woodring was extremely anxious to uncover any graft and corruption that might exist in state government, especially if it could be attributed to the Republicans, he realized that a probe might produce certain undesirable consequences; but the legislators had failed to take this into consideration. For example, because no new contracts could be let, nor could projects under contract but not yet under construction be permitted to start, the seven or eight months required for a highway investigation would delay the employment of hundreds of road-construction workers, set the road-construction program back at least a year, and result in the loss of a $2.2 million federal highway grant. The last would result from the stipulation that funds not used for the stated purpose by 1 September 1931 would revert to the federal government. Therefore, in order to put large numbers of unemployed men back to work, to prevent delay in the highway construction program, and to save more than $2 million in federal aid, Woodring vetoed the Bradney resolution.[25]

With this unexpected action, which came on 13 March, the next-to-last day of the session, "Kansas beheld the strange spectacle of a Republican legislature voting to investigate the activities of a Republican administration and being thwarted by a Democratic governor."[26] Legislative reaction to the veto was mixed, the most bitter criticism coming from those leaders of both parties who had worked to push the resolution through. Senator Bradney angrily denounced the action, claiming that "Governor Reed's friends demanded their 'pound of flesh' for voting for Woodring last fall, and Governor Woodring paid . . . by protecting Reed's highway commission."[27] Beyond the legislative halls, however, reaction to the governor's action was overwhelmingly positive. The most famous editorial writer in Kansas, William Allen White, not only got out of his sick bed to write a laudatory editorial for his *Emporia Gazette,* but he also sent a personal telegram to Woodring, calling his veto "one of the manliest things I have ever seen come out of any governor in all my forty-five years I have known Kansas politics."[28] The *Topeka Daily Capital*'s editorial praised the Governor for "passing up a partisan political opportunity, in order to promote the state highway program."[29]

Governor Woodring's second veto, which came on the last day of the session, was to raise more controversy and attract more attention than the first. Early in the legislative session, Democratic Representative Donald Muir of Harper, who hoped to cut the crime rate, introduced a bill restoring the death penalty (Kansas had abolished capital punishment in 1907). At the time the measure was introduced, Governor Woodring, without giving it much consideration, indicated that he would sign the bill if it were passed by large majorities in both houses. The Muir capital punishment bill quickly found its way to the floors of the house and senate, where it was passed by more than a two-thirds majority. As the bill went through the legislative mill and it became increasingly apparent that the responsibility of approving or rejecting the measure would fall ultimately on him, Woodring began to give the matter considerable thought and study.[30] When the bill finally reached the Governor's desk, the legislators expected the approval that had originally been promised. Woodring, however, shocked everyone by vetoing it.[31] In his veto message, which is still a classic condemnation of capital punishment, Woodring used historical and sociological studies to support his contention that "the proposed legislation is unsound in theory, that it has been demonstrated to be bad in practice, and that its adoption would be most unwise from every viewpoint." He saw no need for Kansas to go back to "the dark ages in our criminal laws."[32] This courageous veto was to pay big dividends for Woodring, because it won widespread approval and acclaim for him in Kansas and throughout the nation.[33]

The smoke from the Governor's two vetoes had not cleared when the legislators adjourned, packed their bags, and headed for home. Technically, adjournment would not come until March 17, but by the evening of March 14, to all intents and purposes, the 1931 session was over. In exactly two months the legislative record of the Woodring administration had been created. How successful had he been? Contemporary opinion held that he had done very well. According to political observer Milton Tabor, "The governor batted nearly 1000 per cent in his suggestions for new laws."[34] In a personal letter to the Governor, William Allen White said, "You have come through the Legislature splendidly."[35] Even Clif Stratton, the chief political writer of the pro-Republican *Topeka Daily Capital*, came to the conclusion that "the governor did a right good job of getting a Republican legislature to enact his legislative program into law. In fact a better job than some Republican governors in the past had been able to do."[36] Woodring, too, was pleased. He had seen nearly every request that he had made to the

44

legislature enacted into law, and so it was not surprising when he indicated that "it had been a constructive and outstanding session."[37]

Kansas Republicans and Democrats rarely agree on anything, but in the spring of 1931 they tended to agree that Governor Woodring had done a good job in getting legislation passed.[38] His success rested on several factors. Of great importance was his ability to win the confidence of the lawmakers. This he did almost immediately by showing them that he was an able and competent individual. The legislators who came into contact with Woodring during his first few weeks in office were amazed and impressed by his grasp of legislative, administrative, and political affairs. If they had not known better, they would never have guessed that they were dealing with a man who had just entered politics.

A warm personality was another asset that the new Governor utilized effectively. His pleasant, friendly "let's be pals" attitude was quite different from that of his predecessor, and the legislators enjoyed it. Conveying a sense of sincerity which was quickly translated into a feeling of trust, he was able to convince the members of the legislature and the public at large that he was deeply interested in the welfare of the state and its citizens.[39] When he said, "I am working for only one thing always—the interests of the average and majority citizen," people believed him.[40]

Woodring's accessibility was just as important to his success as were his ability and personality. It did not take legislators of either party long to discover that getting in to see the Governor was no problem. Furthermore, once they got to see him they always received a warm welcome. He was always willing to listen to their views and ideas and to explain his stand on a certain issue. The Governor's "open door" policy was not limited to public officials, for anyone wanting to see and talk with him on any subject received the opportunity. The open door was more than a gesture. Even during the long, busy days of the legislative session he would take time out from his hectic schedule to visit with job seekers, newspaper reporters, handshakers, and school children. The number of visitors generally averaged more than one hundred a day and sometimes reached three hundred. Woodring's accessibility both impressed those who met with him and endeared him to many Kansans who read in the newspaper about this busy man who always had a "handshake and a smile for everyone."[41]

Personal attributes were responsible for much of the smooth sailing experienced by the Governor during the legislative session, but considerable credit must also go to his decision to delay questions of patronage. When the legislature convened, the Governor announced that, with one or two exceptions, he was not going to submit appointments that needed senatorial approval until late in the session, and appointments not requiring approval

45

would be made only after the session was over. One major benefit of this action was that it discouraged thousands of Democratic job seekers from pressing their claims at that particular time, thereby freeing the Governor for more important and pressing matters. It also left the senate free to concentrate on vital issues. Most importantly, it avoided much of the controversy, ill will, and anger that nearly always develop in legislative bodies when political appointments are considered. The decision was also sound from a public-relations viewpoint, because "the average citizen took it to mean here was a Governor who thought more of the state's business than he did of patronage."[42]

Finally, a great deal of credit for the former banker's quick and successful transition from private to public life, as well as for his legislative success, must go to several very capable advisers. Guy Helvering, the master politician, continued to be the guiding light on political affairs, but he was inexperienced in state legislative matters.[43] In the latter area, however, the Governor's private secretary, Leslie Wallace, and his legislative counsel, Carl Rice, provided much of the valuable advice and assistance that enabled him to carry out his legislative responsibilities so successfully.[44]

No sooner had the session ended than Woodring turned to the problems of patronage. Before the senate adjourned, it had approved his appointees to a half-dozen important positions, but the bulk of the positions were yet to be filled. The Governor had at his disposal about a dozen really important jobs, primarily on key commissions and boards, and several hundred other positions such as inspectors, clerks, stenographers, and game wardens.[45] There was no dearth of applicants to fill those few hundred positions, for more than six thousand job-hungry Democrats appealed to "Harry" to repay them for their role in putting him in the governor's mansion.[46] After all, each would claim that it was his efforts that had given Woodring the votes needed to squeak out the victory. The Governor was literally besieged: on some days there were so many expectant appointees that it was nearly impossible for anyone to get in and out of his office.[47]

The Governor used great care in making his appointments, generally relying on proven businessmen and attorneys, nearly always those who had actively supported his bid for the governorship.[48] Woodring was always a good judge of men, and this was reflected in his appointees, most of whom won high praise from both parties.[49] One appointment, however, caused considerable controversy: that was the State Highway Commission's appointment of Woodring's choice, Guy Helvering, as State Highway Director. Republicans were especially upset, because this gave the Democratic State

Chairman control of the patronage in the largest state agency.[50] While such fears were to prove well founded in that Helvering did use the department for political purposes and while, as will be seen, his actions were to become a major issue in the 1932 election, the state highway program did make great progress under his leadership. Helvering proved to be just as effective in administering the Highway Department as he had been in administering a political campaign, and, as a result, Kansas surfaced more miles of highway (3,321) in 1931 than did any other state in the union.[51]

Of all the problems facing Governor Woodring when he assumed office in 1931, the most pressing revolved around the calamitous conditions in the Kansas oil industry. In the late 1920s Kansas retained its number four ranking among the oil-producing states; however, the industry was experiencing difficulties. The basic problem was overproduction: Kansas, like the other oil states, was "drowning in oil."[52] Consequently, crude oil that sold for $2.31 a barrel in 1926 was down to $1.00 a barrel in the summer of 1930. Following the discovery of rich deposits in eastern Texas in the fall of 1930, it fell to $0.18 a barrel. On top of the low prices, Kansas oil producers received another blow in December 1930, when the Prairie Oil and Gas Company announced that, due to surplus stocks, it would stop purchasing crude oil in Kansas and Oklahoma as of 1 January 1931. The consequence of this was to shut down thousands of shallow "stripper" wells in eastern Kansas. Working to save the strippers were the Independent Petroleum Association (I.P.A., an association of small producers) and a special state-appointed three-man committee headed by Alfred M. Landon, an Independence, Kansas, oil man. Efforts of the I.P.A. and Landon to negotiate an agreement with Prairie and other companies to purchase the "distress" oil failed, and when New Year's Day, 1931, arrived, Prairie shut down. During the following weeks all efforts to provide markets for the stripper production were unsuccessful.[53] It was at this point that Woodring assumed his responsibilities as the state's Chief Executive.

The new Governor was vitally concerned by the turn of events, because Prairie's action had shut down nearly fifteen thousand Kansas oil wells. This not only added to unemployment, it also deprived more than six hundred operators, and ultimately the state, of the economic benefits of the "black gold."[54] Woodring faced two problems: the need to find markets for the stripper wells and the need to provide some sort of long-range solution whereby Kansas oil production could be held in line with demand. An immediate solution to the first problem was absolutely essential, because if the strippers were shut down for any length of time, salt water would breach the wells and permanently destroy them. As Governor-elect, Woodring had pledged to assist the troubled oil industry. Although he was aware of the critical nature of the oil situation, Woodring, whether due to more pressing problems or to negligence, waited for more than two weeks after assuming office before taking any action. When he did go to battle, it was on three fronts: first, against Prairie, for it to continue purchasing the stripper oil; second, against Standard Oil of Indiana, which was the largest ultimate purchaser of stripper production; third, against President Hoover, who could use his position to help the troubled producers.[55]

On 28 January, Woodring sent telegrams to President Hoover and to E. G. Seubert, president of Standard Oil of Indiana, saying that he was "astonished and appalled" that twelve thousand oil wells were being allowed to be destroyed. He asked President Hoover to use his influence to bring about a settlement, and then he added: "If the great leaders of the oil industry, moved by avarice and self-interest, refuse to adjust the intolerable situation confronting the Kansas fields then a tariff on oil holds out the only hope in sight as the solution to our problem."[56] The Governor also appealed to Seubert, as the biggest purchaser of Kansas oil, to use his influence to settle the stripper problem by February tenth. If he failed to do so, Woodring warned, "every resource of the Kansas government will be invoked to get the desired results."[57] Two days later, following an unproductive conference with Prairie's president, W. S. Fitzpatrick, an angry Woodring fired off two more telegrams, one to Fitzpatrick and another to Seubert. After reminding both men of their moral obligations to Kansas producers and chiding them for attempting to pass the buck, he made some subtle threats. To Fitzpatrick, whose firm was contemplating retail sale of oil in Kansas gas stations, he indicated his conviction that if a settlement were not forthcoming, such products "would not be received favorably." To Seubert he hinted at the possibility of a state probe into the relationship between the supposedly separate Standard Oil Company of Indiana and Standard Oil Company of Kansas.[58]

Apparently this last warning had the impact that Woodring had hoped for, because Seubert immediately sent a negotiator to Topeka to confer directly with the Governor about terms of a possible settlement. Some headway was made on these negotiations, and on February seventh, Governor Woodring was able to announce that a temporary solution to the stripper problem had been found and that the prospects for a permanent settlement were good.[59] The temporary settlement, by which Standard of Indiana agreed to purchase 300,000 barrels of stripper oil in the next sixty days, was of great significance, because it enabled the wells to start pumping again, and it gave the Governor time to work out long-term agreements. Woodring took full advantage of the extra time he had won, and in March and April he successfully concluded agreements with Standard and other major companies to purchase nearly all of the state's stripper production.[60] Although he relied heavily on the advice and assistance of Alf Landon and Thurman Hill of the Public Service Commission, Woodring personally did most of the negotiating with the oil company representatives.[61]

Finding markets for the oil from the stripper wells solved the immediate problem, but Woodring was now interested in ways to protect the industry in the future. He increasingly came to accept the idea of an oil tariff as a solution to the domestic problem; thus, he actively supported efforts of Kansas Congressmen to such ends, and he continued to urge President Hoover to support an oil tariff or to use the flexibility of current tariff legislation to ease the burden.[62] Another solution that he supported, but not so enthusiastically, was state proration. Landon and independent Kansas producers were urging that state machinery be established to control oil production by the allotment of quotas (proration). Such control could be used to conserve oil resources and, more importantly, to raise prices by limiting production. In early March a proration law, which gave the Public Service Commission the power to set quotas, was passed by the house but killed in senate committee. Reaction from the small oil producers revived the measure, and it was subsequently passed.[63] Although Woodring was hesitant about approving the bill because he was "unable to reconcile restrictions on the production of natural resources in Kansas with the free importation of oil," he nevertheless signed it because of the widespread support it had among the state's independent oil men.[64] With the passage of the bill, Kansas became the first state in the nation to provide an effective proration system, and other oil-producing states soon followed the Kansas example as they passed laws giving state agencies power to control oil production by alloting quotas.[65] Woodring also continued to work for the oil industry by actively supporting the activities of the loosely knit Oil States Advisory Committee, which made one of the first attempts to bring order to the oil industry by interstate cooperation.[66] Although he by no means solved all the problems of the Kansas oil industry, Woodring did perform a valuable service by finding markets for stripper production, by providing for oil conservation and higher prices through proration (oil was back to eighty-five cents a barrel by the end of 1931), and by helping to lay the basis for interstate cooperation in meeting oil problems.

In the meantime Woodring had started a battle for reduction of utility rates—an endeavor that would ultimately provide him with his greatest public support, favorable nationwide publicity, satisfying victories, and demoralizing setbacks. Woodring had long been bothered by the fact that since the World War the citizens of his state had witnessed a decline in the cost of nearly everything except utilities. This meant that Kansans were paying the same utility rates in bad times as they had in good ones. Furthermore, technological developments had lowered the operating cost of the utilities, but the resultant savings were being passed on to the stockholders rather than to the consumers. The new Governor wanted to correct this "undesirable" situation.[67]

That Woodring intended to challenge the utility companies became apparent in his opening message to the legislature. In it he asked that the Public Service Commission (P.S.C.) be given "sufficient funds to properly perform its functions," which would "result in lower rates for all public utilities."[68] While failing to finance the project as he had suggested, the legislature did provide a major weapon to fight the utilities when it appropriated $100,000 to the P.S.C. to be used specifically for securing lower gas and electric rates. A companion law gave the commission the authority to examine the books of holding companies associated with utility companies operating within Kansas. Although the state now had the financial and legal tools to help bring about reductions in rates, Governor Woodring did not wish to use them except as a last resort. Because he hoped to reach his objective by getting the companies to act voluntarily, he conferred with officials of various gas and electric companies and requested that they reduce consumer rates by at least 10 percent.[69] This "soft" approach was extremely successful, for during 1931 more than two hundred cities and towns benefited from lower rates for electricity, and more than fifty experienced reductions in gas rates. The following year was even more successful, with nearly six hundred communities seeing reductions in rates for electricity, and eighty having lower gas rates. In all, nearly two out of every three communities in the state profited from voluntary reductions in rates.[70]

There was, however, one important and powerful individual who would not go along with the reductions—Henry L. Doherty, president of the Cities Service Company, which supplied gas to nearly one hundred Kansas cities and towns, including most of the larger ones. Henry L. Doherty's life was a real rags-to-riches story. Born in Columbus, Ohio, in 1870, he quit school at the age of twelve in order to go to work as an office boy for the Columbus Gas Company. Serving later as an engineer and manager for various utility companies, he soon amassed a sizable fortune. Then in 1910 he formed Cities Service Company, a conglomerate which by 1931 had grown to include more than one hundred utility companies with assets of more than $660 million. The headstrong multimillionaire watched over his empire like a mother hen, making all major decisions himself; therefore, if one wanted to deal with Cities Service, he did not deal with a vice-president or some other underling: he dealt with Doherty.[71] Woodring was determined to get the Doherty interests to lower their gas rates, not only because of the large

50

Lt. Harry H. Woodring at Camp Colt, Gettysburg, Pennsylvania, 1918.

Governor Harry H. Woodring campaigning for reelection in Kansas, 1932.

James A. Farley, James Roosevelt, and Harry H. Woodring (left to right) planning for the 1932 Democratic National Convention.

number of communities that were involved, but also because their rates were higher than those of any other company in the state.

Realizing that Doherty would never come to Kansas to see him, Woodring decided to go to New York. In late April 1931 the Kansas Governor traveled East to meet with the utility magnate. Armed with data on gas rates throughout the state, Woodring appealed for Doherty to adopt a plan that would provide lower consumer rates through a reduction in the "gate-rate." Doherty listened attentively, promised to consider the proposal, and indicated that he would probably send representatives to Kansas to confer on the matter.[72] Pleased with the tenor of the meeting, Woodring returned to Topeka to await the Cities Service negotiators. Time passed, but nothing happened. Every time Woodring asked the Doherty people to begin discussions, they asked for a delay. Six, eight, and then ten weeks passed after the New York meeting, and still no negotiators appeared.

As the days of June ticked off, Woodring's patience began to wear thin, and he became increasingly convinced that Doherty had no intention of reducing his rates. Finally the Governor came to the conclusion that it was time to act, and on June twentieth he instructed the P.S.C. "to proceed to force reductions."[73] This announcement alarmed Doherty at least enough to have H. C. Caster, his general counsel in Kansas City, open negotiations. On 26 June, Woodring informed Caster that he was tired of the delays and was giving Doherty until the second of July to cut his city "gate-rate" from forty to thirty cents per thousand cubic feet; if such action were not taken, he would have the P.S.C. take steps to force the reduction.[74] Whether it was wise for Woodring to issue such an ultimatum is open to question. On the one hand, it ended any hope for voluntary reduction, because it made Doherty determined to avoid taking any action that might make it appear that someone else was telling him how to run his business. On the other hand, it seems unlikely that Doherty would ever have taken action voluntarily. Had he been sincere about voluntary reductions, he had had plenty of time to institute them.

When the 2 July ultimatum date arrived, Doherty's representatives asked, as they had so many times in the past, for an extension of time. The angry Harry Woodring refused their request and announced that all peaceful negotiations were off and that the P.S.C. was being ordered to proceed. He served notice on the Cities Service Company that it could expect a real battle. "We are in this fight to obtain reasonable gas rates," he said, "and when the smoke clears away and the casualties are counted, the gas company may find that it is not as big as the state of Kansas."[75] Later that afternoon, Blue Sky commissioner Carl Newcomer announced that he was banning the sale of all Cities Service stock, except first preferred, in Kansas. While

Woodring, in all likelihood, coordinated this latter action, he publicly denied that he had had anything to do with it. He did, however, indicate that he would support Newcomer's position.[76]

The irate Henry Doherty immediately swung into action. On 3 July he not only sought an injunction to stop the state of Kansas from banning the sale of Cities Service stock, but he also utilized the application for injunction to charge "His Excellency" (Woodring) with conspiracy to "compel and coerce" him to accede to demands for lower rates. Several days later, Doherty lashed out again, this time with a three-thousand-word telegram to Woodring condemning his "arbitrary and reprehensible" actions to bring about reductions. He also blamed Woodring for inaugurating and forcing an unnecessary fight. The lengthy telegram then proceeded to accuse the Kansas Governor of being a tool of the *Kansas City Star*. The crusading but generally responsible *Star* had been quite vocal in urging rate reductions, and Doherty was convinced that the paper was out to "impair Cities Service's credit and to cripple its operations."[77] Doherty won a partial victory on 14 July, when the United States Supreme Court said that Kansas could not halt the sale of Cities Service stock.[78] Nevertheless, the real winner of this July 1931 clash was Woodring, for a major result of the affair was a great deal of favorable publicity for him in Kansas and throughout the nation. Newspapers in every state, including the *New York Times*, carried a blow-by-blow account of the encounter.[79] In nearly every news story Woodring was portrayed as a warm-hearted champion of the little man who was being pitted against the cold-hearted "Robber Baron," who was out to exploit the consumer for his personal gain. Such stories served to increase the antagonism between Woodring and Doherty, and this was to play a major role in the 1932 gubernatorial campaign.

While Woodring and Doherty engaged in bitter rhetoric, the P.S.C. prepared to open hearings to assist it in determining what a fair rate would be. The proceedings were originally scheduled to begin on 18 August 1931, but lawyers from both sides needed extra time to prepare, and so it was October sixteenth before the hearings finally got underway. This marked the start of legal maneuvering that was to last throughout Woodring's term and well into that of his successor. The gas-rate hearings continued for five months, with Doherty's lawyer claiming that the forty cents per thousand gate-rate was reasonable, and the attorneys for the state claiming that the charge was excessive. Finally, in mid March 1932, the testimony came to an end, and the commission retired to consider its findings and determine what the rate should be.[80] During the hearings, Doherty offered to cut his price from 40 to 35 cents per thousand, but Woodring refused to accept and ordered the commission to proceed. On 19 July the commission ordered a gate-rate reduction of 10.5 cents per thousand—from 40 to 29.5 cents.[81] At this point it appeared as if Woodring had won his fight for lower rates; however, Doherty was not through. With a battery of topnotch corporation lawyers, he took the case into the federal courts, where on 5 January 1933, just four days before Woodring left office, a three-judge panel ruled that the 40-cent rate was not unreasonable and therefore could stand. At that time the crushed Harry Woodring said, "I am rather disgusted with the whole attempt at regulation of utilities."[82] The Governor had made a very creditable record in rate reductions, but he grieved because he had let the "big one" (Doherty) get away. Although the ruling of the federal court was a blow to Woodring, it was only a temporary setback for Kansas, because when Alf Landon became governor in 1933, he continued the fight against Doherty, and in 1936 he succeeded in getting Cities Service to reduce its rates by 20 percent.[83]

Of all the problems that Woodring faced as Governor, none were more continuous and pressing than taxation and economy—two problems that went hand in hand. As the depression deepened in 1931 and 1932, Kansans found it increasingly difficult to meet their tax obligations; thus, as tax delinquency increased, state revenue decreased. This situation created several difficulties for the Governor: first, it subjected him to considerable pressure to lower taxes; second, it made it extremely difficult for him to balance the budget. In spite of the difficulties, Woodring was convinced that he could do both.

When farm prices dipped to disastrous levels in the summer of 1931, a ground swell arose for the convening of a special session of the legislature in order to provide relief for suffering Kansans. Numerous legislators, "general store" politicians, well-meaning citizens, and crackpots had ideas about how to provide the necessary relief, but they rarely agreed with one another. Some wanted to lower taxes and cut state salaries; others wanted to raise taxes and provide more work relief; while still others wanted to raise the gasoline tax or shorten the working day of state employees. There was no dearth of ideas as to how the state legislature might improve the situation.[84]

While Woodring was sympathetic with the aims of those people who were calling for a special session, he resisted their pressures, because he was convinced that such action would create more problems than it would solve. In spite of his announcements that he would not call the legislators back to Topeka, the demands for such action continued. By fall the most vocal calls were coming from two leading Democrats, former Governor Jonathan Davis and State Representative Donald Muir, both of whom were demanding lower taxes by legislative action. When Davis and Woodring exchanged harsh words over the subject of a special session, the former joined with Dr. John Brinkley to try to compel the Governor to take the desired action. In mid October, Davis and Brinkley secured the use of Representative Hall in the Statehouse for a meeting of the Taxpayers Education League. When Davis used that occasion to "call" a special session of the legislature and suggested that the legislators not only lower taxes but also impeach Governor Woodring, a real fight for the 1932 Democratic primary appeared to be shaping up between the two men. Woodring continued to resist such pressure, and when the sixty-year-old Davis remarried in December 1931, his interest in politics temporarily subsided, and he stopped pressing for the session.[85]

Woodring's reasons for refusing to call the legislators back were not limited to his belief that they could accomplish little; they were also due to his feeling that he could effectively bring about tax relief by other means. Although he had no direct control over the state tax levy, he could use his influence with the members of the State Tax Commission to get what he desired. When Woodring took office, the state levy was 1.43 mills, but declining collections were pressuring the Tax Commission to make up the loss by raising the rate to 1.75. Violently opposed to any tax increase at that time, the Governor went before the commission in August 1931 and pledged to reduce state expenditures to a point where such a raise would not be necessary. Convinced of his sincerity and determination, the commission decided to retain the 1.43-mill level. The next year he repeated the performance, and this time he was so convincing that it cut the levy to 1.33 mills, the lowest rate since 1916.[86] Woodring was also instrumental in securing another break for taxpayers when, in February 1932, he used his influence to get the Tax Commission to lower the assessed value of real estate by 14 percent on farm property and by 8 percent on city property.[87] While the tax rates went down only slightly under Woodring, nevertheless they did go down. But at the same time that tax reductions helped relieve distress, they also created a bigger problem: lower taxes meant lower state revenue, which in turn made the problem of balancing the budget extremely difficult.

How to balance the budget—that was the question. There were two general means that could be employed: increase revenue, or reduce expenditures. Woodring saw no real choice, because it was evident that the tax burden was already more than most Kansans could bear. This left the other alternative—reduction of state expenditures. Since state appropriations were less than $10 million a year, there did not appear to be much fat that could be trimmed off.[88] Nevertheless, Woodring was determined to succeed, and shortly after taking office, he instituted an austerity program unlike any that the Sunflower State had ever seen. By eliminating a number of state jobs, by forcing certain institutions to use surplus funds, and by postponing construction, repairs, and improvements at state colleges and universities, Woodring succeeded in saving the state $900,000 during his first year in office. This record pleased but did not satisfy him; thus, he announced his intention to cut expenditures by $2 million during his second year in office. He hoped to do this by reducing salaries and drastically cutting operating expenses at state institutions. In the early spring of 1932 the Governor announced that he was voluntarily reducing his $5,000 salary by 10 percent, and he asked all other state employees to do the same. After he used a "big stick," all the personnel in departments under his control quickly complied, and they in turn were followed by paid members of state boards and commissions. The last holdouts were elected Republican officials. While there was no legal way that the Governor could reduce their salaries, he succeeded in getting them to fall into line by indicating that he would make a campaign issue out of their refusal to cooperate in his economy program.[89]

State penal institutions also contributed to the economy drive by cutting expenses, but higher education made the biggest sacrifice. The Kansas Board of Regents reduced the budgets of the five state schools more than $900,000 by cutting faculty salaries 10 percent, reducing extension work, closing certain departments, not filling faculty vacancies, postponing building programs, and doing minimum repair work. Through such means during his second year in office, Woodring succeeded in saving the state $2 million and, consequently, in balancing the budget.[90] Unfortunately, cutbacks of institutional funds had adverse effects on the programs and facilities of nearly all institutions—especially those of higher education. Public-school children did, however, receive a break from the state when Woodring convinced the State Schoolbook Commission, which was already under fire as a result of the legislative investigations, to reduce the price of schoolbooks by 25 percent.[91]

As Governor, Woodring took a very active interest in the National Guard, but he was very pleased that he never had to call on it for other than disaster duty. It was his interest in the Guard that led to the organization of the 35th Division. This division had not become a reality, because ever since 1918 the three states designated to form the unit—Kansas, Nebraska, and Missouri—had been unable to agree on a Division Commander. With Woodring leading the way, a Commander was agreed upon, the division was completely reorganized, and it subsequently became one of the most effective National Guard divisions.[92] The Governor's interest in the Guard and the American Legion helped to keep him abreast of military and national-defense developments—matters in which he was soon to become deeply involved.

The headaches, heartaches, and pressures of being Governor were tremendous; but Woodring did not mind, for he enjoyed his new position. He loved the give-and-take of politics as well as the sense of importance and power that came with the post. But politics also brought at least one major change in his personality, and that was a diminishing ability to forgive and forget. Perhaps it was the nature of the job which made him increasingly hostile to those people who crossed swords with him.[93] At the same time that he began to display intolerance and vindictiveness toward those who would not play ball with him, he was developing a deep sense of obligation toward those who assisted and supported him. The Governor increasingly became a man who believed that when he did someone a favor, that person should return the favor whenever he was in a position to do so. The person who failed to reciprocate was no friend of Harry Woodring's. This was a reaction that he was to continue to have throughout his political career.[94]

In most ways Woodring remained the same. This was certainly true of the high moral standards that he both maintained and demanded of those who worked in his administration. Although he no longer attended church regularly, he continued to exhibit the precepts of Christian morality that his family had instilled in him. He appeared to have especially strong feelings about drinking. As he put it, "Being Kansas born, I naturally believe in prohibition and in the strictest possible enforcement of it." Whether this statement represented political expediency or a true feeling is uncertain, but while there may be some room for doubt concerning his moral view on the use of alcohol, there is no question of his abhorrence for and intolerance of anyone who drank to excess. Just as repulsive to him as the drunk was the man who could not do his job. Consequently, he did not tolerate incompetency in any position, and he did not hesitate to remove or call for the removal of any man, regardless of his background, who was not doing his job.[95]

Woodring worked hard at being Governor, frequently putting in ten or more hours a day, six days a week, at his office; but he also enjoyed his leisure. After a hard day at the office, the nattily dressed bachelor would hop into his new 12-cylinder black Cadillac (the first 12-cylinder car in the state) and head for the governor's mansion, a three-story, Victorian style house of brick and terra cotta. Since it had thirty-two rooms, it was more than big enough for Harry and Lida, so they frequently invited old friends to come to Topeka and spend several days with them.[96] When company was present, the evening would usually be spent in consuming a home-cooked meal and playing bridge. If there were no houseguests, Harry liked to go to a movie, a concert, or, occasionally, a party. Although the bachelor Governor enjoyed a full and active social life, he was by no means a man about town.

If the Governor wished to engage in some physical activity, he went to the executive stable, saddled up "Governor," and went for a short ride. Being a competent horseman, he frequently took a ride in the morning and evening; however, except for his riding, he received very little exercise. He gave up tennis and hoped to begin playing golf; but the latter never caught his fancy, so he abandoned it. Woodring maintained his interests in sports, but as a spectator rather than as a participant. Every year he traveled to several horse shows as well as to the Kentucky Derby. Football increasingly caught his attention, and he became quite interested in the gridiron fortunes of Washburn University in Topeka.[97]

Being Governor required considerable travel—an aspect of the job that Woodring thoroughly enjoyed. Any Governor is highly sought-after as a speaker, and he was no exception. During his term in office he traveled to nearly every county in the state, speaking before professional meetings, church groups, veterans organizations, agricultural clubs, and scores of other service and civic organizations. His position also required out-of-state travel to such places as French Lick, Indiana, and Richmond, Virginia, for governors' conferences; to New York City to see Henry Doherty; and to Washington, D.C., to confer with various officials on federal-state matters. But the out-of-state place that the Governor visited more than any other was one that few people had yet heard of—Hyde Park, New York.

4

The Governor Plays Politics

While Governor Woodring's duties kept him extremely busy, they did not prevent him from playing politics. The governorship carried with it many official responsibilities which entailed obligations to the entire state and all its citizens. Because he was a Democratic Governor, however, Woodring also had a number of unofficial duties and obligations to his political party. As the Governor of Kansas, he was traditionally recognized as the titular head of his party, but whether or not he was to become the true leader of that party remained to be seen. That Woodring should emerge as Democratic leader of Kansas in early 1931 was only natural in light of several factors: he was the man most responsible for the creation of the present state organization, feeble though it may have been; he held the highest elective post in the state; and he was the only Democrat to hold a statewide elective office. Under these circumstances, Kansas Democrats expected him to provide the party with leadership, and he did not disappoint them.

As soon as the 1931 legislative session ended, Woodring set out to build a strong party organization. His first and most effective means to that end was the appointment of Guy Helvering as head of the Highway Department. The wearing of two hats, those of Highway Director and State Democratic Chairman, enabled Helvering to utilize patronage to build the state's largest agency into an effective arm of the state Democratic party. With regular contributions, which many called assessments, coming into the campaign fund from those individuals appointed by Helvering, the party

58

was soon on a sound financial basis.[1] Although there was no doubt that Guy Helvering was the guiding genius of the Democratic organization, he and Woodring worked closely as a team, and the Governor was clearly the captain. Political opponents were to shout time and again that Helvering was running the party and the state; however, responsible newsmen and those close to the Governor maintained, and still maintain, that Woodring was his own man. The Governor relied heavily on the advice of his State Chairman and good friend, but they frequently disagreed over issues, and when they did, there was never a question as to who the decision maker was.[2]

While Helvering was concerned with exerting greater political strength within the state, Woodring became increasingly interested in wielding influence on the national scene. The latter idea does not seem so outlandish when one realizes that at that time only three of the seventeen states west of Missouri had more electoral votes or sent more delegates to the Democratic National Convention than Kansas did; only California, Texas, and Oklahoma exerted more power.[3] This meant that the Sunflower State could provide valuable Western support to any individual seeking the Democratic presidential nomination in 1932. In addition to realizing that his state could play a major role in the making of a nominee, Woodring knew the importance of supporting the right man at an early date. Such a course held certain dangers, for if he backed a particular candidate who fell along the way, he would be out in the political cold; however, the other extreme of waiting and climbing on the bandwagon offered little in return, since a presidential candidate seldom rewards a Johnny-come-lately.

Early in 1931, after careful consideration, Woodring made a fateful decision. He would support Governor Franklin D. Roosevelt of New York as the Democratic nominee for President. This was a gamble, because Roosevelt was maintaining that he was not candidate.[4] At that particular time the man considered by many to be the Democratic front runner was Governor Albert C. Ritchie of Maryland. Other prominent names that were being mentioned were Roosevelt; the 1928 nominee, Al Smith; the Speaker of the House, John Nance Garner of Texas; industrialist Owen D. Young; Governors William M. ("Alfalfa Bill") Murray of Oklahoma and George White of Ohio; Chicago businessman Melvin A. Traylor; and several favorite sons.[5] Just who would survive or who would emerge and ultimately win the nomination was a big question mark in the spring of 1931.

Woodring's interest in and support of Roosevelt for the nomination actually went back to 1929, when he had begun to follow with interest the activities of the newly elected Chief Executive of the Empire State. Although the Neodesha banker had never met Roosevelt, he became convinced that the New York Governor would make a good president. Soon he was telling his

Democratic friends and former servicemen that Roosevelt should be the party's nominee in 1932.[6] After his election in 1930, Woodring busied himself with legislative matters, but less than a month after the 1931 legislative session ended, he publicly predicted that Roosevelt would be "the next Democratic presidential candidate—(at least as far as Kansas is concerned)."[7] This 13 April 1931 statement made Woodring one of the first public figures to come out openly for FDR; thus, he became one of the original Roosevelt supporters. FDR was pleased when he heard of this unsolicited support, and he immediately asked Woodring to visit him in New York. Less than two weeks later, on 29 April, Woodring, who had gone East to see Henry Doherty concerning gas rates, traveled to Hyde Park to be FDR's dinner guest.[8] This meeting marked the beginning of a long and warm relationship. At such encounters Roosevelt was at his best, and Woodring left Hyde Park more convinced than ever that he was backing the right man.[9] Almost immediately the newspapers were speculating that the prospective presidential nominee was looking for a "strong Middle West Democrat for a running mate" and that Woodring "could well be that man."[10] Upon his return to Topeka, Woodring refused to comment on the possibility that he might be the vice-presidential nominee, but he continued to sing the praises of the New York Governor.[11]

In early June the two Governors met again, this time at the annual governors' conference at French Lick, Indiana, where Woodring addressed the opening session on matters of taxation. In private they talked about the political situation, but in rather vague terms, since Roosevelt was still not an active candidate.[12] In July, FDR sent James A. Farley, his good friend and New York Democratic State Party Chairman, on an eighteen-state tour to sound out and gain support for his nomination. In Topeka, Woodring and Helvering welcomed Farley with open arms and promised their political and financial support to the Roosevelt cause. Farley thanked them for their pledge, and told them to sit tight.[13] Five months later, Woodring, Helvering, and Carl Rice accepted an invitation to spend the weekend at Hyde Park, and so in early December the three Kansans headed East.

The trio went first to Washington, D.C., where the Governor had been asked to address the National Women's Democratic Club. Before that group, on 11 December 1931, Woodring gave his famous "Grandsons of the Wild Jackass" speech, which brought him much favorable publicity and thus did much to lay the basis for national recognition.[14] The following day the Kansans joined one of Woodring's old army friends, Captain Floyd Parks, to attend the Army-Navy football game, and afterward they went to Hyde Park. The most important result of this conference with Roosevelt and Farley was Woodring's promise to see that the state convention pledge all twenty of its delegate votes to the New York Governor.[15] Six weeks later, on 23 January 1932, Roosevelt declared that he was a candidate, and in the months that followed, Roosevelt, Woodring, Farley, and Helvering were in frequent contact regarding Kansas support at the Democratic National Convention.[16]

Fulfilling his pledge to Roosevelt to deliver all twenty convention votes was not to be an easy task for Woodring, since there was little support among Kansas Democrats for the New York aristocrat. Opposition to Roosevelt was based on geography, his wealth, and the fact that he was considered a wet. As 1932 dawned, John Nance Garner appeared to be the front runner among Democrats in the Sunflower State. Not far behind was former Secretary of War Newton Baker. On down the line came Al Smith, Roosevelt, Ritchie, Murray, and Traylor.[17] Woodring's task was further complicated by the fact that Jouett Shouse, his friend and fellow Kansan who was chairman of the National Democratic Executive Committee, was aligned with the National Democratic Chairman, John J. Raskob, in opposition to Roosevelt. Shouse and Raskob hoped to see Smith get the nomination. To help achieve that goal, Shouse hoped to become Permanent Chairman at the national convention; however, to qualify for that position he had to be a delegate, and this meant that the Kansas state convention would determine whether or not he would be eligible for the convention post.[18]

Rumblings were first heard in Kansas Democratic circles in February and March, when Woodring and Helvering sent word to all county central committees that they should endorse Roosevelt; if that were impossible, they should at least send uninstructed delegates to the state convention in May. Many Democrats fell into line, and a number found that when they did not, "the Woodring faction had to run the steam roller over its opponents."[19] Despite such tactics a large number of anti-Roosevelt delegates were chosen for the state gathering. Nevertheless, Woodring remained optimistic that he could deliver the votes as promised. In late April, after a serious setback in the Massachusetts primary, a somewhat alarmed Roosevelt wrote to Woodring, expressing hope that he would "have the Kansas delegation instructed because . . . the minority opposition will claim that they own or can control any and every uninstructed delegation."[20] The actions to be taken by the state convention were of growing importance to the national picture.

As Kansas Democrats began to gather in Lawrence for their May 16 meeting there was no doubt that a bitter fight would ensue if Woodring tried to push "down the throats" of the anti-Roosevelt forces a resolution endorsing the New York Governor. While most of the 1,760 delegates apparently felt that Woodring had the strength to secure the endorsement, they believed that his doing so would badly split the party.[21] In spite of such a prospect, Woodring's commitment to Roosevelt remained firm, and he made it clear that he intended to "rise or fall" on that issue. He was, however, willing to make one concession in the interest of party harmony, and that was to accept Jouett Shouse as a delegate-at-large to the national convention.[22]

In the stormy sessions that followed, the convention took a strong stand for prohibition; reelected Dudley Doolittle, an anti-Roosevelt man, as national committeeman, but only after he made a speech supporting the New Yorker; selected sixteen delegates with one vote each and eight delegates-at-large with a half vote each to send to the Democratic National Convention; and instructed the delegation to cast all its votes for Roosevelt. It was the last two actions that caused all the difficulty. Opposition first appeared when it came time to approve the eight delegates-at-large, all of whom had been personally appointed by Governor Woodring (among the eight were Woodring, Helvering, and Shouse). The anti-Roosevelt forces tried to block adoption of the slate, but in a voice vote, Convention Chairman Guy Helvering ruled in favor of the Woodring choices. The same voices of protest were again raised upon the introduction of the resolution instructing the delegates to vote for Roosevelt, but after considerable arguing and name-calling, the resolution was adopted.[23] Why the *New York Times* called it "one of the stormiest political conventions Kansas has seen since the old Populist days"[24] can be understood from the colorful account of a reporter on the scene:

> The selection of delegates came after a day of the wildest jockeying and fighting in the history of the party in this state. . . . So loud and long were the protests over being "steam-rolled" by the Woodring administration forces, it appeared for a time that a riot squad would be necessary to adjourn the morning session. Harmony prevailed until Chairman Guy T. Helvering called the meeting to order. Then the storm broke and the "dove of peace" flew to Missouri or Oklahoma and was not in evidence again so long as a Democratic delegate remained in town.[25]

Woodring and Helvering had fulfilled their pledge to Roosevelt, but they had done so at the cost of unity in the state party.

With the Kansas convention out of the way, Woodring now looked forward to the Democratic National Convention, which was scheduled to open in Chicago on 27 June. Early that month Farley contacted Woodring and asked him to serve as one of FDR's floor managers; thus, the chairman of the Kansas delegation took on an additional responsibility. Since he had never attended a national political convention before, Woodring traveled to Chicago in mid June and observed the Republicans renominate Herbert Hoover and Charles Curtis, a Kansan. He wanted to familiarize himself with the convention hall and to receive some instructions from Farley concerning his upcoming duties.[26]

As the opening session of the Democratic Convention neared, three important battles were shaping up: who would be Permanent Chairman of the convention; what stand would the platform take on prohibition; and who would be the party's nominee. Woodring arrived in Chicago several days before the convention began in order to meet with Farley, Louis Howe, and other Roosevelt strategists.[27] While the search for delegates continued, the Roosevelt masterminds, Farley and Howe, centered their attention on the problem of selecting the Permanent Chairman. That contest would pit Al Smith's choice, Jouett Shouse, against FDR's choice, Senator Thomas J. Walsh of Montana. Since this would be the first test of strength between the pro- and anti-Roosevelt forces, it would be of great significance, because a victory for either faction was bound to have a big psychological impact on the convention delegates.[28]

The Shouse-Walsh fight put Woodring in something of a dilemma, because Shouse was a personal friend who had helped him to secure the gubernatorial nomination just two years before. On the other hand, the Kansas Governor believed that election of Shouse as Permanent Chairman "would result in the defeat of Roosevelt for the nomination."[29] Most Kansas delegates also had mixed emotions about the Shouse situation, a number feeling that they should vote for him for "old time's sake."[30] Woodring searched for a way out of a difficult situation. A partial solution was found when the delegation decided not to abide by the unit rule in the vote on Shouse. What worried Woodring most about Shouse's becoming chairman was that he would attack Roosevelt in his keynote address, thereby hurting the New Yorker's cause. To prevent that from happening, Woodring, on the day before the convention opened, offered Shouse a deal: Kansas would cast all its twenty votes for Shouse if he would assure Woodring that if he were elected chairman, he would not attack Roosevelt in his speech to the convention. The incensed Shouse rejected the offer by telling Woodring to "Go to Hell."[31] Consequently, the Governor got out his "steam roller." In a closed session on the opening night of the convention, the Kansas delegation, with Shouse absent, voted to cast 13½ votes for Walsh and 6½ for Shouse. The following day the convention cast its votes, and Walsh was elected 626-to-528. Woodring made no secret of his position as he proudly proclaimed, "I voted for Walsh."[32] A number of Kansas Democrats were riled by Woodring's refusal to back Shouse, some because they felt that he was being disloyal, and others because they felt that the action would further stir the feud that had begun at the state convention.[33]

On 29 June the members of the Kansas delegation again crossed swords, this time over the plank in the platform calling for the repeal of the Eighteenth Amendment. On the issue of prohibition, Woodring was free to take any position he wanted, because Roosevelt was maintaining a position of neutrality.[34] In line with his past position, Woodring took a strong stand against the repeal of prohibition, even though he fully expected the convention to support repeal. Although he frequently stated that he felt the Kansas delegation should vote dry, because that would express the majority sentiment of the state, he exerted no pressure on the delegates to do so. Subsequently, the Kansas delegates voted 12-to-8 against repeal, but they were out of step with the rest of the convention, which voted in favor of repeal 935-to-214.[35]

During the convention, Woodring was not only busy with the problems facing the Kansas delegation, but was also deeply involved in working for the Roosevelt cause. As a member of the Roosevelt strategy board, he met with Farley, Howe, and a dozen other strategists twice each day in order to evaluate the situation and update plans.[36] Countless hours were also spent in trying to win the support of uncommitted delegates and in convincing others not to panic but to sit firm if Roosevelt did not win on the first few ballots.

On the afternoon of 30 June the convention finally got down to its primary task of selecting the presidential nominee. During the next twelve hours, Roosevelt, Smith, Garner, Baker, Ritchie, and five others were nominated and seconded with all the hoopla and fanfare that the enthusiastic Democrats could muster. Because of Woodring's work at the convention and his friendship with Roosevelt, the strategy board gave him the honor of making one of the half dozen nominating speeches. Picked to represent the Midwest, the Kansas Governor spoke on the plight of the farmer, called for economic stability and social justice for rural Americans, and gave assurance that the "New Commoner" could provide the leadership necessary for the "rehabilitation of agriculture."[37] The hastily written but well-delivered speech impressed both those in the hall and those listening at home.[38] John W. Davis, the 1924 Democratic presidential nominee, who was a delegate from New York, called it "the most sensible speech that has been made in this convention."[39]

Finally, at four o'clock on the morning of July first, the balloting began. The convention was operating under the two-thirds rule, since a maneuver by the Roosevelt forces to bring about its repeal had caused such an uproar that they were forced to back down.[40] This meant that 766 votes were needed to win the nomination. When the roll call on the first ballot reached Kansas, Woodring proudly cast the state's twenty votes for Roosevelt. But not enough other state delegations followed suit, and the first ballot ended with Roosevelt getting only 666 votes. Although this put him well ahead of his two closest competitors—Smith with 201 and Garner with 90—he still needed a hundred more votes.

On the second ballot, FDR picked up a mere ten votes as all forces held firm.[41] At this point, with a deadlocked convention a possibility, spokesmen for Governor Ritchie approached Woodring and offered him the vice-presidency if he would switch the Kansas delegation to the Ritchie camp on the third ballot. Ritchie hoped that the defection of several Roosevelt delegations to him at that particular time would cause a number of convention delegates to panic and jump on a "Ritchie Bandwagon." Although Woodring liked and respected Ritchie, his loyalty to Roosevelt and his conviction that the Ritchie plan was unlikely to get anywhere caused him to reject the offer.[42] After the third ballot, which was almost a carbon copy of the second, the convention adjourned until that evening.

During the day, Farley, working through Congressman Sam Rayburn of Texas, offered the vice-presidency to John Garner in return for the release of the California and Texas delegations. Garner accepted, and when California switched its votes on the fourth ballot, the Roosevelt opposition crumbled, and the New York Governor received 945 votes and the nomination.[43] On the following day, Garner received the second spot on the ticket by acclamation. Woodring was somewhat disappointed by the Roosevelt-Garner deal, because in the past year he had frequently been mentioned as a vice-presidential possibility, and even in the early days of the convention he had been one of a dozen men frequently mentioned for the spot.[44] He had even gone so far as to suggest the possibility to Farley, who immediately rejected the proposition.[45] However, any disappointment that he may have felt over the selection of Garner was probably overshadowed by his joy over the nomination of FDR.

Woodring emerged from the Chicago convention with a prestige and respect that he had not expected. According to the *Kansas City Star*, "A new national Democratic leader has arisen on the political horizon of Kansas."[46] While the *Topeka Daily Capital* said, "Whether one likes it or not the fact remains that Woodring made a place for himself among the national Democratic leaders for the part he played both on the convention floor and on the board of strategy."[47] There was no question that the Kansas Governor had played an important role in the nomination of Roosevelt. He had given not only moral, verbal, and political support but financial assistance as well. When Farley had first visited Kansas in July 1931, he had appealed to Woodring and Helvering for monetary support, and they had been able to respond readily, because their control of the state organization had enabled them to channel party funds where they desired. During the convention, Farley again approached the Kansans with a plea to help replenish the nearly exhausted Roosevelt funds. The Woodring-Helvering organization had accumulated a rather sizable war chest to be used for the Governor's reelection campaign, but Woodring heeded the request and turned over a large sum of money. These contributions came at times when the Roosevelt organization was in great financial need, and FDR and Farley were never to forget that fact.[48]

Several weeks after the convention, Woodring wrote to Roosevelt and explained the importance of having a concrete proposal for farm relief if he were to carry Kansas or any other farm state. At that time Roosevelt, who had already decided to travel West in quest of farm votes, decided that, in view of his friendship with Woodring and the importance of Kansas as a farm state, he would make his views on farm policy known in a speech at Topeka.[49] On 14 September, Woodring sat on a platform with a host of leading Democrats, including John Nance Garner, as Roosevelt gave one of his major campaign addresses. Roosevelt's speech, which included a number of ideas from Woodring, promised a reorganization of the Department of Agriculture, along with tax relief and easy credit for farmers, and it hinted at a kind of voluntary domestic allotment plan to handle the surplus problem.[50] After the speech Roosevelt openly acknowledged Woodring's assistance, saying, "He [Woodring] has been of very great assistance to me, because I have felt—I think very rightly—that he understands the whole agricultural problem of the country about as well as anybody in the United States."[51] While in Topeka, FDR was the personal guest of Woodring, who took him to the State Fair, showed him around town, and honored him with a state dinner at the executive mansion. This visit left no doubt about the respect and warm friendship that existed between the two men.[52]

For the remainder of the 1932 presidential campaign, Woodring was a leader of the Roosevelt forces in the Midwest, and since he was a Democratic Governor in a normally Republican state, his words continued to carry considerable weight with Farley, Howe, and other party strategists. Although Woodring was deeply concerned with the presidential campaign, his participation and his role in it were practically nil, because he was seeking reelection, and therefore had a contest of his own to conduct.

In looking at Woodring's gubernatorial record in the fall of 1932, one could find many positive accomplishments. He had been quite successful in getting his legislative program enacted: he had lowered taxes, balanced the budget, found markets for stripper oil, and brought about reductions in utility rates in most Kansas towns. He had some other factors that would aid in a bid for reelection. These included a growing national reputation; con-

John Nance Garner and Franklin D. Roosevelt, with Governor Harry H. Woodring (left to right), on their 1932 campaign visit to Topeka.

Harry H. Woodring being sworn in as Assistant Secretary of War by Assistant Chief Clerk Frank Hoadley, April 1933; Secretary of War George H. Dern on the left, and Chief of Staff Douglas MacArthur on the right.

President Franklin D. Roosevelt signing the proclamation establishing the government of the Commonwealth of the Philippines; standing, left to right: Secretary of State Cordell Hull, Chief of Staff Malin Craig, and Acting Secretary of War Harry H. Woodring.

trol of an effective state party organization; the opportunity to use his position to obtain publicity; a reputation as a hard-working, competent, yet likable individual.

With such an array of assets, it would seem that reelection would not be difficult; however, the path to a second term was strewn with obstacles. First, there was considerable bitterness and division within the Democratic party. This anger stemmed from various factors, such as Woodring's refusal to heed the requests of Jonathan Davis and Donald Muir for a special legislative session, his "steam roller" tactics in getting the Roosevelt endorsement through the state convention, and his refusal to support Shouse at the national convention. Second, the Republican split of 1930 was rapidly healing as the party began to rally behind the candidacy of the affable and capable Alf M. Landon. Furthermore, the Republicans could now attack Woodring's record as he had attacked theirs two years before. The third obstacle was the old bugaboo of the last election, the candidacy of John R. Brinkley. Finally, there was the deepening Depression, with its accompanying suffering and growing discontent. To the citizens of the Sunflower State, "the bottom of the cycle was only too evident when corn became cheaper to burn than coal and a barrel of crude oil cost less than five gallons of purified drinking water."[53] Economically, things were much worse than they had been two years before.

From the time that Woodring entered the governorship in January 1931 there had never seemed to be any doubt that he would seek reelection. Although he was in office more than a year before he officially made his intentions known, he continually acted like a candidate and made no effort to refute those who said he would run again. In the fall of 1931 it appeared that the bad blood developing between Harry Woodring and Jonathan Davis over the calling of a special session would lead to a fight in the 1932 primary election.[54] In early December, however, another critic of Woodring, Donald Muir, announced that he would seek the Democratic nomination for Governor. This pleased Woodring, because Muir and Davis appealed to the same group of disgruntled party members; should they both enter the primary, the Governor's opposition would be badly divided. Things did not work out that way, because in late December, Davis, who was a widower, remarried, and for the next few months his interest was in his new bride rather than in the governorship. Davis's temporary loss of interest in politics caused his supporters to rally behind Muir.[55]

The 1932 Democratic primary was to be the young crowd–old crowd contest of 1930 all over again, except that Muir rather than Bowman was the leader of the opposition. Although Woodring waited until Friday, 13 May 1932, to file for candidacy (he considered Friday the thirteenth to be a lucky day), he and Muir started campaigning months before that time. The two Democrats took opposite views on nearly every major issue, thus giving the voters a clear-cut choice. Whereas Woodring favored the income tax and tax limitation amendments, Muir opposed them both, claiming that more economy rather than more taxation was the way to solve the state's economic ills.[56] On the matter of forcing reductions in utility rates, Muir attacked the Governor for " 'persecuting' that great and good man, Henry L. Doherty."[57] Muir also lashed out at the power and influence of Guy Helvering, being especially critical of his practice of assessing state employees 5 percent of their salaries for political purposes. Both Woodring and Helvering openly acknowledged that "voluntary contributions" were being collected, but they maintained that it was better to finance a campaign with a large number of small donations than with a few large gifts from persons or corporations who would expect something in return. They also pointed out that in collecting funds as they were, they were merely following a precedent established years before by the Republicans. Muir likewise criticized the work of the Woodring "steam roller" at the state convention and the abandoning of Shouse at Chicago. While the Democratic challenger continually lashed out at Woodring, the latter did not do the same to his opponent, because he was afraid that such action might antagonize the Muir supporters and ultimately drive them to Brinkley.[58]

Muir conducted a vigorous campaign, traveling around the state making numerous personal appearances, and using the radio extensively. Woodring, on the other hand, exerted little effort in the primary. He did not hit the campaign trail; instead he remained in Topeka and utilized the radio as his major weapon.[59] In early July he initiated a daily radio program. Each day at 12:20 P.M., when businessmen and farmers were supposedly home for dinner, the strains of Woodring's campaign theme song, "Let Me Call You Sweetheart," would usher in a thirty-minute program entitled "Under the State House Dome." While the purpose of the privately financed broadcasts originating from the Governor's office was ostensibly to keep Kansans informed on state affairs, Woodring used them primarily as a campaign tool.[60]

As the primary contest progressed, the Governor acknowledged that he was not campaigning very hard. He justified his inaction by saying the people were fed up with politics and were not interested in hearing a lot of campaign rhetoric.[61] Actually, Woodring saw no reason to spend valuable time and money on a contest that he was sure he would win. He had defeated the old crowd two years before, and since then his organization had been greatly strengthened, while theirs had grown weaker. Another Democrat, Walter Eggers of Bird City, was campaigning for the nomination in western Kansas, but he was doing it more as a lark, and no one took him

68

seriously. All in all, the primary was an extremely dull affair, and in the voting on 2 August, Woodring won a clear and decisive victory over Muir, 91,037-to-42,786.[62] With the primary out of the way, the Governor prepared to square off against his two opponents in the general election, Alf M. Landon and John R. Brinkley.

The August primary that witnessed Woodring triumph also saw Republican Alf M. Landon win a clear-cut victory over his conservative opponent, Lacey Simpson. Two years before, no one would have expected Landon to emerge as a gubernatorial candidate, for it was in the 1930 primary, when he was Republican State Chairman, that his candidate, Governor Clyde M. Reed, had been defeated. At that point it had appeared that Landon was "politically dead," because there did not seem to be much demand for "a politician who could not win renomination for his governor."[63] Early in 1931, when friends suggested that he seek the governorship, Landon expressed no desire to do so. This attitude extended into the spring and was in part attributable to his belief that "Woodring has given pretty general satisfaction and I am afraid will be a hard man to beat."[64]

In the months that followed, more and more representatives of the progressive wing of the Republican party began to put Landon forth as a possible nominee. By fall, Landon, who was continually calling for party unity, sounded more and more like a candidate, and on 20 January 1932 he finally announced that he would seek the nomination. Several days later the conservatives put forth their candidate, Lacey Simpson, a farmer from McPherson. No major issue divided the two men; both were for efficiency, economy, economic recovery, lower taxes, and an oil tariff. Although the two candidates conducted a vigorous campaign, they failed to create any enthusiasm among the voters. Landon, however, was successful in convincing a number of conservative leaders that he was the man who could best unite the party; consequently, he handily defeated Simpson, 160,345-to-59,326.[65] The man from Independence had won the nomination, and he had done so without splitting the party.

In late August, when Landon and Woodring were preparing their strategy for the campaign ahead, their attention was not centered so much on each other as it was on the independent candidate, John Brinkley. Less than three months after his defeat in the 1930 gubernatorial contest, Brinkley, who had continued broadcasting over KFKB pending the outcome of his suspension appeal, sold his station and relocated at Del Rio, Texas. Securing authority from Mexican officials, he built a powerful 50,000-watt transmitter right across the Rio Grande River at Villa Acuna; and in March 1931 he began to broadcast over station XER. He soon had thousands of listeners throughout the Middle Western states, including Kansas. Although Brinkley spent considerable time in Texas, he maintained his legal residence in Kansas, which made him eligible to hold public office in that state.

From the time of his November 1930 defeat, Brinkley never left any doubt that he would run again in 1932. Throughout 1931 Brinkleyism was quite evident in Kansas as hundreds of Brinkley Platform Clubs, Brinkley Good Government Clubs, and Brinkley Cowboy and Cowgirl Ranch Clubs sang the praises of the goat-gland doctor and everything that he stood for. An official newspaper, *Publicity*, which was edited by Elmer J. Garner of Wichita, kept the supporters informed of the activities of their illustrious leader and presented a biased account of what was happening in state politics. Occasionally "Doc" would address a Brinkley rally, and when he did, there was always a large gathering—one such event at Milford in February 1931 drew a crowd estimated at twenty thousand.[66]

In January 1932 Brinkley made his formal announcement of candidacy. He explained that he was taking such action not so much because he wanted to but because it was his duty to come to the aid of his fellow Kansans. As an independent candidate, he was not subject to the primary; consequently, he was able to get a jump on the opposition. On 4 June he came out with a twenty-five-point platform that promised something for everyone: free schoolbooks, medical care for the poor, aid to the aged, more and better roads, a state hospital for Negroes, and an artificial lake for every county. To top it all off, he would do all this and more while still providing economy in government. He never really explained how he would accomplish this fantastic feat, and his trusting followers never asked. Brinkley also continued to play his old role of the martyr as he continually reminded his listeners how he had been persecuted by Kansas authorities.[67] When the campaign began in earnest in September of 1932, Brinkley had a large statewide following, and this time his name would be on the ballot; thus, there was no question that he was a power to be reckoned with.

Woodring's strategy for the general-election campaign was quite simple: he would stand on his record of the past two years, fight for the income tax and tax limitation amendments, and promise to provide the same sound leadership in the future that he had in the past. Beyond that, he decided to wait and see what course the opposition followed. In late August the Democratic State Committee, meeting in Topeka, reelected Guy Helvering as State Chairman and adopted a platform calling for reorganization of state and county government (so as to effect economy by avoiding duplication of efforts), passage of the two tax amendments, cheaper textbooks, curbing of public utilities, continuation of the highway program, development of industry, and the placing of public welfare on a high plane. The platform, which was drawn up by Woodring, Helvering, and Rice, was more an endorsement of past actions than a "promise of things to come."[68]

Woodring was now ready to try to accomplish what no previous Democratic Governor of Kansas had been able to do—get reelected. On 12 September he opened his second campaign, as he had his first, with a speech in Ottawa. In this keynote address he touched on the issues that he was to dwell on throughout the contest. Economy and lower taxes received the most attention. He pointed out that his program to reduce expenditures had been so successful that "for the first time in history, the governor of Kansas spent less than the amount appropriated by the legislature." He told how he had saved the state $1 million dollars during his first year in office and would save it $2 million during the second. Such savings, Woodring maintained, had made it possible to reduce the state levy, but the tax burden was still "intolerable," and relief could be provided only by the passage of the proposed tax amendments which would distribute the burden in an equitable manner. He called attention to the reductions in utility rates that had already been brought about, and he vowed to continue his fight against the Doherty interests. He also cited accomplishments in highway surfacing and in aid to crippled children. In closing, he chided the Republicans for refusing to support the tax limitation amendment, and he critized the independent candidate who "promises of free this and free that" and then says he will reduce taxes.[69]

By the middle of September the three gubernatorial candidates were campaigning in earnest. The contrasting personalities and styles of Woodring, Landon, and Brinkley made for a most interesting contest. Woodring, accompanied by his driver, a county chairman, and one or two people from state headquarters, usually traveled from town to town in the Governor's black 12-cylinder Cadillac. Upon arrival, the Governors' companions would start passing out "Win with Woodring" windshield stickers, campaign buttons, and thimbles as the jovial, smiling candidate would walk down the main street, shaking hands, patting backs, and kissing babies. This was the part of campaigning that he liked most: he enjoyed meeting the people, and they seemed to enjoy meeting him. Returning to the town square, he would mount a platform and give one of his rousing political speeches. Then he would be off to the next town; and this sequence would usually be repeated four or five times a day.[70]

If Woodring's pace seemed hectic, it was nothing compared to that of Landon, who generally visited from eight to ten towns daily. Arriving in town with little or no fanfare, the shy, retiring Republican would stroll the streets, exchanging pleasantries with everyone he met. His warm, folksy manner impressed those he stopped to chat with, but Alf never seemed to enjoy this aspect of campaigning as much as his Democratic counterpart did. When it came to making a speech, Landon was at his worst; he was no public speaker. But while he may have stumbled through his speech in a low monotone, his points were well taken, and he left no doubts about his position on a particular issue.[71]

The most aloof, yet the most exciting and colorful of the three candidates, was Brinkley. Displaying a flair for political showmanship the likes of which had never been seen, the independent candidate attracted some of the largest crowds in the political history of Kansas—frequently between ten thousand and fifteen thousand people. Everyone knew when Brinkley was coming to town, because station XER had been announcing it almost hourly the week before. Not only did they know he was coming, but they knew when he arrived, because the event was heralded by a mighty blast on the "five-mile horn" located atop "Ammunition Train No. 1," a wildly painted truck with a sound system and speaker's platform, which was used to carry his entourage. Brinkley then arrived in one of his airplanes or in his custom-built 16-cylinder Cadillac. After several songs, including a rendition by the cowboy singing star Roy Faulkner of Brinkley's theme, "He's the Man," the red-bearded demagogue would appear and say a few prayers, reiterate his numerous promises, and lambaste his opponents and their respective parties. After his speech, he would quickly disappear; he never ventured into a crowd or walked the streets greeting people.[72] A *New York Times* editorial cited an account in which a reporter called Brinkley a man "without personal contact with the common people, a man of mystery."[73] This aloofness was probably the result of his fear that he might be the victim of an assassin's bullet.[74] In terms of activity, his pace compared to that of Woodring, for he visited four or five towns daily. While his newspaper advertising was about the same as that of his opponents, his billboard advertising was considerably more, and his radio time was several times greater, because he was able to utilize his own station at no cost.

Until the campaign was well under way, Woodring aimed his attack primarily at Brinkley. This decision was based in part on his desire to keep the discontent vote from going to the rabble-rousing redhead, but the major reason seems to have been that anger over certain statements made by Brinkley caused him to turn the contest into a personal feud. The memories of the 1930 campaign had planted the seeds of hate. When Brinkley called Woodring a dog; referred to Thurman Hill, Democratic member of the P.S.C., as " 'a pup'—presumably the son of the dog"; and criticized the Chief Executive for buying new silverware for the governor's mansion when Kansans were going hungry, Woodring became furious and began to retaliate. He accused Brinkley of opposing the income tax amendment because he "probably has one million dollars worth of bonds and securities put away" on which he did not have to pay tax under the current laws. The Governor also claimed that in spite of the "Doctor's" tremendous property holdings, he did not pay a cent of real-estate taxes. The two men argued continually over such matters, as well as over the question of whether the state should provide free schoolbooks.[75] Unfortunately, the angry personal exchanges that took place did nothing to shed light on the major issues.

Not all the Woodring-Brinkley charges and countercharges were over petty matters, for on 21 October the Governor exploded a major bombshell. In a speech at Pittsburg he presented "evidence" to back up his previous allegations that Brinkley's campaign was receiving financial support from Henry L. Doherty, who was determined to bring about Woodring's defeat because of his fight over gas rates. After pointing out that Doherty had purchased a major interest in the *Kansas City Journal-Post* the year before in order to fight him and the *Kansas City Star*—a fact already known by most Kansans—Woodring claimed that Doherty had put an "experienced politician" in charge of an operation to channel funds from a mysterious account, J-329, to the *Journal-Post* and to the *Wichita Beacon* for Brinkley advertising that was designed "to destroy the confidence of the people in my administration." More than $75,000 had been spent for such purposes. Woodring claimed to have the sworn testimony of eye witnesses and photostatic copies to back up every statement. He also threatened to turn the evidence over to the proper authorities for legal action—although he never did so.[76] Both Brinkley and Doherty denied the specific charges but not the general allegations; moreover, they were unwilling to file libel suits against the Governor. Throughout the rest of the campaign, Brinkley attacked Woodring's rate war on Doherty and defended the Cities Service Company. The revelation of the Brinkley-Doherty connection appears to have helped Woodring and hurt Brinkley, for after that time the Governor, who had been running well behind the other two candidates, gained ground while Brinkley slipped.[77] Brinkley's declining support in late October was also due to the activities of the Republicans, who had decided to concentrate on him until the last two weeks of the campaign and then turn on Woodring.[78] To offset the effects of Brinkley's newspaper, *Publicity*, the Republicans utilized one of their own, *The Pink Rag*. The *Rag*, a sort of political underground paper, was especially vicious in its attacks on Brinkley.[79] Landon also lashed out at Brinkley, and as the campaign entered the home stretch, the effects of the Republican and Democratic barrages began to take their toll.

Until the last two weeks of the campaign, Landon generally avoided direct attacks on Woodring; instead he addressed himself to issues—pledging lower taxes and economy, criticizing Helvering's operation of the Highway

Department, and questioning Woodring's stand on prohibition.[80] Since Woodring supported the first two matters, he only had to address himself to the latter two. He met the criticism of Helvering's conduct with the fact that in the previous year Kansas had surfaced more roads than any other state and had still cut its operating cost by $250,000. Concerning Landon's charges that Helvering had gathered party funds through 5 percent assessments on state employees, the Governor merely asked if Landon himself had not done the same thing when he was State Chairman.[81] Landon did not reply. With reference to prohibition, Landon charged the Governor with being "wet in Albany and dry in Kansas," but Woodring proclaimed his allegiance to the drys and denounced the national Democratic party's stand on repeal of the Eighteenth Amendment. Although the wet-dry question arose several times, it did not become a real issue in the state election.[82]

Not all of Woodring's challenges came from the other candidates and their followers. One of his major problems came from Kansas public-school teachers. The trouble stemmed from the Governor's support of the tax limitation amendment, which would have prevented the levying of a general property tax in excess of 2 percent of the assessed property valuation. Schoolteachers and school officials opposed this, because the levy of many school districts already exceeded that rate and therefore, if the limit were imposed, a major source of school revenue would be taken away.[83] In early October, Frank L. Pinet, secertary of the Kansas State Teachers Association, writing in the organization's magazine, *The Kansas Teacher*, called for the defeat of the amendment and of Woodring himself, because the Governor had shown "no sympathy for the schools of Kansas."[84] Woodring criticized Pinet for involving the association in partisan politics, and he argued that while the schools might suffer initially, in the long run they would benefit from the new, sound tax policies. Kansas teachers were not impressed, and they continued to fight the proposal and its sponsor. On election eve, thousands of school children, following their teachers' instructions, distributed doorknob pamphlets urging people not to support Woodring or the tax limitation amendment.[85] Another source of difficulty came from a member of the Governor's own party. The old troublemaker Jonathan Davis, his extended honeymoon over, turned on Woodring, joined the Brinkley forces, and urged other Democrats to do likewise. How many of the old guard he carried with him is unknown, but there is no question that his defection hurt Woodring to some extent.[86]

The last two weeks of the campaign saw the Republicans launch a full-scale attack on the Governor.[87] Jesse Greenleaf, Republican member of the P.S.C., claimed that Woodring's attack on Doherty had actually prevented lower gas rates in Kansas, because the P.S.C. was about to negotiate reductions when the Governor intervened in the hope of furthering his own political career.[88] Landon's campaign manager, Frank Carlson, again brought up the prohibition question by claiming that "Woodring wants to appear wet outside of Kansas and dry inside of this state."[89] Landon, too, unloaded his guns on the Governor, questioning his claims about economy, reduction of taxes, and reduction of utility rates. According to Landon, Woodring was "the greatest little claimer Kansas has had in a long time."[90] Woodring struck back by charging that the Republican candidate was using "half-truths and distortions."[91] Their bitter exchanges in the last week of the contest were of a political nature and led to no personal antagonism between the two men.[92] In closing his campaign at Leavenworth on 7 November, Woodring merely reiterated what he had done during the past two years and then asked the voters to choose between his accomplishments and the promises of his opponents. Having taken his fight to each of the state's 105 counties, a tired and non-too-confident Harry Woodring returned to Neodesha to await the election.

Kansas political forecasters were a little more bold in 1932 than they had been two years before. Nearly all of them picked Landon to win, but they were divided about fifty-fifty on whether Woodring or Brinkley would come in second. There was general agreement, however, that Woodring had been rapidly gaining support in the last two weeks of the contest.[93] That final surge brought Woodring close to victory, but not close enough, for Landon took an early lead and never relinquished it. Final tabulations showed Landon gathering 278,581 votes to Woodring's 272,944 and Brinkley's 244,607.[94] The Kansas precedent of never reelecting a Democratic Governor was still intact.

Why had Woodring failed? Why was it that in spite of a fine record, an effective state organization, and vigorous campaigning, he had not been reelected? Before answering these questions, it should be noted how extremely close the election was. In a contest that saw eight hundred thousand votes cast, less than six thousand separated the winner and the runner-up. Had less than one-half of one percent of those voting cast their ballot for Woodring instead of Landon or Brinkley, the victory would have gone the other way. What had kept the Governor from getting the small number of additional votes that could have changed the outcome? There were a number of crucial factors. First, and most important, was the fact that the Republicans were reunited. This was especially important, because Kansas was a Republican state. Second, Woodring had antagonized many members of his own party by his refusal to call a special session of the legislature, as Jonathan Davis had asked him to do, and by his actions at the 1932 state and national Democratic conventions. The defection of Davis and some of his followers to Brinkley also hurt. Third, by tying himself firmly to the tax limitation amendment, which also went down to defeat, the Governor frightened and antagonized Kansas schoolteachers, who fought him vigorously. Fourth, the Brinkley vote, which took votes from both of the regular party candidates, appears to have hurt Woodring more than it hurt Landon.[95] Finally, Woodring was unable to get the farm vote. While he sympathized with the plight of the farmers, he did not know what to do about it. Believing that agricultural relief should be a federal responsibility, he had done nothing; thus, he could not appeal to the rural voter. The relative importance of each of these factors in the outcome of the election is uncertain, but together they spelled defeat.

Although Woodring had been rebuffed on 8 November 1932, it had been a very good day for Democrats throughout the nation. In Kansas they had had one of their most successful election days ever, as they returned George McGill to the United States Senate, sent three men to Congress, and elected sixty representatives and seventeen senators to the state legislature.[96] The big story of that day, however, and the one most pleasing to Woodring, was the presidential victory of his friend Franklin D. Roosevelt. Carrying forty-two states, including Kansas, Roosevelt rolled up an impressive 472-to-59 margin in the electoral college, thus becoming the thirty-second President of the United States.

While his defeat by Landon was disheartening, Woodring was less upset than one would have expected. With his friend FDR headed for the White House, Woodring knew he was in a good position to share some of the fruits of the presidential victory, and that is exactly what he expected to do. After all, he had been one of the "original" Roosevelt supporters, had channeled funds into the FDR coffers at several critical periods, and had worked hard at Chicago to help the New Yorker win the nomination. He was, therefore, confident that Roosevelt and Farley would reward him accordingly. A more retiring person would have sat back and waited to see what position would be offered, but not Woodring. He did not want just any job; he wanted to be Secretary of Agriculture, and he set out to obtain the position.

Whether Woodring really wanted the Agriculture post or whether he sought it because he felt it was the job that he was most likely to get is uncertain. His only real qualification for the position was the fact that he was Governor of one of the most important agricultural states. Except for lowering taxes, he had, as Governor, made no real effort to aid the farmer; moreover, he had made no specific proposals about how to cope with the problem of farm surpluses or the resulting low prices.[97] Only after FDR's nomination did Woodring begin to think seriously about the farm problem. Perhaps it was Roosevelt's September 14 statement that Woodring understood the problem of agriculture as well as anyone else in the country that boosted the Kansan's ego and motivated him to seek the Agriculture post.

Less than two weeks after Woodring's defeat, his friends and supporters began to conduct a letter-writing campaign to solicit support from politicians, newspapermen, and agricultural organizations for having the Governor appointed as Secretary of Agriculture.[98] On 5 December, Woodring and Helvering, who also expected to be duly rewarded for his support of FDR, traveled to Warm Springs, Georgia, to discuss the farm problem with the President-elect. Although Woodring publicly termed the conference "eminently satisfactory," he privately felt that he had not had adequate time to present his views. Therefore, on 27 December he wrote to Roosevelt, criticizing the various Voluntary Domestic Allotment Plan proposals; presenting the barest outline of his relief program, which would make "the tariff effective on farm products"; and requesting "at least an entire evening's discussion" of his proposals. The requested meeting was set for 12 January 1933.[99]

Before Woodring traveled to Hyde Park, he had to fulfill his final obligations to the state of Kansas by formally turning over the reins of government to his successor. That task was accomplished on Alf Landon's inauguration day, 9 January 1933. At the swearing-in ceremony, Woodring made his farewell address. After citing the achievements of the past two years and praising Landon, his "neighbor and friend for years," he closed by stating that he left the office "with the feeling that I have given my state the very best that was mine."[100] While many Kansans were undoubtedly happy to see him go, a large number probably held views similar to those of the Topeka columnist Charles H. Sessions and the Emporia journalist William Allen White. Sessions wrote, "If it falls to the Democrats ever to elect another governor of Kansas we hope they will show the good sense to elect Harry Woodring."[101] Although White had supported Landon in the election, he paid an editorial tribute to Woodring by sayings:

Governor Woodring should not be lost to public life in this state and in this country. He is a man of exceptional qualities of heart and mind. He is as honest as daylight. He is clear-visioned and courageous. The Democratic president looking over the West for a cabinet officer can find no man better fitted for the honor and for the hard work required of a cabinet-head than Governor Harry Woodring of Kansas. Kansas is as proud of Harry Woodring as though he had overcome the handicap of his Democracy in a Republican state.[102]

After Landon's inauguration, Woodring and Helvering headed for New York, where they spent the entire afternoon of 12 January discussing the farm problem with Roosevelt. At that meeting, as he had done at Warm

77

Springs and in his letter, Woodring voiced violent opposition to the Voluntary Domestic Allotment Plan, emphasizing that he was opposed to restricting production as long as people at home and abroad were going hungry. His solution was to "return to America her foreign [agricultural] markets" by establishing "a program of debenture credit on foreign sales and to exchange agricultural products with foreign nations."[103] Roosevelt listened with interest to these ideas, but he was not yet ready to commit himself to a farm program or to a man to head it. What promises, if any, were made concerning a job in the new administration are unknown, but that Woodring was confident of receiving a good position seems evident from the fact that a week later he completed arrangements to lease a large apartment at the Mayflower Hotel in Washington.[104]

In late January, Woodring returned to Kansas and continued a personal letter-writing campaign to people close to Roosevelt, asking that they urge appointment of him as Secretary of Agriculture.[105] In a letter to Louis Howe, one of FDR's oldest and closest advisers, Woodring boldly proclaimed:

I want to be Secretary of Agriculture. . . . As to future political aspect and success—we must depend on our real friends. One cannot be *elected* President without first being nominated. One cannot be *nominated* only by work of loyal friends. Gov. R. was not nominated by the Wallaces, Peakes [*sic*], Murphys, Ed. O'Neals, Tabors and such bandwagon Roosevelt Republicans. But by Woodrings, Helverings, Farleys and Howes.[106]

The point was clear—he had done something for Roosevelt; now the favor should be returned.

Towards the end of January, reports began to circulate in Washington that Henry A. Wallace of Iowa, an advocate of the Voluntary Domestic Allotment Plan, might be named as the new Secretary of Agriculture. These reports were unsettling to Woodring, but when Roosevelt wrote on 1 February and assured him that no decision would be made on the appointment until just prior to the inauguration, the Kansan's hopes received a boost.[107] Both Howe and Farley were Woodring supporters; but this meant little, for when it came to making cabinet selections, Roosevelt had a mind of his own. As he remarked to the press and to his close advisers, "I regard the cabinet as peculiarly my own official family to be named only by me."[108]

During the second week of February the President-elect decided to offer the Agriculture post to Wallace. After some hesitation the Iowan accepted, and on 22 February the formal announcement was made.[109] The decision to give the position to Wallace rather than to Woodring was a reflection of Roosevelt's policy views rather than a personal matter. He had come to the conclusion that Voluntary Domestic Allotment rather than restoration of world markets offered the best hope for the American agricultural dilemma; thus, he chose Wallace. Although Woodring was not aware of it, he had been given serious consideration for the post of Secretary of War, but in the end Roosevelt decided to appoint former Utah Governor George H. Dern to that position.[110]

Woodring was quite upset when he did not get the cabinet position that he had hoped for, but Farley reminded him that many fine positions were still to be filled and assured him that he would not be forgotten. However, when Inauguration Day arrived, Woodring's future was still undecided. A few days later he was tentatively offered the position of Treasurer of the United States, which would have meant that his signature would have appeared on every piece of United States paper money; but Woodring rejected this idea, because he did not desire what was primarily a clerical job. In the days that followed, there was considerable speculation that he would be named either Governor-General of the Philippines or Comptroller of Currency, but no such offers were forthcoming.[111]

Finally, in late March, Farley approached Woodring about an appointment as Assistant Secretary of War. Woodring's first reaction was one of disappointment; with the domestic and world situation being what it was at that time, the War Department did not sound like a very exciting place to be.[112] There were, however, some factors that made the job appealing to Woodring: his military service had been a very pleasant experience, and he had been quite impressed by the caliber of leaders that he had come into contact with; there would also be considerable opportunity for travel.[113] Furthermore, he had taken an active role in the affairs of the National Guard and of the American Legion—organizations that were vitally concerned with national defense. The new position would give him the opportunity to do something concrete to provide for that defense. He also realized that if he turned this job down, he had no way of knowing what the next offer might be. The position would at least put him in the "Little Cabinet," and it would give him an opportunity to be in a policy-making position. When Woodring hesitated, Farley suggested that he go and talk the matter over with Secretary of War Dern before making his decision. After discussing the nature of his duties with the affable Dern, Woodring decided to take the post.[114] On 30 March he informed the President of his acceptance, and on the following day his name was submitted to the Senate for confirmation. Since there was no opposition, the appointment was quickly approved, and on 6 April 1933, with Secretary Dern and the Army Chief of Staff, Gen. Douglas MacArthur, at his side, Harry H. Woodring took the oath that made him the Assistant Secretary of War.[115] A new and controversial career was about to begin.

5

Assistant Secretary of War

Washington, D.C., was bustling with activity in the spring of 1933 when Harry Woodring assumed his new position as Assistant Secretary of War. There was action throughout the city as the forces of President Franklin D. Roosevelt launched a full-scale attack on the worst depression the country had ever experienced. The eyes of the nation were focused on "FDR" as he pushed through Congress an unbelievable array of legislation—the New Deal was marching in. Bills establishing a host of new agencies, such as the Federal Emergency Relief Administration, Civilian Conservation Corps, Agricultural Adjustment Administration, National Recovery Administration, and the Tennessee Valley Authority, sailed through the legislative branch; and before long, an array of alphabetical designations, such as FERA, CCC, NRA, AAA, and TVA, had become an important part of America's vocabulary. As the citizens grew increasingly aware of the many new agencies and their activities, they also became familiar with the creators and administrators of those programs. Such names as Frances Perkins, Harold Ickes, Henry Wallace, Harry Hopkins, Raymond Moley, and Rexford Tugwell were soon known to most Americans.[1]

As the New Deal advanced, most governmental departments, such as Treasury, Labor, Interior, Agriculture, and Commerce, saw a rapid growth in their activities, obligations, expenditures, and personnel.[2] However, not all departments were experiencing across-the-board expansion; several, most notably the War and Navy departments, saw their responsibilities increased, but at the same time they experienced reductions in budgets and manpower. With the Roosevelt administration engrossed in matters of relief, recovery, and reform, there was little time and even less money for defense. Consequently, the military services, especially the Army, felt the full impact of the nation's economic collapse. That the leaders of the military establishment were able to tolerate such a state of affairs so graciously was primarily a result of the years of military neglect that they had witnessed and experienced.[3]

There is much validity to the adage that in peacetime "we Americans treat our Army like a mangy old dog."[4] Many times in the history of the United States the Army has been permitted to deteriorate to a dangerously low level of effectiveness, but at no time were negligence of and indifference to it greater than during the two decades following World War I.[5] The 1920s saw Army strength dip to a low of 135,000 officers and men (only 35,000 more than the limit imposed on Germany to keep her militarily impotent). Furthermore, the force was not only lacking in manpower, but in equipment and training as well.[6] Dwight Davis, who served as Calvin Coolidge's Secretary of War from 1925 to 1929, referred to the early 1920s as "those discouraging years of curtailment of activities, reductions, demotions and disinterestedness on the part of the public."[7] Although the situation was bad under Presidents Harding and Coolidge, it became even worse under President Hoover, who, when the Depression hit, came to the conclusion that the best place to start reducing government expenditures was the Army. Apathy and economy so decimated the United States war machine in the late 1920s and early 1930s that it soon reached the lowest degree of effectiveness that it had known since before the war. According to the 1933 *Annual Report* of the Chief of Staff, the United States Army ranked seventeenth among the standing armies of the world.[8] Such was the state of military affairs when the Roosevelt administration assumed the reins of government. Although the Republican Chief Executives of the 1920s must bear much of the blame for the decline of the military, the responsibility is not theirs alone, because they reflected the attitudes of both Congress and the American public.[9]

When Woodring entered the War Department in the spring of 1933, it was organized in accordance with the provisions of the National Defense Act of 1920. Heading the organization was the Secretary of War, who was directly responsible to the President for raising and training the Army. Additional military responsibilities included providing for the defense of the insular possessions and the coast of the continental United States, and the developing of new weapons and material. The position also carried with it certain nonmilitary functions, such as the maintenance and operation of the Panama Canal; administration of the government of the Philippines, Puerto

Rico, and the Canal Zone; development of inland waterways and adminis-stration of the Inland Waterways Corporation; formulation and execution of flood-control measures; and the maintenance and administration of the United States Military Academy.[10]

To fill the number one post at the War Department, Roosevelt appointed former Utah Governor George H. Dern. This was not a particularly wise choice, because the affable, soft-spoken Dern had no knowledge of and little interest in the Army. Born near Hooper, Nebraska, in 1872, the strapping young farm boy had gone to the University of Nebraska, where he captained the football team. In 1895 he left college and moved with his family to Utah, where his father became a part owner of a small gold-mining company. Starting out as a bookkeeper, young Dern rose in the ranks, eventually be-coming manager of the Mercur Gold Mining Company, one of the largest in the state. During these years Dern made several major contributions to metallurgical processing—most notably the creation of a vacuum slime filtra-tion process and, in conjunction with Theodore P. Holt, the development of the world-famous Holt-Dern ore-reduction system. In 1914 the then-wealthy and well-known metallurgist ventured into politics, being elected a State Senator. Ten years in the legislature enabled him to learn the ropes of state government, and in 1924 he ran for, and was elected, Governor, a post that he held for eight years. As a progressive Democrat, Dern gained na-tional prominence by sponsoring Workman's Compensation and Public Utilities acts, by instituting tax reforms, and by leading a successful fight to gain recognition of the principle that the water of streams belongs to the states and not to the federal government. In 1931 he became a strong Roose-velt supporter, and as a reward he received the War post rather than the Interior position which he had coveted.[11]

Initially, Dern's appointment created little enthusiasm among military leaders, many of whom considered him a pacifist, but they soon warmed up to him.[12] Unfortunately the new Secretary was able to offer little leadership to the Army during his tenure. His failure stemmed in part from his lack of familiarity with the military and his lack of interest in the activities of the War Department, but the major problem was his deteriorating health. Already failing when he accepted the job, the health of the sixty-one-year-old Secretary became progressively worse with each passing year. High blood pressure and a weak heart sapped more and more of his energy, and as a result, he was frequently away from his office for weeks at a time. Almost from the day that he took office there were rumors that his condition would force him to resign, but he refused to do so, and the warm-hearted Roosevelt could not bring himself to ask for his resignation. Consequently, the War

Department lumbered through Roosevelt's first term with a sick man at the helm.[13]

One step below the Secretary in the departmental hierarchy was the Assistant Secretary of War. The Assistant, who, like his immediate superior, was a civilian, had as his primary responsibility the procurement of all military supplies. His additional major duties included the development of plans and procedures to insure that industry would be able to produce the supplies needed in war time (industrial mobilization), the sale and disposal of surplus supplies, the purchase and sale of military real estate, and the settlement of claims by and against the Army. Furthermore, when the Secretary was absent, the Assistant became the acting head of the department, with all the authority and responsibility that the number one job entailed.[14] With Dern's health being what it was, Woodring frequently found himself carrying the Secretary's burdens as well as his own.

The third-ranking member of the War Department was the Chief of Staff. This post, which was filled by a professional soldier, was, next to that of Commander in Chief, the highest-ranking military position in the United States Army. In addition to serving as the Secretary's immediate adviser on all military matters, the Chief of Staff was responsible for planning and executing the Army's plans for national defense. To assist him in this enormous task he had an Assistant Chief of Staff, General Staff, Special Staff, and numerous other advisory and administrative personnel.[15]

Occupying the position of Chief of Staff when Woodring arrived at the War Department was one of the most able military leaders the United States had ever produced, Gen. Douglas MacArthur. He graduated from West Point in 1903 and then, as a junior officer, served as a military aide to his famous father, Gen. Arthur MacArthur, and to President Theodore Roosevelt. According to Secretary of War Newton D. Baker, he had emerged from World War I as "the greatest American field commander produced by the war."[16] When the conflict was over, MacArthur returned to West Point, where, as the youngest superintendent in the history of the academy, he instituted a number of far-reaching changes in the instructional and physical-training programs. In 1925 his military genius was further recognized when he became the youngest Major General in the Army. Because MacArthur's fame continued to spread, it came as no surprise when, in November 1930, President Hoover appointed him Chief of Staff.[17] During his long military career, MacArthur had come to realize the importance of getting along with his superiors; thus, it was not unusual that he developed a warm and smooth relationship with Secretary Dern and with Assistant Secretary Woodring.[18]

To those promilitary advocates in the nation's capital who hoped that the coming of Roosevelt would bring better times for the United States

Army, the early days of the New Deal brought a rude awakening. Shortly after taking office, the new President shocked them by urging a $144 million cut in Army appropriations, the forced retirement of four thousand officers, and a twelve-thousand-man reduction in enlisted strength. An immediate outcry from the War Department, along with severe criticism from a number of influential newspapers and patriotic organizations, ultimately resulted in the restoration of some of the proposed cuts. Nevertheless, the 1934 budget provided a mere $227 million for military purposes—down more than $52 million from the year before, and the lowest outlay since before the war.[19]

Although Secretary Dern was forced to reduce Army expenditures not just to the bone but "into the bone," he did all that he could to cut spending in the civilian side of the department, so that the military forces, which General MacArthur maintained were already "below the point of safety," would not suffer further.[20] Such efforts, however, achieved only limited success. While the austerity programs did not lead to a reduction of military personnel, as had originally been feared, they did result in a virtual halt in the development of weapons and equipment, the curtailment of training exercises, the continued use of inadequate and obsolete equipment, and reductions in the activities of the Reserve Officers Training Corps (ROTC) and the National Guard.[21] By the mid 1930s the United States Army was nearing an all-time low in terms of national favor, funds, and effectiveness.[22]

While the Army suffered considerably under the impact of the Great Depression, it paradoxically benefited from it via the creation of the Civilian Conservation Corps (CCC). In an effort to help provide economic relief and at the same time preserve the nation's natural resources, Congress, at the President's urging, created the CCC in April 1933. The new program, under the direction of Robert Fechner, started as a joint operation of the Departments of Labor, Interior, Agriculture, and War. Initially the Army had the responsibility of enrolling, supplying, and providing very limited supervision over the conservation activities of more than 350,000 young men located in more than thirteen hundred CCC camps throughout the country. When it soon became evident, however, that the civilian departments were unable to carry out their responsibilities, the mammoth task was almost completely turned over to the Army, even though Fechner remained the director of the program.[23] Consequently, in June of 1933 the War Department turned its attention from the military army to the newly created civilian army. Few officials, military or civilian, were more involved in the CCC than was the Assistant Secretary of War. Purchasing or leasing the land for the camps and providing the necessary food, clothing, blankets, and personal supplies for more than one-third of a million men was no easy task; but Woodring, who spent most of his first eight months in office dealing with CCC matters,

84

proved to be an able administrator, so the massive logistical demands were met successfully.[24]

Toward the end of 1933 the Regular Army personnel who had carried on the bulk of the CCC supervision began to be replaced by specially trained civilian personnel, so that the venture lost a great deal of the military air that it had previously possessed. Whether the CCC activities of 1933 and early 1934 helped or hindered the Army was, and continues to be, a source of considerable speculation. Some War Department officials, including Woodring, tended to emphasize the assets of the program. Those individuals pointed to such benefits as the leadership training that it provided for junior officers and the experience that it provided in mobilizing a moderately large number of men. Others connected with the military, such as Secretary Dern, complained that the CCC took thousands of officers and key enlisted personnel out of the Regular Army, thereby making it useless in the event that it was immediately needed. There was one point on which all those associated with the War Department agreed: the virtual halt of military training and the utilization of reserve war supplies such as clothing, boots, and blankets could have dire consequences in time of emergency.[25] There was no question that the CCC was a mixed blessing as far as the Army was concerned.

Just as the War Department received some benefits from the CCC, it did likewise from projects of the Public Works Administration (PWA) and the Works Progress Administration (WPA). Between 1933 and 1938 more than $250 million was spent on work-relief projects that provided the Army with sorely needed facilities and supplies.[26] Through the PWA and the WPA the Army received such things as hospitals, gymnasiums, ammunition, motor vehicles, aircraft, and new housing for officers and enlisted personnel. While the primary purpose behind such projects was to provide work for the unemployed (pump-priming projects), they did serve to provide the Army with buildings, equipment, and ammunition that, in all likelihood, it would not otherwise have received.

The year 1933 was busy yet relatively uneventful as far as Assistant Secretary Woodring's official activities were concerned; however, in the social realm, an event took place that was to have a profound effect on his subsequent personal and political careers. On 25 July 1933 the forty-six-year-old Kansan's life as a bachelor came to an end when he married Helen Coolidge, the beautiful and talented daughter of Democratic Senator Marcus A. Coolidge of Massachusetts. Helen, whose father had made a modest fortune in the machine-tool business before entering the Senate in 1931, had all the advantages that wealth and social standing could provide. Born in Fitchburg, Massachusetts, in 1906, she had received a fine education at the Mary C. Wheeler School in Providence, Rhode Island, and the Brad-ford Academy in her home state. While showing exceptional talent both as a writer and as a painter, she preferred to pursue a career in the latter; thus, she went to Boston and studied at the Howard Walker School of Fine Art. When her father took his seat in the Senate in 1931, Helen moved to Wash-ington—a place that she found most agreeable. Her fame as an artist quickly spread throughout the capital city, and before long, she was sketching and painting portraits of many of her father's colleagues. Being gifted, attractive, and very personable, she inevitably acquired a large circle of friends and an equally large number of suitors: Helen Coolidge was soon one of the most sought-after young ladies on the Washington social scene.[27]

Since she was the daughter of a Democratic Senator, it was only natural that Helen soon found herself caught up in the activities of the National Women's Democratic Club, and it was through that organization that she first met her husband-to-be. On 11 December 1931 she attended a meeting of the club, at which she heard an address by the Governor of Kansas, Harry Woodring. At a reception afterwards, national Democratic leader Jouett Shouse introduced her to him. Woodring was immediately impressed with her grace and charm, and he promised to call on her the next time he was in Washington.[28]

Six months later, in May 1932, Woodring fulfilled his pledge by stopping off in Washington to spend a few days in the company of Miss Coolidge. On that visit something happened to Harry Woodring that had never hap-pened before—he fell in love. Before departing, he asked her to marry him, but she was unwilling to take such an important step after a courtship of only a few days. The two agreed to keep in touch with one another, and in the following months they corresponded regularly. In January 1933, when Woodring moved to Washington, they began to see each other regularly, and soon she began to feel for him what he had felt for her. Therefore, in June, when he proposed a second time, she accepted. Six weeks later the couple were married in an elaborate ceremony at the Coolidge residence in Fitchburg, and after a honeymoon in Europe the newlyweds took up resi-dence at the Mayflower Hotel.[29]

Because of Helen's charm and grace and Harry's personality and posi-tion, the Woodrings soon became one of the most prominent couples in the nation's capital. They were continually entertaining, and being entertained by, cabinet members, congressmen, generals, ambassadors, and foreign dig-nitaries. Their active social life was instrumental in their acquisition of numerous friends in the administration, on the Hill, at the War Department, and among members of the news media. Official Washington tended to look upon the Woodrings as the perfect couple—a view that especially seemed to

86

be held by FDR.[30] There can be no doubt that Helen Woodring was a major asset to her husband and his career; her importance was to become more evident as the decade rolled on.

Although Woodring's first eight months at the War Department were relatively quiet, routine, and noncontroversial, such a state of affairs was not destined to continue. The year 1934 opened with a bang, and before the end of January the Assistant Secretary of War was one of the most controversial men in Washington. Harry's troubles began when his article entitled "The American Army Stands Ready" appeared in the 6 January issue of *Liberty Magazine*. In this story he claimed that the Army was "the only branch of the government . . . organized and available not only to defend our territory, but also to cope with social and economic problems in an emergency." He then proposed that the activities of the Civilian Conservation Corps be expanded and placed under the control of the military. If this were done, the Army could organize the CCC men, the World War veterans, and the people on relief "into a system of economic storm troops that could support the government's efforts to smash the depression."[31]

To propose such action and to use a phrase like "economic storm troops" at that particular time was quite unfortunate, because the country was becoming increasingly alarmed over reports from Europe concerning the actions of Adolf Hitler's and Benito Mussolini's "storm troopers."[32] In an immediate reaction against the article the White House was flooded with letters and telegrams demanding that the President remove Woodring at once.[33] Typical of the messages received was one from the noted historian Charles A. Beard, who called the article "the first fascist threat from the War Department." Beard warned Roosevelt that such threats "spread distrust of your intentions and your administration." He concluded by asking FDR "to wash your hands of the fascist doctrine and to remove Woodring within fifteen minutes."[34]

In the days that followed, the demands for removal grew in number and intensity. On 24 January a letter signed by some two hundred educators from thirty Eastern colleges and universities was made public in New York. It demanded that Assistant Secretary Woodring "be forced to resign his public office" because his proposals were "not even a thinly veiled advocacy of the German Nazi's dictatorship methods." The signers expressed a fear that if such an attitude prevailed in the War Department, it meant that the country was being prepared for "such an abuse of powers as is intolerable to contemplate." Two days after the letter was released, it and the controversy with which it dealt were brought up on the Senate floor by Senator Thomas Schall of Minnesota; however, they occasioned no debate or discussion.[35] Still, the demands for Woodring's removal flowed into the White House.

When the controversy first arose, the President tried to ignore the matter, but by early February the whole affair had reached such proportions that he asked his Press Secretary, Steve Early, to contact Woodring and straighten the matter out. In the meantime, Roosevelt made it clear that it was his steadfast policy to maintain civilian, not military, control over the CCC camps. When a reporter asked the President if he cared to comment on Woodring's article, he answered in the negative, and then added, "I have been very careful not to read it." In this way he kept from becoming involved. Steve Early, in whose lap the problem now lay, privately criticized Woodring for saying things that gave the impression that the policies of the War Department were at odds with those of the President. Woodring explained to Early and then to Roosevelt that he felt that the whole matter was not as serious as the press and some critics of the administration had made it appear. He maintained that the criticism was due to the placing of a literal interpretation on the term "economic storm troops." According to the Assistant Secretary, "I used this term as a figure of speech just as many people currently refer to the recovery efforts of the government as a war against depression." This explanation apparently satisfied the President, for he did no more than warn the Assistant Secretary to be more careful in the future. The press was also satisfied with Woodring's latest statement, and by mid February the whole matter had been dropped.[36]

The controversy over the CCC article did several things for the Assistant Secretary of War. First, it made him a nationally known figure. Unfortunately, however, the image that he first cast was not a good one, and for years a number of Americans would continue to remember him only as a man with "fascist" ideas. Second, it indicated that it would take a real blunder on Woodring's part to bring the wrath of the President down on him. Receiving only a reprimand probably made the Assistant Secretary feel that he was relatively free to say what he wished. Third, neither Roosevelt nor Woodring was stampeded into action when a vocal section of the electorate became inflamed. This was evident from the fact that neither man considered the public's demand for resignation as a solution to the problem. It would seem that all the furor over the article should have taught the outspoken Kansan to be more careful about what he said, but the next six years were to show that it did not.

While those individuals who were upset over the CCC article were still clamoring for Woodring's scalp, a series of events occurred that was to place the Assistant Secretary in even hotter water. His new problems surfaced on 6 February, when the District of Columbia grand jury began to investigate "irregularities in the awarding of army contracts," specifically those relating to the procurement of motor vehicles and aircraft and to the disposal of surplus materials. On the same day that the grand jury convened, Secretary Dern and President Roosevelt publicly called for a complete investigation in order to determine whether lobbyists or Army officials were involved in any "wrongdoing" in the awarding of contracts.

The announcement of the grand-jury probe came as no real surprise in light of recent rumors floating around the capital that favoritism had become the determining factor in the awarding of millions of dollars worth of Army contracts for trucks, cars, and motorcycles. The contracts in question had been granted in conjunction with two PWA grants that the War Department had received in late 1933; one was for $10 million to be used for motor vehicles, while the other, for $7.5 million, was to be used for aircraft and aircraft equipment. No sooner had the first contracts been let in December 1933, than disappointed bidders began to voice complaints that the awards were unfair because they had been unduly influenced by lobbyists. This questioning of the manner in which the War Department obtained its equipment immediately brought Woodring into the picture, because, as Assistant Secretary of War, he was the individual directly responsible for the procurement and disposal of all army equipment and supplies, including aircraft.

War Department officials were not surprised by the grand-jury inquiry, because they had helped to initiate it. Woodring and Secretary Dern had first heard the rumors concerning contracts in late 1933, and in January 1934 the Secretary asked the Attorney General to investigate the matter. One month later the Justice Department made its findings known to Dern, who in turn made them available to the District Attorney of the District of Columbia. One of the things brought out by the Attorney General's investigation was that the activities of Joseph Silverman, Jr., a New York trader in army surplus goods, were "questionable"; thus, on 5 February, Woodring issued an order barring Silverman from doing further business with the War Department until the grand jury's investigation had been completed. That announcement, which was followed by the President's call for a full inquiry, immediately led to numerous rumors that the District Attorney's probe would reveal a "major scandal" in connection with the awarding of contracts.[37]

The grand-jury investigation, billed as *United States* v. *Silverman and others*, opened on 6 February, with Woodring being the first to testify. In the next three weeks nearly forty witnesses—including Frederick H. Payne, Assistant Secretary of War under President Hoover; Chief of Staff Mac-Arthur; Maj. Gen. Hugh A. Drum, the Assistant Chief of Staff; Ralph T. O'Neil, a former National Commander of the American Legion; and representatives from a number of firms that manufactured automobiles and aircraft—testified in regard to an "alleged conspiracy to defraud the War Department." Although the inquiry started as an examination into the manner in which contracts for motor vehicles had been awarded, it quickly turned to charges that civilian lobbyists were selling their services to industrial firms on the grounds that they could influence the awarding of Army contracts. Inquiry was also made into the way in which surplus Army property was being disposed of. Since each of the areas under scrutiny was Woodring's responsibility, it is not surprising that his personal integrity soon became the object of much speculation, and in most cases the implication was that he personally was involved in some form of graft. Since the testimony before the grand jury was secret, there was room for a great deal of guessing about what was being revealed and what the consequence would be.[38]

The probe was only a few days old when Woodring became "a real storm center in the nation's capital," and rumors abounded that he was on his way out.[39] At the same time, newspapers carried stories that Woodring was not getting along well with Secretary Dern or with General MacArthur. Washington columnists Drew Pearson and Robert S. Allen, whose syndicated column "Washington Merry-Go-Round" appeared in more than 250 daily newspapers, claimed that MacArthur was actively trying to force the Assistant Secretary out of the War Department.[40] The *New York Daily News* did not directly accuse Woodring of any wrongdoing, but it might as well have done so, for it told of the contract controversy and then called Kansas the "center of a group of PWA fund chiseling politicians."[41] The one thing common to nearly all the early stories on the grand-jury investigation was the implication that Woodring was engaged in some wrongdoing. At this point, Harry Woodring's future did not look too promising. Although annoyed by what he called "unfair criticism and insinuations made against me," Woodring made no public statements concerning his guilt or innocence.[42] Privately, though, he expressed his firm conviction that when the "investigations of the War Department activities now underway are completed, my actions and efforts will be fully justified."[43]

As the grand-jury investigation progressed, the story of the alleged conspiracy unfolded. The central figure was Joseph H. Silverman, Jr., a New York exporter who for many years had been buying army surplus supplies, primarily clothing, and selling them abroad. Because of his frequent contact with the War Department, Silverman eventually came to be on good terms with many of its top officials. When Woodring moved into his new apartment at the Mayflower Hotel in 1933, his neighbor happened to be Silverman. Since they were neighbors and came into frequent contact with each other by virtue of their positions, the two men naturally came to be on friendly terms and were frequently seen with each other. The relationship was further strengthened when the surplus dealer secured the legal services of Ralph

90

T. ("Dyke") O'Neil, a Topeka attorney who was a long-time friend of Woodring's and was past National Commander of the American Legion.[44]

In late 1933 Silverman and several of his close associates supposedly began to use both their acquaintanceship with Woodring and O'Neil's long-time friendship with him as ploys in an "influence peddling" scheme. The Silverman interests approached several automobile and aviation firms and offered to represent them at the War Department. For a rather large retainer fee and a 15 percent kickback on the business obtained, they promised to use their "inside influence" to see that their clients received favorable contracts. This would supposedly be accomplished by securing changes in specifications that would assure acceptance of their bid. The impression given to the firms that were approached was that Silverman and O'Neil would be able to use their influence with the Assistant Secretary in order to get the necessary changes in contracts.[45] Of this plan O'Neil had no knowledge.

In preparing his case for the grand jury, District Attorney Leslie C. Garnett discovered that Woodring had previously changed some specifications for motor vehicles; therefore, he wished to ascertain if the changes had been made to give advantage to certain contractors. In testifying before the grand jury, the Assistant Secretary denied, as did O'Neil, any knowledge of the Silverman scheme, but he did admit that he had made a change on the specifications of Army trucks to be purchased under the PWA motorization grant. That change, he explained, which substituted a "full force lubrication system" for the more dated "splash system," was made in order to assure that the contracts would be let on a competitive basis—a practice that had not previously been followed, even though a law requiring "competitive bidding" had been on the books since 1926. In justifying the contract changes, Woodring pointed out that during the Hoover administration 80 percent of the trucks bought by the Army had been purchased from the Chevrolet Motor Company, because Chevrolet was the only truck manufacturer using the splash lubrication system called for in the Army's specifications. Since it was the only company to bid for the trucks, it had always received the contract. A desire to get the most up-to-date lubrication system for Army vehicles, and at the same time to obey the law, had led Woodring to make the change in specifications. Such action enabled a number of new firms to bid on the trucks, and when Chevrolet, which had enjoyed a virtual monopoly for years, lost the contract, it pointed to Woodring and cried conspiracy. Its complaints set in motion the investigation into the Army's contracting procedures.[46]

After hearing testimony on the Silverman scheme and the letting of contracts, the grand jury turned to the question of disposal of surplus materials. This segment of the investigation revealed that shortly after Woodring assumed the War Department post he had agreed to continue the policy of his predecessor that had prohibited the Army from repurchasing supplies that it had previously sold as surplus. In order to implement this policy, the War Department's contracts for sales of surplus materials contained a clause prohibiting the buyer from selling the items in the United States. In July 1933 Woodring, faced with the problem of clothing more than three hundred thousand CCC workers, suspended for one year the "no repurchase" provision as applied to underwear, so that he could repurchase the sorely needed items from Joseph Silverman. While the repurchase price for the seven hundred thousand sets of underwear was nearly double what Silverman had originally paid for them, it was still $750,000 less than the items would have cost had they been purchased new. Woodring, who appeared before the grand jury on three separate occasions, openly admitted that his change in policy had enabled the New York surplus dealer to make a handsome profit, but he justified his action primarily on the grounds that it had saved American taxpayers three-quarters of a million dollars.[47]

While the inquiry into disposal of surplus materials did not indicate any legal wrongdoing on Woodring's part, it did reveal several instances of poor judgment. Shortly after he came to office in early 1933, Woodring had declared large numbers of blankets, shoes, and underwear as surplus and had ordered that they be disposed of. Although several military advisers warned that such declarations were seriously reducing reserve stocks that the Army might ultimately need, Woodring failed to heed their advice. With the rapid growth of the CCC in mid 1933, many of the disposed-of items were in short supply—a situation for which the Assistant Secretary was rightfully criticized. In another instance he made arrangements to swap army saddles and bridles for the sorely needed underwear that Silverman had; however, that deal had been halted by Chief of Staff MacArthur, who claimed that the horse gear was just as essential to the Army as was the underclothing.[48]

On 26 and 27 February the grand jury heard Woodring as the final witness, and then it began to deliberate over the testimony. For the next two weeks the newspapers speculated about the number of indictments that would be returned. On the morning of 12 March, District Attorney Garnett indicated that a decision was near and that he was confident that at least three persons would be indicted. Later that day, however, Garnett received a jolt when the jurists voted 15-to-8 against returning any indictments. That Woodring may have shown some poor judgment in disposing of certain property and that certain lobbyists had shown indiscretions in some of their dealings were

92

of no real consequence to the jury, for no individual involved in the contract controversy had engaged in any sort of illegal activity.

When news of the grand jury's action reached an obviously happy but somewhat subdued Woodring, he indicated that he was "exceedingly gratified" but not surprised by the findings. He then broke his long period of official silence by issuing a prepared statement denying reports that there was any conflict between himself and Secretary Dern or General MacArthur and indicating that, as the chief procurement officer for the Army, he had merely carried out his responsibilities in accordance with the law. He closed by indicating that in the future he would, "in spite of complaints, insinuations and sniping by special selfish interests," continue to safeguard the American taxpayer. Secretary Dern was especially pleased with the jury's decision, hailing it as "a complete vindication of the war department." That evening, scores of Woodring's friends called on him to offer their congratulations on the turn of events, but he did not feel much like celebrating.[49] Even though he had just weathered one investigation, he was currently the central figure in another: a congressional inquiry into the awarding of aircraft contracts.

In early 1934 Congress, caught up in an unprecedented "investigation mania," thoroughly examined dozens of governmental agencies and their activities. The War Department was caught in this onslaught as more than a score of investigating bodies probed into such activities as appropriations, air-mail operations, the status of the Air Corps, alleged profits of the munitions industry, and procurement practices.[50] This last inquiry was the one that most directly involved Assistant Secretary Woodring. Although the investigation was technically undertaken by the House Military Affairs Committee, chaired by Congressman John J. McSwain of South Carolina, the actual work was done by the Rogers Committee, the eight-man Subcommittee on Aviation headed by Congressman William N. Rogers of New Hampshire. On 9 February 1934, three days after the grand-jury investigation of the War Department opened, the Rogers Committee began secret hearings to determine how the Army intended to spend the $7.5 million PWA aircraft grant. In the days that followed, testimony by Woodring; Maj. Gen. Benjamin D. Foulois, Chief of the Air Corps; Brig. Gen. Oscar Westover, Assistant Chief of the Air Corps; Brig. Gen. Henry C. Pratt, Chief of the Material Division; and other military officials revealed that between 1926—when the Aircraft Procurement Act went into effect—and 1933 more than 92 percent of all Army aircraft had been secured by "negotiated bids" rather than by "competitive bids." Under the negotiated-contract system the Air Corps tested any plane made available to it by a manufacturer. If it felt that the craft was satisfactory, it would then negotiate a contract with the producer for the number of aircraft desired. This procedure meant that a handful of top Air Corps officials, especially the Chief of the Air Corps, could and in fact did decide which company or companies received aircraft contracts—a condition looked upon quite favorably by Air Corps leaders and by the manufacturers who received the negotiated contracts.[51]

All went well until late 1933, when Assistant Secretary Woodring decided to implement the section of the Procurement Act requiring that military airplanes be purchased by competitive bidding. Under the new system the Army would seek bids for a plane meeting certain minimum performance requirements. After service tests a contract would be given to the lowest bidder whose craft met the announced standards. Such a move was vigorously opposed by most Air Corps officials, who contended that the new system would not provide as good a plane as did the old system. They argued that in order to get more than one bid on a particular aircraft, it would be necessary to lower the specification requirements, thereby giving the Army an inferior plane to what it could have if it was permitted to secure what it considered to be the best plane regardless of cost.[52] In spite of pressures from within the War Department, Woodring, in December 1933, threw open to competitive bidding the planes that were to be purchased with the $7.5 million PWA grant.[53]

That the disgruntled military men had considerable influence on Capitol Hill became evident to Woodring on 9 February 1934, when he appeared before the Rogers Committee. At that time Congressmen W. Frank James of Michigan and Paul J. Kvale of Minnesota attacked Woodring, asking whether or not he had lowered the performance requirements of new airplanes in order to broaden the competition. Congressman James expressed alarm over reports reaching him that although the performance requirements for a recently advertised military aircraft had originally left the office of Chief of the Air Corps Foulois calling for a minimum speed of 235 miles per hour, a cruising range of 500 miles, and a ceiling of 27,800 feet, when the bids went out of the War Department, they called for a minimum speed of 176 miles per hour, a range of 400 miles, and an 18,700-foot ceiling. "What I am anxious to know," said James. "is whether the Chief of Air Corps' recommendations were changed by the General Staff, your office, or anyone else." "Absolutely not," replied Woodring, who went on to explain that the only change that he had made was to provide for competitive bidding; he had not changed any specifications. Congressman Kvale then voiced support for negotiated bidding and expressed his fear that the policy instituted by Woodring would result in the procurement of slower and inferior aircraft for the Air Corps.[54]

With the question of changes in specifications still unanswered, the

Rogers Committee turned its attention to charges that aircraft firms were making extravagant profits on the sale of military airplanes. On this issue, Woodring came to the defense of the Army and the manufacturers by showing that while the average profit from 1926 through 1933 had been 19.8 percent, the figure had dropped to 8.9 percent in the past three years. The latter figure seemed quite reasonable to Woodring, but to several of the Congressmen it seemed quite high.[55]

The secret hearings of the Subcommittee on Aviation in early February actually raised more questions than they answered, thus casting a shadow of suspicion over the Army's procurement system and its chief administrator, Harry Woodring. Subsequently, on 27 February, John McSwain, Chairman of the House Military Affairs Committee, who was upset because his subcommittee's efforts to investigate procurement practices were being frustrated by "evasions" on the part of certain witnesses, introduced a resolution calling for a full-scale inquiry into "charges of profiteering and irregularities involving the expenditure of public funds for national defense." Three days later the House passed the measure that gave the Rogers Subcommittee $10,000 for expenses, authority to subpoena witnesses, and the power to force private businesses and governmental agencies to make their books and records available to members of the committee.[56]

On 7 March the Rogers group, with its greatly expanded investigative powers, launched a full-scale probe of the procurement practices of the Army. As its leadoff witness it called Harry Woodring. The first topic that the committee considered was a recently released transcript of the 1935 Army appropriations hearings, which contained a statement by General Foulois indicating that specifications for airplanes to be purchased with PWA funds had been "changed in the office of the assistant secretary of war." When asked about this, Woodring acknowledged, as he had several weeks before, that he had had difficulties with Foulois and other War Department officials in instituting the new bidding system, but he strongly denied making any changes. To clarify the matter, the committee immediately sent for Foulois, who denied making the alleged statement and then hedged by stating that if he had said it, he had not meant it.[57] What Foulois left unsaid was that in order to carry out the program of competitive bidding that was demanded of his office, he had to reduce the specification requirements.[58]

After Foulois had finished, Woodring returned to explain exactly how his newly instituted policy worked. First, the War Department publicly advertised for bids for planes with certain specifications and performance capabilities. Companies were then given eight to twelve months to develop such a craft. Any American firm could enter the competition, the only requirement being that its bid had to be accompanied by a sample airplane that had been completed and was ready to fly. After extensive tests by the Air Corps to determine whether the plane could meet the requirements, the bids would be opened, and the company with the lowest per-unit offer would receive the contract. To those committee members who expressed a fear that such a policy would prevent the purchase of more efficient craft which would usually cost more, Woodring explained that the solution to that problem would be to raise performance requirements rather than to eliminate competitive bidding.[59]

In the days that followed Woodring's testimony, Foulois, MacArthur, and other War Department personnel revealed that Woodring had almost single-handedly instituted competitive bidding for aircraft and motor vehicles and that he was in the process of extending the policy to nearly all Army purchases. The members of the committee were favorably impressed by the smooth-talking Assistant Secretary, and on 17 March they indicated their belief that he was "above reproach in handling airplane bids."[60] That good news, which came just five days after the grand-jury "vindication," was followed by more of the same in early May, when the Rogers Committee adopted a report that praised Woodring for his successful attempt to institute competitive bidding for airplanes. It further maintained that while the Assistant Secretary's actions were "required and fully justified," the actions of General Foulois were "in clear violation of existing law."[61] This favorable report did much to offset the earlier bad publicity that Woodring had received. As far as he was concerned, the procurement controversy was over, and he had fared quite well. Both the grand-jury and the congressional investigations started by casting doubts upon his administrative ability and his integrity; yet, they terminated by not only vindicating him but also by convincing the public, Congress, and the President that he was an able and honest public official whose procurement policy benefited both the Army and the taxpayer.

In the latter half of 1934 Woodring further improved the aircraft-procurement policy by providing an evaluation method that placed a "premium upon improvement in performance." This meant that each plane tested by the Air Corps would be awarded bonus points on the basis of a pretermined method of evaluation that was known to the bidder beforehand; ultimately the contract would go to the manufacturer who produced the plane with the highest evaluation. This change, which rewarded performance above the minimum requirements, served as a major incentive for firms to produce aircraft of the finest quality possible. In addition to upgrading the quality of the aircraft, the policy also served as a stimulus to the nation's aircraft industry, in that any company that could produce a plane realized that it now had a chance to win a contract; it was no longer a question of

96

having to know the right people.[62] The subsequent increase in the number of aircraft firms after 1935 was to be of incalculable value in the early days of World War II, for they were to carry the production burden until new facilities could be provided.

By the late 1930s competitive bidding was being used in the procurement of trucks, tanks, small arms, electronic equipment, and hundreds of other military items. The impact of competitive bidding on each of those products was the same as on aircraft: higher quality, lower cost, and more producers.[63] There can be little doubt that Woodring's policy was successful, for it has continued to serve as the basis for Army procurement right down to the present. That the United States Army had such fine equipment to fight with in Europe, the Pacific, Korea, and Vietnam was in no small measure due to the efforts of Harry Woodring.

Although he devoted considerable time and energy to procurement matters, they did not constitute the only area of activity or accomplishment for Woodring. As Assistant Secretary of War, he played a key role in the development of the Air Corps. His close connection with that branch of the Army began on 7 June 1933, when President Roosevelt, as part of an economy move, abolished the post of Assistant Secretary of War for Air and transferred its duties to the Assistant Secretary.[64] Woodring gladly accepted his new responsibilities and then worked ceaselessly to develop air strength. His air-mindedness was quite evident. He loved to travel by air, and his frequent use of military aircraft to go to and from speaking engagements was looked upon with satisfaction by those military men who saw bigger things ahead for air power. Through extensive reading and by continually asking questions, Woodring soon gained an extensive knowledge of aircraft and aeronautics.[65] On one occasion the somewhat surprised J. E. Schaefer, head of the Stearman Aircraft Company, commended Woodring on his "remarkably clear understanding of the technical details incident to aircraft development and aircraft procurement."[66]

It was in his first year at the War Department that the somewhat reluctant Woodring approved the developmental order for an experimental four-engine bomber, which came to be known as the B-17, or Flying Fortress.[67] Woodring later recalled the event:

Back early in 1933 I had only been sitting for a short time as Asst. Sec'y of War and in walked Gen'l Foulois, Col. Conger Pratt . . . and two or three others—all in to my office and laid down some very extensive blue prints and with much conversation and finesse in explaining—covering the first development order for my signature on a four-motored fortress. The order called for the expenditure of millions in the final development—an experiment they assured me—well I was scared to death to sign. But after several days of talk—and several private consultations with Conger Pratt—in whom I had much confidence as to Air Corps matters—I nervously signed.[68]

Approval of the B-17 experimental order was about the only real contact that Woodring was to have with that aircraft as Assistant Secretary, but, as will be seen, it was to present him with numerous problems after he became Secretary of War.

Woodring was interested in the quantity, as well as the quality, of aircraft; thus, in 1934 he, General MacArthur, and General Foulois directed the formulation of plans for a 2,300-plane "Army Air Service 'second to none in quality of planes, pilots and morale.' "[69] Unfortunately, Congress would not go along with the plan, and authorized air strength remained at 1,800 planes. During the next two years, however, he continued to drum up support for a larger Air Corps; and in 1936 he took his case to Congress, where he argued that the number of planes should be increased to 4,000, because "should an emergency arise, this number would undoubtedly be needed." "It is believed, therefore," he continued, "that the interests of national defense, as well as those of national economy, warrant the upper limit in the number of airplanes being left somewhat flexible rather than fixed. However, . . . the number 4,000 does not seem immoderate."[70] Although Congress did not feel that such a large force was needed, it did increase the strength from 1,800 to 2,320 planes. The *Army and Navy Journal* recognized Woodring's role in the expansion by noting that he was "actively helping to put wings on the Army."[71]

As Assistant Secretary of War, Woodring also had a hand in establishing the General Headquarters Air Force (GHQAF), the first real step toward the establishment of an independent Air Corps. Calls for an Air Force separate from the Army went back to the days of World War I, but opposition from within Congress and the military establishment blocked such action; therefore, until well into the 1930s, Air Corps personnel and aircraft were under the control of the area commanders of the Army Corps. Cries for more autonomy for the Air Corps swelled when the 1934 "Air-Mail Fiasco" brought home to Congress and the entire nation the need for reorganization, better aircraft, and more thorough training.[72] The President agreed that the first step in upgrading the Air Corps was reorganization, so on 1 March 1935 the GHQAF was established. The GHQAF, which was commanded by Brig. Gen. Frank W. Andrews and was directly responsible to the General Staff, had under its control all tactical air-combat units and thus could be trained and commanded as a homogeneous force "capable of operating in cooperation with the ground forces in battle or on independent aviation missions."[73]

98

The air arm of the Army now had an independence and a unity that it had lacked heretofore. While a completely independent Air Force was still more than a decade away, the first big step toward that end had been taken. Woodring had enthusiastically supported the new concept, and he and General MacArthur were instrumental in working out many of the details of the new organization.[74] This was the last major project that the two men were to work on, however, because on 1 September 1935 MacArthur stepped down as Chief of Staff and was replaced by Gen. Malin Craig. Woodring and MacArthur had worked well together and had developed a great respect and admiration for one another.[75]

Harry Woodring was proud of the role that he had played as Assistant Secretary of War in the growth and development of army air power, and he had every right to be so. His contributions in aircraft procurement methods, in the development of the B-17, in increasing the air strength, in the creation and organization of GHQAF, and in serving as a spokesman for air power —all served to mark him as a true friend of the Air Corps. Yet, as will be seen, this man, as Secretary of War, was to be frequently and bitterly denounced as being anti–Air Force.

During the years that Woodring filled the number two spot at the War Department, another of his primary responsibilities was to serve as a public-relations man for the Army. In this capacity he traveled throughout the country, delivering scores of speeches to veterans organizations, patriotic groups, and any other gathering that was interested in the Army or in national defense. In these addresses, in which he told what the military was doing, what it planned to do, and what it needed to do, he nearly always focused on one or the other of his two favorite themes: preparedness and patriotism. He maintained that the best way to avoid war was for the United States to be so strong militarily that no nation would dare attack it. As the 1930s rolled on and the power of Hitler and Mussolini grew, and as more nations throughout the world came under arms, Woodring placed even more emphasis on adequate national defense as the best way to avoid a foreign war.[76]

As Europe rearmed, there began to appear throughout the United States numerous antiwar societies which advocated drastic reductions of armaments. Some members of these groups went so far as to pledge that if the country became involved in war, they would refuse to bear arms. Woodring became one of the most outspoken opponents of such groups. Crying out against the threats of "radical organizations" and the "enemy boring from within," he warned Americans that they could not "stand by and watch our great country stripped of its means of defense, ready to be sacrificed on the altar of aggression."[77] When the National Peace Conference, a gathering of thirty-five antiwar societies, met in Washington in 1936, Woodring did not keep silent. He denounced the motives for the conference, and he questioned the loyalty of its participants by saying, "Defense of one's country is the first essential of true patriotism." Such statements were welcomed by conservative groups like the American Legion, but they were bitterly attacked by extreme liberals. The *Nation,* which billed itself as "The leading Liberal Weekly since 1865," called the Woodring attacks "a fascist assault on virtually all the church, labor, pacifist and student groups of the nation."[78] Such criticism did not bother the Assistant Secretary; it only made him more vehement in his condemnation of those "subversive influences opposing adequate military and naval preparedness."[79] Run-ins with various antiwar groups kept Woodring in the news in 1934 and 1935, but they did not place him at the center of any real controversy as the CCC article and procurement investigations had done.

The years that Woodring served as Assistant Secretary of War were especially good ones as far as his personal life was concerned. His marriage to Helen was a most happy one, providing him with a contentment that he had never known. To the happiness of marriage were soon added the joys of fatherhood, with the birth of a son, Marcus Coolidge, on 19 June 1934, followed by that of a daughter, Melissa, on 21 June 1935, and another son, Cooper Coolidge, on 10 February 1937. There was no prouder father in all of Washington, and in the years that followed, Woodring always found time in his busy schedule for his family. The year of Melissa's birth saw the family move to His Lordship's Kindness, a sprawling two-story brick mansion in Prince George County, Maryland; and the next year saw them taking up residence at Woodlawn, a spacious estate near Mount Vernon. These beautiful homes and their surrounding gave Woodring an adequate opportunity to engage in his favorite pastimes: gardening and collecting antiques.[80]

Whereas late 1934 and 1935 were relatively quiet, routine, and noncontroversial so far as Woodring's activities in the War Department were concerned, the situation changed in early 1936, when he became involved in a dispute over the removal of Maj. Gen. Johnson Hagood. The difficulties began in December 1935, when the General, who had a reputation for saying exactly what he thought, was called before a House Appropriations subcommittee to testify about certain War Department appropriations. At that time the subcommittee chairman, Thomas L. Blanton of Texas, assured Hagood that anything he would say would be kept secret. In the candid discussion that followed, the General made several flippant remarks about the WPA, one of FDR's most notable work-relief programs. Speaking of the previous year, Hagood said, "I got a lot of stage money from the WPA. I call it stage money because you can pass it around but you cannot get anything out of it in the end." Two months later, on 10 February 1936, the "secret" hearings were released to the press, and Hagood's charges of "stage money" appeared in headlines across the country—a situation that proved quite embarrassing to Hagood and to the Roosevelt administration.[81]

Two weeks after Hagood's testimony was made public he was relieved as Commander of the Eighth Corps Area, and he was ordered to proceed from his base at San Antonio to his home in South Carolina "to await orders." Just where the Hagood removal order originated was not then, and still is not, clear; however, there was no doubt in the mind of Congressman Blanton that Assistant Secretary of War Woodring was the man most responsible for the "damnable, infamous, dirty and inexcusable" outrage.[82] In a fit of anger, Congressman Blanton took the floor of the House and called for the impeachment of Woodring, Secretary of War Dern, and Chief of Staff Craig; but it was the Assistant Secretary, "the man who has attempted to spank a great major general," that he castigated most vehemently. In the course of his tirade Blanton warned: "Harry Woodring, you are not going to get away with it! You have started something that you are not going to carry through, because I am going to give you the scrap of your life." He then ended with a threat: "Harry Woodring, . . . you had better withdraw this damnable, unjust order to Johnson Hagood, because I am after you."[83]

In spite of a strong desire to strike back at Blanton, Woodring maintained his composure and remained silent. This uncharacteristic action in all likelihood stemmed from a request by President Roosevelt that Woodring refrain from saying or doing anything that would further stir things up. Both the administration and the War Department had hoped that the Hagood affair would fade away, but such was not to be the case, as Congressman Blanton and Senator James Byrnes of South Carolina continued to press for withdrawal of the removal order. Finally, in late March, the President, mindful that it was an election year, moved to end the controversy. He personally met with Hagood on 22 March and 11 April, and after the second meeting he announced that he was restoring Hagood to active duty as Commander of the Sixth Corps Area.[84] With Hagood and his supporters interpreting this action as a vindication, the dispute vanished as quickly as it had appeared, and Harry Woodring gave a sigh of relief. The Assistant Secretary had successfully weathered this controversy just as he had the ones over the CCC article, the grand-jury investigation, the Rogers Committee inquiry, and the encounters with various antiwar groups. Those experiences were extremely valuable to Woodring, because they helped teach him to face, accept, and cope with the kinds of problems, pressures, and criticisms that he would later encounter in an even more crucial government post.

During the years that Harry Woodring served as Assistant Secretary of War, he was involved in a number of controversies that made enemies for him among Congressmen, cabinet officials, churchmen, educators, antiwar leaders, and liberal journalists; however, he had also succeeded in projecting a favorable image to many people in Washington and throughout the country. He impressed many Congressmen as being a young, energetic, and forceful man who had done a masterful job of instituting a competitive purchasing system in the Army.[85] He also won the confidence of many individuals in the War Department; among professional military men he was generally liked and respected. Both Chief of Staff MacArthur and his successor, General Craig, thought very highly of Woodring and developed a very close relationship with him.[86] President Roosevelt, although embarrassed by some of the Assistant Secretary's verbal blunders, still had confidence in him, because the former Kansas Governor had proved to be a very able administrator who could carry out his responsibilities efficiently.[87] Woodring had also won support among members of such powerful organizations as the American Legion, Daughters of the American Revolution, the Reserve Officers Association, and other patriotically oriented groups that looked with favor upon his speeches on preparedness and patriotism.

In the summer of 1936 Harry Woodring could look over the previous forty-nine years with real pride: he had come a long way from Elk City. His success as a banker, Governor, and "Little Cabinet" member revealed that he was a man of administrative ability and political skill. Experience had prepared him for bigger and better things, and all he needed now was the opportunity. That opportunity was just around the corner.

6

Mr. Secretary

On 27 August 1936 Secretary of War George H. Dern died at Walter Reed Army Hospital after a lengthy illness. Five days later, after impressive ceremonies in Washington, he was buried at Salt Lake City, Utah. No sooner had Secretary Dern's death been announced than politicians and newspapermen began to speculate about who would be chosen to take his place. Those mentioned most frequently as possible successors were Frank Murphy, Commissioner to the Philippines; Governor Paul V. McNutt of Indiana; Fiorello H. LaGuardia, Mayor of New York City; and Presidential Secretary Stephen Early. Assistant Secretary of War Harry Woodring's name was occasionally mentioned, but he was not considered a prime contender for the job. Most political observers expected a replacement to be named within a few days and expected Woodring to remain as Assistant Secretary; however, when the early weeks of September had passed, and the President had failed to announce who would fill the position, it came to be felt that perhaps no selection would be made until after the upcoming presidential election.[1] In the meantime, Woodring, who had automatically become Acting Secretary upon Dern's death, continued to fill both the number one and the number two spots in the War Department—as he had during most of the previous three and one-half years. By mid September, President Roosevelt seemed quite satisfied with the existing arrangement and had apparently decided not to fill the post in the immediate future.[2]

In late September the President, who was in the midst of a vigorous campaign for reelection, traveled to his home at Hyde Park, New York, for a few days of relaxation. On Friday, 25 September, he received a message from the Executive Clerk at the White House, calling attention to a letter that had just been received from Attorney General Homer S. Cummings. The letter informed the President of a law that provided that a cabinet position must be filled within thirty days of a vacancy; therefore, it would be necessary to appoint a Secretary of War no later than the following day. Having given little or no consideration to such an appointment, yet being faced with the necessity of fulfilling a statutory requirement, Roosevelt decided to appoint Woodring.[3]

From his home on the Hudson the President immediately wired Woodring, informing him that, since he could not legally remain Acting Secretary for longer than thirty days, he was announcing his "temporary selection" as Secretary. Roosevelt concluded the notification by saying, "I know you will understand my reason for making this a temporary designation."[4] From Washington the obviously happy Woodring quickly replied, expressing his thanks for the appointment and saying, "I fully understand and approve the temporary designation. My wish . . . has been that you would take only such action which gave paramount consideration to your best interests for November."[5]

There seemed to be no doubt that the appointment would be temporary. Roosevelt made that point clear to Woodring, and he wanted it made equally clear to the press.[6] The official announcement from Hyde Park said that the appointment was "temporarily filling the vacancy" left by the death of Secretary Dern, and it emphasized that the law required that the vacancy be filled. When reporters asked for clarification of the statement, especially the "temporarily filling the vacancy" phrase, White House officials declined to give one. The wording of the announcement was therefore taken to mean that Woodring would be only a "temporary" Secretary of War, with a "permament" Secretary being named sometime in the future, in all likelihood after the election.[7] Harry H. Woodring was now the Secretary of War, but for how long was anyone's guess.

By designating Woodring to serve "temporarily," Roosevelt accomplished three politically advantageous feats. First, he gave cabinet recognition to the home state of Republican presidential nominee Alfred Landon just six weeks before the election. Second, he could hold out the secretaryship for possible political advantage in the presidential campaign. Third, he gained campaign support by putting a World War veteran and American Legionnaire into the New Deal cabinet for the first time.[8]

The reaction to the announcement of 25 September was mixed, as is the case with nearly all cabinet appointments. For the most part, Woodring's promotion to the top spot was looked upon with gratification in official and military circles.[9] Within the President's official family the reaction was generally favorable, the only exceptions being Secretary of the Interior Harold Ickes, WPA Administrator Harry Hopkins, and Press Secretary Steve Early.[10] Professional military men were pleased, because it put into office a man whom they knew they could get along with, one who was familiar with the problems and needs of the War Department.[11] In most cases, editorial reaction was in line with that of the *Cleveland Plain Dealer*, which applauded the selection and said that "Secretary Woodring seems to have what it needs in the war office."[12]

The most violent opposition to the appointment of Woodring came from the two-million-member American League against War and Fascism. The national chairman of the league wrote to Roosevelt, criticizing the choice of Woodring because the record showed that "he is a militarist." Many local chapters of the organization also voiced opposition toward the "militarist who prates peace and urges war preparation." One letter expressed fear of the new Secretary because of his "obvious desire for the militarization of our whole system of government." It was apparent that the members of the league remembered well the CCC article that Woodring had written back in 1934.[13] Opposition also came from people who were against war and in favor of disarmament. The *Christian Century* expressed disappointment that the President had selected a man that could "hardly be expected to cooperate with groups interested in promoting disarmament."[14] John Flynn, writing in the *New Republic*, called Woodring "the leader of the jingoes" and expressed fear that he might try to establish a conscript army as Hitler had done.[15] Criticism also came from more moderate quarters. The *Cincinnati Enquirer*, in an editorial, claimed that the new Secretary represented "the professional point of view of the army . . . [and] a different type of mind is needed in the position."[16] On the whole, opposition was not as strong as it might have been, because the appointment was generally looked upon as temporary.

Throughout the fall of 1936 Woodring continued to function as both the Assistant Secretary and the Secretary of War. In spite of such a burden, he still found considerable time to work for an administration victory in the November election. The Secretary had good reasons for devoting so much time to the Roosevelt campaign. First, if the President was not reelected, he would certainly lose his job. Second, if he proved to be a real asset to the party cause and the President was returned to office, perhaps his "temporary" appointment would be made permanent. Consequently, Woodring worked long and hard for a Roosevelt victory in 1936. The Secretary's political labors started in May, when the President sought his assistance in mapping out the strategy for the Kansas campaign. Kansas was considered to be an important state, because it was felt that Governor Landon would probably be the nominee of the Republican party. Because of Woodring's familiarity with Landon's political strengths and weaknesses, he was able to give much valuable assistance in planning the course of the Democratic campaign.[17]

Woodring also put his oratorical skills to good use. In early September he hit the campaign trail, praising Roosevelt and lauding the many accomplishments of the past three and one-half years. The smooth-spoken, aggressive Kansan was one of the first administration figures to take Roosevelt's record to the electorate. In mid September the *New York Times* observed that except for Secretary of Labor Frances Perkins, "Mr. Woodring is the only other high member of President Roosevelt's official family to take up the cudgels for the administration." [18] Throughout September and October, Woodring continued to travel around the country, urging the reelection of Roosevelt. Although personally on good terms with Governor Landon, Woodring did not hesitate to attack him politically. He scoffed at Landon's fiscal record as Governor, and he said that the Republican nominee was offering the American people "a second-hand New Deal at second-hand prices."[19] Wherever Woodring spoke, he was enthusiastically received by large crowds, and both local and state party leaders praised him for the "excellent," "wonderful," and "outstanding" speeches that he made. These reports reached the Democratic National Committee and then the White House, where the fine job that Woodring was doing was noted with pleasure.[20] The new Acting Secretary of War also assisted the party financially by contributing $2,050 to the campaign fund, one of the larger contributions of that year.[21]

As Woodring labored on behalf of the Democratic cause in the fall of 1936, he did so with no assurance that it would be personally profitable, even in the event of victory. In a letter of 9 October to General MacArthur he expressed confidence that FDR would be reelected, but concerning his own future he said:

> No member of the Cabinet has any license to expect a tour of duty in the New Cabinet. I shall be very happy to continue in the service, of course, but my plans are not based on that assurance. New elections bring new obligations and the President's Cabinet is so thoroughly his own personal family of advisers that I would not and am not permitting even a suggestion to be made on my behalf.[22]

One matter that Woodring urged upon the party strategists was the need "to take an advanced stand on the peace issue." He felt that there was a strong sentiment for peace in the West and that, in light of recent events in

106

Europe, the "peace issue" could bring much support.[23] His pleas made little headway with party leaders, because at that time the administration was preoccupied with relief and recovery, not peace. Feeling that this was important, Woodring took up the issue and tried to assure the voters that President Roosevelt was " 'a man who hates war with every fiber of his soul' and who is devoting his life to keeping America at peace."[24] In spite of Woodring's efforts, peace never became an issue in 1936.

In November, Roosevelt was reelected by a landslide, and his administration prepared for another four years in office. The question now arose as to whether the President would make Woodring's temporary appointment permanent or whether he would appoint someone else to fill the post. For six months, from November 1936 to April 1937, Roosevelt did neither: he merely let the matter ride. During that period the status of Secretary Woodring was always in doubt, and as a result, rumors concerning the War post continually filled the air. One day rumor had Woodring being retained in the cabinet; the next day, on his way out. Journalists, relying on "impeccable sources," predicted time and again what the President would do and when, but the dates came and went, and still nothing happened.[25]

At the time of the temporary appointment, FDR gave the impression that he would replace Woodring after the election, but in the weeks that followed the Democratic sweep he made no move to do so. Apparently Roosevelt's failure to act stemmed from certain factors that served to complicate his earlier decision. The fine job that Woodring was doing as Secretary of War, as well as the excellent job that he had done campaigning for the administration, certainly caused the President to have second thoughts about replacing him; however, the primary reason for not appointing a new Secretary was probably the mounting pressure, from many sources, to retain Woodring. The temporary Secretary had gained many friends since coming to Washington, and now they came to his aid.

The strongest pressure for retaining him came from military circles. The *Army and Navy Journal*, a sort of "unofficial" organ of the military services, continually urged that the appointment be made permanent. Such action, it said, "would be greeted with acclaim by the Army." The *Journal* continually praised Woodring, claiming that he was an "extremely efficient Assistant Secretary," who displayed "high qualities of administration" and ran the War Department in a "most capable manner."[26] Other military-oriented publications, such as the *Army-Navy Register*, the *Reserve Officer*, and *Army Ordnance*, also voiced editorial support for Woodring.[27] Some pressure was aimed more directly at the President. Lt. Col. Frank Lowe, National President of the Reserve Officers Association, wrote to Roosevelt: "I do not believe it would be too extravagant to say that every officer . . . of

107

the Army would be *very much* pleased to see Mr. Woodring so rewarded," that is, by making him the permanent Secretary.[28] Edgar H. Taber, Executive Officer of the National Association of Regulars, informed the President that his organization had received "quite a number of letters from servicemen expressing the hope that our present Secretary of War be reappointed to office."[29]

The retention of Woodring was also supported by certain individuals, both military and nonmilitary, whose influence was considerable. The Chief of Staff, Gen. Malin Craig, wanted Woodring to be retained in the top spot because Woodring got along so well with him and the General Staff.[30] Gen. John J. Pershing, who, although long retired, was still looked to for advice by many top military men, said: "I do not see why F.D.R. should not continue Woodring ... he would be better than some man who thought he knew it all."[31] Postmaster General James Farley, whose advice the President often heeded, continually urged that the appointment be made permanent. From the House of Representatives came support from Congressman Lister Hill, one of the most influential members of the Military Affairs Committee. On 28 December 1936 Hill wrote to Roosevelt, stating that he had had the opportunity to observe Woodring's work more closely than anyone else in Congress, and he felt that Woodring had done an outstanding job. Hill then recommended, in the strongest terms, that the President retain Secretary Woodring in his present position.[32] This was a key recommendation, for it seemed to indicate to Roosevelt that his temporary Secretary had the confidence and support of the House Military Affairs Committee.

Throughout November and December the President failed to decide what he should do about Woodring and the War post: he continually wavered between retention and removal. In mid November, Press Secretary Steve Early told the editor of the *Army and Navy Journal* that Woodring would not be reappointed.[33] About this time, moreover, Steve Early and Harry Hopkins, apparently on their own initiative, approached Jesse Jones, head of the Reconstruction Finance Corporation, and asked if he would be interested in becoming Secretary of War. When Jones replied that he would not, they dropped the matter.[34] As 1936 drew to a close, Woodring's status was as uncertain as ever, but the newspapers continued to indicate that he was on his way out.[35] On 23 December, Roosevelt told Secretary Ickes that while he personally thought Woodring was a "nice fellow," he was not going to retain him as Secretary of War.[36] In spite of such indications from Roosevelt that he would remove Woodring, week after week passed, and still he did nothing. In mid January 1937 there appeared the first public indications that Woodring might be retained in the cabinet. On 20 January the *New York Times* reported that Woodring's status was still in doubt, but added,

"There is no certainty that he will be replaced." The following day the same newspaper reported that, except for the possible departure of Farley, no changes were expected in the cabinet and that Roosevelt's second term would probably end "with his 'official family' composed as at present."[37]

As the early months of 1937 slipped by, Secretary Woodring continued to run things at the War Department, and President Roosevelt, who was involved in his fight for court reform, was content to let him do so. While this "temporary arrangement" was working satisfactorily, it could not go on indefinitely, because Woodring had been appointed when Congress was not in session and had therefore not been approved by the Senate. This meant that unless a nomination for Secretary of War was submitted during the present session, Woodring's appointment would expire when the Senate adjourned, thus leaving the position vacant. Such a situation made it mandatory that Roosevelt make some sort of decision about Woodring.

At a White House conference on 19 April 1937, Roosevelt told James Farley that although it was going to be an unpleasant task to perform, he definitely was going to remove Woodring. The President explained that since he had made it clear at the time of the appointment that it would be only temporary, the Secretary would not be surprised by the action. To this, Farley replied: "General Malin Craig was in to see me about Harry; the Army thinks very highly of him. . . . I think Harry is doing a good job and deserves an appointment to prove his fitness for the job."[38] One week later, for reasons known only to himself, President Roosevelt decided to reappoint Woodring as Secretary of War, and on 27 April he sent the nomination to the Senate. The Military Affairs Committee, having no objection to the appointee, reported favorably on the nomination, and on 6 May the Senate confirmed the appointment without debate or objection.[39] At last Harry Woodring was Secretary of War in his own right; the axe that Roosevelt had been holding over his head for the past six months had been removed. The President now faced the problem of finding an Assistant Secretary to take Woodring's old job; however, he chose not to deal with that matter for several months.

Just why the President decided to keep Woodring in the cabinet will never be known, but perhaps a contemporary evaluation of the situation by the nationally known news columnist and radio commentator Boake Carter can give an insight. On 27 April, the day that Woodring's name went to the Senate for confirmation, Carter told his radio listeners:

The President did the nation a good turn; the Army got a good break; and the little clique of "discredit-Woodring" boys pretty high up in the Administration looked not a little foolish this evening, after the President sent the nomination of

109

Harry H. Woodring for a regular cabinet term as Secretary of War, to the Senate. . . . It is pleasing to discover that the President was not impressed by those close about him who sought to set his hand against one who has turned out to be one of the most able of his cabinet and one of the most able and earnest peacetime secretaries of war America has ever had. For a long time, he has been more than simply a figurehead, but on the contrary, an active secretary, who desires to take an earnest interest in his job and not simply rest content to be another shop-window ornament. He has, to his credit, the cleanup of the procurement and supplies smell in the Army of a few years back; an active, rather than simply an academic interest in the Army's Air Corps; the author of plans and methods looking to promoting methods and means of building up stock piles of reserves for industry in case of war. He thinks not in terms of how devilish a death-dealing instrument the Army can be made, but rather of what use it can be put to preserve peace. He will listen to generals, some hide-bound with tradition, and will listen just as willingly to a lowly lieutenant. Pomposity and gold braid do not impress him any more than juvenile irresponsibility. The Army should be tickled that it has this sort of man as boss, and the country that it has this kind of individual as a War Secretary. One hopes that he will wear as well in the future as he has in the past.[40]

When Harry Woodring became the United States Secretary of War, few people knew or cared what he thought about war, peace, the size and make-up of the Army, and its role in national defense. Such ideas, concepts, and principles are important, for they go together to form an individual's "military philosophy." To understand how Woodring looked upon and tried to solve the many problems facing him, especially ones such as military readiness, rearmament, and neutrality, it is essential to know something of the "Woodring military philosophy," for it contained the principles that were to guide his actions during the years that he headed the War Department.

Woodring was different from most earlier Secretaries of War in that his military philosophy was fairly well fixed before he became Secretary. His Army experience, his American Legion activities, his work with the National Guard as Governor, and his three and one-half years as Assistant Secretary of War had caused him to think considerably about the Army and national defense. His having had years to develop his philosophy was beneficial to Woodring, because it made him more sure of himself and gave him confidence that the direction in which he was leading the War Department was the proper one. His outlook was that of both an idealist and a realist. He was an idealist in that he sincerely believed in and hoped for such things as an understanding among people everywhere, cooperation among nations, and world peace. On the other hand, he was a realist in that he did not see the possibility of such things becoming a reality in the near future. Wood-

110

ring felt that with world conditions as they were in the thirties, it would take more than hope and understanding to ensure peace.[41]

During the years that Woodring served in the War Department, he was charged with being "a militarist," "one of the most warlike officials in Washington," and "the leader of the jingoes."[42] Such descriptions caused many Americans to picture the Kansan as a "warmonger," when nothing could have been further from the truth; for if there was one thing that he wanted more than anything else, it was for the United States to remain at peace. Shortly after Woodring became Secretary a journalist asked him what he considered to be the most important requirement for a competent Secretary of War, and without hesitation he replied, "A profound respect for peace."[43] His obsession with this issue was based on his fear that participation in another war would prove disastrous to both victor and vanquished; thus, since United States involvement in another major conflict would lead to the destruction of the nation, he considered it necessary to do everything possible to avoid war.[44] In his first speech as Secretary of War, Woodring pledged: "I shall dedicate my efforts to peace."[45] He did. For nearly four years he warned against, and took action that he felt would prevent involvement in, a foreign war. He was so determined to keep out of war that he ultimately was forced out of office because he would not go along with a policy that he felt might pull the nation into a European conflict. Woodring was a man of peace and was recognized by many as such. The *Washington Times Herald* editorially praised the Secretary of War because "Woodring speaks the language of the people—Peace." Columnist Ernest Lindley referred to him as "a persistent opponent of foreign adventure," and political analyst Ray Tucker called him one of only two "peace-minded men in Roosevelt's Cabinet."[46]

Nearly all Americans agreed with Secretary Woodring that peace was desirable, but when it came to deciding how to maintain that peace, many could not agree with him. Woodring felt that the best way to avoid war was to provide an "adequate national defense which would act as a powerful deterrent against aggression on our shores." He continually stated that peace without security was impossible and that the best security was a military force of sufficient size and strength to keep any nation from even considering an attack. According to him, "peace and security go hand in hand," and the former could not be obtained without the latter.[47] His strong belief in preparedness as the way to ensure peace caused him to come into conflict with those groups and individuals who felt that a strengthening of defenses would be apt to provoke war. Believing that the idea that "preparedness causes war" was a great misconception, Woodring lashed out at anyone who spoke against proposals to strengthen the military forces. Those who urged a de-

111

crease in the size and strength of the Army and the Navy were warned of the "folly [to which] a pacifist policy like this leads." On numerous occasions the Secretary warned his countrymen of what had happened to countries, including the United States in 1917, that found themselves forced into a war when they were woefully unprepared: the result was a loss of life and money far beyond what might otherwise have been; therefore, the nation should never follow such a "foolhardy policy."[48] Woodring was firmly convinced that failure to prepare "would be to ignore all past history and openly invite the possibility of a future national conflagration."[49]

When critics occasionally expressed fears about growing military influence in Washington, Woodring reminded them that the Army had no voice in making laws, shaping foreign policy, or deciding whether or not the nation should go to war. He stated time and again that the Army "sought only to serve, never to dominate the country."[50] Many of the individuals who feared increased military strength were worried about the world arms race that was under way in the mid thirties. They were especially alarmed by Woodring's continuous demands for increased preparedness, because they felt that he was urging the United States to join that contest. That such was not the case the Secretary of War made clear in his *Annual Report for 1937*: "I certainly do not recommend that the United States join in this feverish arms race. . . . However, I do think as insurance against attack we should further strengthen our armed forces."[51]

While Woodring was a strong advocate of preparedness, he did not feel that the country should arm itself beyond its ability to pay, and he spoke proudly of the fact that in 1937 the cost of the United States military establishment was only 3.2 percent of the national budget.[52] To understand this seeming paradox of a desire for stronger defense, on the one hand, and a relatively small defense expenditure and no participation in the arms race, on the other, it is essential to understand Woodring's ideas about the size, make-up, and role of the United States Army.

As Woodring conceived it, the peacetime Army should be a moderate-sized force capable initially of protecting the continental United States, Panama, and Hawaii, yet still able to serve as a nucleus for the raising, training, and equipping of such additional troops as might be needed in an emergency.[53] He favored an Army of quality, not quantity. He never advocated a large military force; in fact, he praised the American Legion because it had made no "fantastic recommendations for a huge standing army."[54] Woodring maintained that the size of the Army was relatively unimportant and that it should be a matter for Congress to determine; he was more interested in providing the military force with the best of equipment and training.[55] Furthermore, he believed that a moderate-sized standing army

112

would be sufficient, because its function would be strictly defensive. In speech after speech he reiterated his belief in the long-standing national policy that contemplated the use of American armed forces only for defensive purposes. As he put it: "The kind of Army we have in mind would be of no use as an expeditionary force such as was sent to Europe in the World War. It is designed purely and simply to defend our own territory."[56]

When Secretary Woodring or other top members of the administration talked of defending the country, they were not thinking of just the continental United States, but of the Western Hemisphere. From 1937 to 1940, plans for the Army were made in accordance with the concept of hemisphere defense that was adopted by the Roosevelt administration.[57] During this period President Roosevelt thought solely in terms of defense of the Americas. For example, when War Department officials in late 1939 presented plans to provide reserves necessary to equip a large expeditionary force for possible use in Europe, the President refused them, saying: "Whatever happens, we won't send troops abroad. We need only think of defending this hemisphere."[58]

Although the Secretary did not consider that the size of the Regular Army was of great importance, he did feel that it should be organized so that it could be expanded rapidly. This would require a well-trained standing force, which could serve as the basis for new units to be made up primarily of personnel from the National Guard and the Organized Reserves. Since a large Army, if it were to be created in time of need, would have to be supplied, Woodring considered supply preparedness vital to the Army's ability to expand. His answer to the supply problem was not to be found in large stockpiles of arms and ammunition, which would deteriorate and become obsolete with age. Instead, his solution was to educate and prepare industry in time of peace for its responsibilities in time of war.[59] This idea was incorporated in the Industrial Mobilization Plan which Woodring labored to perfect, first as Assistant Secretary and later as Secretary.

While Woodring considered military preparedness essential to keeping the peace, there was another factor that he considered to be almost as important. He believed that the American people and all government officials should conduct themselves in such a way as not to incite war or involve the country in one. This, Woodring held, could be done in two ways: by legislation and by moral rearmament.[60] According to him, the legislative means to avoid war were to take the profits out of war and to assure that neutrality was maintained. Since he felt as he did, it is not surprising that from 1936 to 1939 Woodring congratulated Congress on passage of the Neutrality Acts and praised its efforts to take the profits out of war.[61] He favored such legislation, because he thought that it could play a major role in keeping the country from being drawn into war. Woodring thought that if another European war came, there would be demands within the United States for the benefits that would come from the war trade, as well as cries for the preservation of neutral and international rights. He warned Americans to avoid the mistakes of 1914–1917 and to avoid getting involved in a European conflict again, because "the temporary profits of war and the protection of a national vanity are not worth the horrors of war." The Secretary maintained that if Americans wanted to trade with countries at war or to travel on their ships, then they should do so at their own risks. He went even further when he claimed that if war came to Europe, isolation might be thrust upon the United States as the only alternative to becoming involved. Should this happen, he said, he was confident that the American people would accept it and "make this additional sacrifice for the sake of peace."[62] After war came to Europe in 1939, he changed his views to some extent, indicating that because the social, moral, and economic consequences of the war could not be avoided, the country could not "retreat tortoise-like" within its borders. He continued, however, to maintain that it was possible to insulate the country from Europe militarily. Woodring was an isolationist only in that he wished to keep the nation isolated from war. On other matters he was an internationalist; thus, he continuously advocated increased foreign trade and urged international cooperation to solve some of the world's social and economic problems.[63]

Whereas Woodring viewed adequate military defense and proper legislation as essential to the ensuring of peace, he also felt that the nation needed "something more." That something was "Moral Rearmament." Included in this concept was an understanding of one another; recognition of each other's rights; tolerance of other's habits, customs, and religious views; development of a spirit of justice and self-control; and "more of the spirit of brotherly love."[64] The Secretary of War believed that "Moral Rearmament is a great, tremendous influence for good, and it ought to be encouraged." Furthermore, "it is because the war to end selfishness has never been fought that the war to end wars has never been won." Although Secretary Woodring felt that this concept had great merit, he considered it more in terms of a hope for the future.[65] He still believed that a well-trained Army and proper legislation were the hopes for the peace of the present.

In addition to the ideas that made up the "Woodring military philosophy," there was a principle that the Secretary always followed, even though it sometimes meant going against his own philosophy. The principle was that military men, not civilian leaders, should make decisions on matters that were primarily military in nature. When Secretary Woodring was forced from his post in 1940, the *Baltimore Sun* said, "It cannot be recalled that Mr.

Woodring has ever opposed any of the purely military suggestions of his chiefs of staff."[66] That Woodring was proud of this fact was quite evident in a letter that he wrote five years after leaving office:

I have that feeling that I was right in the Office of Secretary of War in following and leaving the military decisions to the General Staff and would like to . . . [see vindicated] that principle of National Defense rather than the Civilian Commander-in-Chief idea knowing more than professional military strategists who made it a life study and profession.[67]

Although Woodring was a "yes man" when it came to what he considered to be strictly military matters, he certainly was not when it came to decisions in the political-military area, and that is where the bulk of his decisions lay. From the time that he became "permanent" Secretary of War in 1937, the outspoken Woodring made it clear to the President, the cabinet, members of Congress, and other officials that he had a mind of his own. Several ideas and concepts, then, made up Woodring's military philosophy and served as guidelines for his policy decisions: (1) the country must remain at peace at all cost except aggression; (2) an adequate defense is the best way to avoid war; (3) the government is not and should not be militarily oriented, and thus it should not have a large standing Army or enter into the arms race; (4) the Army is to be used strictly for defensive purposes; (5) while the size of the standing Army is relatively insignificant, it is essential that it be adequately equipped and trained and that it be capable of rapid expansion; (6) proper legislation can be a key factor in keeping the country out of war; (7) only military isolation is desirable; (8) on economic and social matters the country should cooperate with foreign nations; (9) moral rearmament is the hope for the peace of the future; and (10) military decisions should be made by military men. The effects of this philosophy were quite evident in the policies of the War Department from 1936 to 1940.

When Harry Woodring became Secretary of War in 1936, there were at work throughout the nation certain forces that served to make his job more difficult than it might otherwise have been: those forces were isolationism and the Depression. The former began to appear after World War I, when the United States attempted to turn its back on Europe. Rejection of the League of Nations and refusal to join the World Court were indicative of the growing feeling that the United States should not become involved in European affairs. Throughout the twenties and early thirties, isolationism became the accepted policy of the President, Congress, and the majority of the American people. This sentiment was further strengthened in the mid thirties, when the Nye Investigating Committee and certain historians, such as Walter Millis and Charles Beard, succeeded in convincing the American

115

people that the United States had entered World War I in order to provide for and safeguard the financial interests of a few bankers and munition makers. Feeling that the mistakes of the past could be avoided by legislative means, Congress responded by passing a series of neutrality acts, which it felt would ensure that the country would not again be drawn into war. These acts prohibited the exportation of arms, ammunition, and other war commodities to belligerents; forbad the extension of loans and credit to warring nations; and made it unlawful for Americans to travel on ships of belligerent nations.

With the passage of the neutrality legislation there developed a complacent feeling that the chance of being involved in a foreign war had been virtually eliminated; therefore, prior to 1939, Congress and the American people showed little or no interest in the War Department or its military activities. Even those individuals who were concerned about the nation's defenses paid little attention to the Army, because they considered the Navy to be the bulwark against aggression. Woodring found such complacency difficult to combat.

The Great Depression also contributed to the difficulties of the Secretary of War. Since Roosevelt, Congress, and the public were still primarily concerned with economic recovery as late as 1938, they had little time for or interest in national defense and foreign affairs. Even if the interest had been there, the funds were not. With little concern over defense and with an administration economy drive under way, it was not surprising that the Army experienced severe budgetary problems. After all, if government expenditures had to be cut in some areas, what better place to do so than in the War Department? Roosevelt himself had exemplified this feeling upon entering the presidency, when he had urged Congress to cut the Army's budget by $144 million.[68] Furthermore, it was no secret that Roosevelt, a former Assistant Secretary of the Navy, had a pro-Navy outlook; thus, when he found it necessary to request additional defense funds, it was the Navy, not the Army, that received first priority. With the President, Congress, and most Americans in an isolationist mood and with government spending being slashed, Secretary Woodring faced a real challenge in securing the appropriations and legislation that were necessary in order to strengthen the United States Army. This, however, was to be just one of many problems that Harry Woodring was to face in his four years as Secretary of War.

116

7

Working for Military Readiness

When Harry Woodring became Secretary of War in the fall of 1936, he found himself in charge of a small, ill-equipped, and poorly trained Army. Well aware of the existing deficiencies, the new Secretary immediately set out to rectify them. His goal was to prepare a military force that could successfully meet any challenge from the outside world.

The basis of the United States military program at that time was the National Defense Act of 1920.[1] That act provided for a voluntary citizen Army to be composed of three echelons: the Regular Army, with an authorized strength of 280,000 enlisted men and 18,000 officers; the National Guard, of approximately 430,000 men; and the Organized Reserve, of about 540,000.[2] In the years following the passage of the act, the apathetic Congress never did appropriate funds necessary to implement it and the strength that was provided for never came close to the authorized figure. In 1936 the Regular Army numbered 147,000 enlisted men and 12,000 officers—about half of the minimum number set forth in the 1920 Defense Act. The year before (1935), Congress had appropriated funds to provide for 165,000 enlisted men, but President Roosevelt had released enough money for only 147,000.[3] At the same time the National Guard numbered 189,000, rather than the 430,000 called for; and the Organized Reserve was even worse off, for instead of a force of half a million men, it contained less than 120,000, all of whom were officers. For a nation of 130 million people, the United States military establishment was quite small; its 159,000-man Regular Army placed it in seven-

117

teenth place among the world's standing armies—in a virtual tie with Portugal.[4]

Although the Army was small, its size did not bother Secretary Woodring. Just before he became Secretary, Congress had appropriated funds to provide for 165,000 enlisted men and 14,000 officers by mid 1937, and Woodring felt that under the world conditions prevailing at that time, such a figure would be quite adequate.[5] Although he was not concerned with the size of the Army, he was quite concerned with its efficiency. He desired a well trained and fully equipped force that would be ready to move into action immediately.

Military men generally acknowledge that an army's readiness can be judged by examining the speed and quality of its mobilization, the quality and condition of its equipment and armaments, and the state of training of all its ranks.[6] Unfortunately, in 1936 the United States Army was woefully inadequate in all three areas.

That the Army would be unable to mobilize quickly and efficiently was a fact that the General Staff was well aware of.[7] When Woodring became Secretary, the basis for mobilization was the 1933 Mobilization Plan. This plan envisioned the raising and training of an army of more than one million men within three months of mobilization day (M-Day), a two-million-man force six months after M-Day (M+6), and an army of four and one-half million men twelve months after M-Day (M+12).[8] The plan, which included personnel and supply requirements, had come under fire almost as soon as it had gone into effect. As a new and inexperienced Assistant Secretary of War, Woodring had given his approval to the proposal a few weeks after taking office in 1933, but as he became knowledgeable in the problems of military supply, he soon came to the conclusion that the plan was impractical and could not be carried out.[9] However, Woodring could not convince Secretary Dern of the need for a new mobilization plan, and General MacArthur felt there were more pressing problems facing the Army. Thus, with a lack of impetus from the top, no change was forthcoming. In 1936 the new Chief of Staff, Gen. Malin Craig, whose "greatest concern was the lack of realism in military war plans,"[10] ordered a study on the feasibility of the 1933 Mobilization Plan. After securing reports and evaluations of the plan from commanders at all echelons, the Assistant Chiefs of Staff for Personnel (G-1) and Supply (G-4) concluded that the manpower-procurement rate of the plan was "questionable of attainment and that for this rate the supply demands are doubtful of fulfillment."[11] In October of that same year the Planning Branch, Office of the Assistant Secretary of War, completed a detailed survey of procurement possibilities under the present plan. Their conclusion was that the supply requirements could not possibly be met.[12]

118

As far as the speed and efficiency of mobilization were concerned, the Army was not a ready force, but that was just one of several difficulties. In the quantity and quality of equipment and arms the Army was also lacking. Animal-drawn vehicles and field artillery were still being used extensively, and the War Department continued to maintain that "mounted troops are of great value in certain situations and some horse-drawn light artillery can probably be advantageously used."[13] Furthermore, outdated weapons were the rule rather than the exception. The 1903 bolt-action Springfield rifle was still the basic weapon of the infantry. A new semi-automatic rifle, the Garand 30-cal. M-1, had just been approved as a replacement for the Springfield, but none of them had been issued to the troops. The Browning automatic rifle was being used as a light machine gun, and the World War–vintage heavy Browning machine gun had to function as an antitank gun. Tanks and other self-propelled mechanized weapons were in pitifully short supply, as was ammunition for all classes of small arms and artillery. George Fielding Eliot, perhaps the most widely read American military analyst of the 1930s, concluded that "the condition of the Army as to armament and equipment is far from satisfactory; this is by all odds its worst deficiency."[14]

Unfortunately, many individuals, including numerous Congressmen, did not feel that the Army was lacking in necessary equipment. They pointed to the large surplus of arms, ammunition, and other supplies from World War I that were stored in Army depots throughout the country, and said that those stocks would be sufficient to equip the Regular Army as well as the one-million-man force to be mobilized in the first three months after M-Day. Furthermore, they contended that if war came and the surpluses were not sufficient for a large reserve force, and shortages did develop, the solution would be simple: the items could be secured from commercial sources.[15] Such thinking was deficient in several respects. First of all, it failed to take into consideration the rapid changes being made in military technology, organization, and tactics—all of which served to make many items in the surplus stockpiles virtually worthless in another war. Second, items such as ammunition for small arms and artillery, which had been in storage for over sixteen years, were beginning to deteriorate rapidly, thereby making their reliability questionable. Third, commercial production could not convert to military production overnight. If advance planning were not undertaken, it would take considerable time for commercial sources to begin production of items desired by the military.

Another deficiency of the Army at this time was the poor state of training at all levels. That this problem existed and should be corrected was acknowledged by General Craig in his *Annual Report* for 1936, when he stated that "greater emphasis is necessary on the training of basic units in maneuver and combat exercises."[16] The shortcomings of the Army training program stemmed primarily from the great dispersion of troops, the shortages of funds and equipment, and the lack of time due to the necessity of performing nonmilitary functions. When Secretary Woodring became head of the War Department, the Army was spread from the Philippines to Puerto Rico, from China to the Canal Zone, and across the United States in more than one hundred and fifty posts and stations. Because of such dispersion, it simply was not feasible, tactically or financially, to bring together a sizable number of units for large-scale maneuvers.[17] Moreover, the training of individuals as well as small units was seriously curtailed during the Depression years, because tight budgetary restrictions permitted the use of only a minimum amount of ammunition and other expendable items that were essential for effective training.[18] A shortage of equipment often served to limit the value of training, because only a relatively few individuals could use or work on the actual piece of equipment that they would be utilizing in case of war. A perfect example of this is the fact that as late as 1938 the eighteen National Guard tank companies throughout the country had but one tank each for training purposes.[19]

Another deterrent to training was that many personnel were required to expend all their time and energy on nonmilitary jobs, thus leaving little or no time for military activities. Such functions as care, maintenance, and operation of the Panama Canal; care and improvement of harbors and waterways; responsibilities in the Civilian Conservation Corps; care of national cemeteries; and operation of the Military Academy, along with research and development work and a multitude of other civilian-type tasks, were full-time jobs performed by Regular Army personnel.[20] It was not possible to pull such personnel from their jobs to participate in consolidated field exercises. Even when the time and equipment were available, the training was often impractical and unrealistic. As one soldier put it, "There is too much tendency in the 'field' to take everything along from the barracks . . . including the pool table" and then "too much effort, time and expense is devoted to 'polishing' this and that that should be used to much more advantage in tactical training."[21] There was no question that the training of the United States Army in the mid thirties was deficient in both quantity and quality.

No one was more aware of the Army's lack of readiness than Secretary Woodring, but knowing what needed to be done and getting it done were two different things. The basic reason for the Army's lack of readiness was the failure of Congress to provide sufficient funds; however, Congress reflected the mood of the nation. Because of the isolationist sentiment that prevailed throughout the country during the two decades after World War

120

I, the War Department had not submitted budget requests that it considered sufficient to provide an adequate military force. Instead it merely asked Congress for what it thought it could get. Even then the Army's modest requests were usually slashed to the bone by the President's representatives, the Bureau of the Budget. During these years the bureau rarely called on the War Department to justify the requests it made, but cut those carefully prepared requests on its own judgment. Congress, seeing no threat of war, was generally content to accept the bureau's recommendations.[22] Any individual—civilian or military—who advocated or endorsed increased expenditures for defense was immediately labeled a "jingo" or a "warmonger"; thus, Congressmen found it politically advantageous to avoid defense questions. With the President looking for areas in which to cut expenditures, and with Congress and its constituents bent on isolationism, Woodring considered that the chances of receiving increased appropriations were almost nil. Therefore, he set out to increase the Army's readiness with means available to him at that time.

The first problem that the new Secretary turned to was mobilization. A major step toward realistic planning for mobilization had come late in 1935, when Gen. Malin Craig replaced General MacArthur as Army Chief of Staff. Craig was an extremely capable person who possessed a fine but unheralded military record. Craig, who had graduated from West Point in 1898, had gained valuable combat and administrative experience in the Spanish-American War, the Chinese Relief Expedition, the Philippine Insurrection, and on the Mexican border before serving in the American Expeditionary Force as Chief of Staff of both the Fourth Division and the First Army Corps. In 1925 he became Assistant Chief of Staff, G-3, and after he had completed several assignments as an Army Corps Commander, President Roosevelt appointed him Chief of Staff.[23] The soft-spoken Craig was a man of action rather than words. Since he did not possess a dynamic, forceful personality, his numerous accomplishments were generally not associated with his name. According to the authors of one of the best studies ever made of military mobilizations, "The profound influence which General Craig during his tour as Chief of Staff had on preparing the Army of the United States for World War II has never been widely known or appreciated except by the professional soldiers who were closely associated with him during those years."[24]

Since mobilization requires the recruiting, training, and supplying of the Army, the War Department's 1933 Mobilization Plan had two basic schemes: one for recruitment and training, and another for supply. However, by late 1936 it was apparent to officials in the War Department that the 1933 plan was not satisfactory, for it called for too much too soon after

121

M-Day.[25] Under the initiative and guidance of Secretary Woodring and Chief of Staff Craig there emerged more realistic mobilization plans in the form of the 1936 revision of the Industrial Mobilization Plan and the radically new Protective Mobilization Plan. It was the former that Woodring was to deal with first.

An army cannot merely be recruited and trained; it must also be fed, clothed, equipped, and armed. Realizing the importance of supplying a large military force in time of war, the National Defense Act of 1920 gave to the Assistant Secretary of War not only the responsibility of current Army procurement but also the task of preparing plans for the mobilization of American industry in the event of war. During the 1920s the War Department virtually ignored the formulation of plans for industrial mobilization, but in the 1930s it attempted to work out such a scheme. The solution arrived at was embodied in the 1930 Industrial Mobilization Plan and in revisions of it in 1933, 1936, and 1939. The 1930 plan provided for the creation of four superagencies to handle industrial mobilization: Director of War Industry, Administrator of Labor, Director of Public Relations, and Director of Selective Service. Although the key agency was that of War Industry, which would handle requirements, priorities, and facilities, it was equal to, but not superior to, the others. Coordination of the four agencies was placed in the hands of the President. In 1933 the original plan was revised, and another agency and two independent commissions were added; but the scheme remained essentially the same.[26] Although Assistant Secretary Woodring approved the revision, he soon came to feel that it was too ambitious and thus unrealistic. Consequently, he ordered his staff to begin major revisions of it. As Assistant Secretary of War and later as Secretary, Harry Woodring was quite interested in the Industrial Mobilization Plan, and he devoted a great deal of time and energy to improving it.[27] Woodring continually emphasized the need for "supply preparedness," as he called it. To him this concept meant providing adequate reserve stocks for immediate military needs as well as plans for the rapid mobilization of industries for wartime production. Secretary Woodring indicated his firm belief in the importance of industrial mobilization to military efficiency when he said: "The best general in the world cannot defend his country without troops—the best troops in the world cannot defend their countries without supplies; and supplies cannot be provided without thoroughly efficient preparation and suitable control machinery."[28]

In 1936 the War Department issued a revised Industrial Mobilization Plan. It was ironical that it received its final approval in September from Acting Secretary of War Woodring, who, as Assistant Secretary, had done so much to bring about the new plan. This plan differed from earlier ones

122

in several respects. First, since it dealt solely with matters of industrial mobilization, the selective-service and public-relations provisions of the earlier plans were deleted. Second, the War Resources Administration, which was the new name for the old War Industries Board, was to be established at the outset of war by an executive order, rather than by congressional legislation. Third, when war appeared imminent, the Army-Navy Munitions Board was to assume the functions of the War Resources Administration until that agency was able to undertake its duties.[29] Fourth, the plan showed a greater degree of coordination and harmony between the War and Navy departments than had any previous attempts at cooperative planning. In light of the serious conflicts that had previously characterized joint Army-Navy mobilization planning, this was quite an accomplishment, and one that Secretary Woodring was quite proud of.[30]

For a multitude of reasons the 1936 Industrial Mobilization Plan immediately came under attack: Gen. Hugh Johnson, of NRA fame, claimed that the plan was too detailed and thus inflexible; Bernard Baruch insisted that its provisions should be implemented by civilian experts rather than the military; Secretary of State Cordell Hull felt that controls over exports encroached upon his authority; and numerous political analysts and journalists claimed that the plan provided for excessive regimentation. By 1938 even the War Department was forced to conclude that it contained certain deficiencies, which it hoped to remedy in the next revision of it. In spite of some shortcomings, the plan at least showed an awareness of the complexities of industrial mobilization, and it presented the most sophisticated approach ever designed to meet those complexities. Even a critic like General Johnson concluded that the plan was "a necessary and a very valuable piece of work."[31]

When Harry Woodring assumed the position of Secretary of War in September 1936, he did not immediately leave behind the problems of planning for procurement and mobilization, for he continued to serve as Assistant Secretary. Not until July 1937, when Louis A. Johnson became the new Assistant Secretary, did Woodring give up his dual role. This meant that during his first ten months as Secretary of War, Woodring was still in charge of planning for industrial mobilization. In fact, it was during the period when he was filling both posts that he laid the groundwork for cooperation between the War Department and private industry that later proved to be of such value in the production of certain military items. He did this by pressuring Congress to pass a bill that would enable the War Department to sell, loan, or give to private contractors and firms the drawings, plans, and samples of equipment to be manufactured for the Army in time of war. The bill was designed to familiarize manufacturers with items not directly related to peacetime production, especially items for ordnance and for

123

chemical warfare.[32] Congress, seeing the value of such a program, passed the measure with no opposition. Although this legislation did not go so far as to provide small-scale "educational orders," whereby limited production of certain items would be undertaken, it did give to many industries a better appreciation of what might be involved if they had to convert from civilian to military production.[33] While tremendous progress was to be made in the realm of planning for industrial mobilization after July 1937, it was to come under the leadership of Assistant Secretary Louis Johnson. Unfortunately, Woodring, because of the years he spent as Assistant Secretary, found it extremely difficult to divorce himself from his old post, and, as will be seen, his tendency to advise and guide his new Assistant Secretary was to cause considerable friction between the two and was to seriously affect the operations of the War Department.[34]

As important as Woodring's contributions were to industrial mobilization, they were small in comparison with his contributions to military mobilization. On 8 December 1936 Secretary Woodring initiated a major revision of the Army's plans for military mobilization. On that day he sent the Chief of Staff a memorandum calling attention to the fact that in the first several months of a war the supply requirements for the initial one-million-man force called for in the 1933 Mobilization Plan could not possibly be met. In that case, Woodring contended, it would be useless and wasteful to try to achieve the unrealistic objectives of the plan; what were needed were goals that could be attained. The present mobilization plan provided for the formation of a very large force in a short period of time, and Woodring, General Craig, and the entire General Staff knew that it was just a paper plan, which in reality could not be carried out. The Secretary then suggested that the General Staff consider the "advisability and need for two separate and distinct plans. One, a paper plan based on the Staff's present manpower mobilization tables . . . and a second, based on what I term a 'defensive policy' plan calling for a speedy mobilization of a much smaller force for which material *can be* supplied." What Woodring wanted was a plan that could actually be fulfilled; thus, he favored a scheme that called for mobilization of a much smaller force. He believed that to create such a force and make it effective would require that it be fully trained and completely supplied in peacetime, so that it would be immediately available at the outbreak of war.[35]

The Secretary's directive was all the prodding that General Craig needed to begin work on a new, realistic plan for mobilization. On 16 December he directed the General Staff to begin development of the Protective Mobilization Plan, or PMP. The guidelines presented were quite brief: "The Protective Mobilization Plan will provide for the mobilization of a moderate but balanced force for the protection of the Continental United States including Hawaii and Panama. The size and character of the force should be such as to permit its being speedily and properly armed and equipped." General Craig closed by emphasizing the importance of the plan, and he asked that it be completed as quickly as possible.[36]

It took the War Department two years to complete the PMP. It was written in sections, and as each section was completed in enough detail to be useful, it was published. Thus, the PMP appeared in a handful of installments between February 1937 and December 1938. As a result of the piecemeal release and publication of the plan and its further revisions, it soon became commonplace to read or hear about the 1937 PMP, the 1938 PMP, or the 1939 PMP, when in reality they were all a part of, or a revision of, the same plan.[37]

The PMP introduced a new concept in basic planning for mobilization. According to mobilization experts Marvin Kreidberg and Merton Henry, "The Protective Mobilization Plans were not only the first mobilization plans to be based completely on realism but were also the first plans which successfully achieved real succinctness and simplicity without the sacrifice of coherence."[38] Whereas the earlier plans of 1928 and 1933 had provided for the mobilization of a million-man force three months after mobilization began, the PMP placed reliance on a much smaller but better-equipped and highly trained Army to furnish immediate protection. In the event that additional forces were necessary, the plan called for well-defined steps of expansion which were designed to enable proper equipping and training of new recruits. Under the old plans the order for mobilization brought one million men into the Army at once, whether they were needed or not; but the PMP could mobilize the number necessary to meet the need. The first echelon of defense under the PMP was to be a 400,000-man Initial Protective Force (IPF). This force, which was to include units of the Regular Army and the National Guard, was to be completely ready for combat within one month after M-Day. If it was apparent that the IPF would not be sufficient, a Protective Mobilization Force of more than 700,000 men would then be mobilized. The plan called for this second contingent of troops to be ready eight months after M-Day. In the event that still more troops were needed, the PMP provided for a minimum increase of 150,000 men monthly until a four-million-man force was achieved. The primary weakness of the PMP was that it failed to provide a balanced military force. The Army was to be made up almost solely of infantry; the air force and armored force were virtually ignored. Lack of balance is evident from the fact that the plan provided for only one armored division in a four-million-man force.[39]

Compared to the earlier plans, which called for mobilizing a million men in three months, the PMP seemed to be a step backward; but the goals of the earlier plans could not possibly have been attained, whereas those of the PMP could be. When it is realized that it took the United States fourteen months to put one million men in fighting trim during World War I, the PMP appears more impressive.[40] The plan had its logistical and tactical shortcomings, but in comparison to previous mobilization plans it marked a real step forward. Secretary Woodring was the first to admit that the plan was not perfect, but he did maintain that there was every reason to believe that it was "feasible and will meet our national defense requirements."[41]

While the PMP was being prepared in 1937 and 1938 there was little that Secretary Woodring could do to implement even its first phases, because Congress did not intend to provide funds for a plan that was not yet fully developed. In the meantime Woodring tried in other ways to improve the Army's readiness. In December of 1936 he issued his first annual report as Secretary of War. It indicated a general satisfaction with conditions in the War Department and in the Army. The recommendations made were extremely modest, the most significant being (1) an increase in National Guard strength from 189,000 to 210,000; (2) two weeks of annual training for 30,000 Reserve Officers, instead of the present 20,000; and (3) the establishment of an enlisted reserve of 150,000 men.[42] Woodring felt that such modest demands could certainly be met. The *Washington Herald* stated that the recommendations embraced "a program of minimum requirements," which, even if adopted, would still leave the nation "perilously weak."[43] An editorial in the *Washington Evening Star* maintained that "Congress is not likely to find any of these proposals unreasonable" and recommended that they be given favorable consideration.[44] When the Bureau of the Budget reviewed the increases for the new proposals, they were denied, and, as usual, the Secretary of War was not asked to appear before the bureau or the Congressional Appropriations Committee to justify his budget requests. In the end, Congress performed as it had in the past decade and a half and provided only enough funds to increase the National Guard by 3,000, instead of 20,000; and to give two weeks of training to an additional 2,000 reserve officers, instead of the requested 10,000; and it included no provision for an enlisted reserve.[45]

In spite of his good intentions, Woodring's contributions to improve the Army's readiness were virtually nil in his first full year as Secretary of War. His ineffectiveness stemmed from several factors. First, his dual responsibility as both Secretary and Assistant Secretary, which lasted until July 1937, forced him to divide his time and energy between the two positions. Second, the uncertainty as to whether or not he would be made permanent Secretary caused him to "go easy" so as to not antagonize the President. Third, with the PMP still in preparation and its needs uncertain, he could not yet take steps to implement it. Although he did not bring about any major advancements in the Army during that first year, the Secretary used the period to win the confidence of the President, Congress, and the Army. As a 6 November 1937 editorial in the *Army and Navy Journal* indicated:

Only a Secretary of War could discharge competently these numerous important and responsible duties who has the fullest confidence of the President, and Mr. Woodring has that. Only a Secretary of War could build as Mr. Woodring has built who has the confidence of Congress, and the Secretary has that. We are moved to recite these facts . . . because a year has passed since the responsibility for administering the affairs of the War Department devolved on him. That year has shown his ability and capacity and understanding in connection with national and particularly military needs. These qualities necessarily have earned for him the sincere respect and devotion of the forces which, under the President, he directs.[46]

By the end of 1937 Secretary Woodring was examining the Army more closely than before. This scrutiny resulted from his growing concern over the breakdown of peace throughout the world. Japanese aggression against China, Civil War in Spain, and the growing strength of Hitler and Mussolini caused him to be more critical in his examination of the United States military machine than he had been the year before. In his *Annual Report*, which was released in December 1937, Woodring warned the President that although the Army was more efficient than it had ever been in peacetime, it was "relatively weaker, compared with armies of other great countries, than it was a year ago." The loss in relative strength resulted from the other countries' strengthening of their military forces at a more rapid rate than the United States. Even though Woodring concluded that "at present our Regular Army . . . is too small to accomplish efficiently the task for which it is responsible," he did not ask for a sizable increase; he requested only an additional 7,000 enlisted men and 2,300 officers. He again urged that an enlisted reserve program be established, but this time in much stronger terms than the year before. After warning the President that the nation would be "at a distinct disadvantage during the mobilization period of a major war if we lack trained men to fill key positions in the ranks," he asked that a start be made toward the creation of a 150,000-man enlisted reserve.[47]

With one exception Woodring's recommendations in his *Annual Report* for 1937 were similar to those of the previous year. That exception pertained to his request concerning the quantity and quality of military equipment. Woodring stated, as he was to do repeatedly, that while he did not consider the size of the Army extremely important, he believed that the

127

equipment it had was of the utmost importance. He emphasized the need to reequip the Army "with the latest and best in transportation, means of communication, and weapons." He also emphasized both that the best equipment should be procured and that sufficient quantities should be provided. Although he stressed the importance of and deficiencies in equipment, he urged that a rather conservative approach be used in correcting the shortcoming. He said that he did not want the country to get involved in the arms race, but he did want it to "accelerate" the program for reequipping the Army.[48] Woodring's extremely conservative requests in terms of manpower and equipment reveal one of his major shortcomings as Secretary of War: he continually failed to ask and actively push for what he really believed was necessary in order to create a first-class army. That he was well aware of the deficiencies of the military can be seen in his *Annual Reports*, but when it came to making recommendations, he fell into the old War Department rut of asking for what he thought he could get rather than what was really needed. For this he can be justifiably criticized.

By the time that Secretary Woodring issued his 1937 *Report,* events in Europe had caused President Roosevelt to conclude that it was time to examine the defense needs of the nation very closely. In December and early January the President indicated that he would ask Congress to appropriate a large amount for defense needs.[49] With FDR's growing interest in defense matters, the Secretary of War and the War Department became increasingly optimistic about getting the funds to strengthen the land forces significantly; thus, it was a rather confident Harry Woodring who traveled to the White House on 20 January 1938 to discuss the Army's needs. At that conference, FDR informed Woodring that the Navy, not the Army, was to be the primary beneficiary of his new defense program. A highly distraught Woodring pleaded with the President to give the Army more consideration, and he warned that to ignore the ground forces, as was being done, was a grave mistake. His pleas fell on deaf ears as Roosevelt stuck to his earlier decision. A few days later, Woodring wrote Roosevelt, again asking that the defense program place more emphasis on Army needs, which were "truly justified under the present world situation." He then recommended that an additional $30 million be made available to improve the Army's state of readiness.[50] Woodring felt that if Congress was going to appropriate a vast sum for defense, then the Army should have its fair share. The President, feeling that the needs of the Navy should have first priority, chose to take lightly the advice of his Secretary of War; and in his budget message on 28 January he asked Congress for only $17 million to strengthen the Army. In looking back at this request a few years later, Roosevelt said, "With respect to the Army, I included only those items which had been recommended by the War Department as immediately necessary. It was obviously impossible to do everything at once, and these were the first steps."[51]

While Woodring was generally displeased with the President's 1938 defense program, he was especially resentful of Roosevelt's failure to strengthen the Army Air Corps. Feeling that the Navy was being built up at the expense of the Air Corps, he went to Roosevelt in February 1938 and asked that one hundred planes earmarked for the Navy be given to the Army instead. The pro-Navy Roosevelt listened attentively, but was not persuaded, and the defense program favoring the Navy remained unchanged.[52]

Although Secretary Woodring did not succeed in securing a large share of the defense appropriations for fiscal year 1939, he was successful in bringing about one of his most sought-after goals—an enlisted reserve, or, as it came to be called, the Regular Army Reserve. When the first National Defense Act was passed in 1916, it had included provisions for a reserve of enlisted men; however, after World War I the provision was rescinded because of the large number of veterans that could be called in case of emergency.[53] During the 1920s and 1930s the Citizens Military Training Corps and the ROTC provided a supply of officers that could be tapped in time of war, but there was no program to provide experienced enlisted personnel in such an emergency. From the time that he came into office, Secretary Woodring continually stressed the need for a 150,000-man enlisted reserve; finally, in January 1938, he succeeded in winning the President's support for such a program, but for only a 75,000-man force.[54] Next, Woodring set out to sell the idea to Congress. He indicated to the House and Senate Military Affairs committees that if the Regular Army was called to active duty, it would be forced to take the field with units that were small, depleted, and understrength. Such a dangerous situation could be corrected either by a sizable increase in Regular Army strength or by the establishment of an enlisted reserve. For reasons of economy, Woodring recommended that the latter course be taken.[55] Congress agreed, and in April 1938 it passed the necessary legislation.

The Army Reserve Act provided for the enlistment in the Regular Army Reserve of former Regular Army enlisted men who had returned to civilian life. Since they had previously been trained, no further training was considered necessary. As an inducement to sign up, each reservist was paid $24 a year, and in return he simply had to keep the Army informed of his present address; no weekly or annual training of any kind was required. The Reservists could be called to active duty "only in case of emergency declared by the President." If called, they would receive a bonus of $3 for each month in the Reserves, the total not to exceed $150. An age limit of thirty-five was also established.[56] Plans called for the 75,000-man force to be raised over a period of four years, with the cost running $450,000 the first year and increasing by a like amount annually until it leveled off at $1.8 million after the fourth year. The Regular Army Reserve did not in any way replace or affect any of the reserve forces, such as the National Guard, that were already in existence. Its sole purpose, according to the Senate Military Affairs Committee, was "to bolster the Regular Army so that it can better perform its vital tasks of defense in the first stages of an emergency."[57]

From the time that he became Secretary of War in the fall of 1936 until March 1938, Woodring, while showing a definite interest in increased Army readiness, did not appear alarmed or overconcerned about the shortcomings that he knew existed. As late as February 1938 he indicated that he considered the nation's new defense program modest but adequate.[58] One month later, when Hitler annexed Austria, Secretary Woodring publicly announced that the United States Army was better prepared than at any time in its history for "whatever happens."[59] Apparently, however, he was not as confident as his public utterances indicated, for after the Anschluss he ordered a detailed study to determine the requirements for properly arming and equipping the IPF. While that study was under way he worked hard to convince Congress of the immediate need for an additional two thousand officers for the Regular Army.[60] Congress responded in early April by approving the Secretary's request, and two weeks later the Army Reserve Act, for which Woodring had worked so hard, was passed. Such activities of the Secretary of War were evidently making a favorable impression on the public mind, because in June 1938 Woodring fared very well when the Gallup Poll asked the question: "Do you think the following cabinet members have done a good or poor job in office?" While less than half of those interviewed expressed an opinion on Secretary Woodring, of those that did, five of every six said that he was doing a good job; thus, the conclusion of the pollsters was that "although there is little that peacetime Secretaries of Navy and War can do to win public attention, today's survey shows that [Secretary of Navy] Swanson and Woodring have substantial approval for their work."[61]

In July 1938 the War Department revealed that a careful study showed that there was an immediate and urgent shortage of critical items of equipment for the IPF. To supply those items would cost $142 million.[62] In the weeks that followed, Secretary Woodring and other officials of the War Department tried to educate Congress and the public on the importance and needs of the IPF. Time and again they pointed out that although the quality of the equipment that the units had was good, the quantity was insufficient. Warnings of the consequences of the shortages went unheeded by Congress and the nation, who were convinced that they could avoid another war.

130

Then in September 1938 came the Munich Crisis, followed by Hitler's success at the Munich Conference; and at last the United States was suddenly interested in its Army. The events of September caused Congress and the American people to realize that they had ignored their military establishment long enough and that further delay in upgrading it would be extremely dangerous. At the time that this new crisis atmosphere developed, the IPF was so short of modern arms that had it become involved in combat, it could not possibly have been an effective fighting force. Whereas the PMP called for a minimum of 227,000 semiautomatic rifles, only 12,500 were on hand; of the called-for 1,500 M2-75mm guns, only 141 were available. The story was the same for other new weapons: 60mm mortars—3,750 required, 1 on hand; 105mm howitzers—55 required, 0 on hand; light tanks—244 required, 36 on hand; medium tanks—1,100 required, 319 on hand.[63] General Craig was quite concerned about these shortages, but he was even more alarmed by the fact that "most of these items require in excess of one year to produce." This meant that if the shortages were to be overcome by 1940, it would be necessary to act at once.[64]

In November 1938, six weeks after Munich, Secretary Woodring released his third *Annual Report*. Pessimistically he pointed out that in spite of recent advances, the Army still contained certain "deficiencies in organization, equipment, and personnel which must be corrected before we can be assured of maintenance of a military force fully adequate for our defensive needs." He set as his number one priority the perfection of the 400,000-man IPF. To accomplish that goal he stressed the need for additional equipment and training. Woodring emphasized that the IPF was all important because "if they fail in their protective mission the fate of the reinforcing citizens' armies is sealed." The report also emphasized the importance of properly equipping the forces that would follow the IPF into the field. His conclusion was that there was little need for additional personnel but a great need for additional equipment and training.[65]

Hitler's victory at Munich so impressed Roosevelt that he quickly reached the conclusion that the time had come for the United States to begin rearming extensively. Woodring, therefore, spent November and December working on the President's new rearmament program, which placed heavy emphasis on a greatly expanded Army Air Corps.[66] While considerable attention was given to the air program, other matters of Army readiness were not ignored. On 5 January 1939 Secretary Woodring presented to the President the War Department's recommendations for carrying out the rearmament program and increasing the readiness of existing forces. Because of the recent events abroad, Roosevelt was anxious to strengthen the Army, and therefore he was very receptive to the War Department's proposals.[67]

On 12 January the President sent his budget message to Congress, asking that it appropriate $450 million for the "new needs of the Army." While the bulk of the funds requested was to go for increasing air strength, $110 million were to be used for "'critical items' of equipment which would be needed immediately in time of emergency, and which cannot be obtained from any source within the time and quantity desired."[68] There was no mention of an increase in the Army's manpower. Pleased as Woodring was with the proposed budget, he indicated to the President that there was still reason to be pessimistic, because "while the measures suggested will materially forward the readiness of the Army, nevertheless a serious deficiency of great import to both Army and Navy will still exist after these measures are accomplished."[69] Furthermore, he was pessimistic because there was no certainty that Congress would grant everything that the President requested.

Beginning in mid January 1939, Secretary Woodring made several appearances before the House and Senate Military Affairs committees as well as the Senate and House Subcommittees on Appropriations. Before each committee he emphasized the same thing: "Our main problem, however, is to assure the complete equipment in critical items of our existing Regular Army and National Guard units and the organization of the initial protective force into a force fully capable of shouldering its heavy burden."[70] In the committee hearings, Woodring was usually drawn into a discussion of future as well as present needs of the Army. These discussions saw him and other War Department officials follow the long-standing practice of asking for what they thought they could get rather than what was needed. Woodring told the committeemen that it would be desirable if supplies for the 720,000-man PMF would be made available, but funds for that purpose were not being requested at that time.[71] Recommendations for additional personnel also indicated the War Department's tendency to ask for half a loaf. Woodring informed the Senate Military Affairs Committee that the "War Department has carefully excluded urgent personnel requirements. . . . We prefer at this time to invest such money as is appropriated in matériel."[72] At the same time that such statements were being made by the Secretary of War, the Chief of Staff was expressing alarm because "we urgently need to have always available 5 complete divisions" but at present "we do not have a single division."[73] In spite of the Army's awareness of this shortcoming, no additional troops were requested, and, furthermore, it was made clear that no such request would be made. All military representatives who might conceivably be called to testify before one of the congressional committees were informed by the Chief of Staff that in accordance with "presidential views," no additional increases in ground forces had been requested and that such a position should be maintained by anyone testifying on behalf of the War Department. The memorandum containing this information also contained advice on how to reply to the investigators' questions about the number of ground forces to be provided if and when such an increase should be permitted. The answer to be given was 1,800 officers and 23,000 enlisted men.[74] This information was brought out in most of the hearings.

While members of Congress were debating on how far they should go in implementing the President's 1939 defense program, their minds were made up for them by Adolf Hitler, who on 13 March sent his troops into Slovakia, thus completing the takeover of Czechoslovakia. This act marked the failure of the Munich Agreement and showed the world that Hitler was indeed a dangerous man who could not be trusted. Congress, at last convinced of the need for stronger defenses, was now willing to listen to the suggestions and recommendations of the President, the Secretary of War, and members of the General Staff. During the next three months, Woodring made numerous trips to the Hill to testify before various committees concerning the need for aircraft, training, and "critical items." In one appearance before a House Subcommittee on Appropriations he indicated that he considered the President's proposals "exceedingly conservative and modest" and believed that failure to implement any one of them would endanger the nation's security. He concluded his testimony by saying, "As Secretary of War, I would be sadly remiss in my duty to the American people were I to advise or countenance the reduction of one iota of any item in the President's program."[75]

The jittery Congress did not require much convincing, and in April, May, and June 1939 it passed Army Appropriations Bills for $549 million, including $180 million for new aircraft and $110 million for critical items. It also approved an increase of 2,050 Regular Army officers and authorized an increase in enlisted strength from 165,000 to 210,000 by June of 1940.[76] Woodring was pleased with these legislative victories which marked the biggest military outlays since World War I. It was at about this time that the President expressed himself as "thoroughly satisfied with the administration he [Woodring] has given to the War Department, and particularly the manner in which he assisted . . . in fashioning the Army Expansion Bill and facilitating its passage through Congress."[77]

Because of the new appropriations, Secretary Woodring was now able to carry out some of the programs that he had long been advocating. One of the first problem areas he was to deal with was that of large-scale Army maneuvers. Although the military had long recognized the importance of these exercises in giving valuable experience to all personnel from field grade officers down to privates, the economy drive of the 1930s had virtually eliminated such training. Woodring was especially concerned over the matter of training, because the continual loss from active duty of war-experienced personnel meant that more and more individuals without combat experience were coming into command positions. This factor, he claimed, made large-scale training very important, especially in the United States, "where limited forces, limited facilities and limited funds do not permit those massive peacetime manoeuvres and field exercises which characterize the instructional activities of great armies in other parts of the world."[78] In early 1939, with Congress in a mood to spend money for national defense, Woodring asked for $20 million to expand the Army's training program. Included in this request were funds to conduct the "biggest army maneuvers since 1918." When Congress granted the full amount requested for training, the maneuvers were assured.

Subsequently, in August 1939, Regular Army and National Guard units of the First United States Army gathered at Plattsburg, New York, under their Commander, Gen. Hugh A. Drum, for two weeks of war games. With more than 52,000 men participating, this was the largest peacetime military exercise in the nation's history. When the games opened, General Drum expressed doubts as to the effectiveness of the First Army, claiming that the forces assembled were not an army " 'but a collection of individual units, partially equipped and woefully short' in most of the elements which go to make an army."[79] The two-weeks' exercise did nothing to change his mind, and in a very pointed critique, Drum stressed the "inexperience" of the troops assembled and called the state of affairs that he found "deplorable and inexcusable." The *New York Times* took the statements of General Drum and other Army observers and used them for a front-page story that told of the " 'Deplorable' Lack of Training Especially Evident in [the] National Guard" and came to the conclusion that "Neither It Nor [the] Regulars [Are] Fit for War."[80] At first, Woodring was quite upset over General Drum's revelations, because he felt that they reflected on him as Secretary of War. Soon, however, he came to feel that what Drum had done was a good thing, because the exposure of the Army's lack of training and equipment would help make the public mind more receptive to the adoption of recommendations that he had been making for the past several years.[81]

The summer of 1939 also brought a new era in Army-Navy strategic planning. Prior to that time the War Plans Division of the General Staff had drawn up plans that envisioned a future war with a single nation. These plans were called "color plans," because each possible enemy was designated as a color: thus, War Plan Brown was for war with Germany; War Plan Orange, for Japan; and so forth. The need for more realistic war plans and closer coordination between the two major armed services had long been recognized, but it was not until 30 June 1939 that the Joint Army-Navy Board approved, in general, a new series of basic war plans.[82] The plans, which were known as Rainbow Plans, envisioned waging a war against several foes in more than one area at the same time. The June decision was limited to an outline of the plans; it actually took several years to develop the details.[83] Woodring appears to have taken no part in the preparation of the Rainbow Plans. In part, this was probably because he considered them to be of a strictly military nature and therefore not a matter on which he could advise or guide the Joint Army-Navy Board. Another limiting factor was an order of 5 July 1939 from President Roosevelt to the effect that in the future the Joint Board would report directly to him as Commander in Chief.[84] From that time on, the Secretary of War was usually bypassed when it came to the strategic planning of the Joint Army-Navy Board.

Along with the Army's gains of the summer of 1939 there came a loss. That loss was the retirement of Gen. Malin Craig as Chief of Staff. Although his retirement from active duty was scheduled for 1 September, the stress and strain of the past several years caused him to take terminal leave on 30 June. Considering the strong isolationist and anti-military sentiment that prevailed throughout the country in the mid thirties, General Craig had done an outstanding job in increasing the strength and efficiency of the United States Army, and, most important of all, he had given the Army a realistic mobilization plan.[85] Perhaps the best evaluation of Craig and his contributions to the Army was that given by the noted American military historian Russell F. Weigley, who said, "It is questionable whether any soldier did more than he to make possible American military accomplishments in World War II."[86] When his accomplishments are compared with those of his successor, Gen. George C. Marshall, they seem to be quite small, but when compared with what had been accomplished in the previous fifteen years, they appear to be very substantial. No one hated to see Craig leave more than did Woodring. From the time that Woodring came to the War Department in 1933, these two men had become the best of friends; and later, as Secretary of War and Chief of Staff, they had cooperated to a degree rarely found in military or civilian circles. Woodring, who looked with deep affection upon the General as his "right arm," stated that the relationship he enjoyed with Craig was that of "a brother, and frequently that of a father and son."[87]

In addition to marking Craig's departure from the War Department, August 1939 was to mark the beginning of a new era as far as the United States Army's importance, influence, and significance on the national scene were concerned. With war in Europe appearing imminent, the War Department introduced plans for enlarging and equipping a military force that would be more powerful than any that had ever been contemplated in peacetime.[88] When war finally broke out in early September, interest in the country's defenses became greater than ever. It was at that time that Congress began to scrutinize, as never before, the state of the Army's readiness, and Secretary Woodring and the War Department were, consequently, to emerge as centers of attention and activity. Since August marked the beginning of a new era for the Army, it offers a convenient breaking point for examining Woodring's efforts, up to that point, to improve the Army's readiness.

There seems to be no doubt that the American military machine was much stronger in August 1939 than it had been when Woodring took control of it in September 1936. While it is true that events abroad were in large part responsible for Congress's willingness to strengthen the Army, that situation should not obscure the fact that Woodring, who had the confidence of the President, Congress, and the military, played an important role in securing passage of legislation upgrading the armed forces. In size, planning, training, and equipment the United States Army was better prepared and stronger in August 1939 than it had been at any time since 1919. Whereas in September 1936 there were 147,000 enlisted men and 12,000 officers in the Regular Army, there were 175,000 and 13,200 respectively in August of 1939. More important than these actual strengths was the fact that Congress had just appropriated funds to raise the "authorized strength" of the Army to 210,000 enlisted men and 16,700 officers by June of 1940.[89] Since the Secretary had not actively pushed for such increases in manpower, he can be given little credit for them, but the increases were nevertheless on the way.

In the realm of planning for mobilization, Woodring had played a major role in developing a sensible, workable scheme to provide an adequate protective force and necessary reserves. The Protective Mobilization Plan, with its provisions for an Initial Protective Force and a Protective Mobilization Force, was quite sound; the only problem was that Congress had not seen fit to appropriate the funds that were necessary to implement it. A start, however, had been made in the spring of 1939, when Congress appropriated $110 million for "critical items" and $20 million for training the Initial Protective Force. In addition, Woodring had assisted in the formation of the Regular Army Reserve; had helped to make plans for the largest peacetime military maneuvers; had supervised a major revision of the Industrial Mobilization Plan; had championed the testing and adoption of new weapons, including the Garand semiautomatic rifle; and had contributed significantly to strengthening the defenses of Hawaii and the Panama Canal.

In spite of the progress that had been made, however, the Army was still woefully unprepared to meet any military emergency. Numerically it was far weaker than the army of any other major power, and because of rapid military expansion abroad, it was relatively weaker than it had been several years before. General Craig, in his final report as Chief of Staff, reported that as of 30 June 1939, the Army "was short much of its critical armament and equipment. . . . There were deficiencies in personnel. . . . And there was a serious shortage in immediate war reserves." The result of these deficiencies was: "We have not now a single complete division of the Regular Army [available for instant dispatch to troubled areas]. We have four partial divisions and five brigades in various stages of completion; and only a few special units available." This meant that in the summer of 1939 the United States Army did not have one complete division ready for immediate action.[90] Although Secretary Woodring had accomplished much, there remained a great deal to do, and the road to success was full of military, political, and personal obstacles. It was a combination of the latter two that was to create his greatest problems.

8

Politics Disrupts
the War Department

Throughout its history, both in peace and in war, the United States has been a nation firmly committed to the principle of civilian control of the military. This tenet stems from the belief that "in a democracy all basic policy, including military policy, is made by officials responsible to the people with whom sovereignty ultimately rests."[1] While this principle has held true since colonial times, the American attitude toward the military establishment has continually fluctuated. During periods of war the American people have tended to look upon the military with trust, respect, and appreciation; however, in times of peace a fear of military usurpation and tyranny has caused them to look upon the Army with suspicion and distrust. The widespread fear of the militarization of American society has created an "antimilitary tradition."[2] The public attitude toward the American military establishment has therefore generally been one of admiration and support in time of war, and one of scorn and apprehension in time of peace.

The United States Army has always been expected to provide the nation with adequate security against hostile forces but, at the same time, not be so strong as to present a threat to the society that created it.[3] Such attitudes have placed the American military man in a difficult position, for while his fellow countrymen expect him to defend and, if necessary, die for his country, they also consider him a potential threat to their cherished ideal of civilian control of the government. Out of all this has emerged a widespread belief that the military establishment is a necessary evil. Fear and distrust of American military leaders have caused them to be isolated from other elements of society, so that they have become "a conscious and coherent group within but largely apart from the larger governmental structure. Such a group . . . has its own distinctive entrance and tenure procedures, its own salary system, its own traditions and group attitudes, its own sensitivity and code of privacy."[4] Because of their isolation, military leaders have rarely taken an interest in public affairs and have usually found it expedient to avoid expressing opinions on political matters. However, the officers at the highest echelons have frequently found that they could not avoid becoming embroiled in politics, because they were working under civilians whose decisions were based to a large extent on political considerations. Accustomed to a promotion system based on merit and loyalty, and working within an organization in which the same regulations apply to everyone, the military men have often found it difficult to understand the ways of their politically oriented superiors.

As Harry Woodring soon discovered, carrying out the responsibilities of the Secretary of War was no easy task. The position was a complex and difficult one, not only because of the magnitude of its functions and responsibilities, but also because it placed a politically appointed civilian in charge of an establishment staffed by professional military men. To succeed in the post it was necessary to please and accommodate a politically elected Commander in Chief, on the one hand, and the leaders of the military establishment on the other. As President Roosevelt's representative, Woodring stood for civilian control of the Army; but since the Secretary of War was responsible for the military defense of the nation, he had to represent and attempt to carry out the recommendations of his military advisers. He was in reality a politician doing a military job. In a nation committed to the idea of civilian control of the military, it was extremely difficult to represent and please both those who desired a stronger Army and those who feared the increased influence of the military. In an attempt to please both the civilian and the military, Woodring was forced to walk on the fence that divided the two. To fall or even lean too far to one side always brought the wrath of the other. When he urged Congress and the President to strengthen the nation's Army, he was called a militarist or a warmonger; and when he called for less than the General Staff recommended, military men criticized him for failing to provide an adequate defense. To satisfy completely his superior and his subordinates at the same time was an extremely difficult, if not an impossible, task.

One consequence of having a politically elected Commander in Chief and a politically appointed Secretary of War is that politics comes to play a key role in the decisions, policies, and actions of the War Department. Both President Roosevelt and Secretary Woodring realized that they had the responsibility of providing an adequate military defense, but they also realized that in pursuing that end, they must not do anything to antagonize or frighten Congress or the public, without whose support nothing could be accomplished. In running the War Department, Secretary Woodring had to deal extensively with the President, Congress, the cabinet, and the General Staff. Since the first three of these were politically oriented, it was not surprising that politics came to have a major influence on Woodring's operation of the War Department and eventually came to disrupt its activities. To understand the effects of politics on Secretary Woodring and the War Department, it is necessary to examine his relationships with President Roosevelt, his military advisers, Congress, the Assistant Secretary of War, and those individuals who made up Roosevelt's inner circle of friends.

The personal relationship between Harry Woodring and Franklin D. Roosevelt was an extremely close one from the time they first met in 1931 until the latter's death in 1945.[5] Woodring had the highest respect and admiration for FDR, and he did not hesitate to say so both publicly and privately. Roosevelt was very fond of Woodring, and treasured his friendship. The fact that Woodring was to remain Secretary of War as long as he did was in large part due to his close personal relationship with the President.[6] But while they were always on the best of terms personally, Roosevelt and Woodring were frequently at odds over official matters. Disagreements usually stemmed from the fact that although Woodring was nominally Secretary of War, President Roosevelt always wanted to be, and to a great extent was, his own Secretary of War. The President accomplished this by personal intervention and by delegating tasks to his own personal representatives who were outside of the chain of command.[7] According to Roosevelt's friend Edward J. Flynn, a Democratic leader, "The Boss either appoints four men to do the job of one or one man to do the job of four." He then added that none of the four would know what the others were doing nor would the one man know "the scope of his authority."[8] The *New York Herald Tribune* expressed it more succinctly when it said, "The role of a true executive, functioning through able subordinates possessing both power and responsibility, has never appealed to him [Roosevelt]."[9]

President Roosevelt's desire to run his own show frequently caused difficulty in the War Department, because the Secretary "had his own ideas and he worked hard at putting them through."[10] Woodring was always willing to listen to the other side of an issue, but once he came to a conclusion as to which policy, principle, or line of action to follow, he stuck to it with the utmost tenacity.[11] He liked to tell others what to do, but he was often resentful of another's telling him what to do, even if that other person happened to be his boss, the President of the United States. When he and Roosevelt disagreed on a matter, Woodring would use all his knowledge and oratorical skill to win Roosevelt over; and if the decision was not what Woodring felt it should be, he would often delay in carrying out the President's wishes.

As time passed and Europe headed closer to war, their disagreements over important policies became more frequent, and Roosevelt, in spite of his high personal regard for Woodring, began to consider replacing him. The President, however, was not willing simply to dismiss his Secretary of War; he wished to ease him out of the War Department by offering him another lucrative position.[12] When their disagreements over official matters got to the place where they irritated the President, he began to ignore Woodring, turning to others, both within and outside the War Department. Even when FDR was ignoring Woodring as Secretary of War, he continued to maintain a close personal relationship with him. Although the two men frequently clashed over governmental policies, they never let such disputes interfere with their admiration, respect, and fondness for one another.[13]

Harmonious as Woodring's personal associations with his superior were, his relationships with his military advisers were even better. The close association between Woodring and Chief of Staff Craig was well known; on numerous occasions it was the topic of editorials and news stories.[14] General Craig had a great respect for Woodring, going so far as to say that during the period that he, Craig, was Chief of Staff, Woodring had not "made a single mistake as Secretary."[15] Woodring's relations with Craig's successor, Gen. George C. Marshall, were also very amiable.[16] The General Staff and the heads of the several Service Branches and Combat Arms, as well as the members of their staffs, appear to have felt that Woodring understood their problems and based his decisions on a sincere desire to do what was best for the Army.[17] Another factor that endeared the Secretary to the military leaders was his policy of not interfering in what he considered to be strictly military matters. According to the *Army and Navy Journal*, "Woodring's relations with the military portions of his department have been marked with great consideration and sympathetic understanding. Between him and General Craig . . . there has existed a most cordial relationship and effective cooperation for the good of the military service."[18] Perhaps the best expression of Woodring's relationship with the military appeared in a *Kansas City Star* editorial written after he had been forced from the cabinet: "He had strong support from the military men, who found in the secretary an able business executive, and an open-minded, intelligent and fair department head.

Plenty of testimony to this effect has come from high military sources."[19] The relationship between Woodring and his top military advisers was definitely one of mutual respect and admiration.

In the late thirties, as the threat of Hitler grew larger and larger, the United States turned increasingly to the question of national defense. When this began to happen, Woodring found his relationship with Congress becoming increasingly important. He spent hundreds of hours before the House and Senate Military Affairs committees, made numerous appearances before the War Department Subcommittee of the House Committee on Appropriations, and wrote scores of letters to congressional committees and individual Congressmen, informing them of the Army's needs. He frequently recommended legislation to overcome certain shortcomings, then did all that he could to convince Congress to provide the authorization and the necessary appropriations. In his appearances before the committees, the calm, smooth-talking Secretary usually impressed his listeners with his extensive knowledge of the Army, the Air Corps, the War Department, and national defense.

After war broke out in Europe in the fall of 1939, Woodring adopted a policy of "direct dealing" with the congressional leaders who were responsible for Army authorizations and appropriations. This policy, which consisted of monthly conferences between War Department officials and key House and Senate committeemen, was initiated because Woodring wished "to maintain closer contact between the Department and Congress." At these meetings, Woodring and his military advisers explained what was needed, what was being done, and what the Congress could and should do to assist the Army.[20] One of the major consequences of these meetings was the appearance of a close rapport between Woodring and key members of Congress. This relationship frequently paid big dividends to the Army, such as it did in early 1939 when Woodring gave the Congressmen a chance to observe the highly secret work in radar that the Army was undertaking at the Signal Corps Laboratories at Fort Monmouth, New Jersey; and they responded by providing an additional but unexplained $150,000, which was used for radar research.[21]

Secretary Woodring was highly regarded and respected by a number of important members of the House and the Senate Military Affairs committees. In the House committee, Chairman Andrew J. May, Dow Harter, John Sparkman, and Charles I. Faddis thought very highly of Woodring and were among his most loyal supporters.[22] Faddis, one of the most influential members of the committee, was later to say of Woodring, "He was of the utmost assistance to us in our efforts to bring our military affairs up to date."[23] In the Senate Military Affairs Committee, numerous individuals,

142

both Democrats and Republicans, voiced their confidence in Secretary Woodring. In the fall of 1939 Senator Robert Reynolds of North Carolina told his fellow committeemen, "I have a good deal of confidence in the Secretary, and want the benefit of his advice."[24] At about the same time Senator Josh Lee of Oklahoma, in a committee hearing at which Woodring was testifying, said: "I desire to compliment the present Secretary of War for what he has done in increasing our defense, which I think is due in large part to his efforts."[25] Republican Senator Styles Bridges of New Hampshire, who, as a member of the Military Affairs Committee and the War Department Subcommittee on Appropriations, had considerable opportunity to see Woodring in action, stated on the Senate floor that he found the Secretary "to be an able, capable, conscientious executive and member of the Cabinet."[26] Other important members of the Senate Military Affairs Committee who had confidence in Woodring and considered him to be a strong Secretary of War were Senators Edwin Johnson of Colorado, Lister Hill of Alabama, Bennett Clark of Missouri, and Gerald Nye of North Dakota. The *Army and Navy Journal* summed up Woodring's relationship with the legislative branch by saying, "He has so conducted himself with Congress that he has had little difficulty getting his recommendations adopted."[27]

That Woodring enjoyed a fine relationship with Congress, especially with the more conservative members whose views he best reflected, was evident in a number of ways. First, his recommendations concerning legislation were usually accepted and acted upon. Second, although the discussions in the committee hearings often became heated on both sides, Woodring was never treated in a rude or disrespectful manner. Third, while numerous Congressmen praised him publicly and privately for the job that he was doing, they rarely criticized him. It is doubtful that Woodring could have enjoyed a better working relationship with Congress than he did. This was not to say, however, that he always got what he wanted from Congress. In fact, when it came to appropriations, his meager requests for the War Department were usually slashed even further by the Bureau of the Budget and the Congress, both of whom were heavily influenced by the strong isolationist and antimilitary attitudes of the thirties.[28]

From an examination of Secretary Woodring's personal relationship with President Roosevelt, his associations with military leaders, and his dealings with Congress, one might suppose that he experienced a minimum of political difficulties in running the War Department. Nothing could be further from the truth, for the feuds that Woodring had with his Assistant Secretary, Louis A. Johnson, and a few members of Roosevelt's "inner circle" were of such magnitude and caused so much trouble that they more than offset the gains brought about by his smooth relationships with the President, the military, and Congress. A knowledge and an understanding of Wood-ring's feuds are of utmost importance in understanding this period. Robert Sherwood, author of *Roosevelt and Hopkins*, put it best when he said, "History will achieve no complete understanding of Franklin Roosevelt's Administration without knowledge of the intramural feuds which so frequently beset it. (I do not believe that even history will ever be able to understand why he tolerated them to the extent that he did.)"[29]

After the confirmation of Woodring as Secretary of War in May 1937, the question arose of who would be appointed to fill the post of Assistant Secretary. The names most frequently mentioned for the position were those of two former National Commanders of the American Legion, Louis A. Johnson and J. Ray Murphy. Both men had hoped to get the position of Secretary, and both were greatly disappointed when it was given to Woodring. Johnson was then offered the job of Assistant Secretary, but he turned it down because he did not wish to be in a position where he was a subordinate to Woodring. Murphy was also offered the position, and he likewise turned it down. The President then began a search for a "strictly businessman" to fill the post.[30]

On 7 June, Roosevelt asked Woodring what he thought of William I. Westervelt, vice-president of Sears, Roebuck and Company, as a possibility for Assistant Secretary.[31] Four days later, Woodring reported back that he would be in favor of the appointment; however, the appointment was never made, because in the meantime Louis Johnson had changed his mind and agreed to accept the position.[32] From the time of his initial refusal, Johnson had been under pressure from James Farley and a few high-ranking American Legion officials to change his mind and accept the number two spot.[33] Johnson was hesitant, but he finally agreed to accept the post; his reason for doing so was based on an alleged promise made to him concerning the secretaryship. A knowledge of that alleged promise is extremely important if one is to understand Johnson's actions once he assumed the office of Assistant Secretary.

According to one version of the story, while Johnson was being pressured to accept the job, James Farley called Senator Matthew M. Neely of West Virginia, a friend of Johnson's, and asked him to urge Johnson to take the job. According to Neely, Farley said, "You can tell Louis I think within three or four months he will be made Secretary if he will take the post."[34] Neely passed this information on to Johnson, who then made his decision. Whether correctly or not, Johnson interpreted this as a promise from the President that he would soon be promoted to the top spot. Johnson made no effort to keep the promise a secret, for "almost in the same breath with which he took office . . . he informed intimates that he had been appointed for the express purpose of replacing Woodring in a few months."[35] On numerous occasions Johnson stated that he had been promised the secretaryship. Sometimes he claimed that Roosevelt made the promise, but most of the time he said that Farley had made it on the President's behalf. However, Roosevelt did not recall such a promise, and Farley denied having made any such pledge.[36] Farley termed Johnson's story "absolutely untrue" and told the President that if there was any question about it, he should bring Johnson and himself face to face and ask if such a promise had been made. Roosevelt, wishing to avoid an embarrassing situation, never brought about the confrontation.[37] Whether a promise was actually made is not so important as the fact that Johnson believed, or at least claimed to believe, that he would soon be named to replace Woodring as Secretary of War.

Following a cabinet meeting on Friday, 11 June 1937, the President told Woodring that Johnson had agreed to accept the job of Assistant Secretary, and he asked if Woodring had any objections. When the Secretary replied in the negative, the President said that the announcement would be given to the press.[38] Just whom Woodring supported is unclear, because on the day of the cabinet meeting, he sent two letters to the President concerning the appointment. In one he indicated that he considered William Westervelt "admirably fitted and qualified as to business ability to be Assistant Secretary of War." In a second letter he stated, "I desire to recommend for your consideration the name of the Honorable Louis A. Johnson . . . for appointment as Assistant Secretary of War."[39] It is likely that the letter on Johnson was a mere formality and that it was written after the appointment had been determined. One reason for believing that is was written after the Roosevelt-Woodring meeting is that it seems unlikely that Roosevelt, who was his own boss when it came to appointing key officials, would so readily have accepted Woodring's recommendation.[40]

In deciding on Johnson, FDR followed his time-tested practice of putting "into the same office or job men who differed from each other in temperament and viewpoint."[41] Roosevelt knew that when opposites were placed in the top positions in a department or were put in charge of a major project, their inability to agree or get along insured that "no single view, no single man could achieve undue significance or influence."[42] The result was that major problems could and did end in Roosevelt's lap—exactly where he wanted them. The cabinet members knew that because Roosevelt felt that there were benefits to be gained from departmental quarrels, he was not always anxious to end them.[43] For that reason, Roosevelt gave Ickes and Hopkins control over public works, gave Ickes and Wallace control over conservation and power, placed Sumner Welles in the State Department to offset Cordell Hull, and placed Johnson in the War Department to counterbalance Woodring.[44]

On 15 June 1937 President Roosevelt sent Johnson's name to the Senate for confirmation. Approval was quickly given, and on 29 June he took office. Johnson had been born and reared in Roanoke, Virginia, but after graduating from the University of Virginia Law School in 1912, he went to Clarksburg, West Virginia, to set up practice. He soon entered politics, and by 1917 he was Democratic floor leader of the West Virginia House of Delegates and was considering running for Governor. During World War I Johnson entered the Army, and after receiving a commission, he served in Europe as a captain in the 80th Infantry Division. After being discharged, he returned to his law practice; he also became an active member of the American Legion and was elected National Commander in 1932. In 1936 the staunch Democrat organized the Veterans Division of the Democratic National Committee, and within a year he was rewarded for his political labors with the post of Assistant Secretary of War.[45]

Johnson, who was very energetic and ambitious, set out to supplant Woodring, whom he considered unfit to be Secretary of War.[46] He immediately "set himself to running the War Department, acting very much like a No. 2 man who had been made No. 1 in all but title."[47] Johnson believed that the procurement and economic-mobilization responsibilities conferred upon the Assistant Secretary of War by the National Defense Act of 1920 made him responsible to the Congress and to the Chief Executive, thus making him entirely independent of the authority of the Secretary of War.[48] Such an interpretation, along with the assumption that he would soon be elevated to the top spot, led him to feel that he was entitled to direct access to the President on matters concerning his own office. He also began to present defense programs and estimates publicly without even consulting his chief, Secretary Woodring. To the outspoken Johnson the chain of command meant nothing. Shortly after taking office, Johnson started the practice of announcing that on a certain date he was going to be appointed Secretary of War. When the announced day came and nothing happened, he would wait a few weeks or months, then do the same thing again.[49] According to Woodring, Johnson was soon spending "most of his waking hours in trying to replace me as Secretary of War."[50]

Predictably, Johnson's attitude and conduct soon created difficulties, and with the passage of time the animosity between him and Woodring grew increasingly bitter. At first the two disagreed only over major matters such as selective service, the importance of heavy bombers, and the strength of the Air Corps. But before long they began to bicker and quibble over less im-

146

portant things, and then they progressed to the place where they argued over everything, no matter how insignificant. Eventually the feud got to the place where the two men merely ignored each other.[51]

Evidence of the Woodring-Johnson feud was apparent as early as January 1938. In that month the State Department requested that the Army send six bombers to Buenos Aires, Argentina, on a good-will flight to help that country celebrate the inauguration of its new President. Woodring disapproved of the idea and was prepared to block it. A journalist who wrote for various South American newspapers and who knew the situation in the War Department took the idea to the Assistant Secretary. Johnson liked the idea and took it directly to President Roosevelt, who approved it and instructed Woodring to send the bombers.[52] The flight was made, and it received favorable world-wide publicity, with Woodring receiving most of the credit for ordering the flight to be made—a fact that greatly angered Johnson.

The difficult position in which the Woodring-Johnson feud placed the military leaders can be seen in an incident that took place when the flight to Argentina was under consideration. After Johnson had received the idea of the flight, but before he went to the President, he told General Craig what he was going to do, adding, "Don't tell the Secretary." Craig immediately replied that the Secretary was his chief and that it was his duty to keep him informed of what was taking place. The General then indicated that if he had one quality, it was that of loyalty. Finally Craig asked Johnson, if he were Secretary, what he would think of an Assistant and a Chief of Staff who kept things from him. Johnson did not reply.[53] Such was the situation in the War Department.

Both Secretary Woodring and General Craig were bothered and upset by Johnson's intrigues, but neither was willing to do anything about them. Woodring, who was politically unsure of himself because he did not know what FDR had promised to Johnson, approached Craig in November 1938, asking him to go to the President and explain the condition of the War Department as a result of Johnson's conduct. Craig refused; he did not feel that it was his place to go, since the dispute involved the civilian rather than the military leadership. The Secretary then asked his close friend John C. O'Laughlin, owner and publisher of the *Army and Navy Journal*, to see the President on the matter. O'Laughlin refused, because he felt that Roosevelt would resent an outsider telling him about one of his own departments. The publisher did, however, discuss the matter with Press Secretary Steve Early. Early said that he already knew about the situation in the War Department, adding that "if Woodring had any guts he would ask the President to relieve him or Johnson."[54] Woodring was unwilling to take such action, and Roosevelt continued to tolerate the unfortunate situation.

Woodring began to wonder if Roosevelt's tolerance of Johnson's insubordination indicated that Johnson was indeed to replace him. The first few times that the Assistant Secretary informed General Craig that he, Johnson, was about to be named Secretary, Craig passed the information on to Woodring, who naturally became apprehensive, because he didn't know whether Johnson had made up the story or whether he had actually been so informed. Eventually, after several false alarms, Woodring learned to ignore the announcements. Another of Johnson's irritating practices was to plant in the newspapers information that was favorable to him but detrimental to Woodring.[55]

By the fall of 1939 the War Department, according to one cabinet member, was "making a holy show of itself with Woodring and Johnson each trying to outsmart the other." The situation became so bad that on September 8 Woodring went to see Edwin M. Watson, Roosevelt's Military Aide and Secretary. Woodring complained that "Johnson was running away with the War Department." Watson agreed that the matter ought to be straightened out and that one man ought to be in control; but he did not offer to make such a suggestion to the President, and so Woodring dropped the matter.[56] His failure to take the problem directly to Roosevelt stemmed from a number of factors. First, since his influence with the President was on the wane, he did not feel that he was in a strong enough position to approach FDR on the matter. As the world situation grew worse in the late thirties, the views of Roosevelt and Woodring on how to provide adequate national security became more divergent. The result was that, as time passed, so did Woodring's influence, and with it went his strong support from the President.[57] Second, Roosevelt's growing reliance on Louis Johnson led Woodring to feel that if he asked the President to make a choice between the two, FDR might choose Johnson.[58] The Secretary, unfortunately, did not know that when Roosevelt had been told by James Farley that Johnson expected to be named Secretary, he had replied, "I wouldn't name Louis under any circumstances."[59] Woodring felt that Roosevelt, knowing the situation in the War Department, could take action to correct the situation if he so desired, but apparently he did not wish to do so.

By the time that war broke out in Europe in the fall of 1939, the Woodring-Johnson feud was public knowledge, for newspapers and magazines were printing stories about the bitter quarrel. Typical was a *Time* magazine account of the relations between the two officials: "Only when absolutely necessary do they speak to each other. When official business requires them to communicate, they do so in writing or through harried

148

subordinates. Mr. Johnson despises Mr. Woodring. Mr. Woodring distrusts and despises Mr. Johnson, who for 27 months has gunned for Mr. Woodring's job."[60] At about the same time the *New York Times* reported that apparently a group of New Dealers close to the President felt that the rivalry between Woodring and Johnson "for domination within the War Department had reached a point where the President would have to exert his authority."[61] Still the President, who was willing to ignore or sweep "embarrassing administrative problems under the rug," did nothing.[62]

The unfortunate aspect of the feud between the Secretary and the Assistant Secretary was the disruptive effect that it had on the War Department and, consequently, on military preparedness. The continual bickering and fighting at the top became so bad that the military leaders often did not know who was running the department.[63] One example of how the feuding between the two men affected efficiency was an incident that took place in January 1938. While Johnson was out of town on a trip, Woodring rewrote the procedures by which certain aircraft parts should be purchased. Johnson, upon his return, did not approve of Woodring's changes and halted all transactions concerning the parts until the dispute could be settled. In a few weeks the two antagonists agreed to a compromise, and purchasing resumed; but, in the meantime, valuable procurement time had been lost.[64]

The Woodring-Johnson feud placed Chief of Staff Craig in an especially difficult position. Craig's plight was described by one contemporary as being that of a man "sitting on the fence between these two gentlemen. If he followed the Secretary's instructions he would be in bad odor with the Assistant Secretary, who was quite powerful. If he followed the lead of Mr. Johnson, Mr. Woodring would have him called to account. It was an impossible and tragic situation."[65] It was in large part due to this state of affairs that General Craig left his position as Chief of Staff in June 1939 instead of in September.[66] General Marshall, Craig's successor, found himself in the same difficult position, but, like Craig, he never deserted Secretary Woodring. As Marshall later told Johnson, "Mr. Woodring was Secretary of War and I owed loyalty to him."[67] In 1951 Marshall recalled that working under Woodring and Johnson had been "the most miserable experience of my life." As he described it, "I had to be Chief of Staff to a Secretary . . . and his first assistant who weren't speaking to each other. They not only didn't make any secret of how they hated and despised each other, they ran to the President behind each other's back."[68]

The feud did more than cause difficulty for the Chief of Staff; it also caused partiality among the generals at the War Department. Those military leaders working closest with the Secretary of War usually became "Woodring men," while those working closest with the Assistant Secretary became "Johnson men." Because of this division, relations between the military leaders became increasingly strained, and the work of the General Staff became more difficult.[69] The effects of this division upon the department were later recalled by Brig. Gen. William Ritchie, who served as Woodring's aide and pilot from 1935 to 1938. As he remembered it, Johnson frequently pointed out to top members of the Secretary of War's staff

that they would do well to pay more attention to his policies since he would soon be Boss and calling the shots. Of this Mr. Woodring was fully aware.

It soon became evident in all echelons of the War Department that Mr. Johnson was the aggressor in this top-level feuding and was continually attempting to undermine the Secretary of War's announced policies, especially when he would be away on business trips or a vacation. Mr. Woodring could never afford to miss a Cabinet meeting, since Mr. Johnson would then sit in as Acting Secretary of War. This situation reached a point where I would have to accompany the Woodrings, even on vacation trips, so as to have a plane standing by to fly him immediately to Washington should his Administrative Assistant give him a hurry call. This situation presented a poor spectacle for the military to see the civilian heads of the War Department engaged in political and personal feuding to the overall detriment of the efficiency and image of the entire Department.[70]

In order to gain a better understanding of the interworkings of the War Department during this period, a close examination will be made of the numerous factors that served to influence one major decision. That decision concerned naming a replacement for Chief of Staff Malin Craig. This example is appropriate in that it deals with one of the most important decisions of the period; it also gives a better understanding of the distrust and lack of cooperation that often characterized relationships both within the War Department and between the War Department and the President. In two respects this example is atypical. First, it was one of the few times that Woodring and Johnson agreed on a matter. Second, the decision that was made was an excellent one, and it ultimately benefited the Army and the nation. As will be seen in later chapters, the strained relationship that existed between the War Department and the White House was to result in some decisions that did not serve the best interests of the nation.

Although General Craig was expected to remain as Chief of Staff until September 1939, Woodring had started to think about a replacement for him as early as March 1937. At that time the Secretary asked Gen. Douglas MacArthur, former Chief of Staff, if he would like to return to his old post after Craig's retirement. When MacArthur indicated that he would not consider such an offer under any circumstances, Woodring dropped the matter and never mentioned it to him again.[71] In the months that followed, there was a great deal of speculation, especially among military men, as to who

150

would be the next Chief of Staff. The name most frequently mentioned was that of Maj. Gen. Hugh A. Drum, who had expected to receive the post in 1935 but had been disappointed when Roosevelt surprisingly named General Craig to the position.[72] For reasons that are unclear, Woodring showed little enthusiasm over the possibility of Drum's being appointed, and he began to look for another candidate.[73]

In the spring of 1938 Maj. Gen. Stanley Embick, Deputy Chief of Staff, told Woodring of a brigadier general named George C. Marshall, who might be Chief of Staff material. Embick asked that Marshall be brought to Washington so that his work could be closely observed. After Woodring agreed, Marshall was made head of the War Plans Division of the General Staff.[74] The fifty-eight-year-old graduate of the Virginia Military Institute did an excellent job in his new position, and both Woodring and Craig were greatly impressed; however, they hesitated to make Marshall Deputy Chief of Staff, because he was only a brigadier general and they feared that a number of senior officers might resent taking orders from him.[75] One individual who was not hesitant about advancing Marshall was Assistant Secretary Johnson.

Johnson, who had met Marshall before the latter came to Washington, was greatly impressed by him and actively worked for his appointment as Chief of Staff.[76] In fact, it was Johnson who was responsible for Marshall's being made Deputy Chief of Staff. In October 1938 Woodring was out of Washington, and Johnson was Acting Secretary on the day that the War Council was to meet. Although the Deputy Chief of Staff usually attended such meetings, the position was vacant at that time, General Embick having taken a new command. Before the meeting started, Johnson asked General Craig to appoint General Marshall as Deputy Chief. When Craig tried to side-step the issue by replying that the matter would be worked out, Johnson informed him that there would be no War Council meeting until his, Johnson's, wishes were carried out. Craig left the office for a few minutes, after which he returned, and told Johnson that the orders had been issued.[77] Although Woodring was unhappy at the manner in which the appointment was made, he did not complain, because he was glad to see Marshall in that spot.

In spite of the confidence that Woodring had in Marshall, he was still hesitant to support his appointment as Chief of Staff. Woodring considered the matter of seniority to be quite important, and he was concerned about a possible morale problem should the rule of seniority be ignored. For this reason he leaned, perfunctorily, in the direction of Major General Drum as late as the fall of 1938. Marshall was thirty-fourth in seniority, but a rule that no one could be appointed Chief of Staff who could not serve out a full

151

four-year term before the mandatory retirement age of sixty-four made him the fifth-ranking eligible.[78]

In November, Roosevelt introduced his new air-rearmament program— a program that Woodring and Craig were less than enthusiastic about because of its tendency to ignore the land forces. Such an attitude placed the two men on unfavorable terms with the White House in late 1938 and early 1939. By January 1939 Woodring, apparently alienated by the pressure being exerted by and on behalf of Drum, appeared to have overcome his earlier concerns on the question of seniority and was willing to support Marshall as the new Chief of Staff; nevertheless, the strained relationship with the President kept him and Craig from making such a recommendation for fear that their support would prejudice Marshall's chances.[79] Woodring and Craig recalled that when in 1935 Secretary Dern had made a recommendation as to who should be named Chief of Staff, Roosevelt had rejected it. Woodring therefore decided that he would not recommend anyone unless the President specifically asked him to do so.[80] This decision was based not only on what had happened in 1935 but also on the fact that the President had made it increasingly clear that because he regarded the Chief of Staff as his personal adviser, "he alone would pick the officer that appealed to him personally."[81]

During this period, Johnson continued to push for the appointment of Marshall. This was one of the very few instances in which Woodring and Johnson were in agreement, but at that time they were so at odds and their means of communication were so disrupted that neither was certain of the other's position. General Marshall knew their views, but he was not anxious that they be publicized for fear that either Woodring or Johnson might drop his support if he knew that the other was supporting him. As Marshall described it, "Johnson wanted me for Chief of Staff, but I didn't want Woodring to know he was for me. Craig was for me, but I wanted it kept from the President. Woodring was for me, but I didn't want the others to know."[82] The suspicion, distrust, and ill will that prevailed among the personalities involved in selecting the Chief of Staff reveal that the personal relationships both within the War Department and between the War Department and the Commander in Chief were far from smooth. The President, the Secretary of War, the Assistant Secretary of War, and the Chief of Staff were anything but a team.

During the first week of April 1939 Roosevelt sent for the records of the outstanding General Officers, so that he could consult them before choosing the next Chief of Staff. At that time Woodring broke his earlier silence and recommended General Marshall.[83] Whether he did this on his own or whether he was asked by the President to give his opinion is unknown; nor do we know how forceful his recommendation was. According to Woodring, "I threatened to resign unless he took General Marshall, my nominee."[84] In the light of his own standing with the President at that time, it seems highly unlikely that he would have made such a bold move.

On Sunday, 23 April, Roosevelt called Marshall to the White House and informed him that he was to be the new Chief of Staff. Marshall was the first one to know; the President had not yet told anyone else, including the Secretary of War, of his selection. Just why Roosevelt chose him will never be known for certain, but Marshall felt that favorable words from Woodring and from FDR's close friend Harry Hopkins were primary factors.[85] That Marshall considered Woodring's role to be very important is evident from a personal letter that he wrote to Woodring on 28 April 1939:

My Dear Mr. Secretary:
I got away so hurriedly yesterday that I had little to say to you in appreciation of your action in nominating me to the President for the job of Chief of Staff. The fact that you selected me is the great compliment to my career, but I am more grateful to you for the very special effort you saw fit to evoke in order to bring about my final selection by the President.[86]

What weight Woodring's recommendation might have had will never be known, but it would seem that the realization that the Secretary of War and the Chief of Staff had to work together would have caused Roosevelt to give Woodring's views at least some consideration.

In addition to Woodring's constant dealings with the President, military leaders, Congressmen, and the Assistant Secretary of War, he was in constant contact with his fellow cabinet members. With some, such as Secretary of State Cordell Hull, Secretary of the Navy Claude Swanson, and Postmaster General James Farley, he got along very well. With others, such as Secretary of Labor Frances Perkins, Secretary of Agriculture Henry Wallace, Secretary of Commerce Daniel Roper, and Attorney General Homer Cummings, his association was quite satisfactory. Unfortunately, Woodring's relationship with a group of New Dealers in the cabinet and on the White House staff was not much better than his relationship with Louis Johnson. The leader of that group was Secretary of the Interior Harold Ickes. The feeling between Woodring and Ickes was one of mutual hostility, and from the day that Woodring came into the cabinet until the time he was forced out, Ickes headed an anti-Woodring group that worked almost continually for his removal. In speaking of the efforts to bring about Woodring's removal, Ickes was to say, "I doubt whether any comparable pressure has ever been put on the President in a personal matter."[87]

In his efforts to force Woodring from the cabinet, Ickes enlisted the aid of any individual in Roosevelt's inner circle who did not care for the Secretary of War and wished to see him go. Included in this group at one time or another were Henry Morgenthau, Jr., Secretary of the Treasury; Harry Hopkins, a presidential adviser and later Secretary of Commerce; Sumner Welles, Assistant Secretary of State; Thomas Corcoran, a presidential adviser; Edwin M. Watson, a military aide and adviser to the President; and Steve Early, the President's Press Secretary.[88] Members of this "White House clique," as Woodring and his close friends referred to the group, did not work as a unit, but they were united in a common goal, which was to get a new Secretary of War. Louis Johnson was aware of the clique, and he hoped that it would achieve its goal. But he was not associated with it, because most members of the group held no higher opinion of him than they did of Woodring.

The antagonism between Woodring and Ickes had started in 1933 when Woodring wrote a letter to Ickes, criticizing him for the way in which he was handling certain matters pertaining to public works. After the angry Ickes wrote a strong reply to Woodring, telling him to mind his own business, the battle was on. Several more disputes in the next few years further heightened the hostility between the two. Ickes made no secret of this antagonism; thus, when Woodring was being considered to fill the vacancy created by the death of George Dern, Ickes voiced his disapproval, because he considered Woodring "distinctly second or third caliber material." When the appointment was made, Ickes did not hide his disappointment, and a few days later said about the new Secretary of War: "He struts about with inflated chest more sure of himself and more disagreeable and dictatorial than any man I have met in the Government. He is a damned little upstart with no background and no imagination."[89] It was clear what Ickes thought of Woodring.[90] While Woodring's dislike of the Secretary of the Interior was considerable, he was not so open in saying so.

The first attempt to force Woodring out came in the late summer of 1937, when Ickes confidentially informed a writer for the *Washington Evening Star* that Woodring was on his way out and that he would be sent to the Philippines as High Commissioner.[91] It was hoped that the rumor would make it easier for the President to take such action, since everyone concerned would be more or less expecting it. Woodring's denials that he was leaving the War Department failed to quell the rumors; they did not die until Roosevelt emphatically declared that Woodring would remain.[92] At this time the Secretary of War and the President still saw eye to eye, and things in the War Department were running smoothly; consequently, Roosevelt had no serious thoughts of replacing Woodring. That the War Secretary was satisfied with his present position became evident in the spring of 1938, when, with a rather strong senatorial boom developing for him in Kansas, he punctured the balloon by saying, "I am perfectly happy and completely absorbed in my present work."[93]

In the fall of 1938, however, Roosevelt's ideas on having Woodring remain as Secretary of War had begun to change, for by that time the two men were disagreeing on certain defense matters.[94] The prospect of a new Secretary of War now became more and more appealing. Although Roosevelt would have liked to see Woodring go, he could not bring himself to force him out. FDR was an extremely soft individual when it came to dealing with personal friends; he wanted to be liked, and he did not wish to do anything that might endanger a long friendship.[95] As one contemporary journalist said, "Firing associates is not one of Roosevelt's strong points."[96] Since the President could not bring himself to fire Woodring or ask for his resignation, he hoped to offer him an attractive post, such as an ambassadorship, so that he would willingly step down from his cabinet post. FDR thought that such offers would either be accepted or that they would at least cause Woodring to realize that he was not wanted in his present position and thus would bring about his resignation.[97]

Roosevelt's strategy did not work on Woodring for a number of reasons. First, Woodring did not want to leave Washington. He and Helen led a dazzling life as they set the social pace for the Roosevelt administration. It is doubtful whether any couple in the nation's capital had more friends, did more entertaining, or were entertained more than the Woodrings. They both enjoyed such a life, and they did not relish the thought of giving it up. Furthermore, because the Secretary had three small children, he was somewhat reluctant to move to a foreign country.[98] Second, Woodring considered himself a fighter. If there was anything he did not like, it was a quitter. To resign when the going got rough at the War Department would be the same as quitting, and therefore it was unthinkable. Third, Woodring liked his job; he truly enjoyed all the power, pageantry, and publicity that came with his cabinet post. Fourth, he liked action, and he liked a real challenge. As time passed and the nation began to rearm, his job at the War Department became increasingly important and difficult, and the challenge made him more determined than ever to remain at his post. For all these reasons Woodring refused to resign.[99]

The first time that President Roosevelt actually indicated a desire to ease Woodring out of the cabinet was on 24 December 1938, when he told Louis Johnson that he was going to see if Woodring would be acceptable to Canada as the United States Minister. This idea was part of a larger plan to reshuffle the cabinet. Under the contemplated scheme, which the President had started to formulate in early December when Attorney General

155

Homer Cummings resigned, Frank Murphy, Governor of Michigan, would be named Attorney General; Woodring would be sent to Canada; and Johnson would be made Secretary of War.[100] Then, after a short period, Johnson would be sent to the Philippines as High Commissioner, Murphy would be transferred to the War Department, and Solicitor General Robert Jackson would be made Attorney General. The reason that Jackson was not made Attorney General immediately was that he was a New Yorker, and another New Yorker, Harry Hopkins, had just been named to the cabinet; with two other members of the cabinet from the Empire State, the President feared a public reaction against the lack of geographical balance in the cabinet. When Ickes and Roosevelt discussed this plan on 29 December, Ickes voiced his wholehearted approval, especially for the moves in the War Department, since both Woodring and Assistant Secretary Johnson had "created an unpleasant situation by lining up generals on each side and openly fighting for the place."[101]

The first phase of the President's plan went into effect on 30 December, when he appointed Murphy as Attorney General. Then the scheme ran into difficulty, for when Roosevelt offered Woodring the Canadian post, he turned it down. With Woodring's rejection of the position in Canada, FDR's reshuffling plan came to a halt, since the President was unwilling to force him from office. When Roosevelt's close associates asked him why he did not remove Woodring, he replied that such a move would be politically unwise, because it might result in a loss of the Kansas delegation at the 1940 Democratic convention. Since Roosevelt made such statements even before he was apparently considering a third term, it would seem that he was using the Kansas delegation as an excuse.[102]

At the same time that he turned down the offer of the Canadian post, Woodring told the President that there was one job that he would be interested in—Ambassador to England. At the time such an appointment seemed out of the question, because Roosevelt was pleased with the work of Ambassador Joseph P. Kennedy. Furthermore, it was doubtful whether Woodring could afford the post, because Kennedy was forced to spend $70,000 a year from his own pocket, and Woodring did not have that kind of money.[103] Secretary Ickes contended that Woodring's father-in-law, Senator Coolidge, had agreed to put up half a million dollars to finance the post, but in reality the figure was $5,000 (a good example of Ickes's tendency to exaggerate).[104] That Woodring had an interest in the London job was made evident in a letter of 20 June 1939 to his friend M. M. Levant. At that time he indicated his satisfaction with his present job, but he added that "if the Ambassadorship to the Court of St. James were offered me, it would be quite a temptation, as it would be quite an experience for a country Kansas boy."[105] A short time later, however, he denied having any such interest. In a trans-Atlantic phone conversation with Woodring, Ambassador Kennedy revealed a desire to leave his post, saying, "Anything you can do to get me home is what I want." Woodring stated that he did not want the job, but that he wanted to remain in his present position until 1941.[106] Nevertheless, throughout the summer of 1939 Woodring continued to be mentioned as being under consideration for a diplomatic post in Ottawa or London.

On 30 August 1939 Harlan Miller of the *Washington Post* indicated that Woodring might be induced to take the Canadian position, "but a war crisis involving us might keep him at his present post."[107] Two days later that crisis came when Germany attacked Poland. Any chance that Woodring would voluntarily resign was now gone, for he had always wanted to be at the center of action, and after 1 September 1939 the War Department was such a place. With the outbreak of war in Europe putting new pressures on the military, Roosevelt again toyed with the idea of removing Woodring. Attorney General Murphy, who had come into the cabinet with the understanding that he would soon be named Secretary of War, was getting anxious to make the change, and in early September he asked Ickes to discuss the matter with the President. At that time Roosevelt assured Ickes that Woodring was on his way out; however, the weeks slipped by, and still nothing happened.[108]

Up to this time, Roosevelt's refusal to replace Woodring was due to his reluctance to remove an old friend and possibly to his desire to ensure the support of the Kansas delegation at the next Democratic convention; but after war broke out in Europe, there arose another consideration that made him reluctant to act. That consideration was expressed by columnist Ernest K. Lindley, who said: "By his [Woodring's] spunky stand for a cautious foreign policy he has won many new friends. Any attempt to force him out almost certainly would provoke the open charge that it was because of his wholehearted opposition to dangerous entanglements in the current European war."[109] Woodring, by making strong pledges of noninvolvement, was becoming a well-known spokesman for those individuals who advocated nonintervention at any cost except in the case of aggression against the United States. To remove the Secretary of War would appear to be an attack on the isolationists, and Woodring could well become a rallying point for their cause.[110] For this reason Roosevelt was more reluctant than ever to act.

In November, Ickes went to the President and asked that something be done about the situation in the War Department, where the feuding was becoming a "public scandal." Ickes then offered his advice on how to get rid of Woodring. As he later explained it, "My plan was to build up in Woodring's mind the idea that Dublin was a very important and critical

157

post now on account of the war, that the President wanted a strong man there, and that this job might lead to an even better one." When Roosevelt indicated that he did not think such a plan would convince Woodring to leave, Ickes said, "I think you ought to tell him that he has the choice of Dublin or Kansas." When FDR said nothing, Ickes added, "You just can't do that sort of thing, can you, Mr. President." "No, Harold, I can't," replied Roosevelt."[111] As 1939 came to an end, the President still wanted a new Secretary of War, but "being one who was forever putting off anything distasteful," he would not replace Woodring.[112]

During the early part of 1940 Roosevelt continued his efforts to ease Woodring out. In January, when he learned that William Phillips, United States Ambassador to Italy, was planning to resign, he offered the job to Woodring, who thanked him for the offer but politely declined it. After this incident, Drew Pearson and Robert Allen concluded that "apparently it's going to take more than a sugar-coated hint to dislodge the Secretary of War."[113]

At about this time, Ickes, who now seemed to be obsessed with the idea of removing Woodring, suggested to Roosevelt that he make Woodring Ambassador to France and that he appoint the present ambassador, William Bullitt, as Secretary of War. The President rejected the idea by maintaining that Bullitt was so popular with the French officials and people that he could not possibly make such a change.[114] In February and March, Woodring's name was again mentioned as a possible replacement for Kennedy in London, but Roosevelt persuaded Kennedy to remain at his post, so that possibility faded.[115] Up to this time, all efforts to persuade Woodring to leave his post had failed, and one Washington columnist concluded that Woodring's "defense of his post against all assaults has been a tactical masterpiece which probably will be studied by military men for decades."[116]

After rejection of his plans to send Woodring to Ireland or France, Ickes continued to ponder the question of how to remove him, and in May 1940 he came up with what he called a "brilliant idea" to accomplish his goal. On May 17, a few hours before a regularly scheduled cabinet meeting, Ickes explained his latest plan to the President. At the meeting that afternoon he intended to say in effect: "Mr. President, when you selected us as members of your Cabinet, the world was at peace . . . [but] conditions have so radically changed that I think it is only fair that all of us should resign and leave you free either to revamp your present Cabinet . . . or to constitute an entirely new one." Ickes would then offer his resignation, and when the other cabinet members followed suit, the President could accept the resignations of those men he wanted out and refuse those of anyone he wished to retain. Ickes told Roosevelt what he planned to do, because he felt that

158

if the President did not know about it, he might, in his surprise, say something that would make it more difficult to get rid of Woodring. Although the plan was aimed specifically at Woodring, Ickes did not say so to the President. After Ickes made his scheme known, Roosevelt said, "Why, I couldn't do that, Harold. Some of the members of the Cabinet might think that I don't want them." Feeling that Ickes's proposal would place him in an awkward and difficult position, the President turned it down and then added, "It isn't necessary anyhow, because I am going to ask Woodring's resignation." Ickes, who had heard that story before, laughed impolitely and said, "Mr. President, you will never do it." To this, Roosevelt replied, "You don't know what I can do when I make up my mind."[117] More than a month later Roosevelt finally did what many intimates were convinced that he could never do—force Woodring from office. The factors that finally caused the President to act will be examined in chapter 10.

There can be no doubt that the activities of Johnson, Ickes, and the New Deal clique did much to hamper Woodring's effectiveness as Secretary of War. With an assistant doing everything he could to undermine his superior, there soon developed distrust and confusion throughout the War Department. As a result, overall efficiency suffered. The continual efforts of Ickes and the occasional help of Murphy and Morgenthau in the attempt to replace Woodring indicate that the teamwork and cooperation of the cabinet left something to be desired. Woodring's influence was also undercut by Roosevelt's frequent statements to various officials that he was going to remove him. Such comments indicated to those men around the President that he lacked confidence in his Secretary of War. All of these factors caused Woodring's years as Secretary to be one continuous battle to stay in office. Much of the time and energy that he was forced to use just to keep his job could have been more effectively used in working for the good of the Army. With all the time spent feuding, it was amazing that Woodring was able to accomplish as much as he did. One can only speculate as to what he might have accomplished had those feuds been avoided.

9

Problems of Rearmament

It is impossible to determine exactly when United States rearmament got under way. According to President Roosevelt, his requests of 28 January 1938 for increased armaments "were but the beginning of a vast program of rearmament."[1] That $45 million proposal, however, was aimed primarily at strengthening the Navy, only $17 million being requested for the Army. The Navy's rearmament program was undertaken before that of the Army for several reasons: first, it was generally felt that the Navy would, in all likelihood, be the first force to meet an enemy; second, a longer period of time would be needed to increase materially the size of the fleet; third, President Roosevelt had a great personal interest in the Navy and its activities.[2]

While rearmament was a somewhat gradual process, 14 November 1938 stands out as the most important date in the rearmament of the United States Army or, more specifically, of the Army Air Corps. Upset by Hitler's success at the Munich Conference and alarmed by reports of the growing military might of Germany and Italy, Roosevelt decided to expand drastically the nation's air strength. On 14 November the President called his top civilian and military advisers, with the exception of Secretary of War Woodring, who was on leave, to the White House, in order to reveal his intention to provide a 10,000-plane air force and to establish a productive capacity of 10,000 planes per year. Thus began the rearmament program of the United States Army.[3] Before seeing what actually occurred at the November 1938 conference, the consequences of that meeting, and the role that Woodring played in the new program, it will be valuable to examine Woodring's record and views on air power and the Air Corps prior to the fall of 1938.

As has already been seen, Harry Woodring, as Assistant Secretary of War, had taken a deep and sincere interest in the growth and development of the Air Corps. He had used every possible opportunity to inform the public of the "urgent necessity for additional aircraft," and in 1936 he had played a major role in getting Congress to increase the Army's air strength from 1,800 to 2,320 aircraft.[4] During his first year as Secretary, Woodring continued to emphasize the Air Corps, but he did so, not because he considered it more important than the ground forces, but because he felt it was more deficient and therefore should receive more attention; what he desired was a well-balanced military force. As he told a nationwide radio audience in the summer of 1937: "I have stressed the aviation element of our national defense, not because I regard it of paramount importance. All branches of our defense forces are important. If war unhappily comes to America we must defend ourselves on the sea, on the land, and in the air. A failure in any element might prove fatal."[5]

Woodring foresaw a bright future for military aircraft as an auxiliary to ground forces rather than as an independent weapon. He believed that emphasis should be placed on fighter planes and light and medium bombers that could be used in close support of ground troops or for attacking enemy ships that approached the nation's shores. He looked upon the Army as a strictly defensive force, and the airplane as a defensive weapon. He felt that long-range bombers were "aggressive" rather than "defensive" weapons and therefore had no real place in the Army Air Corps.[6] Such thinking was in line with that of General Craig and most of the General Staff.[7] There were, however, a few military men, such as Gen. Frank Andrews, commander of GHQ Air Force, and Col. Hugh Knerr, his chief of staff, who felt that heavy bombers such as the B-17 were essential for an adequate defense and that they should make up a major percentage of the Air Corps's aircraft.[8]

In addition to his idea of how airplanes should be used militarily, there was another and perhaps more important reason that Woodring favored light and medium bombers over the heavy types—that reason was cost. Until 1939 the funds available to the Army for the purchase of planes were quite small, and Woodring felt that it was better to purchase two twin-engine bombers than one four-engine model. According to Col. James H. Burns, Executive Assistant to the Assistant Secretary of War, Woodring "was interested in numbers only and . . . any arrangement made towards gain in number of planes would undoubtedly be approved by the Secretary."[9] General Arnold expressed the same idea when he said, "The superiority of one

161

B-17 to two B-10's was a mystery which Secretary Woodring . . . never understood."[10]

Secretary Woodring's reluctance to order heavy bombers can be better understood when the cost of them is compared to that of two-engine bombers. For example, in June 1937 the Army ordered more than one hundred twin-engine B-16 bombers at a cost of $65,000 per plane. One month later the War Department let a contract for thirteen Flying Fortresses at a total cost of $3.7 million, or nearly $280,000 per plane.[11] Therefore, the Army could buy four B-16's for the same amount that it would pay for one B-17. The cost of a new four-engine bomber was extremely high because of the excessive cost of "tooling up" and training skilled production personnel. Until the planes were ordered in fairly large quantities, the cost remained excessively high.[12] With less than $37 million to spend on aircraft for the entire year, Woodring understandably favored the much cheaper light and medium bombers.

Woodring's desire for a larger number of planes was also conditioned by his realization that modern aircraft could not be quickly produced.[13] Since construction of planes necessarily took considerable time, he believed that it was necessary to have a peacetime Air Force that would approximate rather closely the wartime requirements. According to Woodring: "In a major war our air arm would probably be engaged almost immediately on the opening of hostilities. Therefore, it is desirable that it be practically on a war footing in time of peace."[14] If the limited appropriations were used on expensive heavy bombers, the 2,320-plane force that was considered essential for the nation's defense could never become a reality.

In June of 1937 Woodring, for the reasons stated above, opposed the purchase of anything but twin-engine bombers for the upcoming fiscal year. In the face of constant pressure, he did retreat and order thirteen Flying Fortresses.[15] Woodring's refusal to provide more heavy bombers was bitterly criticized by Assistant Secretary Johnson and a small group of military men who had great faith in the B-17. This group looked forward with anxiety to the aircraft-procurement program for fiscal year 1939. It was in early 1938, when the new air program was under consideration, that Woodring and Johnson first clashed over the make-up of the Air Corps. The controversy emerged at a meeting in which Woodring presented the General Staff's proposal for 1939. After going over the plan, which provided for only twelve B-17's, Woodring concluded by saying, "That will be the plan." When Johnson began to raise an objection, Woodring said, "We all know you are opposed to it." "Yes I am opposed to it," replied Johnson, who then asked if General Andrews could express his views. The request was granted, and Andrews made a plea for a larger number of heavy bombers; but when

162

The cabinet in 1938 (clockwise from the President): President Roosevelt, Morgenthau, (Treasury), Cummings (Attorney General), Swanson (Navy), Wallace (Agriculture), Perkins (Labor), Vice-President Garner, Roper (Commerce), Ickes (Interior), Farley (Postmaster General), Woodring (War), Hull (State).

Former Secretary of War Patrick J. Hurley, Secretary of War Harry H. Woodring, President Franklin D. Roosevelt, Brig. Gen. Albert L. Cox, and Assistant Secretary of War Louis A. Johnson viewing the Army Day Parade in Washington, D.C., 6 April 1938.

Helen and Harry Woodring leaving for Europe on their honeymoon, July 1933.

Andrews had finished, Woodring pointed to the plan before him and stated: "This is still the program." Determined to have the last word, Johnson replied: "With all due respect to your office, there is a statutory responsibility involved. This is *not* the program until the Commander in Chief approves it."[16] Then, before Woodring could submit the program to the President, Johnson took it to the White House and expressed his disapproval. Johnson urged Roosevelt to place more emphasis on the Air Corps and to increase the number of heavy bombers. At that particular time, Roosevelt, who was not prepared to support the expensive program that Johnson was advocating, accepted the proposal made by Secretary Woodring. The new program called for the building of enough planes in the next three years to bring the Air Corps to its authorized strength of 2,320.[17]

In order to implement the War Department's new aircraft program, in the spring of 1938 Congress appropriated $37 million for the purchase of 450 new planes. Shortly thereafter, however, Secretary Woodring began to feel that the number of planes in the Air Corps should be increased at a more rapid rate than the approved program called for.[18] He decided that the best way to bring about such an increase was to stop purchasing heavy bombers and to use the money to buy a greater number of light and medium bombers; thus, in June he halted the purchase of three heavy bombers and ordered that the money be used toward the purchase of medium bombers.[19] On 29 July, Woodring went even farther and sent a memorandum to Maj. Gen. Oscar Westover, Chief of the Air Corps, informing him that "estimates for bombers in fiscal year 1940 (must) be restricted to light, medium and attack types."[20] This order did not greatly bother General Westover, who "was in favor of large bombers in limited numbers . . . [and] a large number of smaller bombers for close-in support of the Army."[21]

In September 1938 two events occurred that ultimately led to major changes in the program of the Army Air Corps. On 21 September, General Westover was killed in a plane crash, and the Assistant Chief of the Air Corps, Brig. Gen. Henry H. ("Hap") Arnold, was named Acting Chief until the President could make a permanent appointment. White House aides Steve Early and Edwin Watson urged Roosevelt to appoint the GHQ Commander, Gen. Frank Andrews. Both Woodring and Craig opposed the appointment of Andrews because of the great emphasis that he placed on heavy bombers. They favored General Arnold because of his more moderate views on that subject. Arnold, although he was a firm believer in the value of the heavy bomber, tended to favor a balanced air force. When some of Andrew's supporters began to spread rumors that Arnold was irresponsible, unreliable, and an alcoholic, Woodring and Craig came to his defense, assuring the President that there was no truth to such reports and maintaining that Arnold deserved the post. Roosevelt ultimately followed their recommendation, and on 29 September he named Arnold as Chief of the Air Corps.[22]

The second important event of September 1938 was the Munich Conference, at which Hitler received the Sudeten area of Czechoslovakia. The United States Ambassador to France, William Bullitt, immediately returned home and reported to President Roosevelt that Hitler's success was in large part due to French fears of the German Air Force. The conversation with Bullitt, along with similar reports from other officials in Europe, alarmed Roosevelt, causing him to examine more closely the size and make-up of the United States Air Corps.[23] Consequently, October 1938 was to become a key month in the history of Army aviation. Throughout that month the President and the War Department were preoccupied with the question of what role aviation should play in the United States defense system.

During this crucial period, Secretary Woodring was frequently away from his Washington office, making speeches on behalf of Democratic congressional candidates. Two political tours—the first lasting from 7 to 12 October, and the second from 20 October to 2 November—were made in response to a request from President Roosevelt that Woodring serve as an administration spokesman in support of key party candidates. Woodring looked upon his selection as an honor, and he was glad to be of service to the President and the party. His campaigning took him to nine states, where he made a dozen major speeches praising the Roosevelt administration and urging the election of Democratic congressional candidates.[24] Roosevelt's decision to send Woodring on these trips was probably twofold. First, since no other cabinet member possessed more oratorical skill or was a more effective campaigner than Woodring, the President knew that he was sending a man whose speeches would be a credit to the administration and would be beneficial to the candidates. Second, the President, who undoubtedly was giving thought to expansion of the Air Corps, apparently decided that it would be a good time to have the Secretary of War out of town. It was no secret that Woodring favored a balanced military machine, whereas Assistant Secretary Johnson desired a large, powerful Air Corps; thus, Roosevelt knew that it would be easier to gain the War Department's approval of his expansion program if Johnson, rather than Woodring, were in charge.[25]

Before departing on his October political tours, Secretary Woodring took care of one matter that he had been turning over in his mind for a month. On 2 September the President had shown him a confidential letter from Hugh R. Wilson, Ambassador in Berlin, in which he discussed the potential of German air power.[26] In that letter, Wilson warned that anyone who thought "that France, England, and the United States, especially the United States, held at least a small margin of superiority in the air over Germany" was badly mistaken, because "the facts are that Germany . . . has produced an air arm second to none in numbers and quality of first-line fighting airplanes."[27] Because Hitler's success at Munich had convinced Woodring of the validity of Wilson's claim, in early October he asked General Arnold to prepare a plan for expanding the Air Corps by 4,000 planes, thereby creating a force of 6,320 planes. By 19 October, General Arnold had completed the plan and had submitted it to the Secretary's office; however, Woodring was on his political sojourn and did not see it until he returned to his duties in mid November.[28]

In mid October, President Roosevelt began to speak out on the need for a larger air force. Then on 25 October he called Acting Secretary Johnson to the White House and informed him of his desire to expand greatly the Air Corps and aircraft production facilities. Roosevelt told Johnson that he was placing him in charge of a three-man committee, which would include Assistant Secretary of the Navy Charles Edison and the Deputy Administrator of the WPA, Aubrey Williams, to report on ways to increase the production of military aircraft.[29] Since the President did not indicate how much expansion he had in mind, the committee had to use its own judgment about what constituted a major expansion. Three days after the committee was appointed, it submitted a preliminary plan, which provided for the production of 31,000 planes within two years and an annual capacity of 20,000 planes thereafter. Under this plan the existing aircraft industry would increase its production from 2,600 to 11,000 aircraft, and the government would build its own plants to provide the other 20,000. The cost of expanding the facilities and actually producing the planes was estimated at $855 million.[30]

As the President's interest in expanding the Air Corps became apparent in late October, General Arnold drew up a program that represented the views of the Air Corps. On 10 November, Arnold submitted his program to Acting Secretary Johnson. Arnold's primary recommendation was "that at this time, the objective of the Army Air Corps be set at 7,000 planes . . . and an annual production capacity of 10,000 planes, all to be achieved in two years."[31] This plan was not nearly as ambitious as the one put forth by the President's civilian leaders. Which scheme Roosevelt would support was anyone's guess.

On the second weekend in November, President Roosevelt notified a number of key civilian and military leaders of a meeting to be held at the White House on Monday afternoon, 14 November. Present at that all-important conference were Henry Morgenthau, Jr., Secretary of the Treasury; Louis Johnson, the Acting Secretary of War; Harry Hopkins, WPA

Administrator; Robert Jackson, the Solicitor General; Herman Oliphant, General Counsel of the Treasury; Gen. Malin Craig, Chief of Staff; Gen. George Marshall, Deputy Chief of Staff; Gen. Henry Arnold, Chief of the Air Corps; Col. James Burns, the Executive Assistant to the Assistant Secretary of War; Col. Edwin Watson, the President's Military Aide; and Capt. Daniel Callahan, the President's Naval Aide.[32]

At that conference, Roosevelt, to the surprise of nearly everyone in the room, came out in favor of a large air force. According to General Arnold, the President said that a new regiment of field artillery, a new barracks, or new machine tools in an ordnance arsenal "would not scare Hitler one blankety-blank bit. What he wanted was airplanes! Airplanes were the war implements that would have an influence on Hitler's activities!"[33] The President then told the group that he figured that if he would ask Congress for 20,000 planes and a production capacity of 24,000, he would probably get 10,000 planes and a production capacity of the same amount. He indicated that he expected the program to be filled in two years, with commercial plants and seven new government plants producing the planes. The President, who did all of the talking, closed by asking Assistant Secretary Johnson to draw up detailed plans and recommendations for carrying out his proposals. Johnson indicated that he would have the plans ready by the end of the week.[34] Thus ended one of the most important conferences in United States military history. According to General Arnold, the meeting was significant because at that time the Army Air Corps received its Magna Carta.[35]

Where was Secretary of War Woodring when this significant rearmament conference took place? He was a few miles away at his Washington residence, completely unaware that such a meeting was being held. Less than two weeks before, Woodring had returned from his strenuous political tours, after which he had submitted a report to Roosevelt, telling him of his recent activities and giving an estimate of the political situation in the states that he had visited.[36] Having reported to the President, the Secretary of War, exhausted from the hard campaigning, took a two-weeks' leave so that he could rest and spend some time with his family.[37] During this vacation, Assistant Secretary Johnson continued to function as Acting Secretary.

There are several reasons that might explain why Woodring was not informed of the conference on 14 November. First, the President did not want him there because he knew that Woodring would probably object to a program that emphasized the Air Corps and ignored land forces. Furthermore, Roosevelt knew Assistant Secretary Johnson's views on air power, and he felt that Johnson would support the type of program that he, the President, had in mind. A second explanation might be that Roosevelt did not feel that it was necessary to bother with Secretary Woodring, because expansion of the Air Corps was primarily a matter of aircraft procurement, and therefore was the responsibility of the Assistant Secretary rather than the Secretary. Even if this were the case, however, the Secretary should still have been included. If the President had wanted Woodring there, he could have had him, because the Secretary was only ten minutes away from the White House. That Roosevelt did not want Woodring to attend the conference seems evident from the fact that the two men met at an Armistice Day party on Friday, 11 November, and the President did not mention the upcoming meeting.[38]

Louis Johnson's reasons for not informing the Secretary are quite understandable. Neither Johnson nor anyone else scheduled to attend the conference had any idea of what the President would say, and therefore he had no idea that it would be so important. Johnson had been in frequent contact with the President during Woodring's absence, and he saw nothing unusual about being called to the White House on November fourteenth. While it is likely that if Johnson had known what the President had in mind, he would not have wanted Woodring there and might not have told him, the fact remains that he did not know what to expect. General Craig was in the same position as Johnson, in that he had no idea that the meeting would be of such importance and therefore saw no reason for interrupting the Secretary's vacation. In the final analysis it appears that Woodring was not at the conference because President Roosevelt did not want him there, and that his reason for not wanting him there was a fear that the Secretary might oppose his rearmament program.

The meeting of 14 November was highly important, because it was the first time that the President rather than the War Department advocated immediate rearmament. That the Chief Executive supported the movement was important, because he had an influence over Congress that was not possessed by the War Department. President Roosevelt's desire to strengthen significantly the nation's defense system gave Assistant Secretary Johnson and military leaders renewed vigor and enthusiasm, for they now had a man who could make their rearmament plans become realities.

While the professional military men were pleased with the President's willingness to take a big step toward rearmament, they were bothered by the emphasis that he placed on aircraft. The consensus of military leaders was that a well-balanced force was needed. Although the President had specifically asked for airplanes, Johnson and the General Staff, sensing presidential support for a major strengthening of the Army, began to prepare plans that incorporated the concept of a balanced military force.[39] The day after the

White House conference, Johnson asked Craig to supply a detailed two-year program that would provide a 10,000-plane Air Corps, furnish "sufficient stocks of essential supplies to equip and maintain the Protective Mobilization Plan Army," and help to prepare industry for expansion to meet the needs of full mobilization. Although the President had indicated that he expected the cost of the plane program to be approximately $500 million, Johnson failed to mention any such limitation when he requested a detailed plan.[40]

Johnson's memorandum requesting a plan for a balanced force was welcomed by Chief of Staff Craig, who just three weeks before had informed the Bureau of the Budget that "the defense of this country . . . ultimately rests with the ground troops, and to ignore this component is to ignore the lessons of history. We need a further increase in air power, but the deplorable situation of our ground army . . . demands more immediate attention."[41] Essentially the same view was held by Deputy Chief of Staff Marshall, who, according to General Arnold, "needed plenty of indoctrination about the air facts of life."[42] General Craig immediately set his subordinates to work on preparing the plan requested by Johnson, but it was not completed until late November.

While the rearmament plans were being prepared, all coordination and planning both within the War Department and between the department and the White House were carried on through Assistant Secretary Johnson instead of Secretary Woodring. During this period the head of the War Department was virtually ignored. Columnists Drew Pearson and Robert Allen were fairly accurate when they wrote on 1 December: "Secretary Woodring hasn't been consulted on any phase of the defense program. All he knows is what he reads in the paper. Johnson has been Roosevelt's right-hand man in national defense."[43] The intimacy that developed between Roosevelt and Johnson apparently stemmed from their mutual enthusiasm over a large air force. Since early 1938 Johnson had been advocating a 10,000-plane Air Corps that would rely to a great extent on heavy bombers.[44] Therefore, in the fall of 1938, when Roosevelt decided to build a large air force, it was not surprising that he turned to his energetic, aggressive Assistant Secretary of War. In October and November the two men became quite close, and Johnson was a frequent visitor at the White House. This relationship soon gave renewed vigor to the old rumors that Johnson was about to replace Woodring.[45] These were difficult days for the Secretary of War. His status was uncertain, and he had no idea from day to day whether Roosevelt intended to keep him.[46] Furthermore, he was frustrated by the realization that if the President chose to work around him, there was nothing he could do about it; he simply had to wait and see what would happen.

Woodring was not the only War Department official to be snubbed in this period, for Chief of Staff Craig was also receiving the cold shoulder from the Commander in Chief. The only information and advice that Craig and the General Staff were asked to provide were those of a technical nature. Most military leaders considered the President's 10,000-plane program to be "fantastic," and they were reluctant to support it because it placed so much emphasis on the Air Corps.[47] Because of such views, military men were seldom included in the President's discussions of rearmament plans.[48]

If the Secretary of War, the Chief of Staff, and the General Staff were largely ignored, who, then, besides Louis Johnson, was helping Roosevelt formulate rearmament plans? The bulk of the advice was coming from three men who had no military background. These "militarists pro tem" were Thomas Corcoran, a presidential adviser; Harry Hopkins, WPA Administrator; and Aubrey Williams, Deputy Administrator of the WPA.[49] The growing influence of these "ex officio strategists" was upsetting to professional military men, whose advice was not sought. According to one widely read source, during this period General Craig "has peeved in silence, loath to admit in public that he knows little more about the administration's ideas for remaking the Army than ordinary newspaper readers."[50] Throughout November, Craig remained silent as the President continued to consult men like Hopkins and Johnson first, and military men last. By early December he could no longer control his frustration, and during an interview with a reporter, he blurted out that "Hopkins and Aubrey Williams (Hopkins' assistant) are running the defense show."[51] When accounts of Craig's statement and the story behind it were published, he denied that there were any difficulties between the administration and the War Department.[52] Craig's contradiction only served to center more attention on the controversy, and in the weeks that followed, the role of the New Dealers and Louis Johnson received more publicity than ever.[53]

The first of December 1938 marked the beginning of a temporary decline in Johnson's influence with the President and the start of an increase in Woodring's influence. On that day Johnson sent to the President the rearmament plan that had been called for two weeks before. Included were items of $1,289 million for an air program, $421 million for supplies to equip the Protective Mobilization Force, and $122 million for industrial preparedness.[54] Roosevelt immediately called in Johnson, General Craig, and several other military advisers and sharply criticized them for reading too much into the November 14 conference. The angry President chided the group as he noted that he had asked for 10,000 planes at a cost of about $500 million, but instead was presented a $1,800 million plan for strengthening air and land forces as well as for helping to prepare industry for mobilization. Roosevelt then emphasized that he did not feel that he could ask Congress for more than $500 million for rearmament and that it would be necessary to come up with a program that cost that amount.[55]

In spite of the statements made to Johnson at the December 1 meeting, President Roosevelt, in the weeks that followed, became less and less enthusiastic about his 10,000-plane program, until, early in January 1939, he virtually abandoned it. His decision to revamp his original program was in all likelihood due to the poor manner in which Congress and the nation reacted to his proposals. Following the November 14 conference, Johnson, with the President's approval, spoke openly of the need for a large and powerful air arm. A bitter reaction to such statements came from many sources. Senator Bennett Clark of Missouri, one of Woodring's best friends, criticized Johnson's rearmament proposals, saying that such moves would be "covers" for a pump-priming program. Other Senators, such as George Norris, Gerald Nye, David Walsh, and William Borah, expressed similar views.[56] A number of newspapers and magazines also voiced disapproval of establishing such a large air arm. Roosevelt had probably encouraged and approved Johnson's speeches in order to test the public reaction, and when that reaction appeared to be unfavorable, he decided to ease up on his aircraft program.[5]

Thus, from 1 December on, the President moved away from the idea of a large Air Corps and toward the concept of a more balanced armed force. In doing this, he also turned back toward Secretary Woodring, General Craig, and the members of the General Staff who had always urged a proper balance between air and ground forces. By mid December, Woodring was once more in control at the War Department and was working closely with the President in preparing a rearmament program.[58] Roosevelt ultimately gave in to the pressures and advice for balance, agreeing to allot $200 million for the Protective Mobilization Force and $300 million for the Air Corps. Of the latter amount, $120 million was to provide additional personnel and air-base facilities, and $180 million was to purchase aircraft.[59] The details of the revised air program were set forth in January 1939 in the so-called Woodring Plan—a plan that provided for an Air Corps of between 5,500 and 6,000 planes.[60] The basis for the program was the plan that Woodring had asked General Arnold to prepare in October. On 11 January 1939 Secretary Woodring, who had been conferring with the President regularly on the defense program, directed General Arnold to prepare legislation to provide for a 6,000-plane Air Corps.[61] The number was subsequently reduced to 5,500, and the President approved that figure. On the following day, 12 January, Roosevelt asked Congress to appropriate $300 million for the Air Corps. That amount, he said, "should provide a minimum increase of 3,000 planes, but it is hoped that orders placed on such a large scale will materially reduce the unit cost and actually provide many more planes."[62]

In the weeks that followed, the Secretary worked hard to make the Woodring Plan become a reality. On 17 January he went before the House Military Affairs Committee and requested 3,032 additional planes, which, with those previously authorized, would provide a 5,500-plane force by mid 1941.[63] Two weeks later, however, Woodring, having changed his ideas somewhat, wrote to Andrew J. May, chairman of the committee, and called his attention to the fact that procurement of a large number of planes would reduce unit cost, thereby permitting the purchase of more planes than the proposed bill authorized. The Secretary therefore suggested "that the committee give consideration to the removal of the limit on airplane strength, so that a greater number of planes may be procured than now contemplated by the War Department."[64] When the House ignored the recommendation and authorized a force of 5,500 planes, Woodring wrote a letter to Morris Sheppard, who was chairman of the Senate Military Affairs Committee, requesting that no limit be established. The Senate committee decided to compromise between the lower figure set by the House and the absence of a set amount, which was requested by Woodring, and it placed the number at 6,000 planes. The House agreed to the revised figure, and on 26 April the President signed the legislation, which fixed the authorized limit of the Army Air Corps at 6,000 planes.[65] The new figure was far short of the amount originally desired by the President, but when one remembers that until the new legislation was passed, the authorized strength of the Air Force was 2,320 aircraft and the actual strength was about 1,700, the figure of 6,000 is quite impressive.

Throughout 1939 Woodring's and Johnson's influence at the White House rose and fell as the President turned first to one and then to the other. From January through April it was Woodring who held the upper hand; but after the Army Appropriations Bill was passed in late April, the President began again to turn to Johnson.[66] In May and June the warmth that had characterized the Johnson-Roosevelt relationship during the previous November reappeared, and Woodring again found himself on the outside. On 5 July the President moved to weaken Woodring's position even further. On that day he issued an executive order making the Joint Army and Navy Board and the Army and Navy Munitions Board directly responsible to himself. This meant that on numerous defense matters the Assistant Secretaries of War and the Navy and the Military Chiefs of both services could now go directly to the Chief Executive.[67] Whether this action was designed to bring about more efficiency or to provide an easy means of working around the Secretary of War is uncertain, but there is no doubt that it made it easier for the President to by-pass Woodring.

On 3 August, Secretary Woodring, his wife, and his three small children left on a two-week's trip to Panama. Although he planned to inspect the canal and its defense system, the trip was primarily a vacation.[68] In Woodring's absence, Acting Secretary of War Johnson attended the cabinet meeting on 4 August. At that time Johnson requested and received the President's approval for establishing a board of civilians to review the Industrial Mobilization Plan and make recommendations to the Assistant Secretary of War on how to improve it.[69] The new six-man body, which was called the War Resources Board, had as its chairman Edward R. Stettinius, Jr., Chairman of the Board of United States Steel Corporation. The majority of the board members were associated with big business. That Johnson had more in mind for the newly created board than reviewing the Industrial Mobilization Plan became apparent on 9 August, when, in announcing the creation of the board, he said, "In the event of an international emergency the board . . . would become an executive agency of the government with broad powers in many ways similar to those exercised by the War Industries Board of World War days."[70] In the days that followed, Johnson reiterated that view time and again.[71]

In late August the War Resources Board submitted to the President a report stating what it felt its function should be in the event of war. The board declared that it disapproved of the idea for a superagency, and it reaffirmed the authority of the President to coordinate its administration and make important decisions; however, it then proceeded to assign itself extensive economic responsibilities. Such action indicated that the board members were still thinking along the lines of an all-powerful board similar to the one operated by Bernard Baruch during the First World War.[72] The President was displeased with the board's report, because he did not like the idea of granting such broad economic authority to anyone except himself. In discussing the proposals of the War Resources Board with administrative adviser Louis Brownlow, Roosevelt said: "If I were to set up a scheme such as recommended by this report, turning over the sole administration of the economy of the country . . . to a single war administrator—even though he were appointed by me—I would simply be abdicating the presidency to some other person."[73]

Woodring, who found out about the creation of the board while en route to Panama, was quite angry that it had been set up during his absence. He was especially upset because Johnson had not mentioned the matter to him before his departure. At the cabinet meeting on 7 September, Woodring openly expressed his displeasure at the manner in which the board had been

172

established. He added that although he had been back at his office for more than two weeks, Stettinius still had not been in to see him.[74] It was not until 21 September that the War Resources Board finally met with Secretary Woodring.

Angered by Johnson's move to establish the board during his absence, Woodring began to search for a chance to discredit his Assistant Secretary; such an opportunity soon presented itself. During the cabinet meeting of 26 September, Woodring called the President's attention to the foreword that Johnson had written for Leo M. Cherne's recently published book, *Adjusting Your Business to War*.[75] Woodring expressed considerable dissatisfaction over the fact that the Assistant Secretary of War had written the foreword, thus causing many individuals to consider the book to be semiofficial. The result was that headlines such as "U.S. to Regiment All People in Case Nation Goes to War" greeted its publication.[76] After Woodring's blast, Secretary of Labor Perkins joined in, likewise attacking Johnson's endorsement of the book.[77] The President said little at the time, but at the press conference that followed the meeting, he fired two shots at Johnson. First, when asked whether or not Cherne's book had the endorsement of the administration, Roosevelt replied that there was no book on the Army, the Navy, or any military subject that had the imprimatur of his administration. He further added that 90 percent of the books written on such matters were written by people who knew less than nothing about the subject. Then he fired a second shot at Johnson by announcing that the War Resources Board would be disbanded. He said that after the board had submitted its report to him in about ten days, its work would be completed. When the press conference ended, Woodring, who had been in attendance, completed the spanking of Johnson by telling the reporters that the board had never been intended to be a permanent body. He then said, "The War Department is not setting up any permanent war boards and war machinery and I hope we never will."[78]

Roosevelt's statement at the news conference on 26 September left no doubt that Johnson's influence was once more on the wane. Consequently, the press immediately began to speculate that Roosevelt would, as he had in the past, turn back to Secretary Woodring.[79] This time, however, the President turned to his Secretary of the Treasury, Henry Morgenthau, Jr. Roosevelt's reasons for this decision and the consequences of that decision will be seen in the following chapters.

The contributions of Secretary of War Woodring to the United States rearmament program prior to the outbreak of World War II are difficult to

173

evaluate. The 1939 rearmament activities definitely bore the Woodring stamp of a balance between the expansion of land and of air forces. Furthermore, it was the 6,000-plane Woodring Plan that Congress finally approved. It must be remembered, however, that Roosevelt turned to Woodring and the General Staff and accepted their program only after Congress and the public indicated that they did not wish to support the 10,000-plane scheme favored by himself and Assistant Secretary Johnson.

Years later, Woodring was to be bitterly criticized by politicians, journalists, and historians for hindering the development of the Army Air Corps during this critical period. Such critics maintained that if Johnson's proposals had been adopted, the United States military machine would have been much better prepared for World War II. While such statements may be true, they fail to put Secretary Woodring's actions in the proper historical perspective. First, it should be remembered that his views on the proper balance between land and air forces were essentially the same as those of the General Staff (including Generals Craig and Marshall), Congress, and the public at large. Second, even if Woodring had favored the 10,000-plane program, it is highly unlikely that Congress would have approved it. Third, the critics fail to point out the financial limitations placed on Woodring. Funds were extremely tight, and he had to distribute them in an equitable manner; thus, to have channeled nearly all expansion funds into the Air Corps, as the President originally had hoped to do, would have been an unsound and irresponsible act. Finally, those who condemn Woodring usually ignore the advances made by the Air Corps during his tenure as Secretary. When he assumed the post in 1937, the Corps had an authorized strength of 2,320 aircraft and an actual strength of 1,329. Just two years later, however, it had grown to an authorized strength of 6,000 and an actual strength of 3,102.[80] While international events certainly account for some of that growth, a great deal of credit must be given to Secretary Woodring, who determined how aircraft appropriations were actually utilized. Although Woodring cannot be called a major advocate of air power, neither does he deserve the anti–Air Corps label that has so frequently been attached to his name.

10

Problems of Neutrality, 1936-1939

Numerous accounts have been written about the United States and neutrality in the 1930s, in which detailed information has been presented on isolationism, neutrality legislation, and efforts to keep the United States out of a foreign conflict. Nearly all such accounts are similar, in that they tend to look upon the problems of neutrality as the concern of only the President and the State Department. So much emphasis has been placed on the efforts of President Roosevelt and Secretary of State Cordell Hull to handle problems relating to neutrality that there has been a tendency to forget that other top administration officials were also vitally concerned with those matters. One such person was Secretary of War Woodring.

Woodring would have preferred to avoid questions relating to neutrality, because he felt that keeping the country out of war was the "primary concern of the State Department and the Chief Executive," not of the War Department.[1] Although he would have liked to avoid such problems, he could not. As Secretary of War, he soon discovered not only that neutrality was of great interest to him, but also that he could do much to see that it was or was not maintained.

Woodring's influence on neutrality was of both an informal and a formal nature. His informal influence stemmed in part from the fact that he was head of the United States War Department. By virtue of that position, his every statement concerning the Army, national defense, and foreign policy was looked upon as being representative of administration policy or indicative of what that policy might be in the future. A belligerent or offensive statement by such a key member of the executive branch could have a serious effect on the thinking or actions of certain foreign nations, and consequently it could endanger the neutrality of the United States. Another informal influence over neutrality was Woodring's role as a cabinet member. That position gave him ready access to the President; generally he consulted with FDR two or three times every week. That the breakdown of neutrality could ultimately result in the nation's going to war was a fact that Woodring was well aware of, and if there was anything he wanted to avoid, it was war. Therefore, in his capacity as a presidential adviser, he always cautioned against any action that might endanger American neutrality.

Formally, Woodring was able to influence the maintenance of neutrality because the Neutrality Act of 1935 made the Secretary of War a member of the National Munitions Control Board—a body whose purpose was to license and supervise all shipments of arms to foreign countries. As a board member, Woodring had a major voice in determining which war items could or could not be shipped to foreign nations. The Secretary of War had always had the primary responsibility for making decisions about what military supplies were to be sold abroad, but the neutrality legislation of the 1930s made that post more important than it had ever been, especially in regard to maintaining neutrality.

The major problem of neutrality faced by Secretary Woodring centered on the question of selling government arms, ammunition, and implements of war to foreign governments. This had been a problem for Woodring even before he became Secretary, because as Assistant Secretary of War he had been asked by Secretary Dern to recommend what policy the War Department should follow in regard to foreign sales.[2] In preparing his recommendations, Woodring relied on several valuable precedents. A 1920 act had authorized the Secretary of War "to sell to any state or foreign government with which the United States is at peace at the time of the passage of this Act, upon such terms as he may deem expedient, any matériel, supplies, or equipment pertaining to the military establishment . . . which are not needed for military purposes."[3] However, in April 1923 President Harding had established the policy that the government would not sell war equipment to any foreign power. This was done, he said, "to make sure that none of our surplus equipment is employed in encouraging warfare any place in the world." Seven years later, that policy was modified by President Hoover to permit the sale of surplus aircraft and aircraft parts, provided that such sales did not reveal any military secrets and provided that they were approved by the

176

State Department. This decision was motivated primarily by a desire to enhance foreign trade.[4] Based on these precedents, Woodring developed a new policy on foreign sales in August of 1933. According to Woodring, it was to be "the policy of this government to refrain from disposing of arms, ammunitions, and implements of war in possession of this government to foreign powers or to persons who might be presumed to be about to transfer them to foreign powers."[5] This was to be the War Department's contribution to the maintenance of world peace.

Although the War Department refused to sell arms and ammunition abroad, it was not concerned over the sale of such items by United States civilian firms, except when military secrets were involved. The Army not only had no objection to the foreign sale of implements of war made by American manufacturers, it actually encouraged such activity, because this stimulated a number of key war industries. As Woodring explained it, "Such action is considered to enhance the interests of national defense by encouraging the maintenance of facilities for supply in the event of an emergency."[6]

Before 1935 all requests by civilians to export arms and ammunition were handled by the State Department, but they required prior approval from the War Department. When an export request was received, it was forwarded to the Secretary of War, who then informed the Undersecretary of State if there was any objection, on the grounds of "military secrecy," to the exportation of the articles mentioned. If the Secretary of War objected, the State Department denied the request; if he had no objection, the request was approved. The identity of the manufacturer making the request or the identity of the country destined to receive the item made no difference in the decisions of the Secretary of War; the test was strictly one of military secrecy.[7] Such a policy explains why, on 23 October 1933, Secretary Dern approved a request from the Boeing Airplane Company to export B-9 airplanes to Japan, while at the same time he turned down a request to send P-26's to Germany.[8]

In August of 1935 Congress passed the Neutrality Act, which provided that in the event of war between two or more nations, the President would proclaim such a fact; and from that time on, it would be unlawful to export arms, ammunitions, or implements of war to the belligerent nations. The act also made it unlawful to export any war supply without a federal license. To implement this latter provision, Congress established the National Munitions Control Board, which was made up of the Secretary of State, who served as chairman, and the Secretaries of War, the Navy, the Treasury, and Commerce. The board was to supervise and control, through a registration and licensing system, the manufacture, importation, and exportation of all arms and ammunition.[9] The agency created for carrying out the responsibilities of the Munitions Board was the Office of Arms and Munitions Control—an adjunct of the State Department. The functions of the Control Office were basically clerical, since the licensing procedure was clearly spelled out in federal statutes.[10]

In spite of the legislative restrictions placed on it, the Munitions Control Board evolved into an increasingly important body, and with the possible exception of Secretary Hull, Secretary Woodring was to emerge as its most important and influential member. The importance of the board stemmed from the fact that its regulations provided that licenses to export arms could not be issued when doing so would violate the Espionage Act of 1917.[11] This law provided that anyone who turned over to a foreign government or to an individual in a foreign country or to any person not entitled to receive it any "blue print, plan, map, model, instrument, appliance, or note relating to the national defense . . . shall be punished by a fine . . . or by imprisonment . . . or both."[12] This meant that the maintenance of military secrets was the major reason for refusing to grant a license for the exportation of implements of war; furthermore, it was the responsibility of the Secretary of War to make the final decision about whether or not a specific item was a military secret.[13] Thus Secretary Woodring could determine whether or not a particular foreign government would receive a certain type of aircraft, arm, or ordnance item.[14] While the Secretary always consulted the General Staff's G-2 and the Chiefs of the various Technical Services in deciding whether or not an item should be classified as a military secret, he was in no way bound to follow their recommendations. Under the guise of military secrecy, Woodring could, if he so chose, veto the foreign sale of any item that fell in the category of arms, ammunition, or implements of war. As will be seen, however, Woodring used his Munitions Board powers in an impartial and neutral manner, and he ran into difficulty with his superior only when he refused to follow such a policy.

The experience that Woodring gained as Assistant Secretary on matters relating to foreign sales was utilized almost as soon as he assumed the secretaryship. In October 1936 the British Air Attache in Washington called on Woodring and inquired whether it might be possible for the British government to purchase military planes from American manufacturers.[15] Woodring, feeling that British orders would help the sagging United States aircraft industry, favored such sales, provided that the models to be turned over were more than a year old.[16] For the past several years the War Department had followed the policy that no American firm selling planes to the Army could sell similar planes to a foreign government until one year after delivery of the second production plane. It was felt that since experimental

178

A dinner honoring James A. Farley, 1937; seated (left to right): Vice-President John Nance Garner, President Franklin D. Roosevelt, and Farley; standing: Henry Wallace, Harry Woodring, Cordell Hull, Daniel Roper, Henry Morgenthau, Jr.

Secretary of War Harry H. Woodring and Chief of Staff George C. Marshall arriving at the White House for a defense conference, 30 May 1940.

The Woodring family making its farewell visit to the White House, 26 June 1940 (left to right): Marcus, Harry, Melissa, Helen, and Cooper Woodring.

and testing work had been completed and production was well under way by the time the second production plane was received, the United States Air Corps would have the aircraft a full two years ahead of any other country. Some Air Corps leaders, feeling that the release period of one year was too long, wanted to reduce it to six months; but Woodring refused to go along with such a change.[17] The Navy's policy on release of aircraft for export was based on what it called "national defense interests." Since such a phrase could be interpreted in many ways, it meant that the Navy had no set time limit; consequently, some planes were released in six months, while others were held for years.[18]

When the British expressed an interest in buying American-built military aircraft in October 1936, Woodring asked the President to decide on a uniform policy with regard to release; thus, on 11 November, Roosevelt met with Secretary Woodring, Secretary of the Navy Swanson, Acting Secretary of State R. Walton Moore, and Solicitor General Stanley Reed for that purpose. After hearing Woodring and Swanson explain the policies of their departments with regard to the release of aircraft, the President decided that the policy of the War Department should be used by both military services. Although Roosevelt agreed that all Air Corps planes should be considered military secrets for one year, and therefore not eligible for release, he did request that a study be made to see if, in the future, the time limit might be reduced.[19] In late November, Britain temporarily abandoned the idea of purchasing American-built planes, and so, for the time being, the release policy slipped back into a position of relative unimportance.

As Secretary of War, Harry Woodring was determined to ensure that all military secrets, especially those relating to aircraft, remain the sole property of the United States government. Woodring, feeling that since Congress had not authorized an Air Corps of quantity, it was essential that it be one of quality, always attempted to provide the Corps with the latest and most efficient planes available.[20] Occasionally, his determination to protect aircraft secrets became a source of difficulty. Such was the case in October 1936, when Eugene L. Vidal, the Director of Air Commerce, publicly criticized Woodring for refusing to permit representatives from a Latin American air-transport company to visit factories at which Army planes were being produced.[21] With regard to this restrictive visitation policy, as with his refusal to cut the aircraft release period to six months, Woodring was guided by his determination to safeguard American aircraft secrets.

In mid 1936 civil war broke out in Spain, and a few weeks later a number of American airplane manufacturers asked the State Department if they could export planes to Spain, since the Neutrality Act did not impose an embargo in case of civil war. William Phillips, the Acting Secretary of State, informed the manufacturers that sales to Spain "would not follow the spirit of the Government's policy." This "moral embargo" was accepted without question until December.[22] In that month, Robert Cuse, a New Jersey scrap dealer, applied for a license to sell $2.777 million worth of airplanes, airplane engines, and airplane parts to the Spanish government. Since there was no legal prohibition against such sales, the Office of Arms and Munitions Control was forced to issue the export license. The government was widely criticized for issuing the license, but the President explained that nothing else could be done, for although Cuse's action was unpatriotic, it was legal. Criticism then shifted to the Army, when it was revealed that most of the engines to be exported had been sold to Cuse by the War Department in January 1936. Secretary Woodring defended the Army by pointing out that the engines had been sold as surplus because they had already been overhauled three times and would have been unsafe to place in a plane again. He also pointed out that the sale had been completed months before the Spanish Civil War had begun.[23]

In early January 1937 Congress passed a resolution to expand the arms-embargo provision of the Neutrality Act to civil wars, but before the legislation went into effect on 8 January, Cuse was able to export six planes and one engine.[24] Although the furor over the Cuse matter quickly subsided, Woodring was determined that such a thing should not happen again. Therefore, in early March he directed that steps be taken to ensure that in the future, surplus arms, ammunition, and implements of war were to be sold only to citizens of the United States and "then only under a contract specifying that such articles will not be resold, transferred, or mortgaged to any foreign government or power and provided further that such matériel or equipment will not be shipped outside the United States." In the event of resale the same provisions had to be adhered to by the new owner.[25] These principles were incorporated in Army regulations in the spring of 1937, and for the next three years they were implemented without being questioned. Eventually, however, those regulations were to become a major source of controversy between Secretary Woodring and President Roosevelt.

On 1 May 1937 the President signed the 1937 Neutrality Act, which provided the nation with permanent neutrality legislation, the 1935 and 1936 acts having been only temporary. On the same day that the new legislation went into effect, President Roosevelt expanded the list of arms, ammunitions, and implements of war to be included in an embargo. Most of the items added were gases and explosives. The recommendation for expanding the list had come from the Munitions Control Board, but their decision on it had not been a unanimous one.[26] Woodring had voiced opposition to expanding the list on the grounds that a number of the articles

180

and materials to be added were not designed or intended for military purposes. The Secretary of War maintained that restrictions should be placed only on the exportation of items that were definitely for military use. He feared that if the line were not drawn somewhere, the United States might eventually come to define contraband as broadly as Britain had during the World War. In opposing expansion of the embargo list, Woodring stood alone—the board voting 4 to 1 in favor of the new items.[27]

That Woodring did not wish to stand in the way of exports unless they had a definite military advantage to the recipient can be seen by examining his position in the helium controversy of 1937-1938. On 6 May 1937 the German dirigible *Hindenburg*, which was using highly inflammable hydrogen, exploded and crashed as it was landing at Lakehurst, New Jersey, after a trans-Atlantic flight. A few days later the German Zeppelin Company, desiring to utilize a safer noninflammable gas, contacted Secretary of Interior Ickes and inquired whether it could purchase helium from the United States for a second dirigible then under construction. Ickes was consulted because the production and sale of helium was under the control of the Bureau of Mines, which was within the Interior Department.[28]

At a cabinet meeting on 14 May, Ickes informed those who were present of the German request. The cabinet members had mixed emotions concerning the possible sale. With the *Hindenburg* tragedy still fresh in their minds, they tended to look with favor on such a sale for humanitarian reasons, but at the same time they did not wish to sell helium to a foreign government that might use it for military purposes. In order to examine the matter more closely and then make a policy recommendation, the President appointed an ad hoc committee composed of the Secretaries of State, War, Navy, Interior, and Commerce.[29] A week later the committee reported in favor of exporting helium, provided that there were safeguards to ensure that the gas was not used for military purposes.[30] On this recommendation, Woodring was in complete accord with the rest of the group.[31] On 25 May the President, who favored legislation permitting the foreign sale of helium, submitted to key congressional committees the recommendations of his ad hoc committee.[32] Congress was impressed with the report and responded by incorporating its ideas into the Helium Act. Under that measure, which went into effect on 1 September, the Secretary of the Interior retained responsibility for the production and sale of helium, while export control was given to both the National Munitions Control Board and the Secretary of the Interior.[33]

In October the Zeppelin Company requested 17.5 million cubic feet of helium for one year's operations. The Munitions Control Board quickly gave its approval, and on 31 January 1938 the State Department issued an export license. The only thing that now remained was for Secretary Ickes to sell the helium. Ickes, however, refused to do so, because he feared Hitler's intentions and did not want to do anything that might aid the German military machine. Then, when the Germans invaded Austria on 12 March, he was more determined than ever to refrain from selling the gas.[34]

Throughout the spring of 1938 a controversy raged over whether or not Ickes should sell the helium to Germany. President Roosevelt and Secretary Hull pressured him to do so, because the German government was becoming increasingly irritated over the delay, and Roosevelt and Hull wanted to maintain peaceful relations with the Reich.[35] Ickes, however, refused to back down. Woodring also urged that the sale be made, but he did so because he saw no reason to discriminate against a nation merely because one disagreed with its policies. He maintained that since Congress had provided for sale of the gas, any nation requesting it should receive it as long as such action did not endanger the security of the United States. On 4 April and again on 27 April, Woodring wrote to Ickes, urging him to make the sale. Woodring argued that the United States should make the helium available to Germany because of humanitarian reasons, and he assured him that the amount to be sent was "not sufficiently great to represent jeopardy to the National Defense."[36] After the second letter, Woodring saw that he was making no progress with Ickes, and realizing that under the law there was no way of circumventing him, he gave up and stopped pursuing the matter. During the spring and summer, Ickes continued to resist all pressures to make the sale, and in September, after Hitler's success at Munich, those pressures came to an end. In the years that followed, Ickes proudly told how he had helped to curtail the military might of Nazi Germany by denying it American helium.[37] In reality, Ickes did no such thing, because the quantity requested had been so small that it could not possibly have been of any real military value.[38]

In January 1938 a series of events began that marked the beginning of the breakdown of United States neutrality and brought about one of the most controversial issues of the Roosevelt administration. On 16 January, French Senator Amaury de la Grange, a long-time friend of Roosevelt's met with the Chief Executive and asked if France could purchase one thousand planes like those being used by the United States Air Corps.[39] The President pointed out that restrictions of the Neutrality Act would "hinder" French procurement in the event of war, but he indicated a willingness to assist the French all that he could. Upon leaving the White House, de la Grange wrote: "The President will thus be completely in favor of all measures that

182

the French Government might believe necessary to reinforce its air formations in time of peace and in time of war."[40]

France's Minister of Defense, Edouard Daladier, doubted whether Roosevelt would be as helpful as de la Grange had indicated; therefore, he asked the American Ambassador, William Bullitt, to sound out the President on the matter. In February, Bullitt and Daladier's representative, French industrialist Jean Monnet, traveled to Washington in an effort to find out how much support Roosevelt was willing to give France. When Bullitt and Monnet met with the President, he told them of his efforts to repeal the arms embargo and that if war should come before repeal, he would push through such legislation immediately. The President then stated that in the event that he could not bring about repeal of the embargo, he would get around the legislation by sending planes from the United States to Canada, whence they could be sent to France.[41] Since both this meeting and the earlier one, with de la Grange, were confidential, neither Secretary Hull nor Secretary Woodring, nor any other top administrative official, knew what Roosevelt had pledged.

A close examination of the American aircraft industry by French officials revealed that it was barely superior to that of France and that the only American-built plane that could meet their needs was the Curtiss-Wright P-36. When Curtiss-Wright officials were approached by French representatives concerning a sale, they indicated that even if the War Department released the aircraft for export, their limited production facilities would allow no more than one hundred planes to be sent abroad prior to March 1939. Although the number was quite small, Monnet favored making the purchase. A number of technicians in France's Air Ministry were hesitant about buying the planes, because they doubted that the P-36 could stand up against the newest German aircraft; thus, the French Minister for Air concluded that the only way to settle the dispute was to have his leading test pilot, Michael Detroyat, fly the plane and then recommend whether or not the order should be placed.[42]

In early March 1938 the French requested permission for Detroyat to make the flight, but the War Department, following the one-year release policy approved by the President two years before, denied the request. The department also pointed out that since the second production plane had not yet been received, it would be at least a year before such a flight could be made. Chief of the Air Corps Arnold, Chief of Staff Craig, and Secretary Woodring all agreed that the request should be denied.[43] On 10 March the President, acting as Commander in Chief, directed the Chief of Staff to permit Detroyat to fly the P-36. The flight, he said, should be limited to twenty minutes and "should be conducted from some outlying field, with utmost secrecy." The President also directed that anything of a confidential or secret nature should be removed from the plane before the flight.[44] The flight subsequently took place, and when Detroyat reported favorably upon the plane's performance, France's Air Ministry placed an order for one hundred export models of the P-36. The export models, with their name changed to the Hawk 75-A, were essentially the same as those received by the Army Air Corps except for the omission of secret instruments and equipment such as the retractable landing gear.[45]

Nations other than France were interested in purchasing American-built planes at this time, for in March, Britain sent an air mission to explore the possibilities of making such purchases. When the British mission expressed an interest in the B-18 and the War Department refused to permit a test flight because it was still classified as a military secret, the President again overruled his Army advisers and ordered that the British representatives be permitted to make the flight.[46] Unimpressed with the B-18, the British did not order any. However, in June they did place an order for four hundred American-built military aircraft. The planes that were to be supplied, half of which were bombers and half of which were pursuit planes, were no longer classified as military secrets; therefore, there were no problems involved in selling them.[47] Three months after this transaction the Munich Conference took place, and thereafter the British preferred to develop their own aircraft industry rather than to rely on the United States. The British restricted their American purchases, because they feared that if they became involved in a war with Germany, the Neutrality Act would come into effect and cut off all the planes ordered. France, unlike Britain, was willing to take that risk.[48]

On 25 October 1938, while President Roosevelt was in the midst of making plans to expand the United States Air Corps, he met with Ambassador Bullitt, Secretary Morgenthau, and Jean Monnet to discuss the Nazi menace. They discussed what the United States could do to augment France's air strength. Roosevelt told the group that the American aircraft industry could supply France with one thousand pursuit planes and one thousand bombers. Since the French were especially short of bombers, Monnet returned to France and urged Premier Daladier to place a large order. Consequently, on 5 December, Daladier told his Defense Council that there was "the possibility of receiving about 1,000 planes of the latest model in use by the American Army. The American government has formally promised delivery but it must be kept absolutely secret."[49] After a few days of budget juggling, it was decided that Monnet should head a mission to the United States with the funds and authority to purchase one thousand modern aircraft.

When the new French air mission arrived in Washington in mid December 1938, President Roosevelt, remembering the earlier opposition of Woodring, Craig, and Arnold to French efforts to test the P-36, directed Monnet to work through the Secretary of the Treasury. According to Secretary Morgenthau, Roosevelt directed them to his office because "he knew the Treasury [Department] would take a less parochial view of national policy in the sale of aircraft than either War or Navy."[50] The nominal reason given by the President was that the Procurement Division of the Treasury Department was experienced in large-scale purchases.[51]

Secretary Woodring was completely unaware of the presence of the French mission until December 21, when Deputy Chief of Staff Marshall informed him that General Arnold had been requested to grant permission to the French officials to inspect the latest Army planes that were under construction. At a cabinet meeting that afternoon, Morgenthau referred to, but did not discuss, the presence of the Monnet mission. After the meeting, Woodring, Morgenthau, and Acting Secretary of State Sumner Welles held a long discussion.[52] Saying that the French wanted to purchase a thousand of the latest planes, Morgenthau proposed that the French aviation experts be permitted to inspect and test three late models: the P-40, the Martin 166 bomber, and the B-12 Douglas bomber. Woodring immediately objected to the proposal, claiming that it was unwise to show the mission any planes that were under construction or ready to test. Furthermore, he added, the War Department's policy, which the President himself had approved, prohibited the foreign sale of planes until a year after the second production plane had been received. At this point, Roosevelt acknowledged that the French request violated the established policy on sales, but he considered France to be the nation's first line of defense and therefore expected every effort to be made to supply it with the planes it desired. After Woodring again expressed fear that French purchases would interfere with future Army orders, the President wrote on a memorandum of Morgenthau's that for "reasons of state" the French should be permitted to inspect and purchase the planes, provided that procurement of them did not interfere with United States orders. Woodring reluctantly replied that if that was what the President wanted, he would see that it was done.[53]

The following morning, after discussing the President's directive with his military advisers, Woodring was even less enthusiastic about carrying it out. That afternoon he, General Marshall, and General Arnold went to see Secretary Morgenthau. At that meeting, the Army officials reluctantly agreed to release the P-40, because it was already in service and would be eligible for foreign sale in a few months anyway. They did not, however, want to reveal, let alone release, either the newly produced Martin bomber or the Douglas bomber, which was still under development. Woodring and Arnold then argued that if the French were permitted to buy the one thousand planes that they desired, the orders could not be filled in less than eighteen months, which meant that Army procurement would be hindered. Morgenthau said that he intended to carry out the President's order whether the War Department "liked it or not." Woodring replied that he, too, would carry out the President's wishes, but he wanted Roosevelt "to know all the facts and not be mixed in his reasoning" by the information that Morgenthau was giving him.[54] The meeting ended with Morgenthau renewing his pledge to aid the French but agreeing that for the time being there would be no inspection of the secret bombers.[55]

One week later, on 29 December, Woodring wrote to Morgenthau, informing him that the bombers would not be revealed until he was assured of two things: first, that the French had the money to put on the "barrel head" for the planes; second, that the orders would not interfere with future Army orders. Morgenthau considered these demands an attempt by Woodring to place obstacles in the path of the French mission. Therefore, he immediately wrote to the President and informed him, "I am unable to proceed further in this matter as long as Secretary Woodring maintains his present attitude."[56] On the following day, Morgenthau telephoned Woodring and expressed his displeasure with the demands being placed upon him. He charged the Secretary of War with attempting to put him "on the spot by writing a letter placing such limitations . . . on the program of assistance to the French." Woodring replied that he was under pressure from his military advisers not to release the bombers and that he was also afraid that Congress would "raise hell" over their release. He then said, "All I wanted to do, Henry, was simply to protect you in the matter." To this Morgenthau replied, "I don't want to be protected."[57] After an extended discussion, during which the Treasury Secretary mentioned the President's instruction of 21 December, Woodring finally agreed to let the French see the Martin, but not the Douglas, bomber. Two days later Morgenthau informed the French that although it had not been easy to arrange, the mission could inspect the Martin 166. As he explained to Monnet, "The whole United States Army is opposed to what I am doing and I am doing it secretly and I just cannot continue . . . forcing the United States Army to show planes which they say they want for themselves."[58]

During the first two weeks of January 1939, while Morgenthau was on vacation, the French undertook the aircraft inspections. In that period they made a tentative decision to purchase one hundred additional export models of the P-36 and sixty Martin 166 bombers, but they could make no decision on the Douglas bomber, because it remained under wraps.[59] When Morgenthau returned to Washington and found that the War Department was still procrastinating on the matter of the Douglas bomber, he proposed to the President that all purchasing of planes for the United States government be turned over to the Treasury Department. Morgenthau urged such action because it would enable him to release any plane that he wanted to release.[60] The President was unwilling to take such a drastic step, but Morgenthau's protests over the War Department's opposition necessitated his taking some action.

On 16 January 1939 Roosevelt summoned Secretary Woodring, Assistant Secretary Johnson, Secretary Morgenthau, and William Bullitt, the United States Ambassador to France, to the White House. Bullitt opened the meeting by stating that time was running out for France and that the United States should give it all possible assistance. It was especially important, he continued, that the Douglas bomber be made available. Woodring then opposed inspection or release of the bomber because it had secret elements and because it had been built partially with government funds. Its release, he said, "might put the President in an embarrassing position." In the discussion that followed, Roosevelt indicated, but did not actually say, that he favored the release of the plane. Finally, Assistant Secretary Johnson, whose bluntness could occasionally be an asset, said to the President, "Do you mean, sir, that you wish the Douglas light bomber released to the French government?" Roosevelt quickly replied, "I mean exactly that."[61]

The President had made his position clear, and Woodring could hold back no longer. The Secretary directed Johnson to make sure that the War Department cooperated 100 percent with the French air mission, and on that note the meeting ended. A few hours later Johnson informed General Arnold that the members of the French mission should be given access to the Douglas bomber. On 19 January, Arnold telegraphed the military authorities at Los Angeles and informed them that French representatives would arrive the following day. Arnold's telegram concluded: "Authority granted for them to inspect Douglas attack bomber less secret accessories, fly in same, and open negotiations with Douglas Co. relative to purchase."[62] On 20 January three members of the French mission, including the test pilot, Paul Chemidlin, arrived at the Douglas plant in Los Angeles, and on the following day they began to inspect the new aircraft.

"On January 23 all hell broke loose," according to General Arnold.[63] On that day the Douglas bomber, with Chemidlin aboard, crashed in a Los Angeles parking lot, killing the pilot and destroying a dozen cars. Miraculously, Chemidlin survived the crash and was taken to a nearby hospital. At first the Douglas Company attempted to keep the Frenchman's presence on the plane a secret by announcing that the survivor was a company mechanic named Smithins; however, reporters quickly learned the survivor's true identity, and when confronted with the information, the Douglas officials admitted that the French test pilot had been aboard the plane.[64] As the Chemidlin story appeared in newspapers across the country, everyone began to ask the same question. What was a member of the French air mission doing on the experimental bomber?

The crash on 23 January was just what congressional isolationists needed in order to attack the administration, because it was now public knowledge that the executive branch was not being neutral but was assisting the French by granting them special privileges. Isolationist Senator Bennett C. Clark of Missouri had been informed of the presence and activities of the French mission by Secretary Woodring prior to the crash, but he could not mention it publicly without revealing the source of his information.[65] The secrecy that surrounded the French mission prior to 23 January was so tight that not only were newspapermen unaware of it, but even Secretary of State Hull had no knowledge of its activities.[66]

Three days after the crash, at a secret hearing before the Senate Military Affairs Committee, General Arnold, who had been testifying in regard to Air Corps needs for the following year, was placed on the hot seat by Senator Clark, who was quite upset that President Roosevelt had ignored the advice of the War Department and had permitted the French to test the Douglas bomber. During the course of the discussion, Clark turned from the subject at hand and asked why a French aviation expert was on the secret bomber that crashed. Arnold replied: "He was out there under the direction of the Treasury Department, with a view of looking into possible purchase of airplanes by the French mission."[67] The Air Corps Chief then explained that while the visit was under the direction of the Treasury Department, the actual authorization had come from the War Department.[68] After asking Arnold questions whose essence was "Does the Secretary of the Treasury run the Air Corps?" and "Does he give orders about Air Corps procurement?,"[69] Senator Clark asked that the committee call Secretary Morgenthau to appear before it, so that he might explain "what the Treasury Department had to do with authorizing the disclosure to any government, however friendly, of American military secrets."[70]

On the following day, 27 January, Morgenthau and Woodring testified before the committee. Morgenthau told the group that the President had desired that the French be given access to the Douglas bomber, and when informed of this decision, the Secretary of War had directed General Arnold to send the authorization for inspection. When Woodring was asked whether the War Department had declined or discouraged the efforts to make the secret plane available to the French, he tried to side-step the issue

188

by saying that all considerations had been discussed. However, in the grueling questioning that followed, Woodring revealed that he and his military advisers had opposed the plan.[71]

The testimony of Morgenthau and Woodring, which revealed that President Roosevelt had been the man responsible for making the secret bomber available to the French, caused considerable alarm among a number of members of the Senate Military Affairs Committee; thus, they asked their chairman, Morris Sheppard of Texas, to approach the President to get his side of the story. After visiting Roosevelt, Sheppard reported back that "there was absolutely nothing to worry about"; but one pessimistic member stated that if the President was that convincing, then perhaps the entire committee should go to talk to him. To this proposal Senator Sheppard replied, "That's just what you ought to do"—and that is exactly what they did.[72]

On 31 January the entire Senate Military Affairs Committee went to the White House for a private conference with President Roosevelt. At that meeting, the President surprised and alarmed a number of Senators when, after discussing the menace that Hitler presented to Europe and the world, he said, "Our first line of defense is in France."[73] He claimed that France could not be permitted to fall, because if it did, England would be next; and if England fell, Germany could then turn her attention to the world sphere. "Therefore," he continued, "it is to our interest to do what we can to help the French and British maintain their independence." The President then vowed that he would send to the two nations anything and everything that they could pay for. When asked if such a policy was unneutral, Roosevelt replied, "Yes it might be called that," but it was necessary, "because self-protection is part of the American policy."[74] When asked who had actually authorized the French mission to see the Douglas bomber, the President answered:

You need not worry about who authorized that order. . . . I am frankly hoping that the French will be able to get the fastest pursuit planes . . . and the best bombers they can buy in this country. It is not a question of secrecy. We have just one secret, and that is the question of a bombsight and that has not been disclosed to the French and won't. And I hope to God they get the planes and get them fast and get them over there in France. It may mean the saving of our civilization.[75]

To the isolationist Senators present at the White House conference the President's remarks were cause for real alarm. Instead of being convinced that they should curtail their current investigation and support the sale of planes to France, they felt that the President was pursuing a policy that was unwise and dangerous. They considered it unwise because it would take

189

out of the country many airplanes and other valuable military supplies that might ultimately be needed by the United States Army, and they considered it dangerous because such sales might draw the country into a European conflict, much as they had during World War I.[76]

Although the Senators who attended the 31 January meeting had pledged themselves to secrecy, that pledge was immediately broken by a few isolationists who were convinced that the President's policy would lead the nation into war. On 1 February the *New York Times* reported that President Roosevelt had told the conferees "to regard France as the actual frontier of America in an apparently inevitable showdown between democracies and dictatorships."[77] Immediately, there developed widespread criticism of what was called an extension of the American frontier to the Rhineland. The reaction to the President's alleged statement became so bitter that, on 3 February, Roosevelt called a news conference and branded as a "deliberate lie" the claims that he had said anything to the effect that the Rhine was the United States frontier.[78]

The isolationist Senators had forced the President to back down publicly on his Rhine statement, but they were not through. Seeing an opportunity to embarrass him, they continued their investigation of the Douglas-bomber matter for another two weeks. During that period the Military Affairs Committee, meeting in secret session, again called on Woodring, Morgenthau, Johnson, and a number of military leaders in order to rehash the entire story of the French air mission.[79] On 16 February the committee concluded its investigation and began to release portions of the testimony. Two days later the *New York Times* reported that the released transcripts revealed that "President Roosevelt authorized the demonstration to the French air mission of the Douglas 7-B attack bomber . . . against the judgment and over the protests of the War Department."[80] In the weeks that followed, Roosevelt came under heavy attack for pursuing a foreign policy that was anything but neutral.

In February and early March the Monnet Mission placed orders for 555 military planes, including one hundred Douglas and one hundred Martin bombers.[81] On 23 March the mission returned to France, and the controversy surrounding its presence vanished as quickly as it had appeared.

As they concerned Secretary Woodring, the events surrounding the French air mission are significant in that they reveal his determination to ensure the superiority of United States defense and his desire to be neutral in deed. He had opposed release of the Douglas bomber for two basic reasons. First, he wanted to ensure that his country had the best military planes; therefore, he did not want to "give away" to any foreign nation America's latest aircraft. Second, he wished to live up to the spirit of the neutrality legislation—something that he felt the President was not doing. Woodring did not feel that, when it came to the inspection, sale, or release of arms, ammunition, or implements of war, the War Department was "empowered, per se, to discriminate between friendly foreign governments," a friendly foreign government being any nation not at war with the United States.[82]

Although he was more than willing to sell military aircraft to France, Woodring felt that France had to be governed by the same rules and regulations that applied to all other nations. Therefore, he did not wish to show members of the French mission any planes that were still classified as military secrets. Since such views ran counter to those of President Roosevelt, Woodring was overruled. Even though the President was upset by Woodring's opposition to the release of the Douglas bomber to France, the publicity that surrounded the affair after the crash on 23 January made it impossible for him to dismiss his Secretary of War without bringing the wrath of the isolationists down upon himself.[83]

Although Woodring did all that he could to be neutral in deed, he was not neutral in thought. He was sympathetic toward the democratic nations and critical of the fascist countries, and his expression of such views was to cause him considerable difficulty in May 1938. Early in that month he used a speech before the Chamber of Commerce of the United States to criticize, and then warn, Germany, Italy, and Japan that if they continued their present aggressive policies, the Democratic nations might be forced to go to war to stop them. Woodring said: "At present the democracies are strongly pacifistic. They have not always been so. If pressed too far a wave of indignation might sweep over them that would make it extremely difficult to keep the peace."[84] On the next day the press carried accounts of the address under such headings as "War Secretary Warns Dictators to Beware" and "Don't Push Democracies Too Far, Woodring Warns Germany, Italy, and Japan." The controversy was under way. Press reaction was generally hostile, with the Secretary being criticized for "inflaming a bad situation" or confusing "an international picture which is cloudy enough."[85] On the floor of the House, Congressmen Roy Woodruff and Hamilton Fish condemned the Secretary's action; even Congressman Sam D. Reynolds, a Woodring supporter and the chairman of the Foreign Affairs Committee, called the address "ill-timed and ill-advised."[86] Criticism of Woodring's speech was not limited to the United States, however, for the German and Italian Foreign Offices used their semiofficial mouthpieces, *Diplomatische Korrespondenz* and *Giornale d'Italia*, to attack it; and on 14 May, Mussolini himself replied to it by warning that in the event of war, the "totalitarian states will immediately form a bloc and march together to the end."[87] As usual, President Roosevelt made no comment throughout the controversy.[88] Whether Secretary Woodring made the speech on his own or as a trial balloon for the Chief Executive is uncertain, but one thing is clear: it got him into hot water, and from that time on, he carefully avoided making public statements, pro or con, about any foreign government.[89]

Prior to the summer of 1939 Secretary Woodring encouraged foreign nations to purchase American-produced planes, arms, and military equipment. Although he did not want the War Department to become a "purchasing adviser for foreign governments," he did want to see American war industries expanded, and he felt that the best way to bring that about was by increased foreign orders. For that reason he directed his department to do all that it could to put foreign purchasers in touch with American producers.[90] Representatives from nations throughout the world, from Australia to Argentina and Belgium to Bolivia, were authorized to visit American aircraft factories, and Secretary Woodring approved the sale of any model plane to any country requesting it, as long as it was no longer classified as a military secret.[91] However, when a secret was involved or when a request was made to release a certain aircraft or other weapon before the date set for its release, Woodring would refuse to back down.[92] Only when the President overruled him did the Secretary of War make an exception.

By the summer of 1939, because of the threat of war in Europe, the United States government began to receive numerous requests, especially from Britain and France, for airplanes and other war supplies. On 5 July the President gave to the Army and Navy Munitions Board the task of coordinating all foreign purchases. The board established a clearance committee, whose responsibility was to gather information on all foreign orders and, after determining which orders could be filled, decide where to place the orders so that they could best promote American arms and aircraft industries. The establishment of the clearance committee did two things. First, it enabled foreign orders to be secured more quickly than ever before, since the foreign governments no longer wasted time in establishing contacts and negotiating with American producers. Second, orders were distributed to producers in a manner best calculated to build up and strengthen war industries.[93] For example, if one aircraft company had been receiving more orders than it could possibly handle and another such company had been idle because of insufficient orders, the clearance committee could send any new orders for aircraft to the second plant, thereby ensuring that it would have modern equipment and trained personnel, should an emergency arise and rapid expansion be necessary.

In the early morning hours of 1 September 1939 Germany attacked Poland, and withtin a few days all Europe was at war. Roosevelt responded, as required by the Neutrality Act, by applying an arms embargo on all the belligerents; however, he then called Congress into special session and, on 21 September, asked for an immediate repeal of the embargo provision. After six weeks of bitter debate his request was granted on 3 November, with the requirement that all sales of arms, ammunition, and implements of war had to be on a cash-and-carry basis.[94] Secretary Woodring was pleased with the repeal of the embargo, because he was becoming increasingly convinced that the neutrality legislation contained certain shortcomings; thus, as early as 17 July he had written to the House Foreign Affairs Committee that "the arms embargo provision does not actually advance the cause of neutrality and may, under some conditions, serve to involve us in war rather than to accomplish its purpose of keeping us out." Therefore, he asked for its repeal.[95]

When repeal actually came, however, it meant something different to Secretary Woodring than it did to President Roosevelt. To the former it meant that the American arms and aircraft industries could grow and expand as a result of increased foreign orders and, therefore, be better equipped to produce for the United States Army, should war come.[96] The President, on the other hand, saw repeal primarily as an opportunity to help Britain and France arm so that they could successfully meet the Nazi menace.

With the repeal of the arms embargo there came a new flood of orders from Britain and France for military aircraft and other implements of war; thus, on 7 November, Britain established a purchasing commission to facilitate the procurement of American goods. At about the same time, France set up a similar body, but after a few weeks the two groups agreed to merge to form the Anglo-French Purchasing Commission. With a single purchasing commission, Britain and France no longer found themselves bidding against each other for American war goods.[97]

By the end of November it was evident that the Clearance Committee of the Army and Navy Munitions Board could not keep up with the work imposed by the increased foreign orders. Therefore, on 6 December, Roosevelt created the President's Liaison Committee to handle all foreign orders. Remembering the reluctance with which Woodring and Johnson had accepted the French air mission the year before, the President organized the committee so that neither the Secretary nor the Assistant Secretary of War had any control over foreign sales. The President chose Secretary of the Treasury Morgenthau to serve as liaison between foreign purchasers and American producers. In this position Morgenthau had a tremendous responsibility, because he not only had to see that Britain and France received the implements of war that they so drastically needed, but he also had to see that the United States rearmament program did not suffer as a result of the foreign orders.[98] This was a difficult task, and, as will be seen in chapter 12, it was made even more difficult by increasing obstructionism on the part of the Secretary of War.

Secretary of War Woodring was vitally interested in having the United States maintain strict neutrality, because he believed that this was the only way to avoid war. He was afraid that if the country followed a partisan policy and aided the Allies, the ultimate result would be entrance into a war on their side. Therefore, Woodring did everything that he could do to see that the United States government, and especially the War Department, followed a neutral policy when dealing with all foreign governments. An examination of Woodring's actions in regard to the helium controversy, the Spanish Civil War, the March 1938 French and British air missions, and the December 1938 French air mission reveal his determination to see that all nations were treated in a fair and equal manner. He tried to make neutrality a reality.

Beginning in 1938 Woodring's desire to be entirely neutral came into conflict with the views of President Roosevelt, who made no secret of his desire to assist Britain and France. The President had come to feel that the best way to avoid war was to help the European democracies defeat Germany, so that the United States would not have to become involved. The Secretary of War, however, believed that the same ends could best be achieved by not aligning with either side. Throughout 1938 and 1939 Roosevelt and Woodring increasingly came into conflict over the issue of neutrality, but the worst was yet to come. The first six months of 1940 were to bring the controversy to a head and ultimately were to play a major role in the removal of Woodring from the secretaryship in June 1940; but before that was to transpire, Woodring was to make some additional contributions to the strengthening of the United States Army.

11

Toward an "Army in Being"

By midsummer of 1939 Secretary Woodring and his War Department advisers were generally satisfied with developments at home and abroad. Congress had just increased the strength of the Army from 165,000 to 210,000, had appropriated $110 million for "critical and essential war supplies," and had approved an operating budget in excess of $500 million—the largest amount of money ever made available to the Army during peacetime. Along with these developments the possibility of war in Europe seemed to be declining. The growing optimism in government circles over events in Europe was expressed in June by President Roosevelt when he said, "Last winter I thought the chances of war were about three to two, but now they seem to be even."[1] Because of the relaxing of world tensions and because there were no pressing problems facing him, Woodring decided to get away from Washington; therefore, on 3 August he set sail with his family on a two-week's visit to Panama. The trip was more than a vacation, for the Secretary utilized it to inspect the canal and its defense system.[2]

When Woodring departed from the United States, the international scene appeared relatively calm, but that condition soon changed. In mid August, Germany succeeded in engineering a nonaggression pact with Russia. This agreement was of great significance to Hitler, because with it he felt he could now attack Poland without fear of becoming involved in a war on two fronts. Although the official announcement of the pact did not come until 21 August, President Roosevelt and the State Department learned of its imminence on 16 August.[3]

On 17 August Acting Secretary of State Sumner Welles called Acting Secretary of War Johnson, Acting Secretary of Navy Charles Edison, and a few other officials from the State, War, and Navy departments together in order to inform them of the impending Nazi-Soviet pact. At that time, Welles told the group, "The European situation is now so bad that I think we ought to be ready for the worst."[4] Johnson immediately passed the information on to General Marshall, who ordered the General Staff to prepare a detailed plan of action to be taken when war came.[5] On 19 August, Woodring returned to Washington and assisted in the final preparation of the War Department's recommendations. A few days later he sent Roosevelt a memorandum recommending the measures that the Army felt should be taken if and when war broke out in Europe.[6]

The proposals were divided into two groups. First, there were "Immediate Action Measures," which the President could initiate without congressional action; these proposals were designed primarily to speed up procurement. In the second category were "Measures Requiring Congressional Authorization or Appropriations." Included in the latter group were recommendations that the authorized strength of the Regular Army be increased from 210,000 to 280,000 and that the strength of the National Guard be raised from 190,000 to 280,000. It was also proposed that all necessary equipment and a year's supply of munitions be provided for the Initial Protective Force and that certain "critical items" be procured to further implement the Protective Mobilization Plan. Additional aircraft and increased training for National Guard units were also requested. In presenting these proposals to the President, Woodring indicated that they were not mobilization steps but were measures necessary "to place the Regular Army and the National Guard in a condition of preparedness suitable to the present disturbed world situation."[7] Since the measures suggested were to be taken only in case of war and could be implemented only with presidential and congressional support, it was uncertain whether they would ever be carried out.

Having made the Army's desires known to the President, Woodring turned his attention to the Panama Canal. Woodring's deep interest in the canal was based on his firm conviction that it was "the vital link in our chain of national defense."[8] He believed that the canal was of such great importance because the defense of the continental United States rested on the ability of the fleet to move quickly between the Atlantic and the Pacific oceans. If the canal were to be closed, the nation's ability to defend itself would be seriously jeopardized. Therefore, he considered protection of the canal to be "of utmost importance to our national security."[9] This matter of canal security was what led Woodring to embrace the concept of hemisphere defense. He admitted that he did not visualize hemisphere defense as a Pan-American protective alliance, but as a United States defense measure. According to Woodring, "Any hostile air base established anywhere within effective striking proximity of the Panama Canal would prove a vital threat to that waterway—and, therefore, a threat to the very security of these United States."[10] Thus, he concluded that steps would have to be taken to ensure that no such air bases were established.

From the time that he had become Secretary of War, Woodring had continually stressed the importance of the canal and had urged that proper measures be taken to provide for its defense. Such efforts finally paid off, for in 1939 he was the person primarily responsible for getting Congress to appropriate $30 million for air bases, harbor defenses, and antiaircraft guns for the Canal Zone.[11] That same year Woodring achieved a hollow victory when Congress, heavily influenced by his testimony, authorized the construction of a third set of canal locks, but failed to appropriate the funds necessary for constructing them.[12]

As war approached Europe in late August 1939, Woodring became quite concerned over the safety of the canal. What he feared was not an air attack but sabotage.[13] He worried that a German, Japanese, or Italian crew might destroy a ship inside a lock and thereby block the canal. Consequently, in order to reduce the possibility of any such attempt at sabotage, Woodring began on 28 August to advise canal authorities of the make-up, by nationality, of the crews of ships about to go through the canal.[14] This led to especially close observation of those ships having crewmen from the Axis nations. Furthermore, on 29 August he directed that an Army guard be placed on every ship going through the canal. It was hoped that the presence of the military guards would discourage any attempts at sabotaging the ships while they were in the canal.[15]

At a few minutes after three o'clock on the morning of 1 September 1939, Secretary Woodring was awakened by a phone call from President Roosevelt, who informed him that Germany had just attacked Poland.[16] Within thirty minutes, Woodring and Chief of Staff Marshall were at the Secretary's office discussing what action had to be taken immediately. They first notified the Military Commander of the Canal Zone to take extra precautions to ensure the safety of the canal. Next the Commanding Generals of the nine Corps areas and the Hawaiian, Philippine, and Puerto Rican departments were advised of Germany's attack and ordered to take any necessary precautions.[17]

The days immediately following the German attack were especially hectic for Woodring. Daily trips to the White House to confer with the President, as well as numerous conferences with officials of the State, War, and Navy departments, consumed most of his time. During this period a problem that he devoted considerable attention to was the reinforcement of the canal's defenses. By 10 September, Woodring had ordered several thousand troops to supplement the fifteen thousand that were already there, and plans were made to raise the total strength to twenty-two thousand. In addition, more than thirty aircraft, all that could be spared at the time, were sent, and arrangements were made to increase the air strength from one hundred and fifty to three hundred planes as soon as possible.[18]

Increasing air and ground strength in the Canal Zone was a matter on which Woodring could take direct action; however, two other things that he wanted to do could be accomplished only by presidential order. The first thing that he wanted was to have the control of the canal transferred from the Civil Governor to the Military Commander, so that the latter could do a better job of coordinating local defense matters. Consequently, on 5 September the President, acting upon Woodring's recommendation, issued an executive order placing the military in charge of all activities in the Canal Zone.[19] Over this request there was no problem, but over Woodring's second proposal a bitter controversy developed.

In a conference with the President on 1 September, Secretary Woodring asked for authority to let the Army inspect every ship desiring to pass through the canal. The purpose of the inspection was to see that no ship was carrying explosives or other devices that could be used to destroy the canal while it was passing through the locks. Woodring's proposal was bitterly opposed by Undersecretary of State Sumner Welles, who argued that such action might be interpreted by some nations as unjustified harassment and thus might develop into a point of bitter controversy between the United States and the offended nation. Woodring answered Welles's argument by claiming that no nation would have a right to complain, since all ships, regardless of the country from which they came, would be inspected. Furthermore, he added, any protests that might be received were a small price to pay for the security that the inspections afforded the canal.[20] Woodring's arguments ultimately carried the day, and on 5 September the President issued an order granting the Army the authority to make the inspections.[21]

Defense of the Panama Canal was just one of many problems facing Woodring in September of 1939. He had hoped that once war started in Europe, the President would take action to implement the measures that the General Staff had drawn up in August; but, much to his consternation, such was not to be the case. The first setback for the War Department came on the question of increases in troops. Both Woodring and General Marshall

198

considered it essential that the authorized strength of the Regulary Army be increased by 70,000, so as to bring the total figure to 280,000. As far as the National Guard was concerned, they believed an increase from 190,000 to 280,000 was necessary.[22] The President, however, fearing public and political reaction against such large increases, was unwilling to go along with these requests. Consequently, on 8 September he proclaimed a "limited national emergency" and issued an executive order which authorized a Regular Army strength of 227,000, an increase of only 17,000. The same order provided for the National Guard to add only 45,000 men, instead of the 90,000 that the Army had asked for.[23] When Woodring privately expressed considerable disappointment over the small increases that the President had granted, Roosevelt told him that under the present conditions such increases were "all the public would be ready to accept without undue excitement." The President did, however, assure Woodring and Marshall that more troops would soon be authorized.[24]

Other steps taken by the President to meet the "limited national emergency" were just as feeble as the troop increases. A very modest $12 million was made available for the purchase of additional motor vehicles, but virtually no additional funds were made available for "critical and essential" war supplies or for additional training. The only other action taken by the President that approached the recommendations submitted in August was the provision for additional training for the National Guard.[25]

In spite of the President's refusal to provide, or even ask Congress for, anywhere near what the Army had requested, Woodring and Marshall did not give up hope, because by mid September they sensed that there was a growing sentiment in Congress for adequate defense. Their optimism was based on personal assessments as well as on reports from Maj. James McIntyre, the War Department's liaison officer with Congress. In a letter of 20 September to General Marshall, McIntyre stated that after sounding out a number of Congressmen on defense matters, he had concluded: "Now is the time to ask for *everything* the War Department needs. We will get it. Let us strike while the iron is hot."[26] With such encouragement the General Staff prepared an $850-million supplemental armament program, which embodied most of the measures that Woodring and the War Department had previously requested the President to provide in case of war in Europe, but that had not been implemented.[27]

In early October, Woodring presented the new plan to the President and asked that it be implemented immediately. Roosevelt refused, claiming that such vast military expenditures were completely out of the question. To this, Woodring replied that the nation's defense needs would have to be placed first, even if it meant violating the law by creating a financial deficit.

Then he added, "Mr. President, I would rather be impeached for providing the country with means of defense, than impeached in time of emergency for failure to make such provision."[28] In spite of such pleas, however, the President refused to go along with the $850-million program recommended by his Secretary of War and by his Chief of Staff. Finally, in late October, when Roosevelt decided to ask Congress for a supplemental appropriation for the Army, he requested only $120 million, or about 15 percent of the amount that the War Department sought.[29]

Woodring was quite upset that the President had not seen fit to ask Congress for the men and matériel that the Army considered essential in order to provide properly for the national defense. The President felt that the Army was asking for entirely too much, but Woodring considered the requests both reasonable and necessary. Woodring was not one to seek what was not needed, and he continually impressed that idea on his subordinates. During the fall of 1939 he told the General Staff, "We must not take the position of grabbing all we can just because the grabbing is good, but rather ask for what we need to make the military establishment what it should be."[30] It was apparent that the Commander in Chief and the Secretary of War had vastly different views of what the Army needed at that particular time. The War Department had presented a program for increased military readiness that it considered essential and that Woodring did not consider excessive; but in October 1939 the President was not yet ready to accept such a far-reaching program.

With no hope of getting more than $120 million in supplemental funds for the current fiscal year, Woodring, in late October, turned his attention to the Army program for fiscal year 1941. As the General Staff prepared its recommendations, Woodring adopted and began to put into effect a plan to bring about acceptance of them. Whereas the contents of the $850-million program put forth in October had been known only to War Department officials and to the President, the Secretary's new strategy was to give the new plans as much publicity as possible. Woodring felt that by letting Congress and the public know what the Army needed and how much it would cost, he would be able to stimulate interest and support for the new program.[31]

The first thing that the Secretary felt he had to do in order to sell the new program was to convince people that he was a peace-loving man who advocated strengthening the Army for defensive purposes only. Woodring went a long way toward achieving that goal when he made a speech before the National Guard Association on 27 October. In that address Woodring started off by saying, "In all sincerity and in all honesty let me tell you there is no man in public life today who is more determined than your Secretary of War that your sons and my sons shall not march forth to war!" He then went on to claim that while the security of the United States did not demand a military force larger than the peacetime strength provided by the National Defense Act, it did, "demand the maintenance of an Army in being at all times. This force must be fully, perfectly equipped and adequately trained at all times."[32]

Woodring had hoped that his statement concerning an "Army in being" would be the part of the speech that was remembered; however, it was his phrase that American "sons shall not march forth to war" that was singled out and widely publicized. The speech caused columnist Ernest Lindley to write: "For those who believe that this war in Europe is not our war and that we should keep out of it, no matter which side wins or loses, October 27 must be underlined." Lindley then proceeded to discuss the speech, after which he reported that Woodring had vowed to his friends that "no American boys will be sent to fight on European soil so long as I am Secretary of War."[33] Nationwide news coverage, along with Lindley's column on the speech of 27 October, convinced many Americans of Woodring's desire to arm strictly for defensive purposes. The publicity also did much to endear him to those individuals in Washington and throughout the country who leaned toward an isolationist policy. Although the isolationists never counted Woodring among their number and while he never considered himself one of them, there is no doubt that they shared identical views when it came to the question of American involvement in a foreign war. In fact, one of Woodring's statements, "Every man and every dollar necessary for the defense of America, but not one man, not one dollar to fight the wars of other nations," could well have served as the isolationists' creed.[34] According to Woodring, he was a noninterventionist—whose major goal was to stay out of the war in Europe—and not an isolationist.[35] Unfortunately, he was never able to satisfactorily explain the difference between the two. While such a distinction would have been difficult for anyone to explain, it was even more so for Woodring because of his making common cause with such outright isolationists as Senators Wheeler, Clark, and Nye.

Having convinced many Americans that any readiness program that he might advocate would be solely for defense, Woodring was ready to set forth the new program. By early November the Secretary of War, the Chief of Staff, and the General Staff had decided on the broad outlines of the program, but the detailed plans still had to be worked out. At that point, Woodring began to hold conferences with key members of both the House Military Affairs Committee and the Appropriations subcommittee to explain the Army's needs.[36] He recommended that the Regular Army be increased to 280,000 men, but he said that even more important than the number of troops was the need to provide them with proper training and equipment. Woodring warned the Congressmen against authorizing a large force and then failing to provide funds to supply and train it. He then went on to explain that the two objectives that the Army hoped to achieve were a completely trained and equipped Initial Protective Force, and such organization, training, and equipment as would be necessary to provide adequate hemispherical defense.[37] When several Congressmen expressed concern about the high cost of fulfilling the objectives, Woodring sharply replied, "It is time that national defense shall be determined on the basis of our needs and not on a dollar and cents basis."[38] The House members with whom the Secretary talked seemed to be impressed with his views and reasoning, and they indicated a willingness to support his upcoming requests.[39] To further enhance congressional understanding of the Army's needs, the War Department arranged for a total of eighteen members of both the Military Affairs and the Appropriations committees of the Senate and House to make a month-long inspection tour of military installations throughout the United States and the Canal Zone.[40] Most, but not all, of the Congressmen returned from the trip convinced of the need to implement the recommendations of the War Department.

The Secretary of War made the Army's objectives known not only to Congressmen but to the public as well. Throughout November and December, Woodring utilized public speeches and press interviews to expound on what the Army needed and hoped to get from the next Congress.[41] He made clear to the press his determination to have "1,000 percent perfection in training, 1,000 percent perfection in equipment, motorized and mechanized, [and] 1,000 percent in air provision," even if the cost were high.[42]

In mid November the General Staff completed detailed plans and budget requests for Army expansion in the upcoming fiscal year. After granting his approval, Woodring forwarded the recommendations to the Bureau of the Budget and the President, so that they could be utilized in preparing the annual budget message. In addition to operating expenses, the program called for vast expenditures for "critical and essential" war supplies, more arsenal and depot facilities, and additional training. The cost of the entire package was a whopping $1,500 million.[43] The new proposals were received by the President with no more enthusiasm than the supplemental program that had been recommended a month before. Again the primary objection was one of excessive cost. This time, however, Roosevelt chose not to argue the question of military expenditures with his increasingly recalcitrant Secretary of War. Instead, he turned to advisers in the Bureau of the Budget, and together they came to the conclusion that the request for critical items, arsenals, depots, and additional training was unnecessary.[44] Woodring's request for additional supplies and training had once again been rejected by the President.

In spite of this setback, Woodring still had hopes of rallying support for the program of his department. He intended to do that by utilizing one of the strongest propaganda devices at his disposal—the *Annual Report of the Secretary of War*. That document, which was released on 27 December, was short and concise. After quickly reviewing the progress made by the Army in the past several years, Woodring revealed what he considered to be the three most critical needs of the Army: First, the need to further strengthen the defenses of the Panama Canal. Second, the need for a strong Air Corps. Then he came to the third point, the one that he emphasized most: the need for proper equipment and training. In regard to the last he stressed that he was making no recommendation as to military strength, since that was a decision for Congress to make. However, he did say that all American fighting men

must be afforded complete equipment, clothing, supplies, subsistence, transportation, training, and instruction to prepare them for any eventuality presupposed by any military exigency. Whatever . . . the size of our Army . . . I must urgently insist that that force . . . be complete as to personnel, as to matériel, and that it be 100 percent efficient as to training. Our Military Establishment must be an "Army in being!"[45]

From this time on, Woodring always cited an "Army in being" as his major goal.

Woodring hoped that a favorable public reaction to his report might convince the President to change his mind and restore some of the requests made by the Army, but such a reaction did not occur. The newspapers carried accounts of the report on the back pages and failed to comment on it in their editorials.[46] The Secretary placed his final hopes in a nationwide radio broadcast that he made on 31 December. At that time he explained the proposed program for the Army, and he asked for congressional and public support for it.[47] Unfortunately, the broadcast received even less attention than his *Annual Report*. All of Woodring's efforts to create public support for the program had failed—he simply could not convince President Roosevelt of the need for additional funds. Therefore, in early January 1940, when the President presented to Congress the proposed Army budget for fiscal year 1941, he asked for only $853 million—or about 55 percent of what the War Department had requested.[48]

Roosevelt's refusal to accept the War Department's program was in all likelihood influenced by a strong nationwide sentiment that the United States should avoid involvement in the European war at all cost. Going hand in hand with that sentiment was a widespread feeling that the larger the armed forces, the more likely it was that the country would be drawn into a war. For such reasons the President feared a public reaction against large expenditures for the military.[49] Furthermore, there was considerable pressure from Republican Congressmen to hold down all government expenditures.[50] Still another factor that influenced FDR's attitudes was the conduct of the war in Europe. After Germany took Poland in late 1939, the fighting in Europe came to a virtual halt, and the war assumed a "phony" character. As the fear of the Nazi menace began to decline, so did the pressures for materially strengthening the nation's defenses; thus, Roosevelt did not feel so compelled to take action.

Regardless of the reason for the President's decision, the fact remained that he had asked Congress for only about half as much money as the Army had requested. Almost immediately, Woodring indicated that he considered the proposed budget to be inadequate, but he did so in such a way as not to sound insubordinate. On 16 January he appeared before the House Military Affairs Committee, where he discussed the strengths and weaknesses of the Army. At that time he maintained that the Army budget proposed by the President was "a wise step toward the fulfillment of our objectives"; however, he added, "It does not provide for the deficiency of some $300,000,000 worth of critical ordnance and engineer items and a smaller amount of other less critical munitions for the 3/4 million men in the Protective Mobilization Plan."[51] In late February the House opened its hearings on Army appropriations. General Marshall served as the primary spokesman for the War Department, and he did a fine job of explaining the Army's needs.[52] Unfortunately for the Army, the "phony war" had cooled the enthusiasm of a number of Congressmen who, just a few months before, had been so willing to strengthen the Army. Thus, on 4 April the House responded by cutting the President's request from $853 million to $785 million.[53] The measure was then sent to the Senate for action, but before the measure could be considered, events in Europe were to cause a radical change in congressional attitudes.

On 9 April 1940 the phony war came to an end as German troops attacked Norway and Denmark. Suddenly many Americans who had not previously shown an interest in national defense wanted to know what had to be done to provide for adequate national security. At the same time a large number of Congressmen began to ask, not how much a sound Army, Air Corps, and Navy would cost, but how soon they could be provided.[54] On 30 April the Senate, with a new sense of urgency, opened its hearings on the Army appropriations bill.

Ten days after the Senate hearings opened, Germany attacked Belgium

204

and Holland and then moved into France. With that attack, President Roosevelt, who just the day before had received a memorandum from Woodring asking for additional war matériel, decided that the time had indeed come to materially strengthen the Army.[55] After five days of hectic conferences a plan was worked out, and on 16 May the President asked Congress to grant the Army $546 million more than he had previously requested. The new funds, Roosevelt said, would be used "to procure the essential equipment of all kinds for a larger and thoroughly rounded-out Army."[56] Specifically, he asked for an increase in Regular Army strength from 227,000 to 255,000 and for the equipment and munitions required for a Protective Mobilization Force of 750,000 men.[57] At last the President had asked Congress for some of the important things that Woodring had been advocating for the past eight months.[58]

By mid May, alarm over the German advance through the Low Countries made the Senate willing to go even further than the President had suggested, and on 22 May it passed a $1,500 million Army Appropriations Bill. The House responded to the new state of affairs by scrapping its bill of 4 April and adopting the Senate version, and on 13 June the President signed the bill into law.[59] As large as the new appropriation bill had been, it was evident even before its passage that it would not be sufficient. In fact, President Roosevelt had no sooner made his defense speech on 16 May than he realized the need for even further military spending. Therefore, during the last week of May the President and General Marshall discussed the Army's additional needs and what they would cost. Throughout May and June, Woodring, for reasons to be discussed in the following chapter, was again out of favor with the President and thus played virtually no role in these crucial discussions. Consequently, during this time it was Marshall who fought the War Department's battles at the White House.[60] On 31 May, Roosevelt asked Congress for still another $700 million for the Army. Again it responded with more than he requested, this time providing $821 million.[61] This measure—which became law on 25 June—along with the June 13 measure, provided $2,300 million for the Army for fiscal year 1941. Included in these appropriations bills were the funds and the authorization to increase Army strength to 375,000 and to secure an additional 3,000 aircraft. At last the War Department had enough money to create an "Army in being"; however, Woodring never got the opportunity to make that dream become a reality, because on 19 June the President was to ask for, and receive, his resignation.

Although Woodring spent a considerable amount of time from September 1939 to June 1940 seeking more money for the Army, there were other ways in which he sought to provide increased military readiness. One matter to which he devoted considerable attention was that of the reorganization of combat units. For many years there had been talk in military circles of changing the organization of the infantry division. After the outbreak of war in Europe, Woodring decided that the long-overdue change should take place immediately. In mid September the Secretary, acting upon the recommendation of the Chief of Staff, announced that the 22,000-man "square" infantry division would be replaced by a 9,000-man "triangular" division.[62] It was felt that new weapons and mechanization would permit such a reduction in manpower without a corresponding reduction in firepower. The new divisions also offered more command flexibility, since they could be used en masse or as three separate, highly mobile combat teams. Under the new organization, three new divisions were to be formed immediately and two more in the near future. This change in the infantry division was just the beginning of a vast program of reorganization. According to the *Army and Navy Journal* of 21 October 1939, "The Army has plunged into probably the greatest peacetime reorganization in its history . . . sweeping changes are being made in nearly every arm and service."

The reorganization looked good on paper, but the Secretary of War and the Chief of Staff were anxious to see how it would really work. Therefore, in October they drafted a field-training program that called for extensive exercises at the division and corps levels.[63] Several months later, in February and March 1940, the new infantry and cavalry divisions underwent considerable field training, and in April the first corps maneuvers since 1918 were held. The following month seventy thousand men participated in the first corps-versus-corps exercises in the history of the Army. These maneuvers were valuable in that they showed the "triangular" division to be tactically sound; they also revealed a serious need for more tanks as well as antitank and antiaircraft guns at the corps level.[64] The new organization had many shortcomings, some of which would take years to overcome, but at least Secretary Woodring had played a major role in getting this badly needed reorganization under way.

Another problem that Woodring devoted considerable time to was that of eliminating overage and physically unfit officers. He knew that many older officers would be physically unable to carry out their responsibilities should they ever be placed in a combat situation. This problem stemmed from promotion stagnation, which became especially acute in the thirties when a large number of officers who had entered the Army during World War I could not be promoted because there were no openings at the next higher rank. Since promotion was strictly on a seniority basis, it meant that an officer could not be advanced to the next rank until all others with more time in grade had been promoted. Consequently, it was not unusual to find a forty- or forty-five-year-old captain or a thirty- or thirty-five-year-old first lieutenant. When this was the case, it frequently was not because the man was incapable or inefficient but because there simply was no need for more majors or captains. By the late thirties the prospect of remaining in the same grade indefinitely was seriously affecting the morale of many young officers.[65]

To overcome the problem of officers who were overage or unfit, Secretary Woodring, in April 1939, initiated a "vitalization" program. The first part of the program centered on the "Woodring Age-in-Grade Plan." This scheme, which was originated and developed by the Secretary, called for automatic promotion of an officer after a specific number of years in grade.[66] The plan was rejected by Congress, because it was set up in such a way that many able-bodied officers under sixty years of age would be forced to retire.[67] After war broke out in the fall of 1939, Woodring urged that his plan be reconsidered, since, he argued, it was more important than ever that younger officers find their way into the upper ranks. When opposition appeared again, he agreed to a new plan, which provided promotion based on total length of service and grade and did not force the retirement of so many officers. This measure was ultimately passed on 13 June 1940.[68]

The purpose of the second part of Woodring's "vitalization" program was to eliminate those officers who were physically unfit. This was accomplished by administrative action in the spring of 1939. Rigorous physical exams were given to all those in the grades of captain and above, and those who failed the exams were then forced to resign or retire.[69] The "vitalization" program actually had little effect on the Army, because the rapid expansion that began in mid 1940 eliminated the problem of promotion stagnation, and the physically unfit were placed in positions where they could still function. What the Secretary's program did was to pave the way for the next step in promotions reform—a selective advancement system that promoted a man on merit rather than seniority. Such a system was ultimately approved by Congress and was instituted in September 1940, several months after Woodring had left Washington.[70]

In June of 1940 Harry Woodring was forced to resign as Secretary of War, thus ending seven years of continual effort to provide increased military readiness. Much progress had been made under his leadership, first as Assistant Secretary and then as Secretary, and the Army's future looked brighter than ever. Although the strength of the Regular Army was only 257,000, authorizations and appropriations had just been received to raise that figure to 375,000. Funds had also been provided for "critical and essential" items for a 750,000-man Protective Mobilization Force, and provision had been made to secure 3,000 planes above and beyond the 5,500 already on hand or on order. The reorganization of combat units and a more effective training program were also reasons for optimism.[71] It appeared as if Woodring's "Army in being" could, and soon would, become a reality.

The future looked bright, but what was the present status of the Army? How adequate, how prepared, how ready was the United States Army to defend the country when Woodring left office in June of 1940? Perhaps that question could best be answered by Chief of Staff Marshall, who, in describing the state of the armed forces, wrote: "As an army we were ineffective. Our equipment, modern at the conclusion of the World War, was now, in a large measure, obsolescent. In fact, during the postwar period, continuous paring of appropriations had reduced the Army virtually to the status of that of a third-rate power."[72] Several other observers shared the same view. In late May, J. G. Norris, the military editor of the *Washington Post*, reported that recent testimony of ranking War Department officials revealed the well-known fact that the Army "needed many war planes and pilots . . . [and] arms and equipment were sadly lacking in many categories."[73] At about the same time another Washington reporter wrote: "A gloomy view is taken here of our readiness for war. Our Army is so small, so badly equipped that one military leader asserts, 'I would even go to Munich to get a year or more to prepare.' "[74] There seems to be no doubt that in June 1940 the United States Army was far from being an effective military force.

Secretary of War Woodring had labored long and hard to receive the funds necessary to make his "Army in being" a reality, but no sooner had the money for it been secured than he was forced to leave his post. The large appropriations needed to materially strengthen the Army had been sought by Woodring for several years, and he had intensified those efforts after the outbreak of war in Europe. However, prior to the spring of 1940 his pleas to the President, Congress, and the public had gone largely unheeded. Finally, the German attacks on Norway, Denmark, the Low Countries, and France did what Woodring had been unable to do: they convinced the President and Congress that there should be no further delay in strengthening the Army. While it is true that the Army was quite weak in mid 1940, it was not because Woodring had not made every effort to improve it. If the President had followed the advice of his Secretary of War in the fall of 1939, the country could have been well on its way to having an "Army in being" in June of 1940; instead, it was just beginning.

12

Obstructionism Brings Dismissal

When Britain and France declared war on Germany after the latter's attack on Poland in September 1939, President Roosevelt issued a proclamation of neutrality and then, as required by the Neutrality Act of 1937, imposed a mandatory arms embargo on all belligerents. A few weeks later the President, who made no secret of his sympathy for the democratic nations and his desire to aid them, called Congress into special session and asked that legislation be passed that would permit the United States to sell implements of war "abroad." Although he said "abroad," it was clear that he meant to Britain and France. On 3 November, after six weeks of bitter debate, Congress scrapped the mandatory embargo provision of the Neutrality Act and replaced it with a "cash and carry" policy. The United States could now legally make war goods available to the Allies. Unfortunately, however, the President and his Secretary of War had vastly different views as to the extent of the aid that should be made available, and, as a consequence, friction increased between the two men.

As early as January 1939 the President, who felt that the best policy was to help provide Britain and France with the supplies that they needed to defeat Germany, made it quite clear that he was willing to sell the Allies anything that they requested as long as it did not violate the neutrality legislation.[1] By late December of that same year he had gone much further, for he was then so determined to fulfill their requests for war supplies that he was willing to do so even if it meant temporarily denying such goods to the United States Army.[2] Since the President considered Britain and France to be America's first line of defense, his first priority became aid to the Allies, and his second became strengthening the forces of the United States. Secretary Woodring, on the other hand, was opposed to "frittering away" vital war materials by sending them abroad. He felt that the American military machine should be strengthened first, and then aid could be extended to the Allies.[3] He was worried about the disastrous consequences should the United States impair its military strength by sending war supplies to Britain and France and should those nations then fall to Germany.[4] Consequently, he continually advocated that the President reverse his priorities and place the defense needs of the United States first.

It must be kept in mind that in 1940 there was no way of telling which policy—aiding the allies or strengthening America's defenses—could best provide for the nation's security. Roosevelt bet on his "Allies First" policy, and time was to prove that he made the proper decision; thus, Roosevelt became a hero. Woodring, however, advocated a "United States First" policy, and time was to indicate that such a policy might have been fatal to the democratic cause throughout the world. While it is not the place of the historian to speculate as to what might have happened, it is indeed interesting to consider what the present American attitude toward Roosevelt and Woodring might be had Britain been unable to hold out against Germany in 1940.

The story of Woodring's activities in the first six months of 1940 revolves around his disagreements with the President over the questions of supplying American aircraft to the Allies and of turning military surpluses over to them. The disagreements between the two men became so great that Woodring not only failed to cooperate with Roosevelt, but even began to obstruct his policies. As the Roosevelt-Woodring clashes increased in frequency and intensity, the President turned more and more to Secretary of the Treasury Henry Morgenthau to implement his policy of aiding the Allies.

After the 3 November 1939 change in the Neutrality Act had cleared the way for the procurement of American-produced implements of war, both Britain and France set up purchasing commissions in the United States. When it soon became apparent that the two nations were bidding against each other for the limited supply of war materials, they decided to merge their operations. Thus, on 6 December 1939 the Joint Anglo-French Purchasing Commission was established. On that same day the President, upon the recommendation of Secretary Morgenthau, established a special liaison committee, whose function was to coordinate the placing of foreign orders

210

with American firms in such a way that they would not interfere with the United States rearmament program. The committee, which reported directly to the President, was composed of three individuals. The Treasury Department's Director of Procurement was chairman, and the other members were the Quartermaster General of the Army and the Paymaster General of the Navy.[5] The President had deliberately kept Woodring and Johnson off the committee and had made an official of the Treasury Department chairman, so that Morgenthau, who firmly believed in aiding the Allies, would be able to supervise its activities.[6]

Woodring immediately objected to the establishment of the President's liaison committee, because he disapproved of any foreign buying that conflicted, or might possibly conflict, with Army procurement.[7] He also indicated to the President that he felt that the Army and Navy Munitions Board, not the liaison committee, should decide what items should be sold abroad. Assistant Secretary Johnson expressed the same view to the Commander in Chief, who defended his action on the grounds that the Procurement Division of the Treasury was already experienced in large-scale purchases and that over half of the foreign purchases were of nonmilitary, rather than military, items.[8]

The most critical needs of the Allies in the winter of 1939-1940 were military aircraft and aircraft engines. In late December, Arthur Purvis, head of the Anglo-French purchasing commission, informed Morgenthau that a large order would be placed in several months, but that in the meantime the Allies wanted to secure as many military aircraft as they could.[9] Officials of the War and Treasury departments realized that it would be extremely difficult to fill a large order, because production facilities were so limited and because it would take a minimum of nine months to complete the necessary expansion of war plants. Since the Allies wanted the planes as soon as possible and since American manufacturers could not meet the demands of the Army Air Corps and still fill the foreign orders, some sort of priority system had to be worked out. It was over that priority system that President Roosevelt and Secretary Morgenthau, on the one hand, and Secretary Woodring, on the other, were to come into bitter conflict.

In early January of 1940 Morgenthau, who was by then virtually the coordinator of the armament business and the foreign sale of military equipment, approached the President concerning the problems of aircraft production. Since American aircraft factories could not immediately provide Britain and France with the number of planes they desired, Morgenthau believed that every second one of the Army and Navy planes that were currently under production should be given to them. The President was unwilling to accept such a proposal, but he did agree to give the French twenty-five of the first eighty-one P-40's that the Army was scheduled to receive prior to July. Roosevelt also expressed a desire to have an aircraft industry that could quickly expand its production to thirty thousand planes per year, and he and Morgenthau both agreed that Allied purchases could and should be utilized in order to bring about such an expansion.[10]

On 17 January, President Roosevelt called Secretaries Woodring and Morgenthau and Generals Marshall and Arnold to the White House, where he "emphasized the necessity for expediting delivery [of aircraft] to the Allies."[11] The President's instructions were not in line with the ideas of War Department officials who had been giving serious consideration to the difficulties that the American aircraft industry would have in filling domestic and foreign orders. As early as 12 January, General Arnold had written to Secretary Woodring concerning British and French proposals "to set aside work now being done on Army airplanes to expedite foreign deliveries." Arnold vigorously opposed such a course for three reasons: first, it would delay the completion of the Air Corps Expansion Program; second, foreign nations would receive airplanes superior to those of the United States Air Corps; third, such action would antagonize and cause difficulty with Congress.[12] Secretary Woodring was impressed with Arnold's arguments, especially the first two, and he was to use them repeatedly as reasons for opposing a policy whereby planes produced for the Air Corps would be made available to the Allies.

The President's instructions of 17 January had little impact in late January and February, because the plane requests of the Allies were relatively small. Then in early March the Anglo-French purchasing commission presented the liaison committee with the large aircraft order it had previously promised to make. It called for ten thousand planes and twenty thousand engines to be supplied by July 1941.[13] The Allies naturally wanted the very latest planes that could be produced, and Secretary Morgenthau supported them on that matter. Therefore, Morgenthau and Purvis requested that the War Department release the very latest in aircraft, aircraft engines, and superchargers. Secretary Woodring, upon the advice of his military aides, especially General Arnold, refused to release the items, because they were still classified as "secret" and were therefore not eligible to be released. Some of the items requested were not yet in production, and some were in production but had not yet been turned over to the Army.[14]

Woodring had no intention of releasing the items or of changing the release policy so that they could be turned over. Twice in 1939 he had consented to changes in the policy on the release of aircraft. In the spring he had agreed to reduce the time limit for release from one year to six months after delivery of the second production plane. Then in the fall he had approved a new policy, which provided that "military aircraft will not be released for export until they have become identified as production articles." The 1939 changes made it easier for the Allies to receive more modern planes, but they still ensured that foreign delivery of one type of aircraft or aircraft engine would not be permitted until a later type was actually being manufactured for the Air Corps.[15] Now, in March of 1940, Woodring was being asked to release to foreign nations airplanes that were more modern than those possessed by his own Army—and that he was unwilling to do.

On 11 March word of the sale of twenty-five new P-40's to France and of the War Department's opposition to releasing them appeared in Washington newspapers. Congressman Dow Harter, head of the Aviation Subcommittee of the Military Affairs Committee, immediately called for an inquiry into the administration's policy on releasing planes for export. According to Harter, the purpose of the hearing would be to determine whether purchases by the Allies were hampering the United States Army's procurement of aircraft.[16] Chairman Andrew May of the Military Affairs Committee decided that the hearing would be conducted before the entire group, not just the Aviation Subcommittee. Woodring was summoned to testify on the fourteenth, but he requested and was granted a delay until the twentieth. While the House was preparing for its inquiry, Senator Robert La Follette, Jr., was calling for the Senate to do the same.[17]

On 13 March the President, angered by public disclosure of conflict between himself and the War Department over release of military aircraft, called Secretary Woodring, Assistant Secretary Johnson, Secretary Morgenthau, General Arnold, and the newly appointed Secretary of the Navy, Charles Edison, to the White House.[18] At that time Roosevelt informed those who were present of the need for "cooperation and coordination concerning foreign sales of aircraft and accessories," and he made it quite clear that he expected no more resistance from the War Department.[19] He also advised that care be used in answering questions before congressional committees, adding that he had not been pleased with the way in which War Department witnesses had testified in the past. The President then turned to Arnold and said that there were places where officers who did not "play ball" might be sent—like Guam. After the meeting, General Arnold wrote, "It was a party at which apparently the Secretary of War and the Chief of Air Corps were to be spanked and were spanked."[20] The meeting was pleasing to Secretary Morgenthau, who was getting tired of the Army's opposition to aiding the Allies.[21]

The President had emphasized that he wanted to make it easier for Britain and France to get American-built planes. Therefore, it was necessary that the War Department come up with a new policy on the release of aircraft. After the White House meeting on 13 March, Woodring asked Generals Marshall and Arnold to develop a plan that would satisfy the President but not endanger the nation's security. Five days later, on 18 March, they presented their recommendations. What they submitted was a list of all planes currently being produced for the Army, and beside each item on the list there was an indication of whether it should be retained or released. The planes approved for foreign sale were selected in such a way as to ensure that the United States Air Corps would always retain a better model.[22] Woodring approved the plan in principle and asked that it be placed in a form suitable for presentation to the President. This had to be done immediately, because Woodring had to get Roosevelt's approval prior to his appearance before the House committee on the twentieth.

On the morning of 19 March, Secretary Woodring, General Marshall, and General Arnold met in the Chief of Staff's office to discuss the release policy that they would recommend to the President. During the course of that conversation a new idea emerged, which was incorporated into the proposed plan. General Marshall indicated that he felt that the Army Air Corps had more to gain than to lose if it permitted release of its reserve planes to the Allies and subsequently received, in lieu of those craft, later models with improved performance capabilities; this process was known as a "change order" or a "delayed order."[23] Woodring agreed to such a delay in the delivery of reserve aircraft, but not to delays in the delivery of operational aircraft or a small maintenance reserve. At the close of the meeting, Woodring summarized the decisions agreed upon:

1. No military secret or secret development should be divulged or released to any foreign purchaser of military aircraft.
2. No American military plane would be released for foreign sale unless or until a superior plane was actually in the process of manufacture for the War Department.
3. The War Department would negotiate change orders on current contracts so it could obtain refined models.
4. No delivery delays would be tolerated in operating requirement needs or in a 15% maintenance reserve, but delivery delays would be accepted on aircraft scheduled for delivery over and above operational requirements plus a 15% maintenance reserve.[24]

Since the last two provisions had just come out of the present meeting, Secretary Woodring asked that the conferees, plus Assistant Secretary Johnson, meet at his office at seven o'clock that evening to make a final review of the proposed policy before he took it to the President for his approval.

That evening, while Woodring and the others were on their way to the meeting, they heard radio newscasts reporting that at an afternoon news conference President Roosevelt had said that every type of American-built military plane would be released for foreign sale. The President's alleged statement caused considerable concern to the conferees, because it indicated a policy that was quite different from the one that they were about to recommend.[25] In order to determine exactly what the President had said, both a complete transcript of the news conference and a ticker-tape press account were secured. Examination of those documents revealed that the radio reports had been somewhat misleading. The matter of foreign sales had come up at the news conference when a reporter had asked the President to clarify the administration's policy on releasing airplanes and armaments for foreign sale. Roosevelt began by indicating that each case would have to be decided individually. He went on, however, to affirm the vital need for expanding the nation's capacity for producing aircraft, and he added that this could be achieved only with the help of foreign orders. The President also had stated that as far as he was concerned, an airplane was no longer a military secret once it was under production.[26] The implication of such a statement was that he would therefore have no objection to releasing any "secret" aircraft. Roosevelt's statements, plus the fact that he made no mention of delayed orders, seemed to indicate that he intended to release the latest military planes with no strings attached.[27]

While those present at the evening meeting were discussing what the President had really meant by his statements, Secretary Woodring received a phone call from Roosevelt. The Chief Executive, who had been informed of the move to get the stenographic notes of the press conference, told Woodring that his afternoon statements outlined quite clearly the policy that he intended to follow. Next he stated that if there was anyone who did not go along with his program, he would take "drastic" action. Then he issued a warning that he would consider any individual who appeared before the House Military Affairs Committee on the question of release policy to be on trial as far as any statements he might make. Before Woodring could question his superior or explain the new policy that was being prepared, the President hung up.[28] Woodring then informed the group of the President's decision and voiced his dissatisfaction with it. General Arnold, although he was disappointed, stated that since the Commander in Chief had made his decision, there was nothing to do but implement it. For the next three hours, Woodring, Johnson, Marshall, and Arnold argued, debated, and discussed a new release policy. By 1:00 A.M. they had come to agree on a plan that would provide for the release of the latest planes but would assure the Air Corps of receiving improved models at a later date.[29] Before the meeting adjourned, Woodring called Chairman May and asked if his appearance

215

before the House Military Affairs Committee, scheduled for later that morning, could be postponed until 27 March. May consented to Woodring's request.[30]

On the following day, General Marshall presented the new plan to the President. Roosevelt gave it his tentative approval and told Marshall to place it in final form. On 25 March, Woodring, Johnson, and Marshall took a prepared statement on export policy to the White House and got the President's final acceptance of it.[31] Woodring and his military advisers were not pleased with the new policy, but it was what the President wanted, and there was nothing that they could do about it. One contemporary report described the Army's action on the release matter quite well when it said, "Highest War Department officials swung around to the President's view on selling latest model airplanes to the Allies when they discovered that on that issue Mr. Roosevelt's mind was set and determined."[32]

In late March the Secretary of War set forth to defend the new release policy before the House and the Senate Military Affairs committees. In appearing before the House group on 27 March, Woodring explained that the new policy would let the War Department defer the delivery of planes already contracted so that manufacturers could fill their foreign orders. In return, the producers had to agree to deliver a more refined model to the Army at a later date. Such a system would thereby provide aircraft for the Allies, assure the Army Air Corps of receiving planes that incorporated the latest developments, and provide for the expansion of the American aircraft industry. Another provision of the policy was that foreign nations receiving the planes were required to furnish the Army with complete information on the combat performance of the American-built planes so that their shortcomings could be corrected. In the questioning that followed, Woodring assured the committee that the new scheme would not interfere with the procurement of planes needed for the operational requirements of the Air Corps. He also claimed that no secret devices had been or would be released.[33]

In response to further questions concerning his acceptance of the new policy, Woodring denied published reports that he had been opposed to it. He claimed that the entire matter had been worked out with his advisers and without coercion. At that point, Congressman Arthur Anderson asked, "Is it true that Secretary Morgenthau was responsible for this program?" Before Woodring could reply, Chairman May intervened by rapping his gavel and saying that he did not consider the question appropriate. At May's request, Anderson withdrew the question.[34] Thus Woodring was saved from what could have been a very embarrassing situation. After Secretary Woodring's appearance, Assistant Secretary Johnson and Chief of Staff

Marshall further explained and defended the new plan. When the hearing ended, Chairman May issued a public statement in which he said that the testimony clarified all questions concerning the new policy on the release of aircraft and that the Military Affairs Committee considered it to be quite satisfactory.[35]

On the following day, Woodring appeared before the Senate Military Affairs Committee, where he said essentially the same things that he had said the day before. One new matter arose when he was asked whether the new planes would be released only to Britain and France or to any nation. To this, Woodring replied, "Any Government has the right to come here and negotiate and purchase on a cash-and-carry basis. . . . [The War Department] will handle any country and every country on the same basis."[36] In answering the question affirmatively, Woodring was saying the same thing that the President had said several days before;[37] however, while Woodring's answer was probably made in good faith, Roosevelt's sincerity would be open to question. When Woodring had finished testifying, Johnson and Marshall also spoke in favor of the new policy. At the close of the session the committee, by the narrow margin of 5-to-4, rejected a proposal to conduct a formal investigation into the sale of military aircraft to Britain and France.[38]

In spite of Secretary Woodring's attempts to give the impression that the new release policy had not been a source of conflict, the press was well aware of what had been going on. Typical of accounts appearing in news magazines was that of the *United States News*, which said: "[The] breach between President Roosevelt and his War Secretary is widening near to the breaking point. Argument over the question of supplying latest model planes to the Allies really is more bitter inside than has appeared on the surface."[39] Newspaper columnists Drew Pearson and Robert Allen wrote: "Over the vital question of selling latest types of Army airplanes to the Allies, Secretary of War Woodring was in such disagreement with his Chief that there was a near break in the Cabinet."[40] Publisher John C. O'Laughlin, who was in frequent contact with Woodring during this period, reported to General Pershing that a break had been avoided only because Woodring "surrendered, and he did so in order to hold on to his job."[41]

At his meeting with the President on 25 March, Woodring had agreed to accept the new release policy, and in the days that followed, he even defended it before the House and the Senate Military Affairs committees. However, he soon made it apparent that he did not intend to carry it out. On 22 March, Woodring had refused to release for export a General Electric supercharger that was currently being produced for the Army. Even after the new policy had been declared to be in effect, he continued to deny its release. He also refused to sign the orders to release the latest American aircraft for export to the Allies. Assistant Secretary Johnson urged Woodring to sign the releases, but the Secretary refused to do so.[42]

On 9 April, Secretary Morgenthau called Johnson and informed him that the Anglo-French purchasing commission was anxious to complete aircraft contracts with the American manufacturers, but that they could not do so until the War Department signed the necessary releases for the aircraft. Johnson reported that there was nothing he could do. "I'm having all kinds of trouble with Woodring," he said. He then informed Morgenthau that Woodring not only refused to sign the releases, but that he was also threatening to reappear before the House Military Affairs Committee and tell them that he had opposed the new release policy. To this Morgenthau replied, "When the President gives me a job to do, if anybody puts any obstacles in my way I tell the President about it." Morgenthau then stated that he was going to see Roosevelt on the matter, and he suggested that Johnson do the same. Later that day both men informed the President of the Secretary of War's refusal to cooperate. Roosevelt immediately called Woodring and made it abundantly clear that he expected the planes to be released at once. Consequently, the Secretary yielded to the pressure and released the planes. On the next day, arrangements were made to sell to the Allies twenty-four hundred of the latest fighters and twenty-two hundred new bombers. Several weeks later, American manufacturers began to turn over to Britain and France planes that had been built for the United States Air Corps.[43]

Secretary of War Woodring's efforts to keep the latest military aircraft in the hands of the Air Corps, rather than turn them over to the Allies, were paralleled by attempts to keep from selling or turning over surplus military equipment to belligerent nations. On both matters Woodring was motivated by a desire to retain for the United States Army all military items that he considered to be necessary for defense of the nation.

One of many problems facing the War Department was that of disposing of "surplus military property." Prior to 1940 the problem was minimal, because the limited Army budgets created problems of scarcity of supplies, not problems of surplus. Occasionally, however, an Army inventory would reveal that certain supplies and equipment, including arms and ammunition, were in excess of Army needs and were therefore "surplus." When such a situation occurred, it was not unusual for the surplus supplies to be sold to a foreign government. The sales were usually made to Latin American nations; this was done with the encouragement and expressed approval of President Roosevelt, who saw the sales as a way of further implementing his policy of hemisphere defense.[44] While Woodring formally approved of such disposition of surplus, he did so reluctantly, because he felt that the nation was so short of military equipment and supplies that none of it could or should be disposed of. He believed that if war ever came to the United States, every rifle, every mortar, and every artillery piece, regardless of age, would be of value.[45]

After the Soviet Union had attacked Finland in November 1939, the Finnish government requested permission to purchase arms, ammunition, and other implements of war from American producers on a credit basis; however, on 7 February the President decided not to extend such assistance. Although Roosevelt had originally favored aid to the Finns, he yielded to the pressure of Secretary of State Hull and Secretary Woodring, who opposed such a move. Hull did not want to extend direct aid, because he feared the reaction of congressional isolationists and believed that such action might endanger United States neutrality. Woodring's opposition was based primarily on the belief that no military supplies could be diverted abroad without further weakening the nation's defenses.

Following the President's decision to deny Finland the funds to purchase war supplies from American manufacturers, consideration was given to selling, or otherwise providing, surplus war materials to that nation. On 9 February, Roosevelt conferred with Secretaries Hull, Woodring, and Edison on the feasibility of relinquishing surplus war materials to neutral nations so they could in turn sell the items to Finland. Woodring opposed the plan on two counts. First, he claimed that the Army had no surplus war goods to dispose of. Second, since the purpose of the plan was to supply war goods to Finland, it would be an unneutral act which could ultimately lead to involvement in a foreign conflict. In spite of Woodring's pleas, the President decided that the War Department would sell surplus artillery to Sweden, which would in turn sell it to Finland. The President also directed the Secretary of War to determine what other items of military surplus could ultimately be made available. Within a few days, negotiations for the sale of artillery were undertaken, but Finland fell to the Russians before the transaction could be completed.[46]

As a result of the meeting of 9 February, Secretary Woodring asked General Marshall to have G-4, the Supply Division of the General Staff, make a survey to determine what and how much ordnance equipment could truly be declared surplus, so that it could be turned over to foreign governments. On 9 March the survey was completed, and two days later, Woodring was asked to approve the sale price of a list of surplus ordnance materials which would be eligible for sale to foreign governments. Included on the list were 100,000 Enfield rifles, 11,000 machine guns, 237 three-inch mortars, 300 75-mm. guns, and a handful of other weapons in lesser quantities.[47] All of the items listed had been Army property since World War I. Woodring followed the President's explicit instructions and approved the disposition to foreign nations; however, he did so very reluctantly, in part because he believed that the material could not be spared and in part because he felt that the items might not go to neutral nations. His criticism of the means that were being used in disposing of the goods is indicated by the following comment, which he appended to the memorandum asking for his approval of the transaction:

I approve the above paper as a method of carrying out the policy determined by higher authority for the sale of surplus property. But—I continue, as for several years, to absolutely disapprove of the sale of surplus United States Army property. I insist, regardless of any higher authority direction, that if Army surplus property is to be sold, it only be sold by this government to another neutral government.[48]

Woodring's fear that United States Army surplus property might go to belligerent rather than to neutral nations led him to issue a departmental order on 15 March which provided that "no surplus arms or ammunition will be disposed of to any state or foreign government engaged in hostilities." Before taking this action, Woodring had consulted with Secretary of State Hull, who approved of Woodring's action.[49] Sooner or later that order was certain to cause some difficulty, because its provisions were in direct conflict with President Roosevelt's policy of extending aid to nations that were trying to halt Nazi aggression. During the first two months that the order was in effect it caused no problems, because the question of disposing of surplus property did not arise. No problem appeared, because in April, Germany attacked and took control of Norway and Denmark so quickly that the Roosevelt administration did not have time to consider making supplies available to these countries. Consequently, in early May the surplus property that Woodring had released for foreign sale on 11 March was still in Army warehouses.

Germany attacked the Low Countries on 10 May, and in the next few days the rapid advance of Hitler's Army seemed to endanger all of Europe. On the fifteenth of the month, Britain's new Prime Minister, Winston Churchill, sent a message to Roosevelt, telling him of the British determination to meet the Nazi challenge and asking the President to "help us with everything short of actually engaging armed forces." Specifically, Churchill asked for forty or fifty "older destroyers," several hundred modern aircraft, antiaircraft equipment, and ammunition.[50]

Upon receiving Churchill's message, Roosevelt consulted with Secretary Morgenthau on the feasibility of filling the request. Roosevelt then directed

Morgenthau to see what he could get the Army to release. Morgenthau first asked the Chief of Staff and the Chief of the Air Corps if there would be any objection to the immediate release of one hundred pursuit planes that were about to be delivered. General Arnold vigorously opposed such a move, claiming that it would set the development of the United States pursuit squadrons back six months.[51] Marshall concurred with Arnold, and on 17 May he wrote to Morgenthau: "I do not think we can afford to submit ourselves to the delay and consequences involved in accommodating the British Government in this particular manner."[52] In spite of this indication that the Army desired to hold on to everything it could, Roosevelt, on 18 May, sent an optimistic message to Churchill. After informing the British Prime Minister that turning over the destroyers was temporarily out of the question, because it would require congressional approval, the President pledged to "facilitate to the utmost the Allied Governments obtaining the latest types of United States aircraft, anti-aircraft equipment, ammunition, and steel."[53] Roosevelt's willingness to assist the Allies soon led to additional requests for small arms and ammunition, as well as for iron and aluminum.

In his efforts to carry out the President's request to see what the War Department could turn over to the Allies, Morgenthau dealt almost exclusively with General Marshall, rather than with Woodring. This was not only because of the personal dislike that Woodring and Morgenthau had for each other, but it was also because of Woodring's increasing tendency to obstruct the President's policy of actively aiding the Allies.[54] In his desperate search for more war goods, Morgenthau, on 17 May, asked General Marshall if he would conduct a new survey to determine what ordnance materials might be released as surplus without endangering the national defense. Although the last such study had been completed less than three months before, a new one was undertaken. On 22 May the survey had been completed, and a list of surplus items from World War I was turned over to the Chief of Staff. The new report contained many items that had not been included on the surplus list of 9 March, and the quantities on the newer one were much larger.[55] Major discrepancies between the two lists can be seen from the following comparison:

Item	9 March 1940 List	22 May 1940 List
Enfield Rifles	100,000	500,000
.30-caliber ammunition	0	100,000,000 rounds
machine guns and automatic rifles	11,000	35,000
75-mm. guns	300	500
3-inch mortars	237	500

The greatly expanded list of 22 May revealed an attempt on the part of the Army to meet the President's demands to assist the Allies by all means short of war.

On the afternoon of 22 May, General Marshall took the new list of surplus items to the President. He explained that the supplies were available for transfer to the Allies but that the decision on whether or not to make the transfer was up to the President. After expressing approval about the type and quantity of items on the list, Roosevelt directed Marshall to consult with Undersecretary of State Sumner Welles to see if a way could be found to legally turn the material over the Allies.[56]

While efforts were being made to supply critical war items to Britain and France, Woodring continued to maintain that surplus materials could not be turned over to the Allies because they were at war; thus, to aid them in the proposed manner was a violation of the policy of the War Department. He believed it was one thing to permit American industries to manufacture goods and sell them to the Allies, but it was quite another to provide them with war materials that were currently, or had been previously, owned by the United States government.[57] On 23 May, Marshall discussed the transfer of the surplus materials with Welles, who, much to his own dismay, was forced to agree with Woodring's view that under existing legislation the transfer would be impossible.[58] Welles did, however, refer the problem to legal officers in the State Department, and Marshall also asked G-4 to seek a solution to the dilemma.

In an attempt to find a legal means by which the surplus property could be turned over to the Allies, officials in the War and State departments turned to post–World War I legislation governing the sale and disposition of surplus military property and deteriorated ammunition. On 27 May 1940 Gen. Richard C. Moore, the Assistant Chief of Staff, G-4, gave the opinion that the surplus property could be disposed of "in any way that the Secretary of War may deem expedient."[59] The next day the legal opinion of the State Department was set forth by counsel Green Heckworth. He maintained that Army surplus property that was exchanged as part payment for new equipment could be resold by the manufacturers to a belligerent without invloving the neutrality of the United States.[60] This view was further strengthened on 29 May, when Attorney General Robert Jackson informally expressed his agreement with Heckworth's conclusion.[61] These legal opinions seemed to open the way for the War Department to turn in or sell surplus war matériel to a private manufacturer, who could in turn sell it to the Allies. When Welles informed the President of these legal opinions, which would permit disposition of the surplus property to Britain and France, Roosevelt told him to see that the War Department proceeded with the transfer immediately.[62] There remained, however, one obstacle to the transaction—Secretary Woodring.

When Welles informed Woodring of the President's request to turn in the surplus matériel to the manufacturer, Woodring was unwilling to go along with the request. In previously disposing of surplus matériel, Secretary Woodring had always adhered to a ruling by the Comptroller General, which provided that before surplus items could be sold or turned in as part payment on new purchases, they had to first be publicly advertised, and if the amount of the bid was greater than the exchange value, the items had to be sold for cash.[63] Roosevelt, Morgenthau, and Welles opposed such a procedure in the present case, because it was a lengthy process, usually taking several months, and the Allies needed the goods immediately. Furthermore, the three men were antagonized by Woodring's actions, which they saw as just one more attempt to obstruct a policy that he did not favor.

At a meeting of 31 May, Woodring discussed the proposed transfer with Roosevelt. The Secretary informed the President that he had arranged to have inserted into legislation currently under consideration an amendment enabling him to exchange surplus property without previously obtaining bids; but until such legislation was enacted or until the Attorney General issued a formal ruling making it advisable for him to do otherwise, he would continue to proceed as he had in the past. The President, who already knew the Attorney General's view on the matter, agreed to go along with the longstanding policy until a formal opinion could be given by the Justice Department.[64]

That opinion was set forth on 3 June by Acting Attorney General Francis Biddle. His conclusion was: "The provision that such supplies may be sold upon 'such terms as may be deemed best' undoubtedly gives the Secretary of War power to sell without advertisement."[65] After reading the opinion, Woodring agreed to the transfer, the details of which were left to General Marshall.[66] On the following day, Marshall met with Arthur Purvis to determine just what and how much of the surplus goods the Allies desired. After examining Marshall's list (that of 22 May), which included every ordnance item that G-4 had declared to be surplus, Purvis announced that he wanted "the whole damned lot." The Chief of Staff, having anticipated such a request, had already sent orders to arsenals and depots throughout the country, instructing them to pack the equipment and send it to New Jersey for shipment overseas.[67]

On 4 June, Gen. Charles Wesson, Chief of Ordnance, went to see Edward R. Stettinius, Chairman of the Board of United States Steel Corporation. Wesson asked Stettinius, who a few days before had been appointed by the President to serve on the National Defense Advisory Commission, if his corporation would serve as a middleman in the transfer of goods from the War Department to the Allies. Stettinius replied that he could not make such a decision, because his resignation from U.S. Steel was to take effect that very afternoon, but he added that he was almost certain that his successor, Irving Olds, would go along with the idea. After receiving board approval, Olds agreed; and negotiations were undertaken between the War Department and United States Steel Export Company, a subsidiary of United States Steel Corporation. The details were soon worked out, and on 11 June, officials of the Export Company met with Woodring and signed the contracts, which sold all the surplus property on the list of 22 May for $37,619,556. Five minutes later the officials from the Export Company met with representatives of the Anglo-French purchasing commission and sold them the matériel for the same amount that they had just paid for it.[68] The surplus goods then belonged to Britain and France, and within a few days they were on their way to those countries. Before the goods left the United States, Woodring prepared a memorandum for the President in which he requested retention of the 500 75-mm. guns that had been turned over, but for some unknown reason the memo was never sent.[69]

Woodring's reluctance to make American aircraft and Army surplus goods available to the Allies antagonized many top administrative officials who were striving to carry out the President's professed policy of aiding Britain and France.[70] Woodring's actions were more popular with most military leaders, who were opposed to having the nation's small supply of war matériel further depleted but were hesitant to speak out against the policy advocated by the President. Word of Roosevelt's warning to General Arnold about what might happen to officers who did not "play ball" had spread among the military men, and they were not about to jeopardize their careers. General Marshall and his top advisers found themselves in a situation in which the Secretary of War was advocating a policy that they personally favored, but they were bound to carry out the policy of their Commander in Chief—a policy that they were less than enthusiastic about.[71] General Marshall probably revealed the attitude of many military leaders when, during a meeting on 4 June at which Secretary Morgenthau complained about all the difficulty that Woodring was causing him and the President, Marshall said, "Now, everybody in town is shooting at Woodring and trying to put him on the spot and I don't want to see him get on the spot. Everybody is trying to get him out of there and I am not going to be a party to it."[72]

Until early June, Woodring was the only War Department official to speak out against the danger of aiding the Allies at the expense of the United States Army; however, that situation began to change quickly after an announcement made by the President on 11 June that he was ordering a "re-survey" to determine what additional military matériel could be turned back to the manufacturers for ultimate sale to the Allies. At last the military began to speak out. Feeling that to release anything more would endanger the nation's security, the War Plans Division voiced opposition to the President's proposal. General Marshall also came to the conclusion that it was time to call a halt to the disposition of Army material to foreign nations.[73] Therefore, on 22 June he sent the following message to his Commander in Chief: "To release to Great Britain additional war material now in the hands of the armed forces will seriously weaken our present state of defense." He then recommended that "the United States make no further commitments of this sort."[74] Unfortunately, Woodring did not know about this recommendation, because two days before this the President had forced him to resign as Secretary of War.

The President's decision to ask Woodring for his resignation was to come as a surprise to everyone, including Woodring. The only thing more surprising than the forced resignation was that Roosevelt retained his recalcitrant War Secretary as long as he did. On numerous occasions throughout 1939 and early 1940 the President had told close associates that he was about to remove Woodring; however, he had not done so, and by the late spring of 1940 the general feeling was that he never would. There were several factors that made Roosevelt reluctant to act: his extreme distaste for firing anyone, especially an old friend like Woodring; his desire not to antagonize congressional isolationists and noninterventionists; and his yearning to ensure his control of the Kansas delegation at the 1940 Democratic Convention. Nevertheless, in early May the President began to give serious consideration to the appointment of a new Secretary of War. The earlier reasons he had had for retaining Woodring were now being overridden by other factors, but the primary reason for seeking a replacement for him was the increased difficulty that he was having in getting Woodring to carry out his policies. From March 1940 on, Woodring made no secret about opposing the President's policy of aiding the Allies at the expense of the United States. During March and early April he fought against the release of modern military aircraft to Britain and France; then in May he did the same thing in regard to surplus ordnance items. As Woodring's obstructionism increased, the President's fear of antagonizing the isolationists declined, because Germany's successes in Europe had done much to weaken their cause. Another reason for considering removal of Woodring was Roosevelt's desire to unite the country behind him in this period of crisis. The President had come to believe that the best way to provide the national solidarity that he desired was to appoint several prominent Republicans to the cabinet, thereby creating a coalition cabinet.[75]

In order to make the coalition a reality, Roosevelt first had to find qualified Republicans who would be willing to join his administration. One man that the President wanted to have join his team was Frank Knox, the 1936 Republican candidate for Vice-President. In December of 1939 Roosevelt asked Knox to become his Secretary of the Navy, but Knox refused to accept unless another Republican was also appointed to the cabinet at the same time. Because Roosevelt was unwilling to take such a step at that particular time, he asked Knox to let the matter ride for a while.[76]

As the situation deteriorated in Europe in the spring of 1940 and as Secretaries Woodring and Edison continued to lose favor at the White House, Washington was filled with rumors that the President was about to form a coalition cabinet. The names most frequently mentioned as possible appointees were Knox and Alfred M. Landon, the 1936 Republican nominee for President. Landon was invited to the White House, perhaps to be offered a cabinet position, but before he went, he issued a statement saying that he was opposed to a coalition cabinet. On 22 May, Landon visited Roosevelt. At that time the President said that he was looking for replacements for Secretaries Woodring, Edison, and Perkins and that he had a number of men under consideration; however, he did not mention the possibility of a post for Landon. Apparently the anticoalition statement had eliminated the former Republican standard-bearer from further consideration.[77]

It was at about this time that Roosevelt again approached Knox about accepting the Navy post, and again Knox replied, though not as vehemently as he previously had, that he would do so only if another top Republican were appointed to the cabinet at the same time. Thereupon, Roosevelt left the invitation to Knox open, and he began anew a serious search for another capable appointee. The President considered a number of qualified men for that second cabinet position. Knox personally favored William Donovan, who was a distinguished soldier of World War I, a former Republican candidate for Governor of New York, and a former law classmate of Roosevelt's. The President, however, for reasons known only to himself, rejected Donovan.[78] Another possibility, William Bullitt, Ambassador to France, was championed by Secretary Ickes, but the President felt that Bullitt was more valuable in his diplomatic position.[79] Serious consideration was also given to selecting New York's Mayor, Fiorello La Guardia. When word of the possible appointment of La Guardia spread to the newspapers, the conservatives who dominated the House Military Affairs Committee became alarmed because of the "extreme liberalism" of the New Yorker. Therefore,

226

in early June, Chairman Andrew May and Congressman Charles I. Faddis went to see the President. They emphatically informed the Chief Executive that they did not want to have La Guardia made Secretary of War and that if he were appointed, they would refuse to work with him. Roosevelt was angered by such a dictate, but realizing the power and influence wielded by the two men, he assured them that the appointment would not be made.[80]

As the President continued his search for the right Republican to join Knox in his cabinet, the pressure to remove Woodring grew to considerable proportions. In addition to the longstanding pressure from such members of the anti-Woodring inner circle as Harold Ickes, Henry Morgenthau, Steve Early, and Edwin Watson, there now appeared "outside pressure" from the press and the public. Newspaper columnists were especially active in this move. Drew Pearson and Robert Allen continued their long-time criticism of Woodring, calling again for his dismissal. Frank Kent reported the likelihood of the removal of Woodring, adding that he had no idea why the President had retained him for so long. Joseph Alsop and Robert Kintner talked of the lack of leadership in the War Department and called on the President to appoint a new Secretary of War.[81]

In June the calls for replacement of Woodring began to reach the editorial pages. In its edition of 14 June, the *New York Times* contained an editorial criticizing the leadership of the Navy and War departments. In discussing the War Department, it said: "It seems incredible, but it is unfortunately true, that at such a time as this . . . the offices of Secretary of War and Assistant Secretary of War should be occupied by two men who do not see eye to eye, do not pull together, and, reputedly, do not even speak." Mention was then made of the many important defense measures that had to be taken, but "none is more urgently important than the immediate appointment to the top posts in the Navy and War Departments of thoroughly competent, thoroughly non-political and thoroughly cooperative executives."[82] Three days later an editorial in *Life* magazine called for replacement of Woodring, saying that the need for such action was "obvious."[83] The foreign press also got into the act. On 5 June the *London Daily Telegraph* reported that United States aid to the Allies was being delayed by Secretary of War Woodring, who was the leader of American "obstructionists." The article then suggested that perhaps President Roosevelt should "take the risk . . . of kicking out this disloyal member of the Cabinet who has made a hollow mockery of the profession of his chief that the administration's policy was to aid the Allies by every means short of war."[84]

By early June the retention of Woodring in the cabinet was also on the way to becoming a possible political liability to Roosevelt. In a speech on 8 June, New York's Governor, Thomas A. Dewey, who was seeking the

227

Republican presidential nomination, called upon the President to dismiss Secretaries Woodring, Perkins, and Hopkins, who were "symbols of incompetence, disunity and class hatred." Although Perkins and Hopkins were also criticized, the speech was especially critical of Secretary Woodring.[85] Such things as Dewey's speech, along with newspaper and magazine articles and editorials calling for dismissal of Woodring, soon led to a steady stream of letters to the President, asking that he replace his Secretary of War.[86]

One obstacle to the creation of a coalition cabinet was cleared in late May, when Secretary of the Navy Edison was nominated as the Democratic candidate for Governor of New Jersey. This political maneuver, which had been arranged by James Farley at the request of President Roosevelt, provided Edison with a graceful means of stepping aside, and he took advantage of it. On 21 May he submitted his resignation, to be effective 15 June.[87] A position was now open for Frank Knox, but Roosevelt still had not found another prominent Republican to join the administration. Then, at a luncheon on 3 June, Roosevelt's good friend Supreme Court Justice Felix Frankfurter suggested Henry L. Stimson. According to Frankfurter, Stimson would be a perfect choice. He was a well-known Republican; he was well qualified, having served as Secretary of War under Taft and Secretary of State under Hoover; and his views on foreign policy and aid to the Allies were quite similar to those of the President. In the days that followed, Frankfurter continually pressed for the appointment of Stimson.[88]

As the President gave serious consideration to the appointment of Stimson, he also turned to the problem of how to effect the removal of Woodring. It was quite apparent by this time that the Secretary of War would not leave voluntarily. On numerous occasions the President had offered him fine positions, but in each instance the offer had been turned down. As Drew Pearson, writing in mid June, put it: "If there is anything Roosevelt ought to know by now it is that only a blast of TNT will oust his Secretary of War."[89] Furthermore, the President could not bring himself to just call him in and fire him. This left the alternative of finding some pretext for asking Woodring to resign.

On 17 June a series of events started that was to give Roosevelt the excuse for removal that he was seeking. That morning Secretary Morgenthau informed the President that the British urgently needed some four-engine bombers (B-17's). When Roosevelt asked if the Army could spare eight or nine, Morgenthau said that he felt that they could spare ten. "That's fine," Roosevelt replied, "You have been doing grand work and continue to give the English the same help."[90] Later that day, in talking with Gen. Edwin Watson, the President's Military Aide, Morgenthau said that he intended to transfer twelve B-17's and that there was no need to consult the

Army on the transaction. When Watson asked whether the transfer could be made without first asking the War Department, Morgenthau assured him that "we have the authority." At Watson's insistence it was finally agreed to sound out the Army on the proposed transfer of the twelve aircraft.[91] That afternoon Watson informed Woodring that the transfer was under consideration and asked for the Army's reaction.

On the following morning, 18 June, Woodring and General Marshall discussed the consequences of such a transfer. Marshall explained that he strongly opposed the proposed action, because the Army had only fifty-two B-17's, all of which were essential to the defense of the Canal Zone and the Caribbean. Both men agreed that none of the planes should be released. Marshall then wrote a recommendation to that effect and forwarded it to Woodring, who gave it his approval on the morning of 19 June, and then immediately sent it to the White House.[92]

Upon receipt of this memorandum the President decided that the time had come to remove his Secretary of War. Whether his decision was made because he was fed up with Woodring's obstructionist tactics and the B-17 matter was simply the "last straw," or whether he had previously decided on dismissing him and merely seized upon this incident as an excuse, will never be known.[93] Nevertheless, the President sat down and personally wrote, in longhand, the following letter to his Secretary of War:

June 19, 1940

Dear Harry,

Because of a succession of recent events both here and abroad, and not within our personal choice and control, I find it necessary now to make certain readjustments. I have to include in this a change in the War Department—and that is why I am asking that you let me have your resignation.

At the same time it would be very helpful to me if you would accept the post of Governor of Porto [sic] Rico. In the light of the international situation Porto Rico and its administration are of the utmost importance to this country.

Your service as Secretary of War has been carried out loyally and faithfully—and for this I shall ever be grateful to you. This note goes to you with the warmest feeling of friendship on my part—and let me repeat, Harry, that I shall be always thankful to you for your help to me during all these seven years.

Affectionally yours,
Franklin D. Roosevelt[94]

On the next morning the Secretary of War sat down and wrote in longhand a letter which, in spite of the fact that its exact contents were not to be known until years afterward, was to become a source of great speculation and controversy:

229

June 20, 1940

Dear Mr. President,

Your request of yesterday afternoon for my resignation as Secretary of War is acknowledged and you may consider this note compliance therewith.

I assure you that my refusal of yesterday morning to agree to your request for the release of the flying fortress bombers to foreign nations was based upon my own belief, supported by the General Staff, that it was not in the best interests of the defense of our own country.

Fearful of a succession of events to which I could not subscribe I prefer not to accept your proffer of continued service in another post. For the stated reasons I ask that my resignation be considered effective today.

I feel, Mr. President, that I cannot retire with my knowledge of the inadequacy of our preparedness for war without most respectfully urging you to maintain your pronounced non-intervention policy. I trust you will advise those who would provoke belligerency—a state of war for our nation—that they do so with the knowledge that we are not prepared for a major conflict. Billions appropriated today cannot be converted into preparedness tomorrow.

I am indeed grateful to you for having given me this opportunity to serve my country and the President of the United States to the best of my ability. I am also grateful for your kind expression of friendship and believe me I retire with equally warm personal affection. May I remain always most respectfully—

Harry H. Woodring[95]

Accompanying the letter was a note in which Woodring said that he would not make any statement or release any part of the correspondence surrounding the resignation. He asked that any announcements concerning the matter be made by the White House.[96]

A few hours after receiving Woodring's resignation, Roosevelt sent to the Senate for confirmation the names of Frank Knox and Henry Stimson as Secretary of the Navy and Secretary of War. Roosevelt was able to act so quickly because he had offered the War post to Stimson the previous afternoon, and the latter had accepted with the understanding that he could name Judge Robert P. Patterson as Assistant Secretary. (This was accomplished five weeks later, when Assistant Secretary Louis Johnson was forced to resign in order to make room for Patterson.)[97] At the same time that the names of the new appointees were sent to the Senate, Press Secretary Steve Early issued more detailed announcements on the new appointments and on Woodring's resignation. There was one very unusual facet of the news release concerning Woodring—the usual practice of releasing the letter of resignation of an outgoing cabinet member was not followed. The reason for the omission was that the letter to the President was "too personal."[98]

The removal of Woodring and the appointment of Stimson came as a surprise to everyone, including Woodring. Just a few days before, he had

230

told Congressmen May and Faddis that there was nothing to the rumors that he was about to be replaced; in fact, he told the two Congressmen that the President was quite satisfied with the job that he was doing.[99] Assistant Secretary Johnson was both surprised and disappointed; he was surprised that the President had finally mustered the courage to dismiss Woodring, and he was extremely disappointed that he himself had not been made Secretary. After hearing of Stimson's appointment, Johnson went to the White House and expressed his dissatisfaction: "But, Mr. President, you promised me not once but many times," said the angry Johnson.[100] Most Senators were on the chamber floor when the announcement of the impending appointments was made. The shocked surprise of that body was typified by Senator Bennett Clark, who cried out, "Is this true?"[101]

The next morning the *Topeka Daily Capital* carried a story reporting that three weeks before, on 1 June, Woodring had told friends in Topeka that a "small clique of international financiers" was trying to force him from the cabinet because he was opposed to "stripping our own defenses" to aid the Allies.[102] Almost immediately, newspapers throughout the country carried the story from Topeka, and Harry Woodring was once again the center of controversy—this time over his dismissal from the cabinet.

Congressmen and journalists looked at the story coming out of Topeka and at the President's refusal to make public Woodring's letter of resignation, and they concluded that there must be some connection between the two. Congressional reaction was immediate. On the floors of the House and Senate a score of Congressmen praised Woodring for the job that he had done and deplored the President's decision to remove him. Resolutions calling for an investigation into the circumstances surrounding Woodring's resignation, demanding that the President release the controversial letter of resignation, and summoning Woodring to appear before the Military Affairs Committee in order to explain his reason for resigning were introduced in both houses.[103] Although none of the resolutions was passed, the Senate Military Affairs Committee authorized its chairman, Morris Sheppard, to invite Woodring to testify if he cared to. Sheppard made the offer, but the former Secretary of War, in response to a general request from President Roosevelt that he not let his resignation become a political issue, rejected the offer.[104]

The only public statement that Woodring made concerning his resignation was made to reporters on 21 June, when he said, "No one sympathizes with the European democracies any more than I do, but I feel it is America's duty to put our own defenses in order before going to their aid. I simply could not go along beyond the point where I felt we would be jeopardizing our own defenses."[105] With Woodring refusing to tell what had happened

231

and the President failing to release the Secretary of War's letter of resignation, the entire controversy slowly dropped into the background, and Congress and the nation turned their attention to more pressing matters. Although there was never an official explanation as to why Woodring had resigned, it was "universally accepted that he quit rather than go along with Roosevelt's policy of 'anything short of war to help the Allies.' "[106]

One facet of the dismissal that is worthy of examination is Roosevelt's later contention, made in private, that Woodring's refusal to transfer the B-17's to the Allies was in no way connected with the decision to ask for his resignation. In a personal letter written to Woodring on 25 June, the President indicated that he had fully accepted the recommendation not to release the large bombers and that, since they both favored the same course of action, that particular matter could not have been the basis for dismissal. The impression that Roosevelt gave was that by 19 June the time for a cabinet reshuffle had at last come, and the fact that the bomber issue happened to be before Woodring at that particular time was merely a coincidence.[107]

While Roosevelt's explanation could in fact be true, several factors would lead one to think otherwise. First, the President's letter to Woodring asking for his resignation and the call to Henry Stimson offering him the War post were made almost immediately after receiving the War Department memorandum opposing the transfer of the bombers. It is difficult to believe that the memo did not affect the President's decision. Second, in a telephone conversation at 12:52 P.M. on 18 June, presidential aide Edwin Watson told Secretary Morgenthau that Roosevelt had said to him, "If you and Henry think they [the Army] ought to do it [transfer the bombers] go ahead."[108] That conversation, plus a similar one an hour and a half before, indicates that the President, Morgenthau, and Watson were all determined to carry through the transfer regardless of what the War Department said.[109] Yet in a personal letter to Woodring on 22 June, Watson stated, as the President was to do three days later, that the White House had fully intended to go along with the War Department recommendation regardless of what it was.[110] These stated intentions, along with Roosevelt's directive of 20 June to Morgenthau to "lay off on the ten four engine bombers," are quite different from the views expressed by Watson, Morgenthau, and the President in the days preceding Woodring's dismissal.[111] Both the Watson letter and the Roosevelt letter appear to be efforts to lay the basis for a cover-up should the isolationists attempt to make removal of the Secretary of War a cause célèbre. Fortunately, Woodring kept that from happening.

One question remains to be answered, and that is why, after years of threatening to replace Secretary Woodring, did the President finally decide to act? Certainly, political considerations were important; after all, it was an election year, and Roosevelt wanted to bring about national solidarity by forming a coalition cabinet. Furthermore, the President realized that bringing two key Republicans into the administration on the eve of their national convention was bound to cause confusion in the ranks of the opposition.[112] Internal and external pressures were also factors: members of the inner circle, who considered Woodring to be anti–New Deal, continued to urge his removal, and by early 1940 the press and the public were starting to make the same demand. Basic disagreements over policy were also important, but in themselves they were not solely responsible, because the President encouraged different viewpoints and saw certain benefits in having in the same department men with divergent views.[113] That "Woodring was the most outspoken anti-interventionist in the cabinet" was becoming increasingly embarrassing in light of Roosevelt's policies of aiding the Allies.[114] All of the above reasons undoubtedly influenced Roosevelt's decision, but he had tolerated each of them and probably would have continued to do so.

There was one factor, however, that, by June of 1940, could no longer be ignored—Woodring's obstruction of and his delay in carrying out the President's policies. In late 1939 Roosevelt made it abundantly clear that he wished to aid Britain and France by all means short of war, even if it meant a temporary weakening of United States military strength. Woodring, while not necessarily opposed to sales to the Allies, believed that United States defenses should receive first priority. His views were, therefore, completely different from those held by the President. To disagree with his Commander in Chief when a policy decision was being made was, and should have been, quite acceptable. However, once the President had made up his mind and had clearly indicated the policy that he intended to follow, Woodring should have carried it out without delay. Instead, he did what he could to keep that policy from going into effect. In January 1940 the President emphasized that he wanted to provide the Allies with the latest American-built military aircraft, but because of Woodring's obstructionism and delaying tactics this was not done until April. That spring, the turning over of surplus ordnance material to the Allies was also delayed for several weeks because of Woodring's reluctance and near refusal to carry out a policy that he disagreed with. Then, in mid June, when the question of transferring a dozen B-17's arose and Woodring again gave evidence that he was not going to "play ball," President Roosevelt made the decision to replace him with a man whose views were similar to his own.

In attempting to delay the flow of American-built aircraft and of Army surplus goods to the Allies, Secretary Woodring was doing what he sincerely considered to be in the best interests of the United States. His conscience and his military advisers told him to hang on to those items, but his superior told him to turn them over to the Allies. Woodring was inclined to follow the first two rather than the last. In pursuing the courses of action that he did, the Secretary of War was in effect attempting to override the decisions of the Commander in Chief. If there is to be order in a military establishment or in government, a proper superior-subordinate relationship must be understood and carried out at all echelons. Secretary Woodring did not follow that principle. He undoubtedly realized how unfortunate the consequences would be if every American soldier obstructed or delayed in carrying out the orders of his superior; however, he failed to realize that equally disastrous consequences could result if he, the Secretary of War, balked and delayed in carrying out the orders of his superior. Once Woodring had demonstrated that he would not carry out policies that he disagreed with, the President had no alternative to dismissing him. There can be no doubt that Roosevelt had the right and that he had sufficient reason to act as he did.

On 26 June, just one week after his resignation, Harry Woodring, along with Helen and the three children, went to the White House to pay a farewell visit to the President. The atmosphere was relaxed and almost festive as the two men exchanged pleasantries and reminisced about some of the trials and tribulations of the past nine years. Again Roosevelt offered his friend the governorship of Puerto Rico, and again it was refused. After pledging to keep in touch, the men shook hands and said good-by. The following morning the Woodrings piled into the family station wagon and headed for Kansas—Harry Woodring was going home.[115]

13

Years of Frustration

There was no bitterness in Harry Woodring's heart as he, Helen, and their three children—Marcus, Melissa, and Cooper—headed toward Kansas. His seven-and-one-half-year stay in Washington had been an enjoyable and, he felt, fruitful one, and he had no regrets about the recent turn of events. That he was not disappointed was due primarily to the self-satisfaction that he had from knowing that he had stood firm in opposing presidential policies that he felt certain would ultimately draw the United States into the war in Europe. To a man of principle this was very important. Furthermore, while his noninterventionist stand had resulted in the loss of his job, it had not destroyed his personal friendship with Roosevelt; for this he was quite grateful.[1]

Woodring's return to Kansas was also made easier by the fact that he had previously made plans to come home at the end of Roosevelt's second administration, regardless of what the President did. "Win, lose or draw, I am coming back to Kansas to live in 1941," he told his close friends in the fall of 1939 and the spring of 1940.[2] He was returning, he said, "because I have found no place I like so well and I am anxious to give our three children a normal upbringing." When he first began to speak of going back to the Sunflower State, living on a farm, and engaging in banking, many of his friends found it hard to believe, especially in light of rumors that he would accept a lucrative job with a large aviation company when he ultimately left the War Department. Moreover, it was well known that Harry and Helen enjoyed the social life in Washington, and many associates could hardly envision them forsaking that for life in rural Kansas.[3] That Woodring was serious about returning became evident in May 1940, when, after months of searching, he purchased the 262-acre property near Lecompton that had belonged to Governor Frederick Stanton (Territorial Governor of Kansas, 1857) and announced his intentions of refurbishing the old mansion and take up residence there by late 1941.[4] The remodeling plans were under way in June 1940, when his dismissal came. All of these things made coming home much easier than it might otherwise have been.

The leisurely four-day journey from Washington to Topeka ended on 1 July with a welcome that the Woodrings had not anticipated. The family was met at the city limits by a reception committee, which loaded them into open cars and escorted them downtown to the Jayhawk Hotel, where several hundred well-wishers had gathered to welcome them home. After Woodring had witnessed a small parade in his honor, he was swamped by news reporters, who sought a more extensive explanation of events surrounding his dismissal, asked about his political future, and inquired as to whether or not he thought President Roosevelt would be renominated at the upcoming Democratic National Convention. As he had done in Washington, Woodring refused to say anything regarding his dismissal. "Whatever is to be said on that subject," he told the newsmen, "must obviously come from the White House." As to his political future, he stated: "I'll always be interested and active in politics. But they can't run fast enough to get me to take another political job. I've had ten years of public service. That's enough." Concerning the Democratic National Convention, he made it clear that in spite of the recent events involving him, he would still serve as a delegate-at-large from Kansas; but he refused to speculate about what the convention might or might not do in regard to selecting a candidate.[5]

Although the Woodrings actually arrived in Topeka on July 1, the city's formal welcome was to be extended on July 9 at a public dinner sponsored by the Chamber of Commerce. As the dinner drew near and the controversy over his dismissal continued to arouse interest throughout the nation, speculation grew as to what he might say in the upcoming speech. During this period Woodring was receiving about five hundred letters a day—most of which praised him for "relinquishing his post as Secretary of War rather than weaken the Army's power by releasing Army equipment for the use of the Allies."[6]

On 9 July several hundred Woodring associates—both Democrats and Republicans—gathered to honor their fellow Kansan and to welcome him home. After dinner Woodring addressed his guests in a speech that was carried on nationwide radio. After reminiscing about his years as Governor, he noted how the New Deal, under "a determined leader and . . . an equally determined Congress" and cooperating with business, labor, and agriculture, had provided "a broad program of social, political, and economic reforms" which came to be embraced by both political parties. He took a swat, however, at the New Dealers by saying that "simply because some things have been done in the name of the Democratic Party does not mean that I have always approved of many of the methods used in Washington to reach objectives, and I have not approved of some of the brainless, impractical advisers that think our democracy must be tinkered with and made over." Then, after calling for a federal program that would truly provide "rehabilitation to the American farmer," he turned rather abruptly to the matter of foreign affairs. He told his audience that in response to requests from all over the country that he make known his views on American responsibilities to nations involved in the war in Europe, he had this to say: "I have always been, I am now, and I expect to remain a noninterventionist, a noninterventionist in both the military and political controversies of Europe, and I am a strong advocate of keeping this country out of recurring European wars."[7]

While expressing sympathy towards the democracies of the world, he maintained that "our aid should be generous, and upon a strict basis of cash and carry, . . . but only aid to that point that the sale of products to foreign nations does not jeopardize the defenses of our country." He went on to say that "the real decision that confronts our Nation today is whether we have responsibilities or obligations to any warring nations sufficient to cause us to assume an increasing provocative position that eventually will involve us in their war." He told his listeners what he hoped the impact of his resignation might be: "If reaction from my leaving the War Department as a known noninterventionist has caused modification of some policies, and has sobered some of those provocative and meddling advisers of the administration who would strip our own defenses, then I regret that I have only one set of guts to sacrifice on the altar of public service." He also made a plea for expanded military preparedness which he maintained was necessary to "insulate" the nation against war. In closing, he said: "I am grateful, I am appreciative, and I am humble before the President of the United States for the privilege of having served my country to the best of my ability."[8]

To isolationists and noninterventionists alike the speech was quite disappointing, because Woodring had not used the opportunity to reveal the facts surrounding his dismissal or to attack the President and the policies that he was pursuing. Those members of the administration who favored aid to the Allies were relieved that the former War Secretary had not revealed more details on the aid that was being extended. The speech also pleased the President, for it contained nothing embarrassing or disrespectful to him; he was appreciative of the fact that Woodring, out of personal loyalty, had not "told all."

Three days after the dinner honoring his return home, Woodring departed for Chicago, where he was to be a Kansas delegate-at-large to the Democratic National Convention. At this point the Democratic political scene was one of mass confusion. About the only thing that the party members knew for sure was that the Republicans had met in Philadelphia several weeks before and had selected as their presidential and vice-presidential nominees the utility magnate Wendell Willkie and Senator Charles McNary of Oregon. The chaos among the Democrats stemmed from the fact that President Roosevelt had still failed to declare whether or not he would seek or accept the nomination. Although the rank-and-file party members generally supported a "draft Roosevelt" movement, party leaders were bitterly divided over the issue of a third term. Liberal Senators such as George Norris, James Murray, and James Byrnes and administration New Dealers such as Harold Ickes, Harry Hopkins, and Thomas Corcoran were advancing the President's candidacy; while conservatives such as John Nance Garner, James Farley, Senators Carter Glass, and Senator Millard Tydings were strongly opposing such a course.[9]

The Kansas delegation, under instructions from the state convention, was pledged to Roosevelt if he wanted the nomination; but in the event that he did not, the delegates were pledged to Woodring as a favorite son. If the former cabinet officer had any political aspirations at the convention, he did not reveal or attempt to realize them. Instead, he spent his time and efforts trying to get a nonintervention plank into the party's platform. Arriving in Chicago several days before the convention was to begin, Woodring approached a number of party leaders whose views on aiding the Allies were similar to his own. After consulting this group of men, which included James Farley and Senators Burton Wheeler, David Walsh, Patrick McCarran, Bennett Clark, Edwin Johnson, and Gerald Nye, Woodring drew up a proposed foreign-policy plank, which pledged unequivocal support "for a policy of nonintervention in the political and military affairs of the Old World." The proposal was then given to former Kansas Congressman Randolph Carpenter, who presented it to the resolutions committee.[10] The Roosevelt supporters on that committee, realizing the strength of the noninterventionist forces, chose not to challenge the Woodring proposal for fear the controversy might split the convention wide open.[11] It was therefore agreed to write into the platform the statement: "We will not participate in foreign wars, and we will not send our army, naval or air forces to fight in foreign lands outside of the Americas, except in case of attack."[12] The adoption of this plank by the convention was most gratifying to Woodring, for it seemed to give party sanction to the noninterventionist views that he had been championing for the past ten months.

On 17 July, Roosevelt, in spite of the efforts of a number of activitists who were opposed to a third term, received the convention draft that he had hoped for. Although Woodring opposed a third term (he did so on principle, because he felt no man should serve more than two terms as President), he did not openly do so, because of his loyalty to the President and also because he felt that such opposition could not stop the nomination of Roosevelt. The convention's biggest fight came in selecting the man for the second spot on the ticket. Since at the time of the draft the President had not indicated his willingness to run, he had made no mention of a possible running mate; consequently, a number of vice-presidential booms developed. Senator William Bankhead and Paul McNutt, a former Governor of Indiana, came under consideration, and there was even some talk of nominating Woodring. The President, however, indicated that Secretary of Agriculture Henry Wallace was his choice, and after a bitter fight the convention ultimately honored that request.[13]

No sooner had the convention ended than the 1940 campaign got under way, but in that contest Woodring took little interest and no part. His reason for not participating had nothing to with his dismissal from the cabinet but was due to his opposition to the New Dealers who now seemed to be in complete control of the party. Writing to James Farley upon his return from the convention, Woodring said that he felt as if a member of his family had died or his favorite dog had been stolen, because "the Democratic Party and its organization has been stolen from me and my friends . . . by such mavericks that do not have the courage and honesty to step out and organize their own party."[14] He expressed these same views to his old friend John O'Laughlin when he said that the party had been taken away from "orthodox Democrats" by "social reformers with no politics and impractical theories who know no loyalty or party organization. Control taken by such as these does not set well and is my primary resentment in the whole situation."[15] That these anti–New Deal views did not stem from antagonism over his dismissal is evident from the fact that he had been privately expressing such views for more than a year before he was forced from the cabinet.[16]

Once the convention was out of the way, Woodring was able to turn his attention to personal matters. While plans were being drawn up for remodeling the Stanton mansion, the Woodrings moved to Yorkshire Farms, a beautiful suburban showplace just outside of Topeka. Although he was unable to take up residence at the Lecompton farm, which he renamed Rebel

Hill, Woodring did not delay in becoming a farmer. He immediately began purchasing livestock, and by spring of the following year the "Hill" had about eighteen hundred head of sheep, two hundred hogs, some horses and cows, and two hundred chickens. One would hardly expect to find a former banker, Governor, and Secretary of War feeding livestock, ringing the noses of hogs, and cultivating strawberries; but Woodring was doing all this and enjoying it immensely. As one reporter wrote after a four-hour visit to Rebel Hill, "He is not a gentleman farmer . . . but a full-fledged, practical farmer who has found a fuller life in feeding his own livestock and collecting the eggs laid by hens in his flock."[17] While Woodring was adjusting quite easily to his new life, so was his family. Mrs. Woodring found the transition from cabinet wife to housewife and mother not only easy but enjoyable, and before long she was actively involved in various civic and service organizations, most notably the Red Cross. At the same time, Marcus and Melissa were pursuing the joys and frustrations of elementary school, while Cooper's world centered around blocks, toy trucks, and teddy bears.

As a former cabinet member and head of the United States War Department, Woodring was continually sought after by people in public and private life to express his views on matters relating to defense, foreign policy, and politics. Generally, however, he avoided making any public statements on those subjects. Numerous requests from publishing houses, magazines, and newspapers to secure the inside story of his years in Washington and his subsequent dismissal were rejected.[18] He likewise refused to testify before the Senate and House Foreign Affairs committees or to make speeches on behalf of the America First Committee. Woodring did not speak out because of the personal respect and admiration that he held for the man in the White House. He reiterated his earlier pledges of loyalty to the President on 15 January 1941, when he wrote FDR: "I shall never do anything to embarrass your program. I may not always agree 100% but I am always loyal."[19] To this, Roosevelt replied: "I need no pledge of your loyalty. I always assume it as a matter of course."[20] On occasion Woodring expressed his views on a defense matter, as he did in August 1940, when he went on record as being opposed to compulsory military service until the voluntary system received a "fair chance"; however, in such instances he always attacked the idea rather than the administration or the personalities involved.[21]

Throughout 1941 Woodring's interest in his farm and his enthusiasm for remodeling the Stanton home were on the wane. During that time he became increasingly interested in engaging in some sort of business venture that he hoped would lead to quick and substantial financial gains. For a time he sought, unsuccessfully, to be named District Chairman of the Tenth Federal Reserve Bank at Kansas City; and his efforts to purchase a small

Kansas insurance company also failed. By the end of 1941, even though Woodring's life was still involved primarily in farming, he was looking for greener pastures.[22]

After his departure from Washington in mid 1940, Woodring had continued to maintain the noninterventionist stand that he had long advocated. That position, however, was to be abandoned completely on the afternoon of 7 December 1941, when word of the Japanese attack on Pearl Harbor reached Kansas. On the following morning, Woodring sent a telegram to the President, pledging his support and offering his services if they were needed.[23] A few weeks later, in a letter thanking Roosevelt for a Christmas present, Woodring indicated that he would be interested in the ambassadorship to Mexico or in some position in Kansas, but that he preferred not to return to Washington. In that same letter there was also an indication that he might be interested in running against Arthur Capper for United States Senator—a possibility that the President called "interesting and well worth considering."[24]

As the nation went to war, Woodring stepped up the efforts that he had initiated the year before to get the War Department to build a major air base at Topeka. Because of his connections in Washington, the former cabinet official was expected by community leaders to use his influence to do what he could for the area. With regard to this expectation they were not disappointed. Several letters and phone calls to Generals Marshall and Arnold —both of whom owed a great deal to the Kansan for the positions that they occupied—undoubtedly had some influence on the ultimate decision to establish a bomber base near Topeka.[25] According to one source, it was "Harry Woodring, with no delegation to Washington and no more expense than a phone call [to] Hap Arnold," who secured the air base.[26]

Early in 1942 there was speculation that Woodring would seek the governorship again, but when he showed no interest in that position, his party turned to William Burke, Collector of Internal Revenue for Kansas, who was ultimately defeated by Republican Andrew Schoeppel.[27] Woodring's lack of interest in the state situation at that time stemmed from his desire to pursue a course that would have a major impact on the national political scene. His hope was to be the guiding force behind the formation of a third political party.

As has previously been noted, Woodring's opposition to the New Deal, especially its spending policies, went back to his years in Washington, but political expediency and involvement in defense matters had precluded his making such views known. Upon his return to Kansas, he made no bones about his dislike for the liberal mavericks who had stolen the party away. As one Kansas editor noted in August 1940, "Harry Woodring is so out of line with New Deal policies that he is entitled to be classed as an old-time Democrat."[28]

In 1941 and 1942 Woodring became convinced that many Democrats throughout the nation were as disillusioned with their party as he was, but he decided to wait and see if the 1942 elections substantiated his views. When the Republicans made significant gains in both the House and Senate, he felt that the time to act had come; thus, in a speech to the Kansas Grange on 11 December 1942, he outlined his plans for a third party. The new political organization, to be known as the Commonwealth Party of America, was to "offer sanctuary to voters who no longer find solace in the philosophies of the New Deal Democratic party or the currently expressionless Republican party." According to Woodring, the recent gains by the GOP were not the results of the voters' faith in their program but were due to disgust with their New Deal Democrat opponents and their "bureaucratic regulations and Washington paternalism." He expressed the hope that the new party could be sufficiently organized to present a national ticket and possibly state tickets in the 1944 election. Although he was critical of the New Dealers, Woodring carefully avoided any criticism of the President, dismissing him as a possible fourth-term candidate by saying, "Roosevelt will be far too smart and cagey to run as he senses the trend." In closing, he stated, in a none-too-humble fashion, that he would be willing to help create and guide the new party that was needed to accommodate the "millions of politically lost souls."[29]

Woodring's proposal immediately created widespread interest throughout the country. The major wire services picked up the story, and hundreds of newspapers, including all of those in the nation's capital, carried it on the front page. Reaction was generally favorable; hundreds of letters, phone calls, and telegrams expressed hope that the Kansan would be able to carry out the plan that he had set forth.[30] Because James Farley had stopped at Topeka a few days before Woodring gave this speech, there was speculation that the two men had formulated the scheme; however, they had not discussed such a plan.[31] That the President was not upset by the speech seemed evident when he once again sent Woodring a personal Christmas present.[32]

During early 1943 Woodring continued to cite the need for the Commonwealth party, but his involvement in business affairs, plus his family responsibilities, prevented him from making a serious bid to implement his idea. As the year passed and the proposed third party made no headway, Woodring came to feel that the way to end control of the country by New Dealers was not by forming a third party but by recapturing control of the Democratic party. That end, he believed, could be achieved only if someone other than the New Dealers' champion, President Roosevelt, were to be nominated and elected in 1944. Therefore, his major goal soon became the stopping of FDR's bid for a fourth term. Consequently, in the middle of 1943 Woodring's addresses began to take on a new twist. While he continued to be critical of the "state capitalist system" that the New Deal had created, he became increasingly critical of the President, but without mentioning him by name. For example, in a Fourth of July address in Neodesha, he lashed out at the Chief Executive by saying that the voters "must not permit another national election—the election of 1944—to be interpreted as another mandate for absolute and complete domination and control by any President over the executive, legislative and judicial branches of government."[33] In the fall of the year, Woodring contacted Democratic Senator Harry Byrd of Virginia and urged him to lead an anti-fourth-term movement within the party. Sensing the President's strength, Byrd gracefully refused to accept the challenge, saying to Woodring, "You or someone else of our lot would be much better to lead the fight."[34]

As 1944 dawned and it became increasingly apparent that Roosevelt would seek, and in all likelihood receive, the party's nomination again, Woodring concluded that the time had come to make an open stand against the President and the New Dealers who surrounded him. Consequently, in early February, he traveled to Chicago to meet with a handful of state Democratic leaders who were interested in "a reunited Democratic party." Then, in a speech on 4 February to the Chicago Executives Club, Woodring publicly stated that he opposed a fourth term for Roosevelt, and he suggested that the Democrats nominate Secretary of State Cordell Hull. Since the purpose of his speech was to express opposition to a fourth term, the Kansan did not attack the President but praised the social and economic gains that the country had made under "his friend" who would "go down in history as the father of the renaissance of the common man." The problem, Woodring maintained, was not with the man in the White House but with the Palace Guard, "a group of idealistic, misguided, impractical, socially minded, so-called intellectuals" who felt that Democracy had failed and that the nation should be made over.[35]

Immediately after the speech a group of anti–New Deal Democrats from nineteen states announced that they were forming, under the chairmanship of Woodring, the American Democratic National Committee, a group dedicated both to blocking a fourth term for Roosevelt and to regaining control of the party from the "Palace Guard." It was also announced that national headquarters would be opened in Chicago and that a national convention might be held late in April to determine party strategy or select a candidate.[36]

In the weeks that followed, Woodring devoted all of his time and energy to developing the new organization. Operating out of Topeka, he spent time

243

selecting state committeemen and committeewomen, raising money, and developing political strategy. Although the course agreed upon was to "stop Roosevelt," it was decided that because of the late date, no effort would be made to try to elect delegates to the National Democratic Convention.[37] In late February, when Woodring traveled to New York seeking funds and political support, he openly admitted to reporters that the strategy of the group was not firm, because its actions were dependent on whether or not the President was nominated again. He indicated that several options were open: they could wait until after the major party conventions and then endorse one of the nominees, or they could nominate their own candidate. The only alternative that was rejected outright was that of supporting the Democratic ticket if Roosevelt was nominated. After Woodring had spent several days in New York talking to Eastern Democrats with anti-Roosevelt sentiments, he announced plans to organize in every state and to spend $1.5 million in an effort to block the President's reelection. No particular candidate, he said, was being championed by the committee.[38] It was at this point that he indicated to a close friend that the movement "has passed the laughing stage. It is greater and more important than smug Washington realizes."[39] As the weeks passed, however, and the likelihood that the Democrats would go with Roosevelt increased, Woodring began to speak more in terms of a third-party candidate, and he mentioned such possibilities as James Farley, Charles Edison, Senator Harry Byrd, Senator Alben Barkley, Senator Walter George, and several others.[40]

Although Woodring unleashed the same dynamic energy that had made him a champion campaigner more than a decade before, his movement made little headway; and as March progressed, the enthusiasm of the previous weeks quickly waned. The problems hindering the American Democratic National Committee were both political and economic. Politically, they gained little support, because few Democrats were willing to oppose the President, especially when he seemed to have so much going for him: he was extremely popular, the war was going well, and after having spent nearly twelve years in the White House, he was practically becoming a national institution. Even among those party leaders who were opposed to a fourth term, and there were many, few were willing to challenge FDR, because they did not feel that he could be stopped. This situation contributed to the financial difficulties, because people were not inclined to contribute money to a cause that appeared to have little chance of success; thus, the committee was caught in a vicious circle in which a lack of political support made it impossible to get the funds that were needed to carry on a campaign to win more support.[41] Thus, things were at a standstill.

One thing that Woodring had insisted on from the inception of the

American Democratic National Committee was that President Roosevelt not be personally attacked. He always maintained that his opposition to a fourth term was based on the principle that no President should serve more than two terms and on his belief that the government could be saved from the totalitarian state that was being set up by the New Dealers only if the President and his followers were driven from office.[42] What Woodring never explained, or even attempted to explain, was how he could attack the New Dealers and the "Palace Guard" and not criticize their leader—President Roosevelt. Apparently Woodring's loyalty to the President blinded him to this inconsistency.

By early April 1944, with the ineffectiveness of the stop-Roosevelt movement becoming increasingly apparent, dissension became rampant as the various leaders of the American Democratic National Committee attempted to fix responsibility for the failure of the organization. Some placed the blame on party members who gave lip service but no money. The growing consensus, however, was that there could be no real progress as long as they refused to criticize the President. They therefore urged that the direction of attack be shifted toward Roosevelt and that "a smear campaign against him and his family be carried out."[43] Woodring could not and would not agree to this approach, and so, on 2 April, he resigned the chairmanship of the American Democratic National Committee and severed all ties with it.[44] In giving up the fight, he publicly stated that he was doing so because there was "not sufficient time nor are there sufficient funds to organize the rank and file within all the states to such proportions as I had contemplated." He also criticized those Democrats who were "too timid, politically and economically, to stand up and be counted."[45] After his departure, the committee continued to function right up to election time, but it remained an extremely weak and ineffective political body. Woodring's failure to stop Roosevelt was almost inevitable in light of the fact that while he despised the New Deal, he loved and respected its leader and therefore was unwilling to attack him.[46] In other words, he wanted to battle the "monster" without striking at its head; and consequently, he was able to inflict little damage.

Returning home, the frustrated Woodring awaited the inevitable—the renomination and reelection of Roosevelt. The one note of optimism that he found in the 1944 campaign and election was when his friend Senator Harry S Truman of Missouri became Vice-President.[47] Less than two months after Roosevelt was elected to an unprecedented fourth term he sent a Christmas gift to Woodring, just as he had in the past.[48] Woodring replied with his usual pleasantries, and the friendship between the two continued just as if nothing had happened.[49] That these men could remain the best of personal friends after their numerous political disagreements from 1940 on is a tribute

245

to the character of each of them. Such understanding and tolerance are rare in the political world.

The year 1945 was to be a busy one for Harry Woodring as he temporarily turned his attention from politics back to his family and business interests. The children were all in school now, and that they brought much joy and happiness to his life was evident from the letters he wrote to friends and acquaintances. Business ventures became increasingly important as the former banker searched for a means of boosting his own sagging bank account, which had been lightened by the purchase of a beautiful mansion at 1000 Gage Boulevard in Topeka. In addition to his farm, which was actually becoming more of a hobby than a business, he acquired several Royal Crown Cola franchises, secured the statewide agency for the Overland Civilian Jeep, and invested rather heavily in several wildcat oil ventures.[50] But involved as Woodring was with these numerous pursuits, he could not keep his mind off politics. As early as January 1945 he informed James Farley that he was making public appearances and statements that would lay the groundwork for his candidacy for the governorship in 1946 should he decide to run.[51]

As the war against the Axis powers headed for a successful conclusion in early 1945, the United States turned its attention to the peace that would follow. On this subject Woodring was in complete accord with Roosevelt's call for United States participation in an "International Peace Union." In late March, the Kansan wrote to the President, pledging his support for the peace organization and offering to make speeches urging its acceptance. Roosevelt thanked him for his support and said that he would take up the matter of the speeches with the State Department; but he never did so, because three weeks later, on 12 April, he died—the victim of a cerebral hemorrhage.[52] The news of the President's death stunned and saddened Harry Woodring and the entire nation. When Woodring heard the news from Warm Springs, Georgia, he wept for several hours.[53] He had lost a close and dear friend.

As the shock of FDR's death wore away, Woodring came to the conclusion that things were not as bad as they had at first seemed, because the man that he had championed for Vice-President three years before—Harry Truman—was now President. In fact, the more he looked at the situation, the more he entertained the thought of using his friendship with Truman to return to public life via appointment to a key government post.

On 23 July 1945 Woodring, having learned that the President was about to appoint an Ambassador to France and that General Marshall would probably be called upon to make a recommendation, wrote to Marshall and said that while he did not want a job "as a result of pressure and wire pulling," he would be "tempted" to accept the French ambassadorship or to have "the opportunity of bossing you around again as Secretary of War."[54] On that same day he wrote to his friend John O'Laughlin of the *Army and Navy Journal*, reiterating the same ideas and adding, "I have always felt I did a good job as Secretary of War—and there is the vindication angle that bobs up in my mind."[55] A week later, again in a letter to O'Laughlin, he said: "Marshall could be the actual medium and determining factor in my being named [Secretary of War] if he cared to so advise the President. He owes me his appointment as Chief of Staff." He then asked the publisher to approach the General on this matter.[56] Woodring was confident that "George" would repay the debt that he had incurred years before, but on this point the former Secretary of War was to be sorely disappointed, because Marshall, being the professional that he was, refused to champion anyone for the War post. As the Chief of Staff told O'Laughlin, he could not do such a thing, because to do so would imply that he was dissatisfied with Secretary of War Stimson, and such was not the case. In informing Woodring that he would not discuss the appointment with the President, he said that he could not do so "without seriously compromising my purely military position."[57] What Marshall left unsaid was that after his experience with the Woodring-Johnson feuds of 1938–1940, which he later called "the worst experience of my life," he would probably not have recommended him under any circumstances.[58] On 21 September, Secretary Stimson resigned, and Woodring's hopes for returning to his old War Department post soared; but the subsequent appointment of Robert Patterson dashed those hopes and any further thoughts that he had of returning to Washington.

With the possibility of returning to the national scene now gone, Woodring turned his attention once more to state politics. Longing for the days of glory and excitement that political life had previously given him, he decided to seek the governorship in 1946. He had considered the move since early 1945, but his friends advised him against it, because they feared that there would be a postwar reaction against the Democratic party. They also pointed out that the political machine that he and Guy Helvering had developed a decade and a half before had completely disintegrated, as evidenced by Governor Schoeppel's 1944 reelection over Democratic candidate Robert Lemon by the margin of 231,000 votes. The odds against Woodring were overwhelming, but he could remember overcoming such odds sixteen years before, and so with the dawning of 1946, he began to search for an issue on which to build his campaign. That search did not last long, because he quickly found his cause—prohibition.[59]

The "bone dry" status of Kansas stretched back to the 1880s, when a constitutional amendment prohibiting the sale or possession of intoxicating beverages had been passed. In the years that followed, the residents of the Sunflower State spoke with pride of their refusal to let "demon rum" contaminate their citizenry. Refusal to accept the national amendment to repeal prohibition in 1934 gave evidence that the antidrink attitude was still strong at that date. The war years, however, saw those views start to change, and with the end of the war, returning Kansas servicemen brought with them a desire to purchase alcoholic beverages just as they had been able to do overseas and in other states.[60]

Woodring's political sense quickly told him that the liquor issue was the one subject that could stir the voters; thus, in February he opened his bid for the governorship with a speech that labeled prohibition a "farce" and called for its repeal. Immediately a number of key Democrats began to rally behind the "wet" advocate. In the months that followed, he continually pointed out that while Kansas officially maintained that it was dry, it was in reality wet, and therefore that this "hypocritical condition" should be ended. Then, in mid June he officially became a candidate. The drys in the party, however, were not about to give up, and they put forth as their candidates Fred Hinkle of Wichita and Ewell Stewart of Topeka. A fourth Democrat, Worden Howat of Wakeeney, also sought the nomination. Expecting little difficulty in winning the primary, Woodring did little campaigning, being content to make a few public speeches and several radio addresses.[61]

It was in the midst of this campaign that the Woodrings were to receive what he called "the greatest blow that has ever come in our lives," when their twelve-year-old son, Marcus, died of polio.[62] The boy, who became sick after returning from scout camp, died within three days of the onset of the illness. The sudden death came as a terrible shock to Woodring, and it so crushed him that he was never the same again. Those close to him noted that the once jovial, even-tempered extrovert was thereafter a much more sober, irritable, and withdrawn individual. Several days after Marcus's death, eleven-year-old Melissa contracted the dreaded disease, but fate dealt her a kinder hand, and by the end of the summer she had recovered completely.[63]

Although his son's death virtually ended Woodring's primary campaign, it did not seem to hurt him at the polls, for he won a smashing victory, gathering more than three times as many votes as all the other Democratic candidates combined. In the meantime the Republicans chose as their gubernatorial nominee the six-term Congressman from Concordia, Frank Carlson.[64]

In the subsequent general election campaign, Woodring pursued the same hectic pace that he had back in 1930 and 1932; on some days he gave as many as fifteen political speeches. Although he talked about such things as roads, welfare, and education, his campaign centered on one issue—

prohibition. Woodring succeeded in pushing through a wet plank which advocated that the prohibition amendment be resubmitted to the voters, that the amendment be repealed, that there be state-operated liquor stores, and that there be county option; he then built his campaign around those ideas. When his Republican opponents pointed out that his election would not necessarily assure that the state would go wet, he merely replied that if the voters gave a clear mandate for repeal, he was sure that "the honest men in the legislature . . . would see that the people got what they wanted." He also pointed out what every Kansan already knew, that prohibition was not prohibiting a thing and, consequently, that while bootleggers were becoming rich, millions of dollars of tax revenues that could be used for education and welfare were being lost.[65] Helen Woodring also pitched in, campaigning for her husband and against a "prohibition law which does not prohibit."[66]

Woodring's vigorous campaign and, especially, his wet stand had the Republicans frightened. While there was strong sentiment in the party to embrace the wets, the majority were willing to follow the lead of their aged leader, Senator Arthur Capper, who accused Woodring of "trying to ride a modern Trojan horse" and convinced the GOP to take no stand at all on the prohibition issue. Carlson conducted a rather quiet, colorless campaign in which he avoided the liquor issue other than to say that he would be willing to submit the issue of repeal to the people and let them decide.[67]

On 5 November, Kansas voters went to the polls and rejected Woodring's bid to return to the Governor's chair as they cast 254,283 votes for him and 309,064 for Carlson. Although he had cut the Republican margin of two years before from 231,000 to 55,000, it had not been enough. Woodring conceded defeat on election night with a statement that he had simply been caught in a "Republican tidal wave" that swept the country.[68] Undoubtedly, the age-old story of "Republican Kansas" was a key factor in his defeat. Whether his wet stand hurt or helped him is not clear, because while it enabled him to garner much of the veteran vote, it cost him the support of organized religion; and in "churchgoing" Kansas that was bound to hurt. But if Woodring lost the prohibition battle of 1946, he won the war, because his strong showing helped to convince the next session of the legislature to submit a prohibition-repeal amendment to the voters in 1948, and that measure was easily ratified. Consequently, the following session passed enforcement legislation, and at 3:56 P.M. on 8 March 1949 prohibition in Kansas officially came to an end.[69]

In the years following his 1946 defeat, Woodring maintained an avid interest in both state and national affairs, but it was the latter that he followed most closely. During this period he maintained continual contact with President Truman through occasional visits to Washington and frequent

249

correspondence. Woodring was inclined to express in great detail his views on inflation, price controls, labor problems, foreign affairs, and party politics.[70] After the new Secretary of State, George Marshall, put forth his plan for the economic recovery of Europe in June 1947, Woodring became a major advocate of the program and served as an unofficial spokesman for it in the Midwest. Consequently, in early 1948 Truman arranged for Woodring to make a visit to Germany, France, Italy, and several other European countries in order to observe the situation firsthand. That trip convinced Woodring more than ever that the containment policy was necessary in order to stop Russia from spreading "her doctrine by propaganda, by pushing and shoving."[71]

As the presidential election of 1948 drew near, Woodring continued, as he had in the past, to work actively for Truman's election. In the spring of 1946 he had helped to organize the Kansas "Truman for President Club," the very first one in the country.[72] Thereafter he continued to shout his praise of the President, even when it became unpopular to do so; thus, Woodring was happier than most Democrats assembled in Philadelphia in July 1948 when he witnessed the nomination of the "Man from Missouri." Several days later he went to the White House to congratulate the new nominee and to pledge his support in the campaign. That fall Woodring made several speeches on behalf of his friend, even though a number of fellow Democrats felt that it was foolish to do so.[73] After all, they asked, what chance did Truman have against Thomas Dewey? Nevertheless, Woodring continued to be optimistic. On 14 October he sent a telegram to the President, in which he said, "You are making the greatest, wisest and most effective one-man campaign in the history of Presidential campaigns."[74] Apparently the statement was true, because three weeks later Truman pulled the greatest political upset of all time as he defeated the Republican nominee and earned four more years in the White House. For the next four years Woodring remained a loyal supporter on every policy stand, domestic or foreign, that HST took. For example, he was in complete accord with Truman's Korean policy, because it gave "warning to Russia that no further aggressive conflict in the world will be accepted without a war."[75]

No sooner had Truman won the election of 1948 than Woodring began to search for a man that the Democrats could support for the presidency in the next election. Consequently, it was for that reason that he traveled to Paris in 1951 to see General Eisenhower, who was then serving as commander of NATO. At that meeting, Woodring urged Eisenhower, his friend of thirty-three years, whose political affiliation was unclear at that time, to enter the presidential race as a Democrat. Ike side-stepped the offer by claiming that he did not want to be President; but he did leave the door open to further consideration by stating that he had always served his country in whatever capacity he had been called.[76] Convinced that Eisenhower would not run in 1952, Woodring then urged another old friend, Gen. Douglas MacArthur, to seek the post, even if it meant running as a Republican.[77] This offer was likewise rejected. When in 1952 Eisenhower subsequently became the Republican presidential candidate, Woodring was not only disappointed with his friend's choice of party, but he also found himself in a political dilemma. On the one hand, he considered Ike to be the best man for the job, but in order to support him he would have to abandon the Democratic party. On the other hand, if he maintained his party allegiance, he would be supporting a man in whom he did not have confidence, Adlai Stevenson. Being unwilling to commit himself to either course, Woodring merely watched the campaign while privately hoping for an Eisenhower victory.[78]

When Eisenhower won the 1952 election and moved into the house at 1600 Pennsylvania Avenue, Woodring was quite pleased that, for the third time in a row, one of his friends was occupying that residence. Unfortunately, Woodring was unable to benefit from his friendship with the new President, because he virtually destroyed that relationship in the summer of 1954 when he instigated the Woodring-Marshall-McCarthy controversy.

This incident took place in August of 1954, when a motion of censure against the "great Communist hunter," Senator Joseph McCarthy of Wisconsin, was being debated on the floor of the Senate. During that discussion Senator Herbert Lehman of New York called attention to a 1951 speech in which McCarthy launched an "unwarranted attack" on Gen. George Marshall. At that point McCarthy, in order to back up his claim that the statements in that speech were justifiable, introduced a letter written by Woodring to a friend in New York.[79] In the letter, which McCarthy had reprinted in the *Congressional Record*, Woodring had claimed that when General Marshall went to China in 1946 to try to settle differences between the Communists and the Nationalists, he had known that "he was selling out to the Reds." Woodring then went on to say: "I learned to know him [Marshall] better than most people who have not had the close association, and I can tell you that he would sell out his grandmother for personal advantage; that he would sell out his policies, beliefs, and standards to maintain his political and military position with the powers that be."[80] These charges against a man as well known, respected, and loved as Marshall attracted considerable attention throughout the nation. Immediately, many Americans came to Marshall's defense, but, of all the defenders, none was so effective as President Eisenhower.

Just two days after Woodring's controversial letter was made public,

Eisenhower held a previously scheduled news conference at which the first question asked was what he thought of Woodring's statement. After a few moments of silence, the President launched into an emotion-packed acclamation of Marshall, who, he said, "has typified all that we look for in what we call an American patriot." After calling attention to specific acts of unselfish service that Marshall had rendered to the country, the President concluded, "I think it is a sorry reward, at the end of at least fifty years of service to this country, to say that he is not a loyal, fine American and that he served only in order to advance his own personal ambitions." At no time did Ike mention the man whose statement had started the controversy.[81]

After the President had made his statement, Woodring felt that he had no alternative but to let the matter rest. To make a further statement would have only complicated matters by opening the way for a series of charges and countercharges. Because Woodring felt that his letter, whose authorship he openly acknowledged, had already antagonized too many people, he said nothing. Marshall likewise refused to make a statement, and subsequently the controversy just faded away, but not without having a drastic effect on the Eisenhower-Woodring relationship. From that time on, Eisenhower had very little to do with his fellow Kansan, and when they did meet, as they did in connection with Woodring's later work on the Eisenhower Foundation, their encounters were quite perfunctory.

After the Woodring-Marshall controversy, most Kansans felt (and many hoped) that they had heard and seen the last of Harry Woodring; but they were mistaken, because he had enough fight left in him to make one last attempt to reenter politics. Early in 1956 a number of state Democratic leaders approached Woodring about running for the governorship once again, but he rejected their offer, claiming that he was not interested in returning to political life. As a result, they turned to their unsuccessful 1954 nominee, George Docking, a prominent Lawrence banker. Convinced that they had avoided an expensive and divisive primary campaign, the Democrats began to plan ahead for the general election. Those plans, however, had to be scrapped on 20 June, when, just fifteen minutes before the deadline, Woodring filed as a Democratic candidate.[82] Just why he entered the race never became clear, but several of his closest political associates feel that it was to prove to his family and friends that he still had the ability and stamina to seek, win, and hold a high political office. Others who knew him saw it as an attempt to regain the glory, recognition, and feeling of importance that he had once known as Governor and as a cabinet member.[83]

Publicly, Woodring claimed that he was entering the primary race in response to requests from people throughout the state to "unite [the] party and in the general election unite the state." His move shocked, confused,

252

and divided Kansas Democrats, and while Docking's forces were clearing their heads, Woodring went to work. Although the former Governor stated initially that he would not conduct a vigorous campaign, he did not stick to that pledge, because it simply was not his style. His pace in the weeks that followed was hectic, and it needed to be if he were going to win, since there were just seven weeks between the day he filed for candidacy and the election. The first three weeks were spent raising money and creating a statewide organization. He got former State Chairman Evan Griffith to head his campaign, and together they hammered out a viable force made up of old political allies and party leaders who were still peeved at Docking's failure "to cooperate in perfecting a harmonious organization" in 1954.[84]

On 11 July, just four weeks before the election, Woodring traveled to Hays, where he officially opened his campaign. In the next twenty-eight days the sixty-nine-year-old candidate, with his wife always at his side, set a pace that most observers marveled at. Traveling to six or eight towns a day, he gave between fifty and sixty speeches a week. Such vigorous campaigning appeared to be winning increased support, but the question remained as to whether or not he had time to catch up with Docking. Rather than focus on one issue as he had ten years before, Woodring utilized a broad-based appeal which called for increased aid to education, a statewide probationary system for paroled prisoners, an expanded mental-health program, a new state budgetary system, greater state promotion of tourism and industry, and an updated conservation program. He was also critical of Republican "bickering in state government," and he stated that neither candidate in the opposition party was "fit to be Governor." In appealing to Kansas Democrats, Woodring put himself forth as a "true Democrat"; and while he did not personally attack Docking, he let his supporters note that "Mr. Docking registered as a Democrat for the first time on February 1, 1950." The Docking forces, on the other hand, labeled Woodring a "pseudo-Republican," who had bolted the party in 1944 and attempted to block the reelection of President Roosevelt.[85] These charges, especially with their anti–FDR tone, undoubtedly hurt Woodring to some extent, but they were not as damaging as they might have been had it not been for a letter from James Roosevelt, then a United States Congressman from California, which clarified the relationship between his father and Woodring. That letter, which Woodring widely publicized, said in part:

I have heard . . . that it might be expected that you would be attacked on the grounds that there had been serious differences between you and my father. While I am sure that it is not necessary, I would like to make the record clear that not only were there not any serious differences but to the very end my father considered you as one of his loyal and trusted friends and advisers.[86]

253

Thereafter the Woodring-Roosevelt relationship was not brought up by either side.

In contrast to Woodring's dynamic, aggressive campaign, Docking ran a dignified but low-key contest which was aimed more at the Republicans than at his Democratic opponent. On 7 August more than 150,000 Kansas Democrats, a very large number for that state, went to the polls to select their gubernatorial candidate, and in the end, Docking edged out Woodring by less than 900 votes—76,187-to-75,333.[87] After winning his three previous primary contests, Woodring went down to his first defeat, and with that setback his political career came to an end. Even though his age perhaps hurt him, the telling factor was probably the late date that he entered the contest, for by that time most party leaders had already committed themselves to Docking. Nevertheless, the fact that Woodring could enter the primary just seven weeks before the voting and almost single-handedly wage a battle that was to bring him so close to victory is a tribute to his organizational ability and his political skill. For Woodring's sake it was too bad that he did not win, because it was destined to be a Democratic year for the governorship, since the Republicans were badly split after Topeka attorney Warren W. Shaw defeated Governor Fred Hall rather handily in the Republican primary. Therefore, in November, Docking romped to an easy victory and became only the sixth Democrat to hold the highest elective office in the state.[88]

After the 1956 setback, Woodring resigned himself to the fact that his political career was at an end, but that was not to mean that the years to follow were to be any less active than the first seventy had been. While he continued to pursue a variety of business interests, his search to find that one big financial venture that would bring him a fortune and end his financial worries never came to an end. The boy from Elk City made a fair amount of money in his lifetime, but he spent it about as fast as he could earn it, and thus, in his later years, he continually experienced financial difficulties.[89]

One of the most enjoyable experiences that he had during the 1950s and 1960s was in serving on such advisory agencies as the Franklin Delano Roosevelt Citizens Commission, the Kansas Commission for Constitutional Revision, the Eisenhower Foundation, and the Hoover Citizens Commission. It was through his work on the last-named that he became the best of friends with former President Hoover. Woodring also kept up with developments in the Army through personal contacts with such men as Secretaries of the Army Frank Pace, Jr. (1950–1953) and Cyrus R. Vance (1962–1964). Woodring also served on the Board of Trustees of the Woodlawn Foundation, a group that ultimately succeeded in getting the Virginia mansion that the Woodrings had once lived in established as a public shrine.[90]

As Woodring's involvement in politics declined he devoted more and more time to reading—especially history and biography. One very important task that he started several times during these years, but, unfortunately, never finished, was an autobiography, or a firsthand account, of his controversial political career. Each time one of his old cronies, such as Henry Morgenthau, Jr., Harold Ickes, or James Farley came out with his account of what had happened, Woodring would indicate that he was going to tell his side of the story; but he never did. On a few occasions he began to work on his memoirs, only to turn his attention elsewhere.[91] He rarely commented on his own career or his place in history, and to justify that stand he would say, "Well, history will tell the tale—the man himself will tell on himself."[92]

The fifties and sixties also saw him return to the bridge table—a pastime that he had so enjoyed in his prepolitical days. One of his regular playing partners was his former political rival Alf Landon. They were frequently joined by another of Topeka's most famous citizens, Dr. Karl Menninger, the world-renowned psychiatrist who had become a good friend of Woodring's many years before. These men, along with several friends, would usually get together once a week to play bridge and discuss everything from politics to psychiatry.[93]

Woodring had other joys in these years. One of these was the satisfaction of seeing his children grow up, marry, and have children of their own. Melissa, after graduating from Stanford University, married a geologist and had three children, while Cooper, who graduated from the University of Kansas, became an industrial designer and the father of two children. As the Woodring children were experiencing the happiness of marriage, Harry and Helen were having their difficulties, and in March 1960, after nearly twenty-seven years of marriage, they were divorced. They parted without bitterness, and he stayed in Topeka, while she returned East, going to Wilmington, Delaware, where she resumed the art career that she had given up nearly three decades before.[94]

The years following the divorce were lonely ones for the former political figure. Melissa and Cooper had moved out of the state, and thus they and their children got back to Topeka only occasionally. The number of his friends also declined, due to death and illness, and those who were more active found less and less in common with the worn-out politician. Consequently, Woodring became increasingly reclusive, although he did spend considerable time out of doors, maintaining the extensive and beautiful flower gardens that surrounded his showplace on Gage Boulevard.

To loneliness were added the problems of failing health as the human dynamo began to wear out. In 1958 he became a diabetic, and complications from that condition caused him to be hospitalized from time to time thereafter. In 1963 he required surgery on a broken hip received in a fall, and three years later he suffered a cerebral hemorrhage that nearly resulted in death. The following September, while he was standing near his kitchen stove, his pajamas caught fire, and he suffered first- and second-degree burns over a large portion of his body. Two days later, on 9 September 1967, "a stroke suffered while he was recuperating from the burns" proved fatal. Three days later the Woodring children, along with their gracious mother, who had returned for the funeral, stood in Topeka's Mt. Hope Cemetery as 105-mm. howitzers boomed out the final salute to the eighty-year-old former Secretary of War.[95]

The last twenty-seven years of Woodring's life had indeed been frustrating. Removal from his cabinet post in 1940, followed by an unsuccessful attempt to block President Roosevelt's bid for a fourth term; defeat in the 1946 Kansas gubernatorial election; the death of his young son Marcus; a controversy that cost him the friendship of two long-time friends—General George Marshall and President Dwight D. Eisenhower; defeat in the 1956 Kansas gubernatorial primary; and the end of a once-happy marriage—all served to make these years ones of frustration. Woodring was a man whose political career had peaked when he was still in his forties; thus, when he was forced out of public life at the age of fifty-three, he began a search that hopefully would enable him to recapture the glory and to exercise the power that he had previously known. Although, unfortunately, he was never able to regain those golden days, he was fortunate in having had the opportunity to enjoy them once; that is more than most men can say. Perhaps the most fitting epitaph was provided by Woodring himself in the closing lines of his Topeka address of 9 July 1940, when he said:

The fact that a Kansas country boy, without previously seeking or holding public office, could be elected governor of this great commonwealth of ours, and subsequently serve in the Cabinet of the President, is further evidence that our great democracy does work. . . . It has been a great experience for me in Washington. A Kansas boy has dined with kings and queens, with princes and princesses, ambassadors and foreign diplomats, and has sat at the right hand of the President. But, truly, a Kansas boy has seen Utopia from the mountaintops. But today a Kansas boy returns to heaven.[96]

Notes

The following shortened forms have been used throughout the notes:

Capital   *Topeka Daily Capital*
DDEL   Dwight David Eisenhower Library, Abilene, Kansas
FDRL   Franklin Delano Roosevelt Library, Hyde Park, New York
HSTL   Harry S Truman Library, Independence, Missouri
KSHS   Kansas State Historical Society, Topeka, Kansas
LC   Library of Congress, Washington, D.C.
NA   National Archives
PPF   President's Personal File
PSF   President's Secretary File
RG   Record Group
Star   *Kansas City Star*
WGP   Woodring's Governor Papers
WPP   Woodring's Personal Papers

The dates and places of interviews are listed in a section of the Bibliography.

CHAPTER 1

1. *New York Times*, 21 June 1940.
2. Grace Tully, *F.D.R.: My Boss* (New York: Charles Scribner's Sons, 1949), p. 170; Marquis Childs, "Washington Calling," *Dallas Morning News*, 20 March 1944.
3. *Elk City Eagle*, 3 June 1887; *Kansas-State Census*, 1895, vol. 245, p. 15, Elk City; interview with Overton Davis.

4. From the time that Woodring entered politics in 1930 he always gave his birth date as 31 May 1890. While there is a possibility that he may have been born on 31 May instead of 30 May, there is no question that he knew that he was born in 1887 (he gave his correct age when he entered the Army). Perhaps it was a desire to appeal to the younger members of the Democratic party in 1930 that led him to use the later birth date. See Keith D. McFarland, "Secretary of War Harry Woodring: Early Career in Kansas," *Kansas Historical Quarterly* 39 (Summer 1973):206–19.

5. Lew W. Duncan, *History of Montgomery County, Kansas* (Iola, Kans.: Press of Iola Register, 1903), pp. 532–33; *Elk City Eagle*, 3 June 1887.

6. "Woodring Family History," two-page mimeographed sheet presented to the author by Mrs. Eleanor B. Hungerford, 12 August 1971.

7. Materials on "Woodring Family Tree" contained in the Harry H. Woodring Papers. At the time that they were examined, the uncatalogued personal papers of Harry Woodring were in the possession of his son, Cooper C. Woodring, of Plandome, New York. Hereafter these papers will be cited as WPP.

8. Hines Woodring obituary, *Neodesha Sun*, 15 December 1928; *Neodesha Register*, 20 December 1928.

9. After moving to Kansas, Hines Woodring always claimed that he had enlisted in the Union Army in 1864, but official records indicate that he was enrolled on 31 March 1865 and mustered into service on 7 April 1865. "Statement of the Military Service of Haynes Woodring," issued by Maj. Gen. E. S. Adams, The Adjutant General, to Harry H. Woodring, 21 May 1938, WPP; *History of Montgomery County*, p. 532; *Neodesha Register* 20 December 1928.

10. *History of Montgomery County*, p. 532; obituary of Melissa Jane Woodring, *Neodesha Register*, 15 January 1918; *Neodesha Sun*, 15 December 1928; "Hines Woodring—Recalls Some Aspects of His Life," *Montgomery County Clippings*, vol. 3, p. 163, KSHS; Raydene James Benfield, *Elk City, Kansas: Then and Now* (n.p.: Midwestern Litho, 1964), pp. 2–9.

11. Materials relating to "Woodring Family Tree," WPP; *History of Montgomery County*, p. 533; Benfield, *Elk City*, pp. 4, 8.

12. *Elk City Enterprise*, 30 May 1890 and 8 April 1892.

13. Francis W. Schruben, comp., *Harry H. Woodring Speaks: Kansas Politics during the Early Depression* (Los Angeles, Calif.: Francis W. Schruben, 1963), p. 4.

14. *History of Montgomery County*, p. 533; *Elk City Enterprise*, 24 April and 26 July 1891.

15. Benfield, *Elk City*, pp. 7–9.

16. Interviews with Overton Davis, Frank Dancer, and W. A. Stafford; *Star*,

5 October 1930; William G. Clugston, *Rascals in Democracy* (New York: Richard R. Smith, 1941), pp. 165–66.

17. Woodring to Gabriel Tenaglia, 15 April 1940, box 123, "Secretary of War General Correspondence, 1932–1942," NA, RG 107.

18. *Star*, 5 October 1930; *Elk City Eagle*, 1 July 1904; *Ahepa Magazine*, May 1932, p. 16; interview with Overton Davis.

19. *Washington Post*, 26 September 1936; *Star*, 10 August and 5 October 1930; *Topeka State Journal*, 28 June 1930; *Capital*, 22 January 1956; interviews with Cooper C. Woodring, 10 June and 20 July 1968.

20. *Elk City Enterprise*, 14 May and 21 June 1897.

21. Gladys Sewell Sauer to author, 8 July 1971; interview with Byron D. Drybread, who presently lives in the old Woodring home on Maple Street in Elk City.

22. *Star*, 5 October 1930.

23. Unfortunately, school officials in Elk City and Independence, Kans., were unable to find any of Woodring's records; however, several contemporary accounts refer to him as an "outstanding student." *Montgomery County History*, p. 533; Lila G. George to author, 5 November 1971.

24. Woodring to John C. O'Laughlin, 24 July 1940, John C. O'Laughlin Papers, LC. O'Laughlin, who served as First Assistant Secretary of State under President Theodore Roosevelt and later as the editor and publisher of the *Army and Navy Journal*, was a close friend of Woodring's from 1933 until O'Laughlin's death in 1949.

25. *Star*, 5 October 1930; questionnaire filled out by Woodring for *National Cyclopedia of American Biography*, copy given to author by Cooper C. Woodring; Gladys Sewell Sauer to author, 8 July 1971.

26. *Elk City Enterprise*, 1 January 1904.

27. *Elk City Enterprise*, 8 January 1904.

28. *Elk City Enterprise*, 24 June and 11 November 1904; *Lebanon* (Ind.) *Pioneer*, 30 October 1913; Ralph W. Stark to author, 15 March 1971.

29. Ralph W. Stark to author, 23 February and 1 March 1971. Mr. Stark, of Lebanon, Ind., was of great help in locating information on "Lebanon University," which Woodring frequently listed as part of his educational experience.

30. *Elk City Enterprise*, 28 April 1905.

31. Benfield, *Elk City*, p. 10; *Star*, 5 October 1930.

32. *Star*, 5 October 1930.

33. *Little Bear Tracks: A Book of Pictures, Articles, Records, and Events That Helped to Form Neodesha's 100 Years* (Neodesha, Kans.: Neodesha Printing Co., 1971). pp. 19–21, 28–29.

34. *Star*, 5 October 1930 and 10 September 1967; *Capital*, 22 January 1956; *Neodesha Register*, 15 January 1918.

35. *Star*, 5 October 1930.
36. Rev. Raymond W. Settle to Woodring, 26 February 1937, WPP; interview with Overton Davis.
37. Such delays in interment were not unusual, because the frozen ground made grave-digging impossible in the winter months; thus, caskets would be placed in a mausoleum until the ground thawed and a grave could be dug.
38. Woodring diary, 5 May 1918, WPP.
39. Ibid., 7–11 May 1918.
40. "Eisenhower Report on Camp Colt," Capt. D. D. Eisenhower to the Chief of the Tank Corps, 5 August 1920, DDEL. For Eisenhower's recollections of his assignment at Camp Colt see Dwight D. Eisenhower, *At Ease: Stories I Tell to Friends* (Garden City, N.Y.: Doubleday & Co., 1967), pp. 137–52.
41. Woodring to Lida Woodring, 12 May 1918; Woodring to Shirley Shaffer, 18 May 1918, WPP.
42. Woodring diary, 31 May, 7, 15, and 24 June, and 4 July 1918, WPP.
43. Woodring to Shirley Shaffer, 18 May 1918, WPP.
44. Woodring diary, 12 June and 21 August 1918, WPP.
45. Woodring to Lida Woodring, 21 August 1918, WPP.
46. "Eisenhower Report on Camp Colt," Capt. D. D. Eisenhower to the Chief of the Tank Corps, 5 August 1920, DDEL.
47. Woodring diary, 9, 10, and 16 September 1918, WPP.
48. Ibid., 4 and 24 September 1918; Woodring's Discharge to Accept Commission, 4 October 1918; Woodring to Lida Woodring, 25 November 1918, WPP.
49. Woodring diary, 8 October 1918; Woodring to Lida Woodring, 18 November 1918; Extract—Special Order 269, Headquarters, Camp Dix, N.J., 15 December 1918, WPP; Certificate of Military Service presented to author by Cooper C. Woodring.
50. *Reserve Officer*, May 1933, p. 3; interviews with Helen Coolidge Woodring, 20 July and 28 December 1968; Woodring to Floyd L. Parks, 1 December 1931, WPP. Parks, who was Woodring's company commander at Fort Dix, later advanced to lieutenant general, and during World War II was, among other things, Chief of Staff of the Army Ground Forces, Commander of the First Airborne Army, and Commander of the U.S. section of Berlin.
51. Woodring diary, numerous entires, May through September 1918, WPP.
52. Interview with Arthur B. Shaffer, Woodring's brother-in-law.
53. Woodring diary, 7 January 1919, WPP; *Star*, 5 October 1930.
54. Interviews with Overton Davis and with Lawrence J. Catlin; Clugston, *Rascals in Democracy*, p. 166.

55. Interview with C. A. McCullough; Clugston, *Rascals in Democracy*, p. 166; Col. Edward A. Metcalf, III, to author, 12 July 1972.
56. *Neodesha Register*, 28 March 1929.
57. *Star*, 5 October 1930; *Neodesha Register*, 28 March 1929; Clugston, *Rascals in Democracy*, p. 166; "From Private to Secretary of War," *Recruiting News*, November 1936, p. 9.
58. *Bank News*, 1 August 1928, p. 7; "Address of H. H. Woodring at 1927 Conference" of county farm agents held at Kansas State Agricultural College (n.d.), WPP.
59. "History of Southeast Kansas, Inc.," *Southeast Kansan*, 1 February 1930, p. 2.
60. Woodring to Gov. Ben S. Paulen, 14 June 1927; draft of invitation to Flood Control Conference (n.d.), Folder—"Flood Control Conference," Gov. Ben S. Paulen's Papers, KSHS; *Star*, 29 and 30 June 1927.
61. *Democratic State Handbook* (1932) (Salina, Kans.: Democratic State Committee, n.d.), p. 3; *Neodesha Sun*, 4 January 1928; *Neodesha Register*, 7 March 1929.
62. *Star*, 5 October 1930; interview with Ralph Crowder.
63. *Star*, 5 October 1930; Rev. Tom Parish, Jr., to author, 17 June 1971.
64. *Star*, 5 October 1930.
65. F. C. Cooley to Joe W. Allen, published in the centennial issue of the *Neodesha Daily Sun*, 15 June 1971.
66. For a good account of Woodring's Legion activities, as well as the role and importance of that organization in Kansas, see Richard J. Loosbrock, *The History of the Kansas Department of the American Legion* (Topeka: Kansas Department of the American Legion, 1968).
67. Loosbrock, *History of the Kansas Department*, pp. 83–84; interview with Lawrence J. Catlin.
68. Loosbrock, *History of the Kansas Department*, pp. 83, 265.
69. Ibid., p. 83; *Minutes, Kansas Department, the American Legion*, 3–5 September 1928, Pittsburg, Kans. (Kansas City: Benson Brown Reporting Service), p. 71, WPP; *Neodesha Sun*, 5 September 1928; *Neodesha Register*, 6 September 1928.
70. Loosbrock, *History of the Kansas Department*, p. 84.
71. Confidential communication.
72. *Neodesha Sun*, 15 December 1928; *Neodesha Register*, 28 March and 4 April 1929; *Star*, 5 October 1930. On a visit to Neodesha, I was unable to learn more of the controversy that erupted over the sale of the bank, but many old-timers recalled that much "bad blood" resulted between Woodring and his former associates.

CHAPTER 2

1. *Neodesha Register*, 28 March 1929; C. R. Bennett to Woodring, 30 July 1937, WPP; confidential communication.
2. Republican strength in Kansas can be seen in the results of the 1928 election, in which Herbert Hoover polled 513,672 votes to Al Smith's 193,003, Clyde Reed defeated Democrat Chauncey B. Little for Governor by more than 200,000 votes, seven of eight Kansas congressional seats went to the Republicans, and the entire Republican state-wide ticket emerged victorious. William F. Zornow, *Kansas: A History of the Jayhawk State* (Norman: University of Oklahoma Press, 1957), p. 243.
3. Confidential communication.
4. *Iola Daily News*, 14 February 1928; interview with Lawrence J. Catlin.
5. Confidential communication.
6. Interviews with Lawrence J. Catlin and with C. A. McCullough.
7. Confidential communication.
8. The three Democratic Governors of Kansas prior to this time were George W. Glick, 1883–1885; George H. Hodges, 1913–1915; and Jonathan M. Davis, 1923–1925.
9. *Capital*, 10 January 1930; *Pittsburg* (Kans.) *Headlight*, 10 January 1930.
10. *Capital*, 25 and 26 January 1930.
11. *Star*, 10 August and 5 October 1930.
12. *Independence Reporter*, 7 April 1930; *Capital*, 8 April 1930; *Neodesha Register*, 10 April 1930; confidential communication.
13. *Pittsburg Headlight*, 11 April 1930; *Capital*, 17 and 27 July 1930; Schruben, *Harry H. Woodring Speaks*, pp. 3–4.
14. *Capital*, 17 and 27 July and 1 August 1930.
15. Democratic campaign literature for the 1930 gubernatorial campaign, WPP.
16. Of nearly two dozen Woodring acquaintances who were asked about his oratorical skill, all but one indicated that they considered him to be a very effective public speaker, and more than half felt that his speaking ability was an important, if not his most important, political asset; *Star*, 5 October 1930; *Capital*, 4 November 1932; confidential communication.
17. *Capital*, 20 April 1930.
18. *Capital*, 4 and 13 July and 5 August 1930.
19. *Capital*, 17 and 27 July and 7 August 1930; Schruben, *Harry H. Woodring Speaks*, p. 3; Francis W. Schruben, *Kansas in Turmoil, 1930–1936* (Columbia: University of Missouri Press, 1969), p. 27; Joseph H. McDowell to author, 14 June 1971.
20. The statement of campaign expenses, which had to be filed with the Secretary of State, placed Bowman's expenses at $6,280.90 and Woodring's at $375.85. While these figures undoubtedly indicate different interpretations

of "campaign expenses," they are probably indicative of the relative expenditures. *Capital,* 7 September 1930.

21. *Capital,* 4 July 1930; *Star,* 5 October 1930.
22. Printed copy of "Fox Movietone speech made June 8, 1930"; printed program of radio station WREN (Lawrence) for the week of 27 July to 2 August 1930, WPP.
23. *Capital,* 20 July 1930.
24. *Capital,* 5 August 1930.
25. Kansas Secretary of State, *Twenty-Seventh Biennial Report* (Topeka, Kans.: State Printer, 1930), p. 37.
26. *Capital,* 8 August 1930.
27. For an account of Kansas politics in the twenties see A. Bower Sageser, "Political Patterns of the 1920's," in John D. Bright, ed., *Kansas: The First Century* (New York: Lewis Historical Publishing Co., 1956), 2:71–88.
28. Zornow, *Kansas,* pp. 244–45.
29. For an excellent account of the 1930 campaign and election see chap. 2, "The 'Short Count' Election," in Schruben's *Kansas in Turmoil;* for interesting but less detailed accounts see Clifford R. Hope, Sr., "Kansas in the 1930's," *Kansas Historical Quarterly* 36 (Spring 1970):9–12; William B. Bracke, *Wheat Country* (New York: Duell, Sloan & Pearce, 1950), pp. 164–75; Loosbrock, *History of the Kansas Department,* pp. 85–86.
30. *Star,* 5 October 1930; *Hutchinson News,* 4 August 1930.
31. *Capital,* 7 September 1930; *Star,* 5 October 1930.
32. *Capital,* 8 August 1930.
33. Clugston, *Rascals in Democracy,* p. 169.
34. Dudley Doolittle to Woodring, 13 August, 1930, WPP; *Capital,* 8 August 1930; confidential communication.
35. *Capital,* 24 and 25 August 1930; Schruben, *Kansas in Turmoil,* p. 27.
36. Schruben, *Kansas in Turmoil,* p. ix.
37. Clugston, *Rascals in Democracy,* pp. 167–69; Goerge Templar, "The Federal Judiciary of Kansas," *Kansas Historical Quarterly* 37 (Spring 1971): 12–13. Helvering did avoid "big politics" until the late twenties, when he ran for and was elected mayor of Salina, a position that he still held when he was appointed to the state chairmanship.
38. James D. Callahan, ed., *Jayhawk Editor: A Biography of A. Q. Miller, Sr.* (Los Angeles: Sterling Press, 1955), pp. 226–27.
39. *Capital,* 25 August 1930; confidential communication.
40. *Capital,* 7 September and 18 October 1930; confidential communication.
41. *Capital,* 24 and 25 August 1930; *Hutchinson News,* 26 August 1930.
42. *Capital,* 27 August 1930.
43. *Capital,* 25, 27, and 31 August 1930.

44. *Capital*, 2 September 1930; Loosbrock, *History of the Kansas Department*, pp. 87–88.
45. Although negotiations were undertaken to get Reed to support Woodring, he never openly did so; however, in return for pledges to retain some of his appointees, Reed did "cross swords" with Haucke on several occasions during the general-election campaign. In this way Reed indicated that he did not wish his sheep to return to the fold; confidential communication. For examples of Reed-Haucke clashes, see the *Capital*, 21 and 28 October 1930. On page 16 of his anti-Landon book entitled *The Tale of a Fox* (Wichita, Kans.: B. Comer, 1936) author Burt Comer tells of a meeting between Woodring and Reed's representative Alf Landon in which the former agreed to split the patronage 60–40 in return for Reed's support. While Comer's details and the names of the actual participants may not be accurate, I have strong reason to believe that such a meeting did in fact take place.
46. *Capital*, 13 September 1930.
47. *Capital*, 7 September 1930. On 6 August, the day after the primary, the *Capital* ran a large picture of Haucke on the front page with the caption "Next Governor of Kansas."
48. *Capital*, 5 October 1930.
49. *Capital*, 5, 23, and 26 October and 2 November 1930.
50. *Capital*, 21 September 1930.
51. *Capital*, 5 October 1930.
52. Hope, "Kansas in the 1930's," p. 9.
53. A number of works on Brinkley and his political activities have appeared, but perhaps the best two accounts are to be found in Francis Schruben's *Kansas in Turmoil*, pp. 28–46, 79–103, and in Don B. Slechta's "Dr. John R. Brinkley: A Kansas Phenomenon" (Master's thesis, Fort Hays Kansas State College, 1952); also see Gerald Carson, *The Roguish World of Doctor Brinkley* (New York: Holt, Rinehart & Winston, 1960).
54. Schruben, *Kansas in Turmoil*, pp. 28–29; Bracke, *Wheat Country*, pp. 166–68; Walter Davenport, "Gland Time in Kansas," *Collier's*, 16 January 1932, p. 49.
55. After a 20–22 June 1930 hearing, the Federal Radio Commission refused to renew Brinkley's broadcasting license; however, legal appeals delayed the suspension until after the election. Consequently, Brinkley was able to utilize his station throughout the campaign.
56. Schruben, *Kansas in Turmoil*, p. 29; Bracke, *Wheat Country*, pp. 167, 169; *Capital*, 20 September 1930.
57. *Capital*, 20 September 1930; *Hutchinson News*, 20 September 1930.
58. *Capital*, 2 and 5 October 1930; *Hutchinson News*, 3 October 1930.
59. Frank ("Chief") Haucke to author, 24 May 1971.

60. *Capital*, 7, 12, 23, and 26 October 1930.
61. *Capital*, 23 October 1930.
62. *Capital*, 22, 26, 29, and 31 October 1930.
63. Schruben, *Kansas in Turmoil*, pp. 34-35.
64. Ibid., pp. 33-34; *Star*, 5 October 1930.
65. *Capital*, 1, 18, and 22 October 1930.
66. Schruben, *Kansas in Turmoil*, pp. 32-33.
67. *Capital*, 26 October 1930. Emphasis was placed on "J. R. Brinkley" because that was the name by which he was registered as a candidate, and, in light of a ruling by the Kansas Attorney General, it was felt that any other write-in variation would either be invalid or that each variation would be counted as a vote for a separate person. Schruben, *Kansas in Turmoil*, pp. 30-31.
68. *Capital*, 23 and 26 October 1930.
69. Clifford Stratton in the *Capital*, 26 October 1930.
70. *Capital*, 26, 30, and 31 October 1930; *Hutchinson News*, 29 October 1930.
71. *Capital*, 31 October 1930.
72. *Capital*, 31 October and 4 November 1930.
73. *Capital*, 26 October 1930; the *Hutchinson News* of 3 November reported: "There is general agreement on the theory that Mr. Woodring's candidacy has blown up on account of the defection to Brinkley."
74. *Capital*, 5-14 November 1930.
75. Schruben, *Harry H. Woodring Speaks*, p. 5.
76. Socialist candidate J. B. Shields polled 3,866. Kansas Secretary of State, *Twenty-Seventh Biennial Report*, p. 103.
77. Schruben, *Kansas in Turmoil*, pp. 38-43.
78. The reason that a recount was not requested is not clear, but perhaps Don Slechta, in his Master's thesis, "Dr. John R. Brinkley: A Kansas Phenomenon," gives us the best explanation (pp. 131-32): "The Republicans were afraid to ask for a recount that . . . would show that a gigantic fraud had kept the governorship from John R. Brinkley." As to Brinkley: "His advisers talked him out of the idea, because it was felt that he might not get a square deal on the recount and because of the tremendous cost involved." According to historian Donald R. McCoy, Brinkley could not request a recount because he was not on the ballot. Donald R. McCoy, *Landon of Kansas* (Lincoln: University of Nebraska Press, 1966), p. 92. Contemporary accounts made no reference to such a prohibition as McCoy cites.
79. *Capital*, 19 November and 9, 11, 12, and 29 December 1930.
80. Although Woodring had initially predicted that the tax question, especially the income-tax amendment, would become a major issue, it never did, because neither he nor Haucke wanted to stir up the voters on the controversial issue; they both contented themselves by going on record in favor of

the tax amendment but rarely mentioning it in their campaigning. Brinkley, on the other hand, actively urged defeat of the "vicious proposal," which would just add to the tax burden of already overburdened taxpayers. The income-tax amendment was defeated by about 236,000 to 228,000.

81. *Capital*, 5 and 23 November and 12 December 1930 and 4 January 1931; *Hutchinson News*, 5 January 1931.
82. *Capital*, 6 January 1931.
83. *Capital*, 11 December 1930.
84. *Capital*, 4 January 1931; *Hutchinson News*, 26 December 1930.

CHAPTER 3

1. *Capital*, 11 and 13 January 1931; *Hutchinson News*, 12 January 1931; *Inaugural Address of Harry H. Woodring, Governor, January 12, 1931* (Topeka: State Printer, 1931).
2. *Star*, 5 October 1930; *Capital*, 12 January 1931.
3. *Capital*, 13 January 1931; *Hutchinson News*, 16 January 1931.
4. Schruben, *Kansas in Turmoil*, pp. 47–50, 69–71; Hope, "Kansas in the 1930's," pp. 1–8.
5. Schruben, *Kansas in Turmoil*, pp. 65, 71–72.
6. *Capital*, 23 November and 28 December 1930.
7. *Capital*, 19 and 30 November and 9, 11, and 12 December 1930 and 4 and 6 January 1931.
8. *Message of Governor Harry H. Woodring to the Kansas Legislature of 1931* (Topeka: State Printer, 1931).
9. Zornow, *Kansas*, p. 247; *Capital*, 28 December 1930.
10. *Message of Governor Harry H. Woodring to the Kansas Legislature of 1931*; *Capital*, 15 January 1931.
11. *Emporia Daily Gazette*, 15 January 1931.
12. *Star*, 15 January 1931; *Abilene Reflector*, 19 January 1931.
13. *Capital*, 15 January 1931.
14. *Capital*, 6 February 1931.
15. *Capital*, 8 February 1931.
16. *Capital*, 6 and 8 February 1931; *Hutchinson News*, 7 February 1931.
17. *Special Message to the Legislature from Governor H. Woodring, February 16, 1931* (Topeka: State Printer, 1931).
18. *Capital*, 14 and 15 March 1931; *Hutchinson News*, 13 March 1931.
19. *Capital*, 20 March 1931.
20. *Capital*, 22 March 1931.
21. Woodring to R. Norris Miller, 7 January 1933, WGP, KSHS.
22. *Capital*, 14, 15, and 20 March 1931; Zornow, *Kansas*, p. 249.
23. *Capital*, 22 March 1931; *Hutchinson News*, 18 March 1931.
24. Ruth Friedrich, "The Threadbare Thirties," in *Kansas: The First Cen-*

tury, ed. John D. Bright (New York: Lewis Historical Publishing Co., 1956), 2:92; Clugston, *Rascals in Democracy*, pp. 169–72.

25. *Capital*, 14 March 1931; *Hutchinson News*, 13 March 1931.
26. Friedrich, "The Threadbare Thirties," 2:92.
27. *Hutchinson News*, 14 March 1931.
28. Telegram, William Allen White to Woodring, 14 March 1931, William Allen White Papers, Manuscript Division, LC.
29. *Capital*, 15 March 1931.
30. *Capital*, 15 March 1931.
31. Technically the legislature could still have passed the bill over his veto; however, this was highly unlikely, because when the legislators recessed on Friday, 13 March, most of them, considering the session over, returned to their homes. *Hutchinson News*, 14 March 1931.
32. *Capital*, 15 March 1931.
33. *New York Times*, 15 March 1931; *Literary Digest*, 2 May 1931, p. 22; *Christian Science Monitor*, 16 March 1931.
34. *Capital*, 15 March 1931.
35. White to Woodring, 19 March 1931; William Allen White Papers, LC.
36. *Capital*, 12 April 1931.
37. *Capital*, 20 March 1931.
38. *Emporia Daily Gazette*, 2 April 1931; *Atchison Globe*, 29 April 1931; *Capital*, 12 April 1931; *Douglas County Republican*, 13 August 1931.
39. *Capital*, 19 November 1930, 12 January, 22 February, 20 March, and 5 April 1931; interview with Alfred M. Landon; news clipping, *Washington Times-Herald*, n.d. (probably April 1933), in WPP; *Ahepa Magazine*, May 1932, p. 16.
40. Woodring to William H. Gascher, 4 August 1931, WGP.
41. *Capital*, 22 February 1931 and 12 June 1932.
42. *Capital*, 5 April 1931.
43. Clugston, *Rascals in Democracy*, p. 171; *Capital*, 5 April 1931.
44. *Capital*, 4 and 12 January, 22 February, and 1 April 1931; *Hutchinson News*, 26 December 1930; State Democratic Committee, *Democratic State Handbook* (1932), p. 7.
45. *Capital*, 9 December 1930, 14 and 17 March 1931.
46. Woodring to Dr. N. W. Robinson, 21 July 1931; Woodring to Anthony Savito, 3 August 1931, WGP.
47. *Capital*, 20 March and 6 June 1931.
48. Woodring to Horace H. Rich, 23 September 1931, WGP; *Capital*, 12 December 1930.
49. *Capital*, 12 January, 29 March, and 12 April 1931.
50. *Capital*, 1 April 1931; *Hutchinson News*, 31 March and 1 April 1931; Clugston, *Rascals in Democracy*, pp. 171–74.

51. *Capital,* 3 September 1932; *Topeka State Journal,* 10 September 1932; *Horton Headlight Commercial,* 19 September 1932.
52. Avis D. Carlson, "Drowning in Oil," *Harper's Monthly,* October 1931, p. 608.
53. For a detailed account of the oil problem in this period, and especially of Landon's efforts to help solve the crisis, see Donald R. McCoy, "Alfred M. Landon and the Oil Troubles of 1930–1932," *Kansas Historical Quarterly* 31 (Summer 1965):113–37; essentially the same account appears in McCoy's *Landon of Kansas,* pp. 67–90.
54. McCoy, *Landon of Kansas,* p. 74.
55. *Capital,* 29, 30, and 31 January 1931.
56. McCoy, *Landon of Kansas,* p. 79; *Capital,* 29 January 1931.
57. McCoy, *Landon of Kansas,* p. 79; *Capital,* 29 January 1931.
58. *Capital,* 31 January 1931; *Hutchinson News,* 31 January 1931.
59. *Capital,* 8 February 1931; *Hutchinson News,* 9 February 1931.
60. *New York Times,* 28 March 1931; *Hutchinson News,* 27 March and 13 April 1931; *Capital,* 27 March, 11 and 12 April 1931 and 24 May 1932.
61. *Capital,* 8 February 1931, 24 May and 18 October 1932; *Hutchinson News,* 27 March, 13 April, and 23 May 1932.
62. *Capital,* 29 January and 20 September 1931; *New York Times,* 30 May 1931; Woodring to Congressman M. C. Garber, 21 February 1931, WGP.
63. McCoy, *Landon of Kansas,* pp. 80–82.
64. *Hutchinson News,* 16 March 1931. In the summer of 1931 the P.S.C. cut back state production in order to force an increase in oil prices. Woodring, who was pushing more and more for an oil tariff, criticized the proration, saying: "I am against the Mid-Continent states closing the windows against a shower while Washington opens the doors to a flood." *Capital,* 2 September 1931.
65. McCoy, *Landon of Kansas,* p. 81.
66. Ibid., pp. 84–86; Keith L. Bryant, Jr., *Alfalfa Bill Murray* (Norman: University of Oklahoma Press, 1968), p. 199.
67. *Message of Governor Harry H. Woodring to the Kansas Legislature of 1931,* pp. 9–10.
68. Ibid.; *Capital,* 17 February 1931.
69. Schruben, *Harry Woodring Speaks,* pp. 9–10; Woodring to William H. Gascher, 4 August 1931, WGP; *Capital,* 23 June and 1 July 1931.
70. *New York Times,* 24 July 1931; *Hutchinson News,* 20 and 24 July 1931; *Democratic State Handbook* (1932), p. 28.
71. David Lawrence, "American Business and Businessmen," *Saturday Evening Post,* 26 July 1930, p. 34; *Who's Who in America, 1930–1931,* 16:697; *Business Week,* 22 July 1931, pp. 20–21.
72. *Capital,* 30 April and 2 May 1931.

73. *Capital*, 21 June 1931.
74. *Capital*, 23 and 27 June 1931; *Hutchinson News*, 27 June 1931.
75. *Capital*, 3 July 1931.
76. *Capital*, 3 July 1931; *New York Times*, 3 July 1931. Woodring soon became disenchanted with Newcomer, and in February 1932 he tried unsuccessfully to force him to resign. Woodring to Henry K. Koeneke, State Bank Commissioner, 20 February 1932, WGP.
77. *Capital*, 4 and 7 July 1931; *New York Times*, 7 and 8 July 1931. On 6 July, Doherty filed a $12-million libel suit against the *Kansas City Star*, claiming that it was involved in a conspiracy to destroy his business and maintaining that its articles and cartoons influenced Woodring and the P.S.C. to undertake the gas-rate investigation. At the same time, Doherty sent a telegram to Secretary of Commerce Robert P. Lamont, asking him to "proceed against" Woodring because of the Governor's threats "to throw certain Cities Service subsidiaries into receivership" and because of his action banning the sale of Cities Service stock in Kansas. *Capital*, 7 and 11 July 1931; *Outlook and Independent*, 19 August 1931, pp. 483–84.
78. *New York Times*, 14, 15, and 17 July 1931.
79. *New York Times*, 3, 7, 8, 14, 15, and 17 July 1931; *Capital*, 3, 4, 7, 8, 9, 15, and 16 July 1931; *Newton Journal*, 16 July 1931; *Hutchinson News*, 3, 4, and 7 July 1931.
80. *Capital*, 8, 16, and 18 August and 8 and 10 December 1931, 6 February and 22 March 1932; *Hutchinson News*, 16 October and 3 November 1931.
81. *Capital*, 19 and 20 July 1931.
82. *Capital*, 1, 2, 17, and 18 September and 27 October 1932 and 6 January 1933. While the Doherty interests were fighting the reduction in the courts, Woodring, in September 1932, ordered his Attorney General to take action to "bring ouster and receivership proceedings" against ten subsidiary Doherty companies in Kansas, but federal court injunctions halted any such action. Woodring to Attorney General Roland Boynton, 16 September 1932, WPP.
83. McCoy, *Landon of Kansas*, pp. 169–70.
84. *Capital*, 15 June and 27 September 1931.
85. *Capital*, 20 and 22 August, 6 and 27 September, 13, 16, and 18 October, 3, 6, 15, 16, and 27 December 1931; John R. Finger, "The Post-Gubernatorial Career of Jonathan M. Davis," *Kansas Historical Quarterly* 33 (Summer 1967):161.
86. *Capital*, 9 August 1931; Frederick Palmer, *This Man Landon* (New York: Dodd, Mead & Co., 1936), p. 121; *Democratic State Handbook* (1932), p. 21.
87. *Capital*, 6 February 1932.

88. Legislative appropriations were $9.546 million for fiscal year 1932, and $9.033 million for 1933.
89. *Capital*, 1 October 1931 and 17, 18, and 20 March, 17 April, 11 May, 5 and 22 June, and 13, 15, and 31 July 1932.
90. *Capital*, 17 April 1932.
91. Woodring to George E. Rogers, 4 September 1931; Woodring's statement to the School Book Commission, 3 September 1931, WGP; *Capital*, 31 January, 9 July, and 12 August 1932.
92. *Capital*, 13, 14, and 16 August 1931 and 26 April, 7, 18, and 23 August, and 23 December 1932; *Reserve Officer*, May 1933, p. 3; memorandum for Governor Woodring from Brig. Gen. M. R. McLean, The Adjutant General (Kansas), 18 April 1932, WGP; *Army and Navy Journal*, 8 April 1933.
93. Confidential communication.
94. This characteristic appears to be evident when one examines Woodring's career; it was further confirmed in interviews with more than a dozen people who were very close to him, including members of his immediate family.
95. Woodring to Helen Goddard, 1 April 1932, WGP. Woodring's views on drinking were put forth clearly in January 1932, when he fired a hard-drinking State Representative whom he had appointed as a weighmaster in the Grain Department. At that time he said: "I simply will not tolerate drunkenness, any wild parties, or lack of attention to duty . . . if one of my appointees, no matter how influential he may be, thinks he can . . . neglect his duties he has another thought coming." *Capital*, 3 January 1932.
96. *Capital*, 27 March and 23 May 1931; Federal Writers Project, *Kansas: A Guide to the Sunflower State* (New York: Viking Press, 1939), pp. 288–89.
97. *Capital*, 25 March and 23 May 1931; Ernest E. Bearg to Woodring, 25 February 1932, plus numerous newspaper clippings telling of Woodring's visits to horse shows, the Kentucky Derby, football games, etc., all in WPP.

CHAPTER 4

1. *Capital*, 7 and 8 January, 23 February, 22 July, and 25 August 1932; interviews with James A. Farley and with Alfred M. Landon; Joseph H. McDowell to author, 14 June 1971; Clugston, *Rascals in Democracy*, pp. 171–75.
2. Interviews with James A. Farley and with Georgia Neese Clark Gray; confidential communication. That Woodring was not a Helvering puppet appears evident from his subsequent career, because after he went his separate way in the Roosevelt administration in 1933, the former Governor proved to be an effective administrator and politician. During his career in Washington no one ever questioned that Woodring was his own man.

3. After the 1930 reapportionment, Kansas had nine electoral votes, compared to Texas's twenty-three, California's twenty-two, and Oklahoma's eleven. At the 1932 Democratic National Convention, Kansas had twenty delegate votes, while Texas had forty-six, California forty-four, and Oklahoma twenty-two.
4. James M. Burns, *Roosevelt: The Lion and the Fox* (New York: Harcourt, Brace & World, Inc., 1956), pp. 125–26.
5. Frank Freidel, *Franklin D. Roosevelt*, vol. 3, *The Triumph* (Boston: Little, Brown & Co., 1956), pp. 244–45; James A. Farley, *Behind the Ballots* (New York: Harcourt, Brace & Co., 1938), pp. 92–93; James A. Farley, *Jim Farley's Story: The Roosevelt Years* (New York: McGraw-Hill, 1948), pp. 12–13.
6. *Star*, 3 July 1932; interview with Lawrence J. Catlin.
7. *Capital*, 14 April 1931.
8. *Capital*, 28 and 30 April and 4 May 1931.
9. *Capital*, 4 May 1931. The deep impression that the Roosevelt charm could have on an individual in a one-to-one encounter is evident from the experience of Senator Clarence C. Dill of Washington, who recalled that during this period Roosevelt invited him to dinner in Albany, where "I talked with him three hours and came away a devoted and enthusiastic booster." Cited in Burns, *Roosevelt: The Lion and the Fox*, p. 130.
10. *Capital*, 3 May 1931; *New York Times*, 3 May 1931.
11. *Capital*, 5 May 1931; *Hutchinson News*, 4 May 1931.
12. *Capital*, 1 and 2 June 1931; *New York Times*, 30 May and 1, 2, and 3 June 1932.
13. Interview with James A. Farley; *Capital*, 16 July 1931; Clugston, *Rascals in Democracy*, pp. 175–76; Burns, *Roosevelt: The Lion and the Fox*, pp. 126–27; Farley, *Behind the Ballots*, pp. 84–87.
14. *Capital*, 12 December 1931; *New York Times*, 12 December 1931.
15. Capt. F. L. Parks to Woodring, 1 December 1931, WPP; *Capital*, 12 and 17 December 1931; *New York Times*, 14 December 1931; confidential communication.
16. Between April 1931 and June 1932 Woodring visited with Roosevelt six times—on four trips to New York and at two governors' conferences; in addition, Guy Helvering and Carl Rice also made several visits to Hyde Park. Roosevelt to Woodring, 2 February 1932, WPP; *Capital*, 22 March and 9 and 26 June 1932; Callahan, *Jayhawk Editor*, pp. 227–28.
17. *Capital*, 22 February 1931.
18. *Capital*, 19 July 1931, 10 February, 20 March, and 5 April 1932; Freidel, *Franklin D. Roosevelt: The Triumph*, pp. 244–45.
19. *Capital*, 7 February and 3 and 6 April 1932.
20. Roosevelt to Woodring, 3 May 1932, WPP.

21. *Capital*, 15 and 16 May 1932; *New York Times*, 17 May 1932.
22. *Capital*, 12 and 16 May and 8 June 1932; *New York Times*, 17 May 1932.
23. *Capital*, 17 and 18 May 1932; *Hutchinson News*, 17 May 1932; *New York Times*, 17 May 1932; Freidel, *Franklin D. Roosevelt: The Triumph*, p. 287.
24. *New York Times*, 17 May 1932.
25. *Capital*, 17 May 1932.
26. *Capital*, 19 June 1932.
27. Telegrams from Farley to Woodring, 23, 25, and 27 June 1932, WPP; *Capital*, 22 June 1932.
28. Woodring to John W. Young, 14 June 1932; Woodring to Charles G. Nevins, 23 June 1932; Robert Jackson to Woodring, 11 June 1932; I. B. Dunlop to Woodring, 18 June 1932, WPP; *Star*, 3 July 1932.
29. Woodring to Charles G. Nevins, 23 June 1932, WPP.
30. *Capital*, 22 and 25 June 1932; *Hutchinson News*, 23, 24, and 25 June 1932.
31. *Capital*, 26 June 1932.
32. After the convention, Woodring wrote: "There was no personal feeling against Mr. Shouse . . . nor was there any intent to humiliate him. The vote on permanent chairman was the first real test of strength on the Roosevelt following and was so looked upon by both sides." Woodring to Cora G. Lewis, 6 July 1932. Essentially the same thing was said in a letter to Richard Rohrer, 23 July 1932, WPP; *Capital*, 27 and 29 June 1932; Farley, *Behind the Ballots*, pp, 126–27.
33. *Capital*, 2 and 10 July 1932.
34. Roosevelt had come out against prohibition in 1930; however, because of the divisive nature of the issue, he decided to take a neutral position in 1932; Burns, *Roosevelt: The Lion and the Fox*, p. 126; *Capital*, 15 December 1931.
35. Woodring to Charles G. Nevins, 23 June 1932, WPP; Ewing Laporte, comp., *Official Report of the Proceedings of the Democratic National Convention, Held at Chicago, Illinois, June 27th to July 2nd, 1932* (Chicago: n.p., 1932), pp. 188, 192; Farley, *Behind the Ballots*, pp. 127–28; *Capital*, 19 and 28 June and 1 and 6 July 1932.
36. *Capital*, 26 June 1932.
37. *Official Report of the 1932 Democratic National Convention*, pp. 237–38; *Capital*, 28 June and 1 July 1932.
38. In referring to the speech, Woodring claimed: "I drafted it in about ten minutes while the convention was in session." Woodring to B. F. Brittain, 19 July 1932, WPP.
39. *Capital*, 2 July 1932.
40. The Roosevelt forces, knowing that they commanded a majority of delegates but not the two-thirds necessary for nomination, attempted to repeal the two-thirds rule. When it appeared as if the plan would succeed, the

Roosevelt opposition became so indignant that Roosevelt felt compelled to back down. Woodring strongly supported repeal of the rule. Freidel, *Franklin D. Roosevelt: The Triumph*, pp. 299–300; Burns, *Roosevelt: The Lion and the Fox*, pp. 134–35; Samuel I. Rosenman, *Working with Roosevelt* (New York: Harper & Brothers, 1952), p. 75.

41. *Official Report of the 1932 Democratic National Convention*, pp. 300, 314.
42. *Capital*, 22 June 1956; interviews with Cooper C. Woodring, 10 June 1968, and with Helen Coolidge Woodring, 20 July 1968.
43. Farley, *Behind the Ballots*, pp. 132–39; Freidel, *Franklin D. Roosevelt: The Triumph*, pp. 308–11; Bascom N. Timmons, *Garner of Texas: A Personal History* (New York: Harper & Brothers Publishers, 1948), pp. 165–67; *Official Report of the 1932 Democratic National Convention*, p. 329.
44. *Capital*, 27, 28, and 30 June and 3 July 1932.
45. Interview with James A. Farley.
46. *Star*, 3 July 1932.
47. *Capital*, 3 July 1932.
48. Interview with James A. Farley; Joseph H. McDowell to author, 14 June 1971; confidential communication; Clugston, *Rascals in Democracy*, p. 175.
49. Freidel, *Franklin D. Roosevelt: The Triumph*, p. 346.
50. *Capital*, 15 September 1932; Edward L. Schapsmeier and Frederick H. Schapsmeier, *Henry A. Wallace of Iowa: The Agrarian Years, 1910–1940* (Ames: Iowa State University Press, 1968), pp. 155–56.
51. *Star*, 15 September 1932.
52. *Capital*, 15 September 1932; *Hutchinson News*, 14 September 1932; *Time*, 19 September 1932, p. 11.
53. Schruben, *Kansas in Turmoil*, p. 47.
54. *Capital*, 22 October and 1 and 8 November 1931.
55. *Capital*, 3 and 6 December 1931; Finger, "The Post-Gubernatorial Career of Jonathan M. Davis," p. 161.
56. *Capital*, 3 December 1931 and 14 May 1932.
57. *Capital*, 22 October 1931.
58. *Capital*, 21 February, 22, 24, and 27 July, and 7 August 1932; *Hutchinson News*, 21, 23, 26, and 27 July and 1 August 1932.
59. *Capital*, 11, 17, 24, and 27 July 1932.
60. Kansas Governor, *Under the Statehouse Dome: Our State Government*, Radio speeches of Governor Harry H. Woodring, broadcast from his desk in the capitol at Topeka, July to September 1932 (Topeka, 1932); *Star*, 31 May and 5 July 1932; *Capital*, 11 and 29 July 1932; *New York Times*, 12 June 1932.
61. *Capital*, 17 July 1932.
62. *Capital*, 27 August 1932.

63. McCoy, *Landon of Kansas*, p. 66. McCoy deals extensively with the 1932 gubernatorial campaign, centering his attention on Landon, pp. 91–117.

64. Ibid., p. 93.

65. Ibid., pp. 93–102; Palmer, *This Man Landon*, pp. 55–58; *Capital*, 3 and 21 January and 27 August 1932.

66. Schruben, *Kansas in Turmoil*, pp. 80–84; Bracke, *Wheat Country*, p. 173; Richard H. Bailey, "Dr. Brinkley of Kansas," *Nation*, 21 September 1932, p. 254.

67. *Capital*, 16 January and 1 and 5 June 1932; Zornow, *Kansas*, p. 250. Francis Schruben, in his *Kansas in Turmoil*, has an entire chapter on the 1932 gubernatorial campaign, with special emphasis on Brinkley.

68. *Capital*, 31 August 1932.

69. *Capital*, 13 September 1932; *Democratic State Handbook* (1932), pp. 20–21.

70. Woodring campaign literature, 1932 gubernatorial contest; 1932 Woodring campaign photographs, WPP; McCoy, *Landon of Kansas*, p. 108; interview with Alfred M. Landon.

71. McCoy, *Landon of Kansas*, p. 108; Palmer, *This Man Landon*, p. 58; Schruben, *Kansas in Turmoil*, pp. 86–87.

72. Schruben, *Kansas in Turmoil*, p. 89; *New York Times*, 17 and 23 October 1932.

73. *New York Times*, 31 August 1932.

74. Slechta, "Dr. John R. Brinkley," p. 145.

75. *Capital*, 24 and 29 September 1932; Schruben, *Kansas in Turmoil*, pp. 92–93.

76. *Capital*, 21 and 25 October 1932; Schruben, *Harry Woodring Speaks*, pp. 9–11; Schruben, *Kansas in Turmoil*, p. 94; McCoy, *Landon of Kansas*, p. 109.

77. *Capital*, 28 and 30 October 1932.

78. Interview with Alfred M. Landon; Schruben, *Kansas in Turmoil*, p. 96.

79. Zornow, *Kansas*, p. 250; Schruben, *Kansas in Turmoil*, p. 96.

80. Interview with Alfred M. Landon; Schruben, *Kansas in Turmoil*, pp. 96–97; McCoy, *Landon of Kansas*, pp. 106–9; *Hutchinson News*, 4, 6, 8, 11, and 14 October 1932.

81. In discussing political contributions, Woodring said: "I have no apologies to offer . . . for the 5% voluntary contributions which have been received from my employees. These people who have benefited from their jobs have signified their confidence in my administration by such contributions." *Capital*, 12 July and 12 October 1932; the Independent Voters League of Kansas came to Woodring's defense by claiming that the Woodring-Helvering method of collecting campaign funds had been "used by every administration in the last 29 years." *Capital*, 7 October 1932.

82. Schruben, *Kansas in Turmoil*, p. 99; McCoy, *Landon of Kansas*, p. 36.

83. *Capital*, 6 and 21 February, 10 March, 26 July, and 8 October 1932.
84. *Kansas Teacher*, October 1932, pp. 50–51; *Capital*, 6 October 1932; *Hutchinson News*, 14 October 1932; Keith McFarland, "Teacher Political Power, 1932-Style," *Kansas Teacher*, May 1974, pp. 15–16, 28–29.
85. *Capital*, 19 October 1932; *Hutchinson News*, 14 and 15 October 1932; Joseph H. McDowell to author, 14 June 1971. In March 1932, when the school interests began their fight against Woodring and the tax-limitation amendment, the Governor announced, "I will rise or fall on this tax amendment."
86. *Capital*, 30 October and 2 November 1932. On Davis's action in the 1932 campaign see Finger, "Post-Gubernatorial Career of Jonathan M. Davis," pp. 161–63.
87. Apparently the Republicans were still quite concerned about Brinkley even at the end of October, because on the thirtieth they ran a full-page ad in the *Topeka Daily Capital*, which read: "LANDON or BRINKLEY. The Next governor of Kansas will be either Alf M. Landon or Dr. John R. Brinkley. Past history . . . has shown that no Democrat ever has been re-elected governor of Kansas. . . . Woodring will fail. The issue therefore is Landon or Brinkley."
88. *Capital*, 24, 26, and 28 October 1932.
89. *Capital*, 26 October 1932; *Hutchinson News*, 25 October 1932.
90. McCoy, *Landon of Kansas*, p. 110.
91. *Capital*, 5 November 1932.
92. Interview with Alfred M. Landon; *Capital*, 2 November 1932.
93. *Capital*, 23 and 30 October and 4, 6, and 8 November 1932; *Hutchinson News*, 22 October and 2, 4, and 7 November 1932.
94. *Capital*, 27 November 1932.
95. Years later, Woodring indicated his belief that "Brinkley was the determining factor that took the vote away from me by the thousand." Schruben, *Harry H. Woodring Speaks*, p. 11.
96. Zornow, *Kansas*, p. 251. The effectiveness of the Helvering organization is evident when one compares the 1930 and 1932 campaign expenditures. The cost of the 1930 state Democratic campaign was $17,000, while the 1932 contest cost $81,000. In the latter campaign the Republicans spent $20,000 and Brinkley $56,000. Helvering to Woodring, 3 December 1930, WPP; *Capital*, 8 December 1932.
97. Writing to William Allen White on 10 August 1931, Woodring, in reference to the plight of the Kansas farmer, said: "I am at a loss after much study and attention to the subject, just what might be done to afford some immediate relief." William Allen White Papers, LC; *Capital*, 22 September 1932; clipping from *Pittsburg Sun*, (?) December 1932, WPP.

98. Alice Horan to James A. Farley, 23 November 1932; C. A. Bowman to Emory Thomason, 25 November 1932, WPP.
99. Woodring to Roosevelt, 27 December 1932; Roosevelt to Woodring, 29 December 1932, WPP; *Capital*, 6 and 8 December 1932. The Roosevelt-Woodring correspondence of December 1932 and January 1933 can also be found in the "Records of the Democratic National Committee, 1928–1933," box 231, folder entitled "Kansas after Election," FDRL.
100. *Capital*, 10 January 1933.
101. Charles H. Sessions, "Topeka Tinklings," *Capital*, 8 January 1933.
102. *Emporia Gazette*, 11 November 1932.
103. Woodring to Louis Howe, (?) January 1933, "Records of the Democratic National Committee, 1928–1933, Kansas," box 231, FDRL; Roosevelt to Woodring, 1 February 1933, WPP; Franklin Delano Roosevelt, *F.D.R.: His Personal Letters, 1928–1945*, ed. Elliott Roosevelt (New York: Duell, Sloan & Pearce, 1950), 1:323–24; *Capital*, 10, 13, and 17 January 1933.
104. R. L. Pollio, manager of the Mayflower Hotel, to Woodring, 20 January 1933, WPP.
105. Woodring to Patrick Ewing, 5 January 1933; Woodring to R. Norris Miller, 7 January 1933, WPP.
106. Woodring to Howe, (?) January 1933, "Records of the Democratic National Committee, 1928–1933, Kansas," box 231, FDRL.
107. Roosevelt to Woodring, 1 February 1933, WPP; also in Roosevelt, *F.D.R.: His Personal Letters, 1928–1945*, 1:323–24.
108. *Capital*, 31 January 1933; Lela Stiles, *The Man Behind Roosevelt: The Story of Louis McHenry Howe* (Cleveland, Ohio: World Publishing Co., 1954), p. 231; Richard F. Fenno, Jr., *The President's Cabinet: An Analysis in the Period from Wilson to Eisenhower* (Cambridge, Mass.: Harvard University Press, 1959), p. 58.
109. Schapsmeier and Schapsmeier, *Henry A. Wallace of Iowa*, pp. 161–62.
110. Interview with James A. Farley.
111. *Capital*, 8, 23, and 26 March 1933.
112. Interview with James A. Farley.
113. Joseph H. McDowell to author, 14 June 1971.
114. Interview with James A. Farley; *Capital*, 26 and 30 March 1933; Ralph T. O'Neil to Louis Howe, 26 March 1933, Official File 25-A, "Endorsements for Assistant Secretary of War," FDRL; *Army and Navy Journal*, 1 and 8 April 1933.
115. *Capital*, 30 March and 5 and 7 April 1933; *New York Times*, 7 April 1933; *Congressional Record*, 73d Cong., 1st sess., vol. 77, pt. 1, p. 1095, and pt. 2, p. 1205; Henry Cabot Lodge to author, 28 June 1968. Less than a month after Woodring took office, President Roosevelt appointed Guy Helvering to be the Commissioner of Internal Revenue—a position that he held for

eleven years until his appointment as federal judge of Kansas in late 1943. Templar, "The Federal Judiciary of Kansas," p. 13.

CHAPTER 5

1. Dick West, "Cabinet Names? One Man's Memory Bank Now Bankrupt," *Dallas Times-Herald*, 13 December 1972.
2. William E. Leuchtenburg, *Franklin D. Roosevelt and the New Deal, 1932–1940* (New York: Harper & Row Publishers, 1963), pp. 41–76.
3. C. Joseph Bernardo and Eugene H. Bacon, *American Military Policy: Its Development since 1775* (Harrisburg, Pa.: Military Service Publishing Co., 1961), pp. 387–89.
4. Robert E. Sherwood, *Roosevelt and Hopkins: An Intimate History* (New York: Harper & Brothers, 1948), p. 76.
5. Russell F. Weigley, *History of the United States Army* (New York: Macmillan Co., 1967), pp. 402–3.
6. Bernardo and Bacon, *American Military Policy*, pp. 387–88.
7. Charles G. Washburn, *The Life of John W. Weeks* (Boston: Houghton Mifflin Co., 1928), p. 274.
8. Mark S. Watson, *United States Army in World War II: The War Department: Prewar Plans and Preparations* (Washington, D.C.: U.S. Government Printing Office, 1950), p. 24. An excellent study of the effects of the Depression on the military is contained in a Ph.D. dissertation, "The Impact of the Great Depression on the Army, 1929–1936," by John W. Killigrew (Indiana University, 1960).
9. *New York Times*, 4 December 1930; Selig Adler, *The Isolationist Impulse* (New York: Abelard-Schuman Ltd., 1957), pp. 227, 249; Bernardo and Bacon, *American Military Policy*, p. 389.
10. *Official Duties, Department of War* (Washington, D.C.: U.S. Government Printing Office, 1934), pp. 1–2; War Department Orders E of 28 November 1933, prescribing the classes of business to be acted on by the Secretary of War, the Assistant Secretary of War . . . (Washington, D.C.: U.S. Government Printing Office, 1933), p. 1.
11. *National Cyclopedia of American Biography* (New York: James J. White & Co., 1937), 26:9.
12. *Army and Navy Journal*, 2 May and 3 June 1933 and 29 August 1936; Douglas MacArthur, *Reminiscences* (New York: McGraw-Hill Book Co., 1964), p. 100.
13. *New York Times*, 28 August 1936; *Army and Navy Journal*, 27 January and 10 February 1934; Maj. Gen. George Van Horn Moseley to Gen. Douglas MacArthur, 4 September 1936, "Moseley File," MacArthur Papers, MacArthur Memorial Bureau of Archives, Norfolk, Va. That Dern was frequently absent from his post is evident from the large volume of cor-

respondence that left his office between 1933 and 1936 signed "Harry H. Woodring, Acting Secretary of War."

14. *Official Duties, Department of War* (1934), p. 2; War Department Orders E of 28 November 1933, pp. 2–3.
15. To assist the Chief of Staff there was a General Staff, which was charged with the preparation of plans and policies for recruiting, mobilizing, organizing, supplying, equipping, paying, and training the Army. The General Staff was divided into five divisions: Personnel (G-1), Intelligence (G-2), Operations and Training (G-3), Supply (G-4), and War Plans Division (WPD). For a further explanation of Army organization at this time see Watson, *Prewar Plans and Preparations*, pp. 64–75. Senate Military Affairs Committee, "Army of the United States," *Senate Document No. 91*, 76th Cong., 1st sess., pp. 11–16; *United States Statutes at Large*, vol. 41, pt. 1, 1919–1921, p. 765; *Official Duties, Department of War* (1934), pp. 3–4.
16. *National Cyclopedia of American Biography*, vol. G., pp. 26–27.
17. Ibid.
18. MacArthur, *Reminiscences*, p. 100; telegram from MacArthur to Woodring, 2 October 1935, MacArthur Papers, MacArthur Memorial Archives; MacArthur to Woodring, 15 July 1937, WPP.
19. Bernardo and Bacon, *American Military Policy*, p. 403; Walker S. Buel, "The Army under the New Deal," *Literary Digest*, 26 August 1933, pp. 3–4; Samuel Grafton, "The New Deal Woos the Army," *American Mercury*, December 1934, p. 441; MacArthur, *Reminiscences*, pp. 100–101; *Army and Navy Journal*, 24 June 1933.
20. Buel, "The Army under the New Deal," p. 4.
21. Ibid.; *Army and Navy Journal*, 30 December 1933; *New York Times*, 28 August 1936.
22. Weigley, *History of the United States Army*, p. 402.
23. John A. Salmond, *The Civilian Conservation Corps, 1933–1942: A New Deal Case Study* (Durham, N.C.: Duke University Press, 1967), pp. 26–27, 30, 40–41, 45; Dorris Clayton James, *The Years of MacArthur*, vol. 1, *1880–1941* (Boston: Houghton Mifflin Co., 1970), pp. 418–21.
24. *Annual Report of the Secretary of War, 1934*, pp. 28–29; *Army and Navy Journal*, 30 December 1933; *New York Times*, 28 August 1936; *Topeka State Journal*, 27 May 1933. Woodring's involvement in supplying shoes, boots, and clothing and other necessities to the CCC stemmed from his responsibility for "supervising and acting upon matters pertaining to . . . the sale of surplus supplies." Before the Army could turn over any supplies to the CCC, the goods had to be declared "surplus," and only Woodring had the authority to make such declarations.
25. Marvin A. Kreidberg and Merton G. Henry, *History of Military Mobilization in the United States Army, 1775–1945* (Washington, D.C.: U.S.

Government Printing Office, 1955), pp. 462–63; Grafton, "The New Deal Woos the Army," p. 439; *New York Times*, 28 August 1936.

26. Sherwood, *Roosevelt and Hopkins*, p. 76.
27. *New York Times*, 10 June and 26 July 1933; *Baltimore Sun*, 10 June 1933; *Army and Navy Journal*, 29 July 1933.
28. Interviews with Helen Coolidge Woodring, 20 July 1968 and 14 June 1969.
29. Ibid.; *Baltimore Sun*, 10 June 1933; *Army and Navy Journal*, 29 July 1933; *Independence* (Kans.) *Reporter*, 18 July 1933; telegram from Dwight D. Eisenhower to Woodring, 27 July 1953, PPF, 841, DDEL. Woodring's best man was his good friend James Roosevelt, FDR's oldest son. Also in attendance was another friend, Maj. Dwight D. Eisenhower, who was currently on duty at the War Department.
30. Marquis W. Childs, *I Write from Washington* (New York: Harper & Brothers, 1942), p. 161; interview with Gerald P. Nye.
31. Harry H. Woodring, "The American Army Stands Ready," *Liberty*, 6 January 1934, pp. 7–11. Little did Woodring expect the article to cause such a furor: writing to his sister Lida on 13 November 1933 (WPP), he said: "Here comes real good news—I have written an article on the army etc. and sold it to the Liberty . . . I got a very large price for it—I am going to try another on finance and ask $2,500 for it." It is not surprising that he never wrote the other article. During the years that followed, he was offered "substantial sums" for articles on national defense, but he refused them. Woodring to Ralph Wallace, 14 April 1939, WPP.
32. Arthur M. Schlesinger, Jr., *The Coming of the New Deal* (Boston: Houghton Mifflin Co., 1958), p. 339.
33. For numerous examples of such correspondence see box 39, PPF 25, "War Department, 1933–1945," FDRL.
34. Ibid.; Charles A. Beard to Roosevelt, 20 January 1934.
35. *Congressional Record*, 73d Cong., 2d sess., vol. 78, pt. 2, p. 1416.
36. Press Conference #95, 7 February 1934, PPF 1-P, 3:134–36; Steve Early to Woodring, 5 January 1934 (?); Woodring to Louis Howe, 24 February 1934, box 1, "War Department, 1933–1945," OF 25, FDRL; *New York Times*, 8 February 1934; *Army and Navy Journal*, 10 February 1934; *Capital*, 8 February 1934; Charles Beard and Mary Beard, *America in Midpassage* (New York: Macmillan Co., 1939), p. 571.
37. *New York Times*, 6, 7, and 8 February 1934; *Army and Navy Journal*, 10 February 1934; *Capital*, 7 and 8 February 1934.
38. *New York Times*, 7, 8, 9, 10, 13, and 22 February 1934; *Capital*, 7, 8, 9, and 10 February 1934.
39. *Army and Navy Journal*, 10 and 17 February 1934; *Capital*, 8 and 13 February 1934.
40. *Army and Navy Journal*, 10 and 17 February 1934; *Capital*, 8 and 13 Feb-

ruary 1934; *New York Times*, 13 March 1934; James, *Years of MacArthur*, 1:439–40.

41. *New York Daily News*, 8 February 1934.

42. *New York Times*, 13 and 14 March 1934; *Capital*, 8 February 1934.

43. Woodring to William Allen White, 21 February 1934, William Allen White Papers, LC.

44. Portions of the transcript of testimony in the grand-jury investigation of *United States* v *Silverman and others*, in WPP; *Capital*, 8 and 9 February 1934.

45. *Capital*, 8 and 9 February 1934; *New York Times*, 8 and 9 February 1934.

46. *Kansas City Times*, 9 and 14 March 1934; *Star*, 17 March 1934; *Army and Navy Journal*, 10 February 1934.

47. Woodring to the Honorable Charles Curtis, 22 May 1933; Woodring to the Brimley Corporation, 29 May 1933; memorandum for the Secretary of War, 23 August 1933, memorandum from Woodring to the Secretary of War, 2 July 1934, memorandum from Woodring for the Executive Assistant to the Secretary of War, 24 July 1934, box 177, "Silverman," and box 181, "Surplus Property," "Secretary of War General Correspondence, 1932–1942," NA, RG 107; *New York Times*, 22 and 23 February 1934.

48. *Capital*, 8 February 1934; *Star*, 21 June 1940; Drew Pearson and Robert Allen, "The Washington Merry-Go-Round," *Washington Herald*, 5 June 1937; Grafton, "The New Deal Woos the Army," p. 442.

49. *New York Times*, 13 and 14 March 1934; *Kansas City Times*, 13 March 1934; *Star*, 13 March 1934.

50. *Army and Navy Journal*, 24 March 1934.

51. *Army and Navy Journal*, 10 and 17 February 1934; *New York Times*, 10 February 1934; *Capital*, 9 February 1934.

52. *Army and Navy Journal*, 17 February 1934; Benjamin D. Foulois, with C. V. Glines, *From the Wright Brothers to the Astronauts: The Memoirs of Major General Benjamin D. Foulois* (New York: McGraw-Hill, 1968), pp. 263–64.

53. *New York Times*, 7 and 10 February 1934; *Army and Navy Journal*, 10 February 1934; Woodring to Congressman William N. Rogers, 10 April 1934, and Woodring to Congressman W. Frank James, 31 May 1934, box 2, "Airplanes," "Secretary of War General Correspondence, 1932–1942," NA, RG 107.

54. *Army and Navy Journal*, 10 February 1934; *New York Times*, 10 February 1934; *Capital*, 10 February 1934; Irving B. Holley, Jr., *Buying Aircraft: Matériel Procurement for the Army Air Forces* (Washington, D.C.: U.S. Government Printing Office, 1964), pp. 113–27.

55. *New York Times*, 10 February 1934; *Capital*, 10 February 1934.

56. *Washington Star*, 14 February 1934; *Capital*, 15 February 1934; *New York*

Times, 28 February and 7 March 1934; *Army and Navy Journal*, 24 February and 3 March 1934.

57. *New York Times*, 8 March 1934; *Army and Navy Journal*, 20 March 1934.
58. Years later Foulois wrote: "The only way Woodring could achieve his purpose [competitive bidding], however, was to force us to lower our specifications for the planes we wanted by reducing speed, range, and altitude requirements. This I refused to do. It would have meant buying new but obsolete planes." Foulois, *Memoirs*, p. 264.
59. *New York Times*, 8 March 1934.
60. *New York Times*, 18 March 1934; *Army and Navy Journal*, 10 March 1934; *Star*, 10 (editorial) and 17 March 1934. For an excellent account of Woodring's handling of Congress over the procurement question see Holley, *Buying Aircraft*, pp. 128–31.
61. *New York Times*, 4 April 1934; *Army and Navy Journal*, 12 May 1934. On 15 June the Rogers Subcommittee issued a formal report of its investigation (*House Report 2060*, 73d Cong., 2d sess., also printed in *Army and Navy Journal*, 23 June 1934). The report was extremely critical of Foulois and called for his removal as Chief of the Air Corps. In one of his most courageous acts as Secretary of War, George Dern, who felt that the General was being made into a scapegoat, refused to heed the committee's request, and Foulois remained at his post until he retired in the fall of 1935.
62. Woodring to Congressman John J. Cochran, 10 October 1934, box 2, "Airplanes," "Secretary of War General Correspondence, 1932–1942," NA, RG 107; George H. Dern to Congressman J. J. McSwain, 15 August 1935, McSwain Papers, Perkins Library, Duke University, Durham, N.C.; Woodring to the Honorable Millard Tydings, 28 September 1935, William P. Lane Papers, Perkins Library, Duke University; Harry H. Woodring, "Better Planes, Faster Procurement Foreseen," *Army and Navy Journal*, 22 August 1936. Competitive bidding did have some drawbacks; for an analysis of its shortcomings and the modifications to Woodring's policies in the 1930s see Holley, *Buying Aircraft*, pp. 132–46.
63. *Annual Report of the Secretary of War, 1937* (Washington, D.C.: U.S. Government Printing Office, 1937), p. 27; Ralph E. Smith, *The Army and Economic Mobilization* (Washington, D.C.: U.S. Government Printing Office, 1959), pp. 216–17, 242; James A. Huston, *The Sinews of War: Army Logistics, 1775–1953* (Washington, D.C.: U.S. Government Printing Office, 1966), p. 66.
64. *New York Times*, 8 June 1933; *Army and Navy Journal*, 10 June 1933.
65. "With the Secretary of War in His Flying Office," *Star*, 23 January 1938; interviews with Brig. Gen. William L. Ritchie, Woodring's former military aide and pilot, and with Dow W. Harter, a former member of the House Military Affairs Committee and a member of the Rogers Subcommittee.

66. J. E. Schaefer to Woodring, 25 February 1936, box 3-A, "Air Corps," "Secretary of War General Correspondence, 1932–1942," NA, RG 107.

67. Edward Jablonski, *Flying Fortress: The Illustrated Biography of the B-17s and the Men Who Flew Them* (Garden City, N.Y.: Doubleday & Co., 1965), pp. 4–6; telegram from Woodring to Roosevelt, 25 February 1942, PPF 663, "Harry H. Woodring," FDRL.

68. Woodring to Generals George C. Marshall and Henry H. Arnold, 8 January 1941, WPP.

69. *New York Times*, 28 July 1934.

70. *Senate Reports*, 74th Cong., 2d sess., vol. 7, "Committee on Military Affairs Report No. 2131," p. 2.

71. *Army and Navy Journal*, 15 August 1936.

72. The so-called Air Mail Fiasco began in February 1934, when President Roosevelt, alarmed over alleged irregularities and monopolistic practices in the granting of air-mail contracts, canceled all existing agreements and ordered the Army to fly the mail until new contracts could be negotiated. Bad weather, poor equipment, and lack of training turned the affair into a near disaster, with nine Air Corps pilots killed and twelve planes lost in the first month of operations. The fiasco, which ended in May when the Army stopped carrying the mail, did serve to awaken the President, Congress, and the public to the critical needs of the long-ignored Army Air Corps. For an inside view of these events see Foulois, *Memoirs*, pp. 235–61.

73. David H. Popper, "American Defense Policies," *Foreign Policy Reports* 15 (1 May 1939):45.

74. Watson, *Prewar Plans and Preparations*, p. 284; *New York Times*, 28 July 1934.

75. Telegram from MacArthur to Woodring, 2 October 1935, box 35, "Chief of Staff," "Secretary of War General Correspondence, 1932–1942," NA, RG 107; MacArthur to Woodring, 15 July 1937, WPP; Woodring to MacArthur, 26 May 1937 and 28 February 1952, MacArthur Papers, MacArthur Memorial Archives.

76. *Army and Navy Journal*, 20 and 27 May 1933; *Army and Navy Register*, 11 July 1936; *New York Times*, 12 November 1934, 24 September 1935, and 31 May 1936.

77. *New York Times*, 12 November 1934.

78. Paul W. Ward, "The Inexcusable Woodring," *Nation*, 29 April 1936, p. 539; "New War Secretary Pacifist Enemy," *Christian Century*, 14 October 1936, p. 1373.

79. Interview with Helen Coolidge Woodring, 20 July 1968; *New York Times*, 17 May 1936; *Army and Navy Register*, 11 July 1936.

80. *New York Times*, 20 June 1934, 22 June 1935, and 11 February 1937; "The

Home of the Harry Woodrings," *Democratic Digest*, April 1935, pp. 5–6; *Washington Post*, 22 June 1935.

81. *New York Times*, 11 February 1936; *Time*, 9 March 1936, p. 14.
82. *New York Times*, 25 February 1936. According to Arthur Krock in his column in the *New York Times* of 26 February, the decision to remove Hagood "presumably" originated with President Roosevelt himself.
83. *Congressional Record*, 74th Cong., 2d sess., vol. 80, pt. 3, pp. 2712–13.
84. *New York Times*, 27, 28, and 29 February, 23 and 24 March, 12 and 14 April, and 3, 5, and 6 May 1936. On 2 May, Hagood assumed command of the VI Corps Area, and two days later, having felt vindicated, he resigned from the service.
85. Interviews with Dow W. Harter and with Charles I. Faddis; Lister Hill to author, 14 August 1968; John H. Sparkman to author, 29 April 1968; Gerald P. Nye to author, 25 July 1968; Edwin C. Johnson to author, 27 April 1968.
86. MacArthur to Woodring, 15 July 1937, WPP; John C. O'Laughlin to Gen. Malin Craig, 1 September 1939, box 35, John C. O'Laughlin Papers, LC; MacArthur to General Craig, 16 September 1937, MacArthur Papers, MacArthur Memorial Archives.
87. *Army and Navy Journal*, 3 October 1936; transcript of Boake Carter's radio broadcast of 27 April 1937, WPP.

CHAPTER 6

1. *New York Times*, 28 August and 2 September 1936; *Washington Evening Star*, 28 August 1936; *Army and Navy Journal*, 12 and 19 September 1936.
2. *Army and Navy Journal*, 19 September 1936.
3. Tully, *F.D.R.: My Boss*, pp. 196–97; memo of letter, Cummings to Roosevelt, 24 September 1936, OF 62, "Precedents Index" (retained in White House), FDRL.
4. Telegram, Roosevelt to Woodring, 25 September 1936, PPF 663, "Harry H. Woodring," FDRL.
5. Telegram, Woodring to Roosevelt, 25 September 1936, box 38, PSF, "Woodring," FDRL.
6. Memo of telegram, Marvin H. McIntyre to Stephen Early, 25 September 1936, box 4, OF 25, "War Department and Cross Reference," FDRL.
7. *New York Times*, 26 September 1936.
8. *New York Herald Tribune*, 26 September 1936; *Army and Navy Register*, 3 October 1936; *Newsweek*, 3 October 1936, p. 20; Frederic W. Wile, "Washington Observations," *Washington Evening Star*, 28 September 1936.
9. *New York Times*, 26 September 1936.
10. Harold F. Ickes, "My Twelve Years with F.D.R.," *Saturday Evening Post*, 5 June 1948, p. 90.

11. *Army and Navy Journal,* 3 October 1936.
12. *Cleveland Plain Dealer,* 27 September 1936.
13. *New York Times,* 8 October 1936; Flatbush Branch (Brooklyn, N.Y.) of the American League against War and Fascism to Roosevelt, 17 December 1936, and Trenton Branch of American League against War and Fascism to Roosevelt, 16 December 1936, box 25, OF 25, "Misc. War Department," FDRL.
14. "New War Secretary Pacifist Enemy," p. 1373.
15. John Flynn, "Other People's Money," *New Republic,* 28 October 1936, p. 350.
16. *Cincinnati Enquirer,* 28 September 1936.
17. Memorandum by Woodring, 6 May 1936, OF 300, "Democratic Committee, 1933–1945, Kansas," FDRL.
18. *New York Times,* 12 September 1936.
19. Interview with Alfred M. Landon; *Washington Evening Star,* 18 October 1936.
20. Letters praising Woodring's campaign activities, OF 25, "Misc. War Department, 1936–1940," FDRL.
21. *New York Times,* 17 December 1936.
22. Woodring to Gen. Douglas MacArthur, 9 October 1936; Woodring File, MacArthur Papers, MacArthur Memorial Archives.
23. Harold L. Ickes, *The Secret Diary of Harold L. Ickes,* vol. 1, *The First Thousand Days: 1933–1936* (New York: Simon & Schuster, 1953), p. 682.
24. *New York Times,* 21 September 1936.
25. *Army and Navy Journal,* 7 and 28 November 1936 and 30 January 1937; *Washington Evening Star,* 17 December 1936; *New York Times,* 18 December 1936.
26. *Army and Navy Journal,* 7 and 28 November 1936 and 30 January 1937.
27. *Army and Navy Register,* 5 September 1936; *Reserve Officer,* October 1936, p. 3; *Army Ordnance,* November/December 1936, p. 166.
28. Lt. Col. Frank Lowe to Roosevelt, 16 September 1936, OF 25-A, "War Department Endorsements for Secretary Harry H. Woodring," FDRL.
29. Edgar H. Taber to Roosevelt, 22 December 1936, OF 25-A, "War Department Endorsements for Secretary Harry H. Woodring," FDRL.
30. John C. O'Laughlin to Gen. John J. Pershing, 26 December 1936, box 57, O'Laughlin Papers, LC.
31. Gen. John J. Pershing to John C. O'Laughlin, 28 December 1936, box 57, O'Laughlin Papers, LC.
32. Congressman Lister Hill to Roosevelt, 28 December 1936, OF 25-A, "War Department Endorsements for Secretary Harry H. Woodring," FDRL.
33. John C. O'Laughlin to Gen. Douglas MacArthur, 28 November 1936, box 54, O'Laughlin Papers, LC.

34. Jesse H. Jones, with Edward Angly, *Fifty Billion Dollars: My Thirteen Years with the RFC* (New York: Macmillan Co., 1951), p. 256; Bascom M. Timmons, *Jesse H. Jones: The Man and the Statesman* (New York: Henry Holt & Co., 1956), p. 251.

35. *New York Times,* 18 December 1936; *Washington Evening Star,* 17 December 1936.

36. Harold L. Ickes, *The Secret Diary of Harold Ickes,* vol. 2, *The Inside Struggle: 1936–1939* (New York: Simon & Schuster, 1954), p. 24.

37. *New York Times,* 21 January 1937.

38. Farley, *Jim Farley's Story,* pp. 80–81.

39. *Congressional Record,* 76th Cong., 1st sess., vol. 8, pt. 4, p. 4253; Henry Cabot Lodge to author, 28 June 1968.

40. Transcript of Boake Carter's radio broadcast of 27 April 1937, WPP.

41. *New York Times,* 7 March 1938; "'Army in Being,'" *Time,* 1 January 1940, p. 12.

42. *New York Times,* 8 October 1936; Ickes, *Secret Diary,* 1:682; Flynn, "Other People's Money," p. 350.

43. *Young Democrat,* January 1937, p. 7.

44. *Army and Navy Journal,* 12 March 1938.

45. *New York Times,* 5 October 1936.

46. *Washington Times-Herald,* 30 October 1939; Ernest Lindley, "An Example of Sanity," *Washington Post,* 27 October 1939; Ray Tucker, "Washington Letter," *Living Age,* December 1939, p. 381.

47. Woodring to Mrs. Josephine A. Russell, 29 January 1937, box 193, "Wars," "Secretary of War General Correspondence, 1932–1942," NA, RG 107; Harry H. Woodring, "Supply Preparedness," *Army Ordnance,* March/April 1937, p. 263.

48. Woodring to Mrs. John Robertson, 23 September 1938, box 122, "National Defense," "Secretary of War General Correspondence, 1932–1942," NA, RG 107; *New York Times,* 18 April 1939; Harry H. Woodring, "Our Power for Defense," *National Republic,* December 1934, pp. 1–2.

49. Woodring to Mrs. John Robertson, 23 September 1938, box 122, "National Defense," "Secretary of War General Correspondence, 1932–1942," NA, RG 107.

50. Woodring, "Supply Preparedness," p. 265; *New York Times,* 15 June 1938.

51. *Annual Report of the Secretary of War, 1937,* p. 2.

52. *Army and Navy Journal,* 10 July 1937.

53. Woodring to Congressman Lister Hill, 22 May 1939, box 176, "National Defense," "Secretary of War General Correspondence, 1932–1942," NA, RG 107.

54. *New York Times,* 23 September 1937.

55. *Foreign Policy Bulletin*, 24 November 1939, p. 4; *Army and Navy Journal*, 30 December 1939.
56. *New York Times*, 19 November 1939.
57. David H. Popper, "The United States Army in Transition," *Foreign Policy Reports* 16 (1 December 1940):216.
58. Joseph Alsop and Robert Kintner, *American White Paper: The Story of American Diplomacy and the Second World War* (New York: Simon & Schuster, 1940), p. 65.
59. Woodring, "Supply Preparedness," pp. 263–65.
60. Woodring to Mrs. Josephine A. Russell, 29 January 1937, box 193, "Wars," "Secretary of War General Correspondence, 1932–1942," NA, RG, 107.
61. *Congressional Record*, 76th Cong., 3d sess., vol. 86, pt. 13, p. 557.
62. *Army and Navy Register*, 12 September 1936.
63. *Congressional Record*, 76th Cong., 3d sess., vol. 86, pt. 13, p. 557; *Congressional Record*, 75th Cong., 3d sess., vol. 83, pt. 11, pp. 2318–20.
64. *Army and Navy Journal*, 7 November 1936.
65. " 'Army in Being,' " p. 12.
66. *Baltimore Sun*, 21 June 1940.
67. Woodring to John C. O'Laughlin, 30 July 1945, box 71, O'Laughlin Papers, LC.
68. *New York Times*, 18 April 1933.

CHAPTER 7

1. *United States Statutes at Large, 1919–1921* (Washington, D.C.: U.S. Government Printing Office, 1921), 41:759–812.
2. Popper, "American Defense Policies," pp. 41–42; Popper, "The United States Army in Transition," p. 217; "Who's in the Army Now?" *Fortune*, September 1935, pp. 39–48.
3. Kreidberg and Henry, *History of Military Mobilization*, p. 451.
4. *Annual Report of the Secretary of War, 1936*, pp. 2–6; "America Is Arming," *Nation*, 8 April 1936, p. 436.
5. Secretary Woodring—questions and answers from reporters for *Army-Navy Journal*, 30 September 1936, box 176, "Secretary of War General Correspondence, 1932–1942," NA, RG 107.
6. Malcolm Wheeler-Nicholson, *Battle Shield of the Republic* (New York: Macmillan Co., 1940), p. 42.
7. Kreidberg and Henry, *History of Military Mobilization*, pp. 466–70.
8. Ibid., p. 443.
9. Ibid., pp. 466–67.
10. "Annual Report of the Chief of Staff, 1939," printed in *Annual Report of the Secretary of War, 1939*, p. 23.
11. Kreidberg and Henry, *History of Military Mobilization*, p. 472.

12. Ibid., p. 475.
13. *Annual Report of the Secretary of War, 1937*, p. 6.
14. George Fielding Eliot, *The Ramparts We Watch* (New York: Reynal & Hitchcock, 1938), pp. 314–15.
15. Kreidberg and Henry, *History of Military Mobilization*, p. 447.
16. "Annual Report of the Chief of Staff, 1936," printed in *Annual Report of the Secretary of War, 1936*, p. 37.
17. Eliot, *The Ramparts We Watch*, pp. 312–13.
18. "Annual Report of the Chief of Staff, 1933," printed in *Annual Report of the Secretary of War, 1933*, pp. 21–25.
19. Eliot, *The Ramparts We Watch*, p. 315.
20. "Army of the United States," *Senate Document No. 91*, 76th Cong., 1st sess., pp. 11–12.
21. Corp. Leon Denis, "Training for the Next War," *Infantry Journal*, May/June 1936, p. 225.
22. Kreidberg and Henry, *History of Military Mobilization*, p. 451.
23. *National Cyclopedia of American Biography* (New York: James T. White, 1951), 37:184; Weigley, *History of the United States Army*, p. 415.
24. Kreidberg and Henry, *History of Military Mobilization*, p. 476.
25. "Arms before Men," *Time*, 22 August 1938, p. 23.
26. Albert A. Blum, "Birth and Death of the M-Day Plan," in *American Civil-Military Decisions*, ed. Harold Stein (University, Ala.: University of Alabama Press, 1963), pp. 66–67.
27. *Reserve Officer*, 1 January 1937, p. 13.
28. Woodring, "Supply Preparedness," pp. 264–65.
29. *Industrial Mobilization Plan*, Revised 1936 (Washington, D.C.: U.S. Government Printing Office, 1936), pp. 15–18.
30. *Army and Navy Journal*, 12 December 1936.
31. Kreidberg and Henry, *History of Military Mobilization*, p. 530. For more on the Industrial Mobilization Plans of the 1930s see Byron Fairchild and Jonathan Grossman, *The Army and Industrial Manpower* (Washington, D.C.: U.S. Government Printing Office, 1959), pp. 7–14.
32. *Army and Navy Journal*, 5 December 1936 and 24 July 1937.
33. As Secretary of War, Woodring continued to push Congress and the President for authorization and funds to place "educational orders" with certain manufacturers. Congress responded favorably in the summer of 1938, and a limited program was instituted. "Arms before Men," p. 25.
34. For the causes and consequences of the friction between Woodring and Johnson see chap. 8.
35. Memo for Chief of Staff from the Secretary of War, 8 December 1936, "Chief of Staff," 13984-262, NA, RG 165.

36. Memo from the Secretary of the Chief of Staff for the Assistant Chief of Staff, G-3, 16 December 1936, "Chief of Staff," 13984-263, NA, RG 165.
37. Kreidberg and Henry, *History of Military Mobilization*, pp. 479–80.
38. Ibid., p. 480.
39. Ibid., pp. 480–92; Popper, "American Defense Policies," pp. 43–44.
40. "Arms before Men," p. 23.
41. *Annual Report of the Secretary of War, 1938*, p. 1.
42. *Annual Report of the Secretary of War, 1936*, pp. 1, 2, and 6.
43. As quoted in the *Army and Navy Journal*, 5 January 1937.
44. *Washington Evening Star* (editorial), 23 December 1936.
45. *Annual Report of the Secretary of War, 1937*, pp. 7–8.
46. *Army and Navy Journal* (editorial), 6 November 1937.
47. *Annual Report of the Secretary of War, 1937*, pp. 1, 2, 7, and 8.
48. Ibid., p. 2.
49. *New York Times*, 7 December 1937 and 6 January 1938.
50. Woodring to Roosevelt, 24 January 1938, box 38, PSF, "Woodring," FDRL.
51. *The Public Papers and Addresses of Franklin D. Roosevelt, 1938: The Continuing Struggle for Liberalism* (New York: Macmillan Co., 1941), p. 71.
52. Daily Air Corps Record, 1938–1939, 28 February 1938, box 56, Official File, 1932–1946, Henry H. Arnold Papers, LC.
53. *Senate Reports*, 75th Cong., 2d and 3d sess., vol. 1, report 1414, pp. 3–4; *House Reports*, 75th Cong., 2d and 3d sess., vol. 1, report 1828, pt. 2, p. 4.
54. *Washington Post*, 29 January 1938.
55. *Senate Reports*, 75th Cong., 2d and 3d sess., vol. 1, report 1414, pp. 3–4; *House Reports*, 75th Cong., 2d and 3d sess., vol. 1, report 1828, pt. 2, p. 4.
56. *United States Statutes at Large, 1938* (Washington, D.C.: U.S. Government Printing Office, 1938), 52:221–22.
57. *Senate Reports*, 75th Cong., 2d and 3d sess., vol. 1, report 1414, p. 3.
58. *Army and Navy Register*, 12 February 1938.
59. *New York Times*, 16 March 1938.
60. *Senate Hearings*, Committee on Military Affairs, 76th Cong., 1st sess., "National Defense," pp. 250–53.
61. *New York Times*, 3 July 1938.
62. *Army and Navy Register*, 23 July 1938; "Arms before Men," p. 23.
63. Memorandum for Colonel Watson from Chief of Staff, 19 November 1938, "Status of Certain Critical Arms and Material," AG580 (10-19-38), NA, RG 407.
64. Ibid.
65. *Annual Report of the Secretary of War, 1938*, pp. 1–5.
66. The development of the air rearmament program will be dealt with in chap. 9.

67. Woodring to Roosevelt, January 1939, box 38, PSF, "Woodring," FDRL.
68. *The Public Papers and Addresses of Franklin D. Roosevelt, 1939: War and Neutrality* (New York: Macmillan Co., 1941), pp. 71–72.
69. Woodring to Roosevelt, January 1939, box 38, PSF, "Woodring," FDRL.
70. *House Hearings*, Subcommittee of the Committee on Appropriations, 76th Cong., 1st sess., "Military Establishment Appropriation Bill for 1940," p. 3.
71. *Senate Hearings*, Committee on Military Affairs, 76th Cong., 1st sess., "National Defense," p. 5.
72. Ibid., p. 6.
73. Memorandum from the Chief of Staff to Assistant Chiefs of Staff, and the Chief of the National Guard Bureau, 7 February 1939, AG320.2 (2-7-39), NA, RG 407.
74. Ibid.
75. *Army and Navy Journal*, 10 June 1939.
76. *New York Times*, 4, 26, and 27 April, 4 May, and 1 and 3 July 1939; Watson, *Prewar Plans and Preparations*, pp. 154–55; Stetson Conn and Bryon Fairchild, *The Framework of Hemisphere Defense* (Washington, D.C.: U.S. Government Printing Office, 1960), p. 15; *Laws Relating to National Defense during Seventy-Sixth Congress* (Washington, D.C.: U.S. Government Printing Office, 1941), p. 4; Popper, "The United States Army in Transition," p. 217.
77. *Army and Navy Journal*, 15 April 1939.
78. *New York Times*, 18 February 1939.
79. *New York Times*, 16 August 1939.
80. *New York Times*, 26 and 27 August 1939.
81. John C. O'Laughlin to Gen. Hugh Drum, 11 September 1939, box 36, O'Laughlin Papers, LC.
82. The Joint Board, whose army components were the Chief of Staff, the Chief of G-4, and the Chief of the WPD and whose Navy personnel included the Chief of Naval Operations, the Assistant Chief, and the head of their WPD, was responsible for "matters of policy and planning." Watson, *Prewar Plans and Preparations*, pp. 79 and 87.
83. Maurice Matloff and Edwin Snell, *Strategic Planning for Coalition Warfare, 1941–1942* (Washington, D.C.: U.S. Government Printing Office, 1953), pp. 6–8.
84. *Federal Register*, vol. 4, pt. 3, July–September 1939, p. 2786.
85. Kreidberg and Henry, *History of Military Mobilization*, p. 476.
86. Weigley, *History of the United States Army*, p. 415.
87. Craig to Woodring, 30 June 1939, and Woodring to Craig, 13 September 1939, WPP; *Army and Navy Journal*, 29 April 1939; interview with Brig. Gen. William Ritchie. Craig's retirement in 1939 was not to mark the end of his military career, for the coming of World War II brought him back

to the War Department as the head of Secretary of War Henry Stimson's Personnel Bureau. He stepped down from that position in 1945, just one year before his death.

88. Conn and Fairchild, *Framework of Hemisphere Defense*, pp. 19–21.
89. *Annual Report of the Secretary of War, 1936*, p. 21, *1940*, app. B., table C.
90. "Chief of Staff's Annual Report, 1939," printed in *Annual Report of the Secretary of War, 1939*, pp. 25 and 35.

CHAPTER 8

1. Harry L. Coles, ed., *Total War and Cold War: Problems in Civilian Control of the Military* (Columbus: The Ohio State University Press, 1962), p. 4.
2. Arthur A. Ekirch, Jr., *The Civilian and the Military* (New York: Oxford University Press, 1956), p. vii.
3. Samuel P. Huntington, *The Soldier and the State: The Theory and Politics of Civil-Military Relations* (Cambridge, Mass.: Belknap Press of Harvard University Press, 1957), pp. 155–57.
4. Walter Millis, *Arms and the State: Civil-Military Elements in National Policy* (New York: Twentieth Century Fund, 1958), p. 6.
5. Evidence of their continued friendship is reflected in the correspondence that the two continued to carry on until March 1945. See PPF 663, "Harry H. Woodring," FDRL.
6. Drew Pearson and Robert S. Allen, "The Merry-Go-Round," *Akron Beacon Journal*, 2 September 1939.
7. Fenno, *The President's Cabinet*, pp. 46–47.
8. Arthur Krock, *Memoirs: Sixty Years on the Firing Line* (New York: Funk & Wagnalls, 1968), p. 202.
9. *New York Herald Tribune* (editorial), 21 June 1940.
10. Senator John Sparkman to author, 29 April 1968.
11. Ibid.
12. Ickes, "My Twelve Years with F.D.R.," 5 June 1948 installment, pp. 81, 90, and 91.
13. Woodring to Roosevelt, 20 June 1940, 18 January 1942, 5 January 1943, 27 December 1944, and 19 March 1945; Roosevelt to Woodring, 19 and 25 June 1940, 29 January and 4 March 1942, and 24 March 1945, PPF 663, "Harry H. Woodring," FDRL.
14. *Army and Navy Journal*, 2 January and 29 May 1937 and 29 April 1939.
15. Gen. Malin Craig to John C. O'Laughlin, 7 September 1939, box 35, O'Laughlin Papers, LC.
16. John C. O'Laughlin to Gen. Malin Craig, 1 and 6 September 1939, box 35, O'Laughlin Papers, LC.

17. *Army and Navy Journal* (editorial), 2 January 1937.
18. *Army and Navy Journal*, 29 May 1937.
19. *Star* (editorial), 21 June 1940.
20. *Army and Navy Journal*, 4 November 1939.
21. Watson, *Prewar Plans and Preparations*, p. 50.
22. Andrew J. May to Roosevelt, 10 November 1938, box 25, OF 25, FDRL; Dow Harter to author, June 1968; John Sparkman to author, 29 April 1968.
23. Charles I. Faddis to author, 28 April 1968.
24. *Senate Hearings*, Committee on Military Affairs, "To Provide for a Sound National Defense," 76 Cong., 1st sess., p. 7.
25. Ibid., pp. 12–13.
26. *Congressional Record*, 76th Cong., 2d sess., vol. 85, pt. 2, p. 278.
27. *Army and Navy Journal*, 18 May 1940.
28. *Star*, 21 June 1940; Kreidberg and Henry, *History of Military Mobilization*, p. 450.
29. Sherwood, *Roosevelt and Hopkins*, pp. 135–36.
30. *New York Times*, 18 May and 4 June 1937.
31. Lawrence Houghterling to Roosevelt, 7 June 1937, forwarded to Woodring with request for opinion, box 38, PSF, "Woodring," FDRL.
32. Woodring to Roosevelt, 11 June 1937, box 38, PSF, "Woodring," FDRL.
33. Interview with James Farley.
34. White House memorandum for President Roosevelt from Senator M. M. Neely, 27 April 1938, OF 25-A, "War Department," "Endorsements for Assistant Secretary," FDRL.
35. Pearson and Allen, "The Merry-Go-Round," *Akron Beacon Journal*, 1 December 1938.
36. Interview with James A. Farley; Eugene Gerhart, *America's Advocate: Robert H. Jackson* (Indianapolis, Ind.: Bobbs-Merrill Co., 1958), p. 164.
37. Interview with James A. Farley.
38. *New York Times*, 15 June 1937.
39. Woodring to Roosevelt, 11 June 1937, OF 25-A, "War Department," "Endorsements for Assistant Secretary," FDRL.
40. Stiles, *The Man Behind Roosevelt*, p. 321.
41. Burns, *Roosevelt: The Lion and the Fox*, p. 372.
42. Elting E. Morison, *Turmoil and Tradition: A Study of the Life and Times of Henry L. Stimson* (Boston: Houghton Mifflin Co., 1960), p. 488.
43. Fenno, *The President's Cabinet*, pp. 45–46; Frances Perkins, *The Roosevelt I Knew* (New York: Viking Press, 1946), pp. 359–60; Cordell Hull, *The Memoirs of Cordell Hull* (New York: Macmillan Co., 1948), 1:205–6; John T. Flynn, *The Roosevelt Myth* (Garden City, N.Y.: Garden City Publishing Co., 1949), p. 55.
44. Burns, *Roosevelt: The Lion and the Fox*, p. 372.

45. "Arms before Men," p. 24.
46. Childs, *I Write from Washington*, p. 161; Brig. Gen. William Ritchie to author, 2 June 1969.
47. "Scandalous Spats," *Time*, 9 October 1939, p. 16.
48. William Frye, *Marshall: Citizen Soldier* (Indianapolis, Ind.: Bobbs-Merrill Co., 1947), p. 254.
49. Smith, *The Army and Economic Mobilization*, p. 102; Troyer S. Anderson, "History of the Office of Under-Secretary of War," MS, Office of the Chief of Military History, chap. 4, p. 3; "The High Cost of Peace," *Fortune*, February 1939, p. 45; John C. O'Laughlin to Gen. John Pershing, 3 December 1938, box 58, O'Laughlin Papers, LC; interview with Helen Coolidge Woodring, 20 July 1968.
50. *Capital*, 11 November 1947.
51. Frye, *Marshall: Citizen Soldier*, p. 252; "Scandalous Spats," p. 16.
52. Pearson and Allen, "The Merry-Go-Round," *Akron Beacon Journal*, 24 February 1938.
53. John C. O'Laughlin to Gen. John Pershing, 12 February 1938, box 58, O'Laughlin Papers, LC.
54. John C. O'Laughlin to Gen. John Pershing, 19 November 1938, box 58, O'Laughlin Papers, LC.
55. John C. O'Laughlin to Gen. John Pershing, 19 November and 3 December 1938, box 58, O'Laughlin Papers, LC; interview with Helen Coolidge Woodring, 20 July 1968; Childs, *I Write from Washington*, p. 161; Ickes, *The Secret Diary of Harold Ickes*, 2:717.
56. Ickes, *The Secret Diary of Harold Ickes*, 2:716–17.
57. John C. O'Laughlin to Gen. John Pershing, 19 November 1938, box 58, O'Laughlin Papers, LC.
58. John C. O'Laughlin to Gen. Malin Craig, 1 September 1939, box 35, O'Laughlin Papers, LC.
59. Farley, *Jim Farley's Story*, p. 114.
60. "Scandalous Spats," p. 16.
61. *New York Times*, 28 September 1939.
62. Forrest C. Pogue, *George C. Marshall*, vol. 2, *Ordeal and Hope, 1939–1942* (New York: Viking Press, 1966), p. 20.
63. Pearson and Allen, "The Merry-Go-Round," *Akron Beacon Journal*, 21 October 1939.
64. Daily Air Corps Record, 1938–1939, 14 January 1938, box 56, Official File, 1932–1946, Henry H. Arnold Papers, LC.
65. Katherine T. Marshall, *Together: Annals of an Army Wife* (Atlanta, Ga.: Tupper & Love, Inc., 1946), p. 41.
66. John C. O'Laughlin to Gen. James G. Harbord, 22 September 1938, box 35, O'Laughlin Papers, LC.

67. Pogue, *Marshall: Ordeal and Hope*, pp. 21–22.
68. Doris Fleeson, "Story behind Marshall Blast by Woodring," *St. Louis Post-Dispatch*, 4 August 1954.
69. Jay Pierrepont Moffat, *The Moffat Papers*, ed. Nancy H. Hooker (Cambridge, Mass.: Harvard University Press, 1956), p. 327; Jonathan Mitchell, "M-Day Man: Louis A. Johnson," *New Republic*, 22 February 1939, p. 65; Frye, *Marshall: Citizen Soldier*, p. 251.
70. Gen. William Ritchie to author, 2 June 1969.
71. John C. O'Laughlin to Gen. John Pershing, 23 March 1937, box 57, O'Laughlin Papers, LC.
72. Frye, *Marshall: Citizen Soldier*, p. 246.
73. Forrest C. Pogue, *George C. Marshall*, vol. 1, *Education of a General, 1880–1939* (New York: Viking Press, 1963), p. 315.
74. Ibid., pp. 314–15.
75. John C. O'Laughlin to Gen. John Pershing, 25 October 1938, box 58, O'Laughlin Papers, LC.
76. Pogue, *Marshall: Education of a General*, p. 315.
77. Ibid., p. 319.
78. John O'Laughlin to Gen. Robert E. Wood, 1 November 1938, box 71, O'Laughlin Papers, LC; Pogue, *Marshall: Education of a General*, p. 327.
79. Pogue, *Marshall: Education of a General*, p. 329; Boake Carter, "New Army Head Personal Choice, Why Selected," n.d., news clipping in WPP.
80. John C. O'Laughlin to Gen. John Pershing, 1 April 1939, box 58, O'Laughlin Papers, LC.
81. *Army and Navy Journal*, 29 April 1939.
82. Pogue, *Marshall: Education of a General*, p. 326.
83. John C. O'Laughlin to Gen. John Pershing, 8 April 1939, box 58, O'Laughlin Papers, LC.
84. Woodring to John C. O'Laughlin, 30 July 1945, box 71, O'Laughlin Papers, LC.
85. Pogue, *Marshall: Education of a General*, p. 326.
86. Marshall to Woodring, 28 April 1939, WPP.
87. Ickes, *The Secret Diary of Harold Ickes*, 3:196.
88. Ibid., 2:127 and 3:12 and 117; Walter Winchell, "Winchell on Broadway," *Akron Beacon Journal*, 8 March 1938; John C. O'Laughlin to Gen. Robert E. Wood, 1 November 1938, box 71, O'Laughlin Papers, LC; *Newsweek*, 27 September 1937, p. 42; Childs, *I Write from Washington*, p. 162. For a rundown on several members of the "inner circle" see Patrick Anderson, *The Presidents' Men* (Garden City, N.Y.: Doubleday & Co., 1968), pp. 7–85.
89. Ickes, *The Secret Diary of Harold Ickes*, 1:101 and 2:135–36; Ickes to Woodring, 2 October 1933, box 1, OF 6, "Interior Department," FDRL.

90. Not all that Ickes said about Woodring was bad. He told of one time that he came to a cabinet meeting after an illness: "The members of the cabinet were very cordial to me and came around to shake hands . . . all except Woodring. He made no pretense of any friendly feeling and I respect him for it. At least he isn't a hypocrite." Ickes, *The Secret Diary of Harold Ickes,* 2:173.
91. *Army and Navy Journal,* 4 September 1937; Farley, *Jim Farley's Story,* p. 135.
92. *Army and Navy Journal,* 4 September 1937 and 15 January 1938; *Boston Globe,* 22 September 1937; *Star,* 17 September 1937; *Newsweek,* 21 August 1937, p. 38.
93. Woodring to Ben S. Paulen, 5 April 1938; Woodring to Charles Deatherage, 18 March 1938, WPP; *Star,* 9 March 1938; *Kansas City Times,* 31 March 1938.
94. John C. O'Laughlin to Gen. John Pershing, 19 November 1938, box 58, O'Laughlin Papers, LC.
95. Interview with James A. Farley.
96. Pearson and Allen, "The Merry-Go-Round," *Akron Beacon Journal,* 26 May 1939.
97. Ickes, "My Twelve Years with F.D.R.," 5 June 1948 installment, p. 90.
98. Childs, *I Write from Washington,* p. 161; Harlan Miller, "Over the Coffee," *Washington Post,* 30 August 1939; *Topeka State Journal,* 14 December 1939. A good idea of the Woodrings' social pace can be gained from examining the numerous invitations sent and received by them during their years in Washington—WPP.
99. Interview with Helen Coolidge Woodring, Cooper C. Woodring, and Melissa Woodring Jager, 20 July 1968.
100. Roosevelt had apparently changed his mind about Johnson, because one year before he had stated that he would not appoint him Secretary of War "under any circumstances." Farley, *Jim Farley's Story,* p. 114.
101. Ickes, *The Secret Diary of Harold Ickes,* 2:537–38; Paul Mallon, "Cabinet Shakeup Whispered in White House Circles," *Washington Times-Herald,* 19 April 1939.
102. Ickes, *The Secret Diary of Harold Ickes,* 2:692; Bernard F. Donahoe, *Private Plans and Public Dangers: The Story of F.D.R.'s Third Nomination* (Notre Dame, Ind.: University of Notre Dame Press, 1965), p. 130.
103. Ickes, "My Twelve Years with F.D.R.," 5 June 1948 installment, p. 90; Miller, "Over the Coffee," *Washington Post,* 30 August 1939.
104. Ickes, "My Twelve Years with F.D.R.," 5 June 1948 installment, p. 90; Senator Marcus Coolidge to Woodring, 12 July 1939; Woodring diary, 12 July 1939, WPP.
105. Woodring to M. M. Levant, 20 June 1939, WPP.

106. Woodring diary, 19 July 1939, WPP.
107. Miller, "Over the Coffee," *Washington Post*, 30 August 1939.
108. Ickes, *The Secret Diary of Harold Ickes*, 3:12.
109. Ernest K. Lindley, "Democratic Candidates," *Washington Post*, 6 November 1939.
110. Gerald P. Nye to author, 25 July 1968.
111. Ickes, "My Twelve Years with F.D.R.," 5 June 1948 installment, p. 90; Ickes, *The Secret Diary of Harold Ickes*, 3:64.
112. Farley, *Jim Farley's Story*, p. 156.
113. Pearson and Allen, "The Merry-Go-Round," *Akron Beacon Journal*, 24 January 1940.
114. Ickes, *The Secret Diary of Harold Ickes*, 3:136.
115. *United States News*, 8 March 1940, p. 40.
116. Miller, "Over the Coffee," *Washington Post*, 25 February 1940.
117. Ickes, "My Twelve Years with F.D.R.," 5 June 1948 installment, p. 92; Ickes, *The Secret Diary of Harold Ickes*, 3:179-80.

CHAPTER 9

1. *The Public Papers and Addresses of Franklin D. Roosevelt, 1938*, p. 71.
2. Kreidberg and Henry, *History of Military Mobilization*, pp. 541-42; Weigley, *History of the United States Army*, p. 417.
3. Watson, *Prewar Plans and Preparations*, pp. 136-39; memorandum for the Chief of Staff from General Arnold, 15 November 1938, OF 25-T, "Army Chief of Staff," FDRL.
4. *Army and Navy Register*, 22 August 1936; for Woodring's contributions to the Air Corps as Assistant Secretary of War see chap. 5.
5. *Congressional Record*, 76th Cong., 1st sess., vol. 81, pt. 10, app., p. 2007.
6. *Army and Navy Journal*, 7 January 1939; Watson, *Prewar Plans and Preparations*, pp. 44-45; Brig. Gen. William Ritchie to author, 2 June 1969.
7. Chief of Staff statement on priorities, 25 October 1938, AG 580 (10-19-38), "Increase of the Air Corps . . . ," NA, RG 407; Henry H. Arnold, *Global Mission* (New York: Harper & Brothers, 1949), pp. 163-64.
8. Thomas H. Greer, *The Development of Air Doctrine in the Army Air Arm, 1917-1941*, U.S. Air Force Historical Studies No. 89 ([Maxwell Air Force Base, Ala.]: Air University, 1955), p. 82; Daily record of events, 9 and 16 June 1937, box 55, Official File, 1932-1946, Henry H. Arnold Papers, LC.
9. Daily record of events, Chief of Air Corps, 23 April 1937, box 55, Official File, 1932-1946; Henry H. Arnold Papers, LC.
10. Arnold, *Global Mission*, p. 167.
11. *New York Times*, 11 June and 27 July 1937.

12. Greer, *Development of Air Doctrine*, pp. 96 and 98; *New York Times*, 23 February 1939.

13. Woodring to Congressman Schuyler Bland, 19 May 1938; Woodring to Charles F. Horner (President, National Aeronautical Association), 10 December 1937, box 3-A, "Air Corps," "Secretary of War General Correspondence, 1932–1942," NA, RG 107.

14. Woodring to Charles F. Horner, 10 December 1937, box 3-A, "Air Corps," "Secretary of War General Correspondence, 1932–1942," NA, RG 107.

15. Daily record, Chief of Air Corps, 9 and 16 June 1937, box 55, Henry H. Arnold Papers, LC; *New York Times*, 27 July 1937.

16. Frye, *Marshall: Citizen Soldier*, pp. 253–54.

17. Greer, *Development of Air Doctrine*, p. 98.

18. Woodring to Congressman Schuyler Bland, 19 May 1938, box 3-A, "Air Corps," "Secretary of War General Correspondence, 1932–1942," NA, RG 107.

19. Memorandum, Assistant Secretary of War for the Chief of the Air Corps, 9 June 1938, "Chief of Staff," 17840-121, "Subject: Procurement of 2-engine Bombardment Planes," NA, RG 165; General Craig to Woodring, 13 July 1938, WPP.

20. Quoted in Watson, *Prewar Plans and Preparations*, p. 36.

21. Daily record, Chief of the Air Corps, 3 September 1938, box 56, Henry H. Arnold Papers, LC.

22. John C. O'Laughlin to Gen. John Pershing, 1 October 1938, box 58, O'Laughlin Papers, LC.

23. Watson, *Prewar Plans and Preparations*, pp. 131-32.

24. *Index, Speeches of Secretary of War Beginning February 19, 1937*, WPP; *Secretary of War Appointment Calendars—Woodring*, U.S. Army Military History Research Collection, Carlisle Barracks, Pa.; Congressman Andrew J. May to Roosevelt, 10 November 1938, box 25, OF 25, "Misc., 1936–1940," FDRL; May to Woodring, 10 November 1938, WPP; telegram, Woodring to Roosevelt, 8 November 1938, box 6, OF 25, "War Department, 1938–1939," FDRL.

25. *Army and Navy Journal*, 3 July 1937; Childs, *I Write from Washington*, p. 161; Frye, *Marshall: Citizen Soldier*, p. 252.

26. Watson, *Prewar Plans and Preparations*, p. 132.

27. Wilson to Roosevelt, 3 July 1938, copy in WPP.

28. Memorandum from General Arnold for Secretary Woodring, 19 October 1938, AG 580 (10-19-38), "Increase of the Air Corps by Aircraft," NA, RG 407.

29. Johnson to Roosevelt, 28 October 1938, and memorandum, Assistant Secretary of War, Assistant Secretary of Navy, and Deputy Administrator of

WPA to President Roosevelt, 28 October 1938, "Increase of the Air Corps by Aircraft," NA, RG 407.

30. Preliminary report on expansion of aircraft production, 28 October 1938, "Increase of the Air Corps by Aircraft," NA, RG 407; John McVickar Haight, Jr., *American Aid to France, 1938–1940* (New York: Atheneum, 1970), pp. 52–53.

31. Memorandum, Chief of the Air Corps to Assistant Secretary of War, 10 November 1938, AG 580 (10-19-38), "Increase of the Air Corps by Aircraft," NA, RG 407.

32. Memorandum for the Chief of Staff from General Arnold, 15 November 1938, box 71, OF 25-T, "Army Chief of Staff," FDRL.

33. Arnold, *Global Mission*, p. 177.

34. Memorandum for the Chief of Staff from Generald Arnold, 15 November 1938, box 71, OF 25-T, "Army Chief of Staff," FDRL.

35. Arnold, *Global Mission*, p. 177.

36. Telegram, Woodring to Roosevelt, 8 November 1938, box 6, OF 25, "War Department," FDRL.

37. *Washington Post*, 12 and 13 November 1938.

38. *Washington Post*, 12 November 1938.

39. Watson, *Prewar Plans and Preparations*, p. 139; Kreidberg and Henry, *History of Military Mobilization*, pp. 542–43.

40. Memorandum from Acting Secretary of War Johnson to the Chief of Staff, 15 November 1938, AG 580 (10-19-38), "Increase of the Air Corps by Aircraft," NA, RG 407.

41. Chief of Staff Craig's statement on priorities to the director of the Bureau of the Budget, 25 October 1938, "Increase of the Air Corps by Aircraft," NA, RG 407.

42. Arnold, *Global Mission*, pp. 163–64; Pogue, *Marshall: Education of a General*, pp. 334–35.

43. Pearson and Allen, "The Merry-Go-Round," *Akron Beacon Journal*, 1 December 1938.

44. Frye, *Marshall: Citizen Soldier*, pp. 252, 254–55, and 259–60; memorandum, General Arnold to Louis Johnson, 24 October 1938, box 2, "Aircraft Production—1938," Henry H. Arnold Papers, LC.

45. Mitchell, "M-Day Man: Louis A. Johnson," pp. 63–65; *Army and Navy Journal*, 19 November 1938.

46. John C. O'Laughlin to Gen. John Pershing, 19 November 1938, box 58, O'Laughlin Papers, LC.

47. *Foreign Policy Bulletin*, 16 December 1938, p. 4.

48. "Rearmament v. Balderdash," *Time*, 19 December 1938, p. 11; *Newsweek*, 12 December 1938, pp. 9–10; *Collier's* (editorial), 28 January 1939, p. 66.

49. "Rearmament v. Balderdash," p. 11; *Foreign Policy Bulletin*, 16 December 1938, p. 4.
50. "Rearmament v. Balderdash," p. 11.
51. *Newsweek*, 12 December 1938, pp. 9–10.
52. *Army and Navy Journal*, 17 December 1938.
53. *Foreign Policy Bulletin*, 16 December 1938, p. 4; *Time*, 19 December 1938, p. 11; *Collier's* (editorial), 28 January 1939, p. 66.
54. Memorandum, Assistant Secretary of War Johnson to Roosevelt, 1 December 1938, AG 580 (10-19-38), "Increase of the Air Corps by Aircraft," NA, RG 407.
55. Watson, *Prewar Plans and Preparations*, pp. 142–43; Haight, *American Aid to France*, pp. 60–64.
56. *Army and Navy Journal*, 3 December 1938; *Newsweek*, 12 December 1938, pp. 9–10.
57. *Cleveland Plain Dealer*, 28 December 1938; *Portland Oregonian*, 10 December 1938; *Army and Navy Journal*, 3 December 1938; John C. O'Laughlin to Gen. John Pershing, 17 December 1938, box 58, O'Laughlin Papers, LC.
58. John C. O'Laughlin to Gen. John Pershing, 17 December 1938, box 58, O'Laughlin Papers, LC; Ernest K. Lindley, "A Cabinet Shuffle," *Washington Post*, 18 December 1938; Miller, "Over the Coffee," *Washington Post*, 23 December 1938.
59. Watson, *Prewar Plans and Preparations*, p. 143.
60. Kreidberg and Henry, *History of Military Mobilization*, p. 546.
61. Memorandum, Secretary of War Woodring to the Chief of the Air Corps, 11 January 1939, AG 580 (12-14-38), "Legislation for Proposed Air Expansion," NA, RG 407.
62. *The Public Papers and Addresses of Franklin D. Roosevelt, 1939*, p. 72.
63. *House Hearings*, 76th Cong., 1st sess., Committee on Military Affairs, 17 January 1939, "An Adequate National Defense," p. 2.
64. Woodring to Andrew J. May, 3 February 1939, box 2A, "Air Planes," "Secretary of War General Correspondence, 1932–1942," NA, RG 107.
65. *New York Times*, 23 February and 27 April 1939.
66. *Army and Navy Journal* (editorial), 15 April 1939.
67. *Federal Register*, 7 July 1939, p. 2786; Watson, *Prewar Plans and Preparations*, p. 66; Smith, *The Army and Economic Mobilization*, p. 42.
68. *New York Times*, 4 August 1939.
69. Fairchild and Grossman, *The Army and Industrial Manpower*, p. 18.
70. *New York Times*, 10 August 1939.
71. *New York Times*, 18 and 31 August 1939; *Washington Post*, 18 August 1939; *Time*, 21 August 1939, p. 13.
72. Anderson, *History of the Office of Under-Secretary of War*, chap. 6, p. 25.

73. Louis Brownlow, *A Passion for Anonymity: The Autogiography of Louis Brownlow* (Chicago: University of Chicago Press, 1958), 2:425.
74. Ickes, *The Secret Diary of Harold Ickes*, 2:720.
75. *Washington Post*, 27 September 1939.
76. Blum, "Birth and Death of the M-Day Plan," p. 83.
77. According to Woodring, it was Miss Perkins rather than himself who brought the matter up. See Pearson and Allen, "The Merry-Go-Round," *Akron Beacon Journal*, 6 October 1939.
78. *New York Times*, 27 September 1939; *Washington Post*, 27 September 1939.
79. *Army and Navy Journal* (editorial), 30 September 1939.
80. *New York Times*, 5 January 1937; *The Aircraft Yearbook for 1946*, ed. Howard Mingos (New York: Lanciar Publishers, 1946), p. 484.

CHAPTER 10

1. Woodring to Congressman Sol Bloom, Acting Chairman, Committee on Foreign Relations, 17 July 1939, box 102, "International Traffic," "Secretary of War General Correspondence, 1932–1942," NA, RG 107.
2. Memorandum for the Secretary of War from the Assistant Secretary of War, 24 August 1933, box 78, "Foreign Governments—Sale of Material," "Secretary of War General Correspondence, 1932–1942," NA, RG 107.
3. *United States Statutes at Large*, vol. 41, pt. 1, p. 949.
4. Memorandum to the Secretary of War from the Assistant Secretary of War, 24 August 1933, box 78, "Foreign Governments—Sale of Material," "Secretary of War General Correspondence, 1932–1942," NA, RG 107.
5. Ibid.
6. Assistant Secretary of War Woodring to Elevator Supplies Co., Hoboken, N.J., 13 September 1934, box 78, "Foreign Governments—Sale of Material," "Secretary of War General Correspondence, 1932–1942," NA, RG 107.
7. Undersecretary of State to the Secretary of War, 19 November 1934, box 78, "Foreign Governments—Sale of Material," "Secretary of War General Correspondence, 1932–1942," NA, RG 107.
8. Secretary Dern to James P. Murray, Vice-President of Boeing Airplane Co., 23 October 1933, box 78, "Foreign Governments—Sale of Material," "Secretary of War General Correspondence, 1932–1942," NA, RG 107.
9. *United States Statutes at Large*, vol. 49, pt. 1, pp. 1081–82.
10. Murray S. Stedman, *Exporting Arms: The Federal Arms Exports Administration, 1935–1945* (Morningside Heights, N.Y.: Kings Crown Press, 1947), p. 17.
11. Ibid., p. 59.
12. *United States Statutes at Large*, vol. 40, pt. 1, p. 218.
13. Woodring to Secretary of State Hull, 6 April 1939, box 102, "International

Traffic in Arms," "Secretary of War General Correspondence, 1932–1942," NA, RG 107.

14. Ibid.

15. Memorandum for files from Col. James Burns, 14 November 1936, box 2, "Airplanes," "Secretary of War General Correspondence, 1932–1942," NA, RG 107.

16. Memorandum of conference held 22 October 1936, box 2, "Airplanes," "Secretary of War General Correspondence, 1932–1942," NA, RG 107; Anthony Eden, *Facing the Dictators: The Memoirs of Anthony Eden* (Boston: Houghton Mifflin, 1962), pp. 544–45.

17. *Army and Navy Journal*, 14 November 1936.

18. *Army and Navy Journal*, 14 November 1936.

19. Memorandum for files from Secretary Woodring, 11 November 1936, box 2, "Airplanes," "Secretary of War General Correspondence, 1932–1942," NA, RG 107.

20. *Congressional Record*, 76th Cong., 1st sess., vol. 81, pt. 10, app., p. 2006; interview with Helen Coolidge Woodring, 20 July 1968.

21. *Army and Navy Journal*, 17 October 1936.

22. Robert A. Divine, *The Illusion of Neutrality* (Chicago: University of Chicago Press, 1962), pp. 168–69.

23. *New York Times*, 29, 30, and 31 December 1936.

24. *New York Times*, 7 January 1937.

25. The Adjutant General to the Assistant Secretary of War, 17 March 1937, box 181, "Surplus Property," "Secretary of War General Correspondence, 1932–1942," NA, RG 107.

26. Stedman, *Exporting Arms*, p. 58.

27. Statement made for the Secretary of War at the meeting of the National Munitions Control Board, 30 April 1937, AG 470 (4-16-37), NA, RG 165.

28. Michael D. Reagan, "The Helium Controversy," in *American Civil-Military Decisions*, ed. Harold Stein (University, Ala.: University of Alabama Press, 1963), p. 45.

29. Ickes, *The Secret Diary of Harold Ickes*, 2:143.

30. *Senate Hearings*, Committee on Military Affairs, 75th Cong., 1st sess., "Conservation of Helium Gas," pp. 123–24.

31. In early April, a few weeks before the crash of the Hindenburg, the House and Senate Military Affairs committees had started hearings regarding legislation on the foreign sale of helium. At that time Secretary Woodring informed both committees that the War Department had no objections to foreign sales. Ibid., pp. 12–13.

32. Ibid., pp. 123–24.

33. *United States Statutes at Large*, vol. 50, pt. 1, pp. 885–87.

34. Ickes, *The Secret Diary of Harold Ickes*, 2:344.

35. Reagan, "The Helium Controversy," p. 51.
36. Ibid., pp. 49–50.
37. Ickes, "My Twelve Years with F.D.R.," 5 June 1948 installment, pp. 82, 84.
38. *Senate Hearings*, Committee on Military Affairs, 75th Cong., 1st sess., "Conservation of Helium Gas," pp. 76, 99.
39. For an excellent account of this conference as well as Roosevelt's subsequent attempts to aid France see Haight, *American Aid to France*.
40. John M. Haight, Jr., "Roosevelt As Friend of France," *Foreign Affairs* 44 (April 1966):518–19.
41. Ibid., p. 520.
42. Ibid., p. 521.
43. Ibid.; Haight, *American Aid to France*, pp. 10–11.
44. Daily Air Corps record, 1938–1939, 10 March 1938, box 56, Henry H. Arnold Papers, LC.
45. *United States Air Service*, February 1939, p. 28; "Armaments Arguments," *Aviation*, March 1939, pp. 69–70.
46. Haight, "Roosevelt As Friend of France," p. 521.
47. Edward R. Stettinius, Jr., *Lend-Lease: Weapon for Victory* (New York: Macmillan Co., 1944), pp. 13–15; *United States Air Service*, July 1938, p. 34.
48. Stettinius, *Lend-Lease*, pp. 13–15.
49. Haight, "Roosevelt As Friend of France," p. 523.
50. Henry Morgenthau, Jr., "The Morgenthau Diaries," pt. 4, *Collier's*, 18 October 1947, p. 17.
51. Ibid.
52. Memorandum of conversation between John C. O'Laughlin and Secretary Woodring, 19 February 1939, box 71, O'Laughlin Papers, LC.
53. Ibid. See also John Blum, ed., *From the Morgenthau Diaries*, vol. 2, *Years of Urgency* (Boston: Houghton Mifflin Co., 1965), pp. 65–66.
54. Ibid.; memorandum of conversation between John C. O'Laughlin and Woodring, 19 February 1939, box 71, O'Laughlin Papers, LC.
55. Blum, *From the Morgenthau Diaries*, 2:67.
56. Ibid., 2:69.
57. Morgenthau, "Morgenthau Diaries," pt. 4, *Collier's*, 18 October 1947, p. 17.
58. Blum, *From the Morgenthau Diaries*, 2:69.
59. Memorandum for the Assistant Secretary of War from the Chief of the Air Corps, 9 January 1939, box 86, "France," "Secretary of War General Correspondence, 1932–1942," NA, RG 107.
60. Blum, *From the Morgenthau Diaries*, 2:70.
61. Morgenthau, "Morgenthau Diaries," pt 4, *Collier's*, 18 October 1947, p. 17.
62. *Senate Hearings*, Committee on Military Affairs, 76th Cong., 1st sess., "To Provide for an Adequate Defense," p. 186.
63. Arnold, *Global Mission*, p. 186.

64. *Washington Post*, 25 January 1939; *New York Times*, 27 January 1939.
65. Gerald P. Nye to author, 25 July 1968; interview with Gerald P. Nye; Pearson and Allen, "The Merry-Go-Round," *Akron Beacon Journal*, 17 February 1939.
66. Memorandum of conversation, Secretary of State Hull and French Ambassador de Saint-Quentin, box 58, "France, 1933–1940," Cordell Hull Papers, LC.
67. *Senate Hearings*, Committee on Military Affairs, 76th Cong., 1st sess., "To Provide for an Adequate Defense," p. 64.
68. Ibid., p. 65.
69. Arnold, *Global Mission*, p. 185.
70. *Senate Hearings*, Committee on Military Affairs, 76th Cong., 1st sess., "To Provide for an Adequate Defense," p. 65.
71. Ibid., pp. 112–15.
72. Gerald P. Nye to author, 25 July 1968.
73. Ibid.
74. Transcript of conference with the Senate Military Affairs Committee, 31 January 1939, box 262, PPF 1-P, FDRL.
75. Ibid.
76. Watson, *Prewar Plans and Preparations*, p. 133.
77. *New York Times*, 1 February 1939.
78. *The Public Papers and Addresses of Franklin D. Roosevelt, 1939*, pp. 112–13.
79. *Senate Hearings*, Committee on Military Affairs, 76th Cong., 1st sess., "To Provide for an Adequate Defense," pp. 197–227.
80. *New York Times*, 18 February 1939.
81. Haight, *American Aid to France*, pp. 100–101; Haight, "Roosevelt As Friend of France," p. 525.
82. Assistant Secretary of War to the Secretary of the Navy, 9 December 1935, box 78, "Foreign Governments—Sale of Material," "Secretary of War General Correspondence, 1932–1942," NA, RG 107.
83. John C. O'Laughlin to Gen. John J. Pershing, 18 February 1939, box 58, O'Laughlin Papers, LC.
84. *Army and Navy Register*, 7 May 1938; *Army and Navy Journal*, 7 May 1938; *New York Times*, 6 May 1938.
85. *New Bedford* (Mass.) *Standard Times*, 6 May 1938; *Utica* (N.Y.) *Observer-Dispatch*, 6 May 1938; *Passaic* (N.J.) *Herald News* (editorial), 6 May 1938; *Washington Post* (editorial), 8 May 1938; *Foreign Policy Bulletin*, vol. 17, no. 3 (10 June 1938), p. 4.
86. *New York Times*, 21 May 1938; *Congressional Record*, 75th Cong., 3d sess., vol. 83, pt. 7, pp. 7198–99; *Philadelphia Inquirer*, 8 May 1938.
87. *New York Times*, 7, 8, 15, and 19 May 1938; *New York Herald Tribune*,

15 May 1938: *Army and Navy Register*, 21 May 1938; Beard and Beard, *America in Midpassage*, p. 498.

88. Privately, F.D.R. did not lose his sense of humor over the turn of events, as is evidenced in a reply to Ambassador William Phillips in Rome. Phillips indicated that in retaliation for Woodring's speech, the Mussolini regime had refused to invite him and his wife to several official gatherings. To this the President replied: "You and Caroline must have been deeply insulted by not being invited to any of the indoor or outdoor functions. I shall have to get Harry Woodring to make another speech!" Roosevelt, *F.D.R.: His Personal Letters, 1928–1945*, 2:785–86.

89. Mrs. Woodring and Harold Ickes believe that Woodring made the speech without consulting the White House, while Senator Gerald Nye and columnists Drew Pearson and Robert Allen maintain that the speech was approved by Roosevelt before it was given.

90. Woodring to the Secretary of the Navy, 6 January 1939, box 2-A, "Airplanes," "Secretary of War General Correspondence, 1932–1942," NA, RG 107.

91. See numerous letters in folders entitled "Foreign Government Official Visits," box 78, and "International Traffic in Arms," box 102, "Secretary of War General Correspondence, 1932–1942," NA, RG 107.

92. Woodring to Secretary of State Hull, 22 April 1939; Johnson to Secretary Hull, 1 April 1939, box 102, "International Traffic in Arms," "Secretary of War General Correspondence, 1932–1942," NA, RG 107.

93. Richard M. Leighton and Robert W. Coakley, *Global Logistics and Strategy, 1940–1943* (Washington, D.C.: U.S. Government Printing Office, 1955), p. 30.

94. For an excellent account of the fight for repeal of the arms embargo see Divine, *The Illusion of Neutrality*, chap. 9.

95. Woodring to Congressman Sol Bloom, Acting Chairman, House Foreign Affairs Committee, 17 July 1939, box 102, "International Traffic in Arms," "Secretary of War General Correspondence, 1932–1942," NA, RG 107. It was similar thinking that caused Woodring to become an opponent of one of the most famous proposals ever designed to keep the United States out of war—the Ludlow Resolution. In 1937, Congressman Louis Ludlow, an Indiana isolationist, laid before the House a resolution to submit a constitutional amendment requiring a popular referendum upon a declaration of war except in case of direct aggression. Woodring spoke out against the proposed amendment, claiming that it was more likely to lead to war than to avoid it, because such a referendum could cause a fatal delay in meeting the threats of a possible aggressor, might be interpreted as a sign of weakness by aggressor nations, and would seriously tie the hands of the President in his conduct of foreign affairs. In January 1938 the measure was barely

rejected by the House, defeat coming only because President Roosevelt personally intervened to prevent its passage. In 1939 and 1940 the resolution was slightly altered and again introduced, but while it had considerable support, it did not pass. On each occasion Secretary Woodring made clear to Congress that he opposed the measure because its passage would "afford encouragement to possible enemies . . . lessen the defensive power of the nation . . . and thus result in a national disaster." *Army and Navy Journal*, 8 January 1938; Woodring to Congressman Andrew J. May, 20 April 1940, box 123, "National Defense," "Secretary of War General Correspondence, 1932–1942," NA, RG 107; Woodring to Senator Carl A. Hatch, 9 June 1939, box 90, "Hearings before Congressional Committees," "Secretary of War General Correspondence, 1932–1942," NA, RG 107.

96. Woodring to Congressman Sol Bloom, 17 July 1939, box 102, "International Traffic in Arms," "Secretary of War General Correspondence, 1932–1942," NA, RG 107.

97. Stettinius, *Lend-Lease*, pp. 20–21.

98. Ibid.

CHAPTER 11

1. Louis B. Wehle, *Hidden Threads of History: Wilson through Roosevelt* (New York: Macmillan Co., 1953), pp. 219–20.

2. *New York Times*, 4 August 1939.

3. William L. Langer and S. Everett Gleason, *The Challenge to Isolation, 1937–1940* (New York: Harper & Brothers, 1952), p. 181; Alsop and Kintner, *American White Paper*, p. 54.

4. Alsop and Kintner, *American White Paper*, p. 55.

5. Secretary of the General Staff for Assistant Chiefs of Staff, 18 August 1939, "Chief of Staff," 21060-8, NA, RG 165.

6. Memorandum for the President from Secretary Woodring, August 1939, box 39, PSF, "War Department, 1933–1945," FDRL.

7. Ibid.; Watson, *Prewar Plans and Preparations*, pp. 155–56.

8. *New York Times*, 20 August 1939.

9. Woodring to Roosevelt, December 1938, box 38, PSF, "Woodring," FDRL.

10. *Annual Report of the Secretary of War, 1939*, p. 2.

11. Pearson and Allen, "The Merry-Go-Round," *Akron Beacon Journal*, 20 December 1939.

12. *Army and Navy Journal*, 5 and 12 August 1939.

13. *Army and Navy Register*, 18 March 1939.

14. Memorandum for The Adjutant General from Assistant Chief of Staff, G-2, 28 August 1939, and copies of radiograms sent to Panama Canal Department, "WPD," 4191, NA, RG 165.

15. *New York Times*, 30 August 1939.

16. Woodring diary, WPP; interview with Helen Coolidge Woodring, 20 July 1968.
17. Miller, "Over the Coffee," *Washington Post*, 8 April 1940; memorandum for the Chief of Staff and the Deputy Chief of Staff, 1 September 1939, "AG 380.3 (9-1-39)," NA, RG 407.
18. *New York Times*, 4, 5, 6, 7, and 10 September 1939.
19. *Army and Navy Register*, 9 September 1939.
20. Interviews with Helen Coolidge Woodring, 20 July and 29 December 1968; *New York Times*, 6 September 1939.
21. Executive Order 8234, 6 September 1939, in *Federal Register*, 7 September 1939, p. 3823.
22. Memorandum for the President from Secretary Woodring, August 1939, box 39, PSF, "War Department, 1933–1945," FDRL.
23. Watson, *Prewar Plans and Preparations*, p. 157; Weigley, *History of the United States Army*, pp. 423–24; *Army and Navy Journal*, 9 September 1939.
24. Watson, *Prewar Plans and Preparations*, p. 157; memorandum from the Chief of Staff to the Deputy Chief of Staff, 8 September 1939, "AG 320.2 (9-8-39)," NA, RG 407.
25. Watson, *Prewar Plans and Preparations*, p. 157.
26. Ibid., p. 161.
27. Ibid.
28. *Army and Navy Journal*, 14 October 1939.
29. *New York Times*, 1 November 1939; Watson, *Prewar Plans and Preparations*, p. 162.
30. *Army and Navy Register*, 18 November 1939.
31. Although Woodring did not actually state his new strategy, his actions of November and December reveal his intention to give the new program the widest possible publicity.
32. *Army and Navy Journal*, 28 October 1939.
33. Ernest Lindley, "Pax Americana," *Washington Post*, 28 October 1939.
34. *Army and Navy Journal*, 28 October 1939.
35. Interview with Gerald P. Nye.
36. *Army and Navy Journal*, 4 November 1939.
37. *Army and Navy Journal*, 11 November 1939; interview with Charles I. Faddis.
38. *Army and Navy Journal*, 4 November 1939.
39. *Army and Navy Journal*, 11 November 1939.
40. *Army and Navy Journal*, 11 November 1939; interviews with Charles I. Faddis and with Dow W. Harter.
41. *Army and Navy Journal*, 11 November 1939; *Army and Navy Register*, 9 December 1939 and 6 January 1940.

42. *Army and Navy Journal,* 11 November 1939.
43. Kreidberg and Henry, *History of Military Mobilization in the United States Army,* p. 565.
44. *House Hearings,* Committee on Appropriations, 76th Cong., 3d sess., "Military Establishment Appropriation Bill for 1941," p. 14; Watson, *Prewar Plans and Preparations,* pp. 163–64.
45. *Annual Report of the Secretary of War, 1939,* pp. 3–4.
46. *New York Times,* 28 December 1939; *Washington Post,* 27 December 1939.
47. *Army and Navy Register,* 6 January 1940.
48. *House Hearings,* Committee on Appropriations, 76th Cong., 3d sess., "Military Establishment Appropriation Bill for 1941," p. 14.
49. Watson, *Prewar Plans and Preparations,* p. 157.
50. *House Hearings,* Committee on Appropriations, 76th Cong., 3d sess., "Military Establishment Appropriation Bill for 1941," pp. 28 and 37–38.
51. *Army and Navy Journal,* 20 January 1940.
52. *House Hearings,* Committee on Appropriations, 76th Cong., 3d sess., "Military Establishment Appropriation Bill for 1941," pp. 2–48.
53. *New York Times,* 5 April 1939.
54. *House Hearings,* Committee on Appropriations, 76th Cong., 3d sess., "Military Establishment Appropriation Bill for 1941," pp. 28–32 and 55–58.
55. Watson, *Prewar Plans and Preparations,* p. 166; Blum, *From the Morgenthau Diaries,* 2:138.
56. *The Public Papers and Addresses of Franklin D. Roosevelt, 1940,* p. 202.
57. *Senate Hearings,* Committee on Appropriations, 76th Cong., 3d sess., "Military Establishment Appropriations Bill for 1941," pp. 405–6.
58. *Army and Navy Journal,* 18 May 1940.
59. *New York Times,* 23 May and 13 and 15 June 1940. In addition to the appropriation, the measure authorized contracts for an additional $257 million worth of military equipment.
60. Marshall biographer Forrest Pogue tells of a very crucial conference at the White House on 13 May and comments that "Woodring sat apart, lending no help to the Chief of Staff." Pogue, *Marshall: Ordeal and Hope,* p. 30.
61. *The Public Papers and Addresses of Franklin D. Roosevelt, 1940,* p. 253. In addition to the regular appropriation, $254 million in contract authorizations were approved.
62. *New York Times,* 17 September 1939; *Army and Navy Journal,* 23 September 1939.
63. *Army and Navy Journal,* 14 October 1939.
64. *Army and Navy Journal,* 27 April 1940; Watson, *Prewar Plans and Preparations,* pp. 159 and 204–5.
65. *Army and Navy Journal,* 26 April 1939 and 1 June 1940; *Army and Navy Register,* 13 April 1940; Watson, *Prewar Plans and Preparations,* p. 247.

66. *Army and Navy Register*, 26 April and 20 May 1939.
67. *House Hearings*, Committee on Military Affairs, 76th Cong., 3d sess., "Promotion of Promotion List Officers of the Army," pp. 3–4; Watson, *Prewar Plans and Preparations*, p. 247.
68. *Army and Navy Journal*, 13 January and 15 June 1940.
69. *Army and Navy Journal*, 20 May 1939.
70. Watson, *Prewar Plans and Preparations*, p. 249.
71. *Army and Navy Journal*, 15 and 29 June 1940.
72. Although Marshall's statement referred to conditions in the fall of 1939, he proceeded to say that conditions were not much better by June 1940. *The War Reports of General of the Army George C. Marshall, Chief of Staff, General of the Army H. H. Arnold, Commanding General, Army Air Forces, [and] Fleet Admiral Ernest J. King, Commander-in-Chief, United States Fleet, and Chief of Naval Operations*, with a foreword by Walter Millis (Philadelphia: J. B. Lippincott Co., 1947), p. 16.
73. *Washington Post*, 26 May 1940.
74. Doris Fleeson, "Washington Views 'Our Vital Interest,'" *Independent Woman* 19 (June 1940):188.

CHAPTER 12

1. Transcript of conference with the Senate Military Affairs Committee, 31 January 1939, box 262, PPF 1-P, FDRL.
2. Blum, *From the Morgenthau Diaries*, 2:115; Watson, *Prewar Plans and Preparations*, p. 138.
3. *Army and Navy Journal*, 13 July 1940; Burns, *Roosevelt: The Lion and the Fox*, p. 420; Warren F. Kimball, *The Most Unsordid Act: Lend-Lease, 1939–1941* (Baltimore, Md.: Johns Hopkins Press, 1969), p. 26.
4. *Star*, 20 June 1940.
5. Memorandum, President Roosevelt to Secretary of War Woodring, 6 December 1939, box 122, "International Traffic in Arms," "Secretary of War General Correspondence, 1932–1942," NA, RG 107.
6. Blum, *From the Morgenthau Diaries*, 2:111–12.
7. The committee was officially called the Interdepartmental Committee for Coordination of Foreign and Domestic Purchases, but was always known or referred to as the President's liaison committee.
8. Blum, *From the Morgenthau Diaries*, 2:112–13.
9. Ibid., pp. 115–17.
10. Ibid.; Langer and Gleason, *The Challenge to Isolation*, p. 291.
11. Blum, *From the Morgenthau Diaries*, 2:116.
12. Memorandum for the Secretary of War from the Chief of the Air Corps, 12 January 1940, box 223, "Aircraft Production, 1939–1941," Henry H. Arnold Papers, LC.

13. Langer and Gleason, *The Challenge to Isolation*, p. 290.
14. Blum, *From the Morgenthau Diaries*, 2:117.
15. *Army and Navy Journal*, 23 March 1940.
16. *Washington Post*, 11 and 12 March 1940.
17. *New York Times*, 14 March 1940.
18. Edison, who had been Assistant Secretary of the Navy since 1937, had been named Acting Secretary in July 1939, when Claude Swanson died, and he was ultimately made permanent Secretary in December 1939.
19. Memo of record by General Arnold, 13 March 1940, box 223, "Aircraft Production, 1939–1941," Henry H. Arnold Papers, LC; Blum, *From the Morgenthau Diaries*, 2:117; Joseph Alsop and Robert Kintner, "The Capital Parade," *Dallas Morning News*, 18 March 1940.
20. Memorandum of record by General Arnold, 13 March 1940, box 223, "Aircraft Production, 1939–1941," Henry H. Arnold Papers, LC.
21. Blum, *From the Morgenthau Diaries*, 2:117; Kimball, *Most Unsordid Act*, p. 36.
22. Memorandum of record by General Arnold, 16 and 18 March 1940, box 223, "Aircraft Production, 1939–1941," Henry H. Arnold Papers, LC.
23. Memorandum of record by General Arnold, 19 March 1940, box 223, "Aircraft Production, 1939–1941," Henry H. Arnold Papers, LC.
24. Report of a meeting held in the Chief of Staff's office, 10:30 A.M., 19 March 1940, "Chief of Staff Binder, March 1940," NA, RG 165.
25. Memo of record by General Arnold, 19 March 1940, box 223, "Aircraft Production, 1939–1941," Henry H. Arnold Papers, LC.
26. *The Public Papers and Addresses of Franklin D. Roosevelt, 1940*, pp. 104–8.
27. Memorandum of record by General Arnold, 19 March 1940, box 223, "Aircraft Production, 1939–1941," Henry H. Arnold Papers, LC.
28. Ibid.; *Army and Navy Journal*, 20 April 1940.
29. Memorandum of record by General Arnold, 20 March 1940, box 223, "Aircraft Production, 1939–1941," Henry H. Arnold Papers, LC.
30. *Army and Navy Register*, 23 March 1940.
31. Government Policy on Aircraft Foreign Sales, 25 March 1940, box 223, "Aircraft Production, 1939–1941," Henry H. Arnold Papers, LC.
32. *United States News*, 5 April 1940, p. 40.
33. Woodring's statement before the House Military Affairs Committee, 27 March 1940, box 102, "International Traffic in Arms," "Secretary of War General Correspondence, 1932–1942," NA, RG 107.
34. *New York Times*, 28 March 1940; *Army and Navy Register*, 30 March 1940.
35. *New York Times*, 28 March 1940.
36. *Senate Hearings*, Military Affairs Committee, 76th Cong., 3d sess., "Purchase of Implements of War by Foreign Governments," p. 10.

37. *The Public Papers and Addresses of Franklin D. Roosevelt, 1940,* p. 108.
38. *New York Times,* 29 March 1940.
39. *United States News,* 29 March 1940, p. 40.
40. Pearson and Allen, "The Merry-Go-Round," *Akron Beacon Journal,* 17 April 1940.
41. John C. O'Laughlin to Gen. John Pershing, 23 March 1940, box 58, O'Laughlin Papers, LC.
42. Record of a conference held in the Chief of Staff's office, 22 March 1940, "Chief of Staff Binder, March 1940," NA, RG 165; Blum, *From the Morgenthau Diaries,* 2:119.
43. Blum, *From the Morgenthau Diaries,* 2:119–20; Morgenthau, "The Morgenthau Diaries," pt. 4, *Collier's,* 18 October 1947, p. 72.
44. Memorandum for the Chief of Staff from the Assistant Chief of Staff, G-4, 9 March 1940, "Chief of Staff," 15270-896, NA, RG 165.
45. *Congressional Record,* 76th Cong., 3d sess., vol. 86, pt. 16, app., pp. 4429–31.
46. Langer and Gleason, *Challenge to Isolation,* pp. 291 and 338–40; Watson, *Prewar Plans and Preparations,* pp. 303–4; *New York Times,* 9 and 10 February 1940; Hull, *The Memoirs of Cordell Hull,* 1:707; Robert Sobel, *The Origins of Interventionism: The United States and the Russo-Finnish War* (New York: Bookman Associates, 1960), pp. 97–100.
47. Memorandum for the Chief of Staff from the Assistant Chief of Staff, G-4, 9 March 1940, "Chief of Staff," 15270-896, NA, RG 165.
48. Note appended by Secretary Woodring to memorandum cited in note 47.
49. Memorandum approved by the Secretary of War and the Secretary of State, 12 March 1940, box 102, "International Traffic in Arms," "Secretary of War General Correspondence, 1932–1942," NA, RG 107.
50. Winston L. S. Churchill, *Their Finest Hour* (Boston: Houghton Mifflin Co., 1949), p. 24.
51. Blum, *From the Morgenthau Diaries,* 2:150.
52. Memorandum from the Chief of Staff for the Secretary of the Treasury, 18 May 1940, "Release of P-36 Type Airplanes . . . to the British Government," "Chief of Staff, Emergency File, 11 May to 16 August 1940," NA, RG 165.
53. Churchill, *Their Finest Hour,* p. 25.
54. Roosevelt's determination to avoid Woodring's obstructionist tactics by working around him became increasingly evident in mid May, when he informed Morgenthau that he wanted him to "expedite the entire military program, particularly the production of aircraft engines." The President then made that position clear to Secretary Woodring in a memorandum of 24 May, which said: "It is of utmost importance that no contracts be entered into from now on either for planes or engines or for the development of new types of planes or engines without coordinating this with the general

program as a rule. For the time being, until the final machinery is set up, this coordination will be cleared through the Secretary of the Treasury to me as Commander in Chief. Please see that this is carried out in toto." Blum, *From the Morgenthau Diaries*, 2:144; memorandum for Secretary of War Woodring from President Roosevelt, 24 May 1940, box 2-B, "Airplanes," "Secretary of War General Correspondence, 1932–1942," NA, RG 107; Kimball, *The Most Unsordid Act*, p. 54.

55. Memorandum from the Chief of Ordnance to the Chief of Staff, 22 May 1940, "Availability of Ordnance Material for Release . . . ," "Chief of Staff, Emergency File, Binder 2," NA, RG 165; Watson, *Prewar Plans and Preparations*, p. 309.

56. Memorandum for the record by the Chief of Staff, 25 May 1940, "Regarding Release of Ordnance Material to the Allied Purchasing Agent," "Chief of Staff, Emergency File for 11 May to 16 August 1940," NA, RG 165.

57. Blum, *From the Morgenthau Diaries*, 2:153; Langer and Gleason, *Challenge to Isolation*, p. 488.

58. Memorandum for the record by the Chief of Staff, 25 May 1940, "Regarding Release of Ordnance Material . . . ," "Chief of Staff, Emergency File, Binder 2, for 11 May to 16 August 1940," NA, RG 165.

59. Memorandum for the Chief of Staff from the Assistant Chief of Staff, G-4, 27 May 1940, "Chief of Staff, Emergency File, Binder 2, for 11 May to 16 August 1940," NA, RG 165.

60. Report from Green Heckworth, Department of State legal adviser, 28 May 1940, box 7, OF 25, "War Department, 1940," FDRL.

61. Handwritten note on memorandum for the Secretary of State from Green Heckworth, 28 May 1940, box 2-B, "Secretary of War General Correspondence, 1932–1942," NA, RG 107.

62. Memorandum from the Secretary of War to the President, 31 May 1940, box 2-B, "Secretary of War General Correspondence, 1932–1942," NA, RG 107.

63. Ibid.

64. Ibid.

65. *Official Opinions of the Attorneys General of the United States*, vol. 39, *Advising the President and Heads of Department in Relation to Their Official Duties*, ed. John T. Fowler (Washington, D.C.: U.S. Government Printing Office, 1941), pp. 445–46.

66. Blum, *From the Morgenthau Diaries*, 2:153–54; Watson, *Prewar Plans and Preparations*, p. 310.

67. Blum, *From the Morgenthau Diaries*, 2:153–54; Stettinius, *Lend-Lease*, p. 70.

68. Stettinius, *Lend-Lease*, p. 26.

69. Memorandum for the President from the Secretary of War, 17 June 1940 (not used), "Chief of Staff, Foreign Sales, Binder 4," NA, RG 165.
70. Morgenthau, Hopkins, Watson, and Early were especially upset with Woodring's attitude toward the Allies.
71. Memo for the Undersecretary of State from the Chief of Staff, 16 May 1940, and memo for the Secretary of the Treasury from the Chief of Staff, 18 May 1940, "Chief of Staff, Emergency File, Binder 2, for 11 May to 16 August 1940," NA, RG 165; *Star*, 21 June 1940.
72. Blum, *From the Morgenthau Diaries*, 2:153–54.
73. Actually, Marshall had officially been expressing such views since mid May. Memo for the Undersecretary of State from the Chief of Staff, 16 May 1940, and memo for the Secretary of the Treasury from the Chief of Staff, 18 May 1940, "Chief of Staff, Emergency File, Binder 2, for 11 May to 16 August 1940," NA, RG 165.
74. Watson, *Prewar Plans and Preparations*, p. 111.
75. Ibid., pp. 166–67; Brownlow, *A Passion for Anonymity*, 2:435.
76. Knox to Roosevelt, 15 December 1939, and Roosevelt to Knox, 29 December 1939, box 1, Frank Knox Papers, LC; McCoy, *Landon of Kansas*, p. 431.
77. Interview with Alfred M. Landon; McCoy, *Landon of Kansas*, pp. 432–36.
78. Knox to Mrs. Knox, 11 June 1941, box 1, Knox Papers, LC; McCoy, *Landon of Kansas*, p. 437. There is evidence that Knox either had dropped, or was on the verge of dropping, his earlier proviso that another Republican be named. See Brownlow, *A Passion for Anonymity*, 2:446.
79. Tully, *F.D.R.: My Boss*, p. 242; Ickes, *The Secret Diary of Harold Ickes*, 2:132–33 and 136. In the *New York Times* for 19 February 1948, Bullitt claimed that on 9 June the President offered him the position of Secretary of the Navy and that he accepted the offer, but when Knox decided to take the position, the President dropped the matter of Bullitt's appointment.
80. Charles I. Faddis to author, 28 April 1968.
81. Pearson and Allen, "The Merry-Go-Round," *Akron Beacon Journal*, 19 June 1940; Frank R. Kent, "The Great Games of Politics," *Baltimore Sun*, 5 June 1940; Alsop and Kintner, "The Capital Parade," *Washington Evening Star*, 20 June 1940.
82. *New York Times*, 14 June 1940.
83. *Life* (editorial), "Will U.S. Mobilize Its Industrial Might in Time?" 17 June 1940.
84. *London Daily Telegraph and Morning Post*, 5 June 1940.
85. *New York Times*, 9 June 1940.
86. See box 25, OF 25 Misc., "War Department, 1940," FDRL.
87. Farley, *Jim Farley's Story*, pp. 212–13; Ickes, *The Secret Diaries of Harold Ickes*, 3:186.
88. Franklin Delano Roosevelt, *Roosevelt and Frankfurter: Their Correspond-*

ence, 1928–1945, annotated by Max Freedman (Boston: Little, Brown & Co., 1967), pp. 524–27.

89. Pearson and Allen, "The Merry-Go-Round," *Akron Beacon Journal*, 19 June 1940.

90. Blum, *From the Morgenthau Diaries*, 2:162.

91. Telephone conversation between Watson and Morgenthau, 18 June 1940, "Morgenthau Diaries (book 272, pp. 280–81)," FDRL.

92. John C. O'Laughlin to Gen. John Pershing, 22 June 1940, box 58, O'Laughlin Papers, LC.

93. James Farley, who was close to Woodring and Roosevelt, believed the latter to be the case. Farley wrote, "I am satisfied that Edison and Woodring would have been eased out on one pretext or another to bring men into the cabinet who were convinced that the United States should enter the war." *Jim Farley's Story*, p. 243.

94. Roosevelt to Woodring, 19 June 1940, WPP; also in box 38, PSF, "Harry H. Woodring, 1937–1940," FDRL.

95. Woodring to Roosevelt, 20 June 1940, box 38, PSF, "Harry H. Woodring, 1937–1940," FDRL.

96. Memorandum from Woodring to Roosevelt, 20 June 1940, box 38, PSF, "Harry H. Woodring, 1937–1940," FDRL.

97. Henry Stimson and McGeorge Bundy, *On Active Service in Peace and War* (New York: Harper & Brothers, 1947), pp. 323–24; *New York Times*, 26 July 1940.

98. *Washington Post*, 21 June 1940.

99. Charles I. Faddis to author, 28 April 1968.

100. Bernard M. Baruch, *Baruch: The Public Years* (New York: Holt, Rinehart & Winston, 1960), 2:277.

101. *New York Times*, 21 June 1940.

102. *Capital*, 21 June 1940.

103. *Congressional Record*, 76th Cong., 3d sess., vol. 86, pt. 8, pp. 8791, 8822, 8855, 8908, 9038, and 9039, and vol. 86, pt. 16, pp. 4280–81; *New York Times*, 21–24 June 1940.

104. Roosevelt to Woodring, 25 June 1940, WPP.

105. *Kansas City Times*, 22 June 1940.

106. *Capital*, 9 July 1940.

107. Roosevelt to Woodring, 25 June 1940, WPP; Roosevelt, *F.D.R.: His Personal Letters, 1928–1945*, 2:1042–43.

108. Telephone conversation between Watson and Morgenthau, "Morgenthau Diaries (book 273, pp. 280–81)," FDRL.

109. Ibid., pp. 278–79.

110. Watson to Woodring, 22 June 1940, WPP.

111. Blum, *From the Morgenthau Diaries*, 2:163.

112. Roosevelt biographer James MacGregor Burns feels that the timing of the removal of Woodring and the appointments of Stimson and Knox was primarily associated with the President's desire to play havoc with the Republican convention; Burns, *Roosevelt: The Lion and the Fox*, p. 424.
113. Benjamin V. Cohen to author, 27 May 1969.
114. *Newsweek*, 1 July 1940, p. 7.
115. *New York Times*, 27 June 1940; *Capital*, 27 June and 2 July 1940.

CHAPTER 13

1. Interview with Helen Coolidge Woodring, 20 July 1968; *Capital*, 27 June and 2, 3, 9, and 10 July 1940; *Pictorial Times* (Topeka), 22 October 1969.
2. *Kansas City Times*, 19 March 1940; *Star*, 12 May 1940; Woodring to Albert A. Searle, 26 March 1940, WPP.
3. *Kansas City Times*, 19 March 1940; *Star*, 12 May 1940; interview with Gerald P. Nye.
4. *Star*, 12 May 1940.
5. *Capital*, 2 and 3 July 1940.
6. *Capital*, 2, 3, and 9 July 1940; *New York Times*, 7 July 1940.
7. *Congressional Record*, 76th Cong., 3d sess., vol. 86, pt. 16, pp. 4429–31; *Capital*, 10 July 1940.
8. *Congressional Record*, 76th Cong., 3d sess., vol. 86, pt. 16, pp. 4429–31.
9. *Capital*, 12 and 14 July 1940; Burns, *Roosevelt: The Lion and the Fox*, pp. 422–27; Leuchtenburg, *Franklin D. Roosevelt and the New Deal*, pp. 314–16.
10. *New York Times*, 11 and 16 July 1940; *Capital*, 3, 12, 14, and 15 July 1940.
11. *New York Times*, 11 and 16 July 1940; *Capital*, 3, 12, 14, and 15 July 1940; Donahoe, *Private Plans and Public Dangers*, p. 171.
12. *Official Report of the Proceedings of the Democratic National Convention, Held at Chicago, Illinois, July 15th to 18th Inclusive, 1940*, p. 154; James F. Byrnes, *Speaking Frankly* (New York: Harper & Brothers Publishers, 1947), p. 10.
13. Burns, *Roosevelt: The Lion and the Fox*, pp. 427–30; *New York Times*, 16, 17, and 18 July 1940; *Capital*, 16 and 17 July 1940.
14. Woodring to Farley, 25 July 1940, WPP.
15. Woodring to O'Laughlin, 24 July 1940, box 71, O'Laughlin Papers, LC.
16. Woodring's personal diary for 1939—16 February, 3 March, 11, 13, and 15 April, 5 May, 24 June, and numerous other dates, WPP.
17. Robert K. Kelley, "On a Historic Kansas Hill a Former Secretary of War Finds Peace and Content," *Star*, 20 April 1941.
18. John C. O'Laughlin to Woodring, 11 July 1940; Woodring to O'Laughlin, 24 July 1940, box 71, O'Laughlin Papers, LC.

19. Woodring to Roosevelt, 15 January 1941, PPF 663, "Harry H. Woodring," FDRL.
20. Roosevelt to Woodring, 21 January 1941, WPP.
21. *New York Times*, 3 August 1940; Arthur Vandenberg to Woodring, 7 August 1940, WPP; *Congressional Digest*, vol. 20, nos. 8 and 9 (August 1940), p. 213.
22. M. S. Eccles to President Roosevelt, 10 February 1941; Woodring to Roosevelt, 15 January 1941, PPF 663, "Harry H. Woodring," FDRL.
23. Telegram from Woodring to Roosevelt, 8 December 1941, PPF 663, "Harry H. Woodring," FDRL.
24. Woodring to Roosevelt, 18 January 1942; Roosevelt to Woodring, 29 January 1941, PPF 663, "Harry H. Woodring," FDRL.
25. Woodring to Generals Marshall and Arnold, 8 January 1941, WPP; Woodring to General Marshall, 19 April 1941, WPP; Marshall to Woodring, 12 January 1942, WPP.
26. Zula B. Greene, "Peggy of the Flint Hills," *Capital*, 19 September 1967.
27. *Outlook*, 26 February 1942; Zornow, *Kansas*, pp. 323–24.
28. *Lyndon* (Kans.) *Herald* (editorial), 8 August 1940.
29. *Topeka State Journal*, 12 and 13 December 1942; *Kansas City Times*, 16 December 1942.
30. *Topeka State Journal*, 12 and 13 December 1942.
31. *Kansas City Times*, 16 December 1942; Farley to Woodring, 16 December 1942, WPP.
32. Woodring to Roosevelt, 5 January 1943, PPF 663, "Harry H. Woodring," FDRL.
33. *Chicago Tribune*, 6 July 1943.
34. Senator Harry F. Byrd to Woodring, 2 November 1943, WPP.
35. *Capital*, 4 and 5 February 1944; *New York Times*, 5 February 1944.
36. *New York Times*, 5 February 1944.
37. *New York Times*, 20 February 1944.
38. *New York Times*, 20, 21, and 25 February 1944; *New York Daily Express*, 22 February 1944.
39. Woodring to John C. O'Laughlin, 15 February 1944, box 71, O'Laughlin Papers, LC.
40. *New York Times*, 5 March 1944.
41. *New York Times*, 3 April 1944; *Capital*, 3 April 1944.
42. P. E. Laughlin to President Roosevelt, 10 April 1944, PPF 8773, FDRL.
43. Ibid.
44. Ibid.; *New York Times*, 3 April 1944; *Capital*, 3 April 1944.
45. *Capital*, 3 April 1944.
46. *New York Times*, 3 April, 13 May, 1 June, 16 September, and 7 November 1944.

47. Harry S Truman to Woodring, 27 July 1944 and 16 March 1945, WPP.
48. Woodring to Roosevelt, 27 December 1944, WPP.
49. Ibid.
50. Woodring to John C. O'Laughlin, 30 July 1945, box 71, O'Laughlin Papers, LC; financial records in WPP.
51. Woodring to Farley, 18 January 1945, WPP.
52. Woodring to Roosevelt, 19 March 1945, PPF 663, "Harry H. Woodring," FDRL; Roosevelt to Woodring, 24 March 1945, WPP.
53. Interviews with Helen Coolidge Woodring and with Melissa Woodring Jager, 20 July 1968.
54. Woodring to General Marshall, 23 July 1945, copy in box 71, O'Laughlin Papers, LC.
55. Woodring to O'Laughlin, 23 July 1945, box 71, O'Laughlin Papers, LC.
56. Woodring to O'Laughlin, 30 July 1945, box 71, O'Laughlin Papers, LC.
57. O'Laughlin to Woodring, 9 August 1945, box 71, O'Laughlin Papers, LC; General Marshall to Woodring, 16 August 1945, WPP.
58. Doris Fleeson, "Story behind Marshall Blast by Woodring," *St. Louis Post-Dispatch*, 4 August 1954.
59. Interviews with Helen Coolidge Woodring, 20 July 1968 and 14 June 1969.
60. Robert W. Richmond, "Kansas in the Late 1940s," in *Kansas: The First Century*, ed, John D. Bright (New York: Lewis Historical Publishing Co., 1956), 2:463–64.
61. Ibid.; Zornow, *Kansas*, p. 327; *Hutchinson News-Herald*, 26 May, 11, 14, and 17 June, and 5 August 1946.
62. Woodring to Milton Eisenhower, 14 August 1946, WPP.
63. *Topeka State Journal*, 19 July 1946; *New York Times*, 20 and 28 July and 7 August 1946; interviews with Helen Coolidge Woodring, 14 June 1969, with William Ritchie, and with Alfred M. Landon.
64. *Capital*, 7 August 1946; *Hutchinson News-Herald*, 7 August 1946.
65. Richmond, "Kansas in the Late 1940s," 2:463–64; *Time*, 9 September 1946, p. 26; *Hutchinson News-Herald*, 20 September and 3 November 1946.
66. *Hutchinson News-Herald*, 30 October 1946.
67. Richmond, "Kansas in the Late 1940s," 2:463–64; *Capital*, 3, 4, and 5 November 1946.
68. *Hutchinson News-Herald*, 6 November 1946; Zornow, *Kansas*, p. 329.
69. Richmond, "Kansas in the Late 1940s," 2:467, 475–76, and 480.
70. Woodring to Truman, 9 March 1945, box 111, "Senate and Vice-Presidential Papers," "Papers of Harry S Truman," HSTL; Truman to Woodring, 21 January, 31 May, and 9 December 1946 and 28 October and 6 November 1947, PPF 1768, "Harry H. Woodring," "Papers of Harry S Truman," HSTL; Truman to Woodring, 16 March 1945 and 20 January 1947, WPP.
71. Woodring to Truman, 5 December 1947; Woodring to Matthew J. Con-

nally; telegram from Connally to Woodring, 10 December 1947; memorandum from Connally to Col. Neal Mora, 10 December 1947—all in OF 249, "Travel by Army and Navy Planes," "Truman Papers," HSTL; President's Appointment Book, 14 January and 12 March 1948, HSTL; *New York Times*, 3 February 1948; *Purchaser*, June 1949, p. 4.

72. Harry M. Washington to President Truman, 27 April 1946, PPF 2656, "Truman Papers," HSTL; Zornow, *Kansas*, p. 331.

73. Telegram from Woodring to Connally, 15 July 1948, and telegram from Woodring to Truman, 14 October 1948, PPF 1768, "Truman Papers," HSTL; President's Appointment Book, 17 July 1948, HSTL.

74. Telegram from Woodring to Truman, 14 October 1948, PPF 1768, "Truman Papers," HSTL.

75. Truman to Woodring, 16 January 1950, and news clipping, n.p., n.d., WPP.

76. Interviews with Helen Coolidge Woodring, Cooper C. Woodring, and Melissa Woodring Jager, 20 July 1968; *Capital*, 9 September 1951 and 22 January 1956; Zornow, *Kansas*, p. 337.

77. Woodring to Gen. Douglas MacArthur, 28 February 1952, MacArthur Papers, Bureau of Archives, MacArthur Memorial, Norfolk, Va.

78. Interview with Helen Coolidge Woodring, 14 June 1969.

79. *New York Times*, 3 and 4 August 1954.

80. *Congressional Record*, 83d Cong., 2d sess., vol. 100, pt. 10, p. 12960; *New York Times*, 3 and 4 August 1954.

81. *New York Times*, 5 August 1954.

82. *New York Times*, 5 August 1954; *Capital*, 4, 5, and 6 August 1956.

83. *Hutchinson News-Herald*, 6, 20, and 21 June 1956; *Capital*, 21 June 1956; interviews with Cooper C. Woodring, 12 July 1971, and with Alfred M. Landon; confidential communication.

84. *Hutchinson News-Herald*, 21 June and 8 July 1956; *United Kansas Democrat*, 30 July 1956.

85. *Hutchinson News-Herald*, 15, 27, and 29 July and 2 and 5 August 1956; *United Kansas Democrat*, 30 July 1956.

86. Congressman James Roosevelt to Woodring, 19 July 1956, WPP; *United Kansas Democrat*, 30 July 1956.

87. *Hutchinson News-Herald*, 8 and 9 August 1956; *Capital*, 9 August 1956; *New York Times*, 8 August 1956.

88. Zornow, *Kansas*, p. 342.

89. Miscellaneous correspondence between Woodring and the Internal Revenue Service, WPP.

90. Memorandum regarding Franklin Delano Roosevelt Memorial Commission, 22 September 1955, OF 101-FF1, "Eisenhower Papers," DDEL; Program of the Annual Meeting, Board of Trustees, the Eisenhower Foundation, 1961, WPP; Hoover to Woodring, 19 December 1949 and 24 August 1956,

and Woodring to Hoover, 26 October 1950, 5 October 1955, and 7 February 1957, Herbert Hoover Presidential Library, "Post-Presidential Papers, 1st Hoover Commission and Post-Presidential Individual—Woodring," Herbert Hoover Library, West Branch, Iowa; *Capital*, 22 January 1956; Frank Pace, Jr., to Woodring, 13 June 1951, and Cyrus R. Vance to Woodring, 1 June 1963, and Woodring to General Eisenhower, 20 June 1949, WPP.

91. *Kansas City Times*, 10 October 1947; *Worcester* (Mass.) *Daily Telegram*, 11 November 1947; interview with Helen Coolidge Woodring, 14 June 1969.

92. *Pictorial Times* (Topeka), 22 October 1969.

93. Interview with Alfred M. Landon; Dr. Karl Menninger to author, 7 January 1971 and 17 August 1972.

94. Interviews with Helen Coolidge Woodring, Cooper C. Woodring, and Melissa Woodring Jager, 20 July 1968; *Time*, 14 March 1960, p. 98; *Emporia Gazette*, 12 September 1967.

95. Maurice E. Fager to author, 8 December 1970; *New York Times*, 2 May 1959 and 31 May 1963; *Capital*, 10 September 1967; State of Kansas, Office of the Adjutant General, "Funeral Arrangements for Former Governor Harry Woodring," 11 September 1967, copy given to author by Cooper C. Woodring.

96. *Congressional Record*, 76th Cong., 3 sess., vol. 86, pt. 16, p. 4431.

Bibliography

Although many primary and secondary sources were extremely valuable for the writing of this book, two of them—the Woodring Personal Papers and the Secretary of War's General Correspondence, 1932–1942—were absolutely essential. For the former collection I am deeply in debt to Mr. Cooper C. Woodring of Plandome, New York, who gave me complete access to these papers, which are as yet uncatalogued. In going through this collection, which I estimate to contain approximately 4,000 letters, 200 telegrams, 5,000 news clippings, 800 pamphlets and published reports, 1,000 photographs, and hundreds of miscellaneous items, I tentatively organized the material into the following categories:

1. Woodring's family—ancestors, parents, sisters, relatives, etc.
2. Pre-1928 Activities
   a. news clippings
   b. letters
3. American Legion Activities
   a. news clippings
   b. pamphlets, programs, etc.
4. Governor
   a. campaign material
   b. published speeches, reports, etc.
   c. personal letters, memorandums, telegrams
   d. news clippings
5. Assistant Secretary of War
   a. official correspondence

b. personal correspondence
c. invitations—social engagements
d. appointment books
e. news clippings
6. Secretary of War
   a. official correspondence
   b. personal correspondence
   c. memorandums
   d. social matters
   e. news clippings
7. Post-1940 Activities
   a. campaign material
   b. personal correspondence
   c. news clippings
8. Photographs
   a. family
   b. official
      (1) Governor
      (2) Assistant Secretary of War
      (3) Secretary of War
9. Miscellaneous letters, newspapers, pamphlets of historical value
10. Political mementoes

This collection was especially valuable in providing information on Woodring's prepolitical career and his activities after leaving public life, but the material from his years as Governor and as a War Department official is rather sketchy and therefore will be of limited value to the in-depth researcher. Nevertheless, when this collection is completely organized and indexed, it should prove of great value to students of both Kansas and United States history.

The Secretary of War, General Correspondence, 1932–1942, which is located in the National Archives, was also indispensable to the study. This collection of several hundred boxes of material contains nearly every piece of official correspondence that crossed Woodring's desk at the War Department between 1933 and 1940.

Other material of value is listed in the following selected bibliography.

ARCHIVAL MATERIAL

War Department, Secretary of War, General Correspondence, 1932–1942. National Archives, Washington, D.C., Record Group 107.

War Department, Records of the War Department General Staff, Chief of Staff, 1936–1940. National Archives, Record Group 165.

War Department, Records of the War Department General Staff, Supply Division, 1936–1940. National Archives, Record Group 165.

War Department, Records of the War Department General Staff, War Plans Division, 1936–1940. National Archives, Record Group 165.
War Department, Records of the Adjutant General, 1936–1940. National Archives, Record Group 407.

MANUSCRIPTS

Henry H. Arnold Papers. Library of Congress. Washington, D.C.
George H. Dern Papers. Library of Congress.
Dwight D. Eisenhower Papers. Dwight D. Eisenhower Library. Abilene, Kansas.
Cordell Hull Papers. Library of Congress.
Frank Knox Papers. Library of Congress.
William P. Lane Papers. Duke University Library. Durham, North Carolina.
Douglas MacArthur Papers. MacArthur Memorial Bureau of Archives. Norfolk, Virginia.
John J. McSwain Papers. Duke University Library. Durham, North Carolina.
Ewing Young Mitchell Papers. University of Missouri Library. Columbia, Missouri.
Henry Morgenthau, Jr., Diaries. Franklin D. Roosevelt Library. Hyde Park, New York.
John C. O'Laughlin Papers. Library of Congress.
Ben S. Paulen Papers. Kansas Historical Society. Topeka, Kansas.
General John J. Pershing Papers. Library of Congress.
Records of the Democratic National Committee—Kansas 1928–1933. Franklin D. Roosevelt Library.
Franklin D. Roosevelt Papers. Official File, President's Personal File, and President's Secretary File. Franklin D. Roosevelt Library.
Harry S Truman Papers. Harry S Truman Library. Independence, Missouri.
William Allen White Papers. Library of Congress.
Harry H. Woodring Governor's Papers. Kansas State Historical Society. Topeka, Kansas.
Harry H. Woodring Personal Papers. In possession of Cooper C. Woodring. Plandome, New York.

INTERVIEWS

Catlin, Lawrence J. Neodesha, Kansas, 9 August 1971.
Crowder, Ralph. Neodesha, Kansas, 8 August 1971.
Dancer, Frank. Independence, Kansas, 8 August 1971.
Davis, Overton. Independence, Kansas, 8 August 1971.
Drybread, Byron. Elk City, Kansas, 7 August 1971.
Faddis, Charles I. Waynesburg, Pennsylvania, 4 August 1970.
Farley, James. New York City, 1 August 1968.
Gray, Georgia Neese Clark. Topeka, Kansas, 6 August 1971.

Harter, Dow W. Washington, D.C., 13 June 1969.
Jager, Melissa Woodring. Wilmington, Delaware, 20 July 1968.
Landon, Alfred M. Topeka, Kansas, 5 August 1971.
McCullough, C. A. Neodesha, Kansas, 9 August 1971.
Nye, Gerald P. Washington, D.C., 13 June 1969.
Ritchie, General William L. Washington, D.C., 13 June 1969.
Shaffer, Arthur B. Independence, Kansas, 8 August 1971.
Stafford, W. A. Neodesha, Kansas, 9 August 1971.
Woodring, Cooper C. New York City, 10 June, 20 July, 28 December 1968; 14 June 1969; 11–14 July 1971.
Woodring, Helen Coolidge. Wilmington, Delaware, 20 July and 28 December 1968; 14 June 1969.
Wright, Vada. Elk City, Kansas, 7 August 1971.

CORRESPONDENCE

Allen, Joe W. 24 February 1971.
Arends, L. C. 2 May 1968.
Black, Hugo. 26 June, 1968.
Catlin, Lawrence J. 9 June 1971.
Cohen, Benjamin V. 22 May 1971.
Crowder, Ralph. 8 June 1971.
Davis, Overton. 20 October 1970.
Dunn, Caroline. 27 November 1970.
Edison, Charles. 15 April 1969.
Erickson, Rev. Charles O. 26 February 1968; 4 November 1970.
Faddis, Charles I. 28 April 1968.
Fager, Maurice E. 8 December 1970.
Farley, James A. 24 July 1968.
George, Lila S. 5 November 1971.
Harter, Dow W. 28 June 1968.
Haucke, Frank ("Chief"). 24 May 1971.
Heller, Ray E. 24 November 1970.
Hill, Lister. 14 August 1968.
Hungerford, Eleanor B. 12 August 1971.
Johnson, Edwin C. 27 April 1968.
Jones, Rev. Ray Carlton. 3 December 1970.
Kilday, Paul J. 31 May 1968.
Lodge, Henry Cabot. 28 June 1968.
McDowell, Joseph. 14 June 1971.
Menninger, Dr. Karl. 7 January 1971; 17 August 1972.
Metcalf, Edward A., III. 12 July 1972.
Nye, Gerald P. 25 July 1968.

Parish, Rev. Tom, Jr. 17 June 1971.
Pogue, Forrest C. 5 June 1968.
Rice, Carl. 27 July 1971.
Ritchie, General William L. 2 June 1969.
Sauer, Gladys Sewell. 8 July 1971.
Shaffer, Arthur B. 15 September 1970.
Sherwood, Leon A. 15 June 1971.
Sparkman, John H. 29 April 1968.
Stark, Ralph W. 23 February and 15 March 1971.
Stockhill, Louis. 19 August 1968.
Wood, Lonnie N. 23 September 1970.

PRINTED PUBLIC DOCUMENTS

Inaugural Address of Harry H. Woodring, Governor, January 12, 1931. Topeka: State Printer, 1931.

Kansas Secretary of State. *Twenty-seventh Biennial Report.* Topeka: State Printer, 1930.

Laws Relating to National Defense Enacted during Seventy-sixth Congress. Washington: U.S. Government Printing Office, 1941.

Message of Governor Harry H. Woodring to the Kansas Legislature of 1931. Topeka: State Printer, 1931.

Official Opinions of the Attorneys General of the United States Advising the President and Heads of Departments in Relation to Their Official Duties. Vol. 39. Edited by John T. Fowler. Washington: U.S. Government Printing Office, 1941.

U.S., *Congressional Record.* Vols. 80–86.

U.S., *Federal Register.* Vols. 4 and 5.

U.S., *Government Manual,* 1933–1940. Washington: Office of Government Reports, 1933–1940.

U.S., House of Representatives. *Documents.* "Second Annual Report of the National Munitions Control Board." House Document No. 465. 75th Cong., 3d sess., 1938.

U.S., House of Representatives. *Documents.* "Third Annual Report of the National Munitions Control Board." House Document No. 92. 76th Cong., 1st sess., 1939.

U.S., House of Representatives, Committee on Military Affairs. *Hearings.* "An Adequate National Defense As Outlined by the Message of the President of the United States." 76th Cong., 1st sess., 1939.

U.S., House of Representatives, Committee on Military Affairs. *Hearings.* "Promotion of Promotion List Officers of the Army." 76th Cong., 3d sess., 1940.

U.S., House of Representatives, Committee on Military Affairs. *Hearings.* "Vitalization of the Active List of the Army." 76th Cong., 1st sess., 1939.

BIBLIOGRAPHY

U.S., House of Representatives. *Reports.* "Reestablishing the Regular Army Reserve." House Report No. 1838. 75th Cong., 3d sess., 1938.

U.S., House of Representatives. *Reports.* "Secretaries of War and Navy to Assist American Republics to Increase Their Military and Naval Establishments." House Report No. 1231. 76th Cong., 1st sess., 1939.

U.S., House of Representatives, Subcommittee of the Committee on Appropriations. *Hearings.* "Military Establishment Appropriation Bill for 1940." 76th Cong., 1st sess., 1939.

U.S., House of Representatives, Subcommittee of the Committee on Appropriations. *Hearings.* "Military Establishment Appropriation Bill for 1941." 76th Cong., 3d sess., 1940.

U.S., Senate. *Documents.* "Army of the United States." Senate Document No. 91. 76th Cong., 1st sess., 1940.

U.S., Senate, Committee on Military Affairs. *Hearings.* "Conservation of Helium Gas." 75th Cong., 1st sess., 1938.

U.S., Senate, Committee on Military Affairs. *Hearings.* "General Staff Corps Eligible List." 75th Cong., 1st sess., 1938.

U.S., Senate, Committee on Military Affairs. *Hearings.* "National Defense." 76th Cong., 1st sess., 1939.

U.S., Senate, Committee on Military Affairs. *Hearings.* "Procurement of Aircraft." 76th Cong., 1st sess., 1939.

U.S., Senate, Committee on Military Affairs. *Hearings.* "Promotion of Promotion List Officers of the Army." 76th Cong., 3d sess., 1940.

U.S., Senate, Committee on Military Affairs. *Hearings.* "Purchase of Implements of War by Foreign Governments." 76th Cong., 1st sess., 1940.

U.S., Senate, Committee on Military Affairs. *Hearings.* "Regular Army Reserve." 75th Cong., 3d sess., 1938.

U.S., Senate. *Reports.* "Reestablishing the Regular Army Reserve." Senate Report No. 1414. 75th Cong., 3d sess., 1938.

U.S., Senate, Special Committee Investigating the National Defense Program, United States. *Hearings.* "Investigation of the National Defense Program." 80th Cong., 1st sess., 1948.

U.S., Senate, Subcommittee of the Committee on Appropriations. *Hearings.* "Military Establishment Appropriation Bill for 1940." 76th Cong., 1st sess., 1939.

U.S., Senate, Subcommittee of the Committee on Appropriations. *Hearings.* "Military Establishment Appropriation Bill for 1941." 76th Cong., 3d sess., 1940.

U.S., *Statutes at Large.* Vols. 41 and 50–54.

War Department, Office of the Secretary of War. *Annual Report of the Secretary of War, 1933–1940.* Washington: U.S. Government Printing Office, 1933–1940.

War Department. *Industrial Mobilization Plan.* Washington: U.S. Government Printing Office, 1936.

War Department. *Official Duties, Department of War.* Washington: U.S. Government Printing Office, 1934.

The War Reports of General of the Army George C. Marshall, Chief of Staff, General of the Army H. H. Arnold, Commanding General, Army Air Forces, [and] Fleet Admiral Ernest J. King, Commander-in-Chief, United States Fleet, and Chief of Naval Operations, with a foreword by Walter Millis. Philadelphia: J. B. Lippincott Co., 1947.

PUBLISHED MEMOIRS, CORRESPONDENCE, AND OTHER PERSONAL ACCOUNTS

Alsop, Joseph, and Kintner, Robert. *American White Paper: The Story of American Diplomacy and the Second World War.* New York: Simon & Schuster, 1940.

Arnold, Henry H. *Global Mission.* New York: Harper & Brothers, 1949.

Baruch, Bernard M. *Baruch: The Public Years.* New York: Holt, Rinehart & Winston, 1960.

Blum, John M., ed. *From the Morgenthau Diaries.* Vol. 1, *Years of Crisis, 1928–1938.* Vol. 2, *Years of Urgency, 1938–1941.* Boston: Houghton Mifflin Co., 1959, 1965.

Brownlow, Louis. *A Passion for Anonymity: The Autobiography of Louis Brownlow.* Chicago: University of Chicago Press, 1958.

Byrnes, James F. *Speaking Frankly.* New York: Harper & Brothers Publishers, 1947.

Callahan, James E., ed. *Jayhawk Editor: A Biography of A. Q. Miller, Sr.* (From the Recollections, Writings, and Papers of A. Q. Miller, Sr.) Los Angeles: Sterling Press, 1955.

Childs, Marquis W. *I Write from Washington.* New York: Harper & Brothers, 1942.

Churchill, Winston L. S. *Their Finest Hour.* Boston: Houghton Mifflin Co., 1949.

Clugston, William G. *Rascals in Democracy.* New York: Richard R. Smith, 1941.

Comer, Bert. *The Tale of a Fox.* Wichita, Kans.: B. Comer, 1936.

Eden, Anthony. *Facing the Dictators: The Memoirs of Anthony Eden.* Boston: Houghton Mifflin Co., 1962.

Eisenhower, Dwight D. *At Ease: Stories I Tell to Friends.* Garden City, N.Y.: Doubleday & Co., 1967.

Farley, James A. *Behind the Ballots.* New York: Harcourt, Brace & Co., 1938.

———. *Jim Farley's Story: The Roosevelt Years.* New York: McGraw-Hill Co., 1948.

Foulois, Benjamin D., with Glines, C. V. *From the Wright Brothers to the Astronauts: The Memoirs of Major General Benjamin D. Foulois.* New York: McGraw-Hill Co., 1968.

Hull, Cordell. *The Memoirs of Cordell Hull.* 2 vols. New York: Macmillan Co., 1948.

Ickes, Harold L. *The Secret Diary of Harold L. Ickes.* Vol. 1, *The First Thousand Days: 1933–1936.* Vol. 2, *The Inside Struggle: 1936–1939.* Vol. 3, *The Lowering Clouds: 1939–1941.* New York: Simon & Schuster, 1953–1954.

Jones, Jesse H., with Angly, Edward. *Fifty Billion Dollars: My Thirteen Years with the RFC (1932–1945).* New York: Macmillan Co., 1951.

Kansas. Governor. *Under the Statehouse Dome: Our State Government.* Radio speeches of Governor Harry H. Woodring, broadcast from his desk in the capitol at Topeka, July to September 1932. Topeka, Kans.: N.p., 1932.

Krock, Arthur. *Memoirs: Sixty Years on the Firing Line.* New York: Funk & Wagnalls, 1968.

MacArthur, Douglas. *Reminiscences.* New York: McGraw-Hill Book Co., 1964.

Marshall, Katherine T. *Together: Annals of an Army Wife.* Atlanta, Ga.: Tupper & Love, Inc., 1946.

Moffat, Jay Pierrepont. *The Moffat Papers: Selections from the Diplomatic Journals of Jay Pierrepont Moffat, 1919–1943.* Edited by Nancy H. Hooker. Cambridge, Mass.: Harvard University Press, 1956.

Perkins, Frances. *The Roosevelt I Knew.* New York: Viking Press, 1946.

Roosevelt, Franklin Delano. *F.D.R.: His Personal Letters, 1928–1945.* Edited by Elliott Roosevelt. 2 vols. New York: Duell, Sloan & Pearce, 1950.

——. *The Public Papers and Addresses of Franklin D. Roosevelt.* Compiled and collated by Samuel I. Rosenman. Vols. 5–9, for 1936, 1937, 1938, 1939, and 1940. New York: Macmillan Co., 1938–1941.

——. *Roosevelt and Frankfurter: Their Correspondence, 1928–1945.* Annotated by Max Freedman. Boston: Little, Brown & Co., 1967.

Roper, Daniel C. *Fifty Years of Public Life.* Durham, N.C.: Duke University Press, 1941.

Rosenman, Samuel I. *Working with Roosevelt.* New York: Harper & Brothers, 1952.

Schruben, Francis W., comp. *Harry H. Woodring Speaks: Kansas Politics during the Early Depression.* Los Angeles: Francis W. Schruben, 1963.

Sherwood, Robert E. *Roosevelt and Hopkins: An Intimate History.* New York: Harper & Brothers, 1948.

Stettinius, Edward R., Jr. *Lend-Lease: Weapon for Victory.* New York: Macmillan Co., 1944.

Stiles, Lela. *The Man behind Roosevelt: The Story of Louis McHenry Howe.* Cleveland: World Publishing Co., 1954.

BIBLIOGRAPHY

Stimson, Henry, and Bundy, McGeorge. *On Active Service in Peace and War.* New York: Harper & Brothers, 1947.

Tugwell, Rexford. *The Democratic Roosevelt.* Garden City, N.Y.: Doubleday & Co., 1957.

Tully, Grace. *F.D.R.: My Boss.* New York: Charles Scribner's Sons, 1949.

Wehle, Louis B. *Hidden Threads of History: Wilson through Roosevelt.* New York: Macmillan Co., 1953.

Welles, Sumner. *The Time for Decision.* New York: Harper & Brothers, 1944.

NEWSPAPERS

Abilene (Kans.) *Reflector*
Akron (Ohio) *Beacon Journal*
Army and Navy Journal
Army and Navy Register
Atchison (Kans.) *Globe*
Baltimore Sun
Boston Globe
Chicago Tribune
Cincinnati Enquirer
Cleveland Plain Dealer
Dallas Morning News
Elk City (Kans.) *Eagle*
Elk City Enterprise
Elk City Globe
Emporia (Kans.) *Gazette*
Hutchinson (Kans.) *News*
Hutchinson News-Herald
Kansas City Star
Kansas City Times
Lebanon (Ind.) *Pioneer*
London Daily Telegraph and Morning Post
Neodesha (Kans.) *Register*
Neodesha Sun
New York Herald Tribune
New York Times
Pictorial Times (Topeka)
Pittsburg (Kans.) *Headlight*
The Times (London)
Topeka Daily Capital
Topeka State Journal
United Kansas Democrat
Washington Evening Star

Washington Herald
Washington Post
Washington Times-Herald

MISCELLANEOUS UNPUBLISHED MATERIAL

Anderson, Troyer S. "History of the Office of Under-Secretary of War." Typed manuscript located at the Office of the Chief of Military History, Washington, D.C.

Certification of Military Service of Harry Woodring. There are two certificates: one for service as an enlisted man; the other for service as an officer. In possession of author.

Index to the Speeches of Secretary of War, beginning 19 February 1937. Woodring Personal Papers.

Kansas State Census, 1895. Volume 245, Elk City, 15. Kansas State Historical Society. Topeka, Kansas.

Killigrew, John W. "The Impact of the Great Depression on the Army, 1929–1936." Ph.D. dissertation. Indiana University, 1960.

Minutes of the Kansas Department of the American Legion, 3–5 September 1928. Pittsburg, Kansas.

Montgomery County Clippings, vol. 3. Kansas State Historical Society. Topeka, Kansas.

Questionnaire filled out by Woodring for *National Cyclopedia of American Biography.* Copy given to author by Cooper C. Woodring.

Secretary of War Appointment Calendars—Woodring. U.S. Army Military History Research Collection. Carlisle Barracks, Pennsylvania.

Slechta, Don B. "Dr. John R. Brinkley: A Kansas Phenomenon." Master's thesis, Fort Hays Kansas State College, 1952.

Statement of the Military Service of Haynes Woodring. Woodring Personal Papers.

Taped interview by Richard Loosbrock of Harry H. Woodring on Woodring's activities in the American Legion. Courtesy of Dr. Loosbrock and Floyd J. Rogers of the Kansas Department of the American Legion.

"Woodring Family History." Two-page mimeographed sheet presented to the author by Mrs. Eleanor B. Hungerford of Washington, D.C.

BOOKS

Adler, Selig. *The Isolationist Impulse.* New York: Abelard-Schuman Ltd., 1957.

The Aircraft Yearbook, for *1936, 1937, 1938, 1939, 1940,* and *1946.* Edited by Howard Mingos. New York: Aeronautical Chamber of Commerce of America, Inc., and Lanciar Publishers, 1936–1940, and 1946.

Anderson, Patrick. *The Presidents' Men: White House Assistants of Franklin D. Roosevelt, Harry S Truman, Dwight D. Eisenhower, John F. Kennedy and Lyndon B. Johnson.* Garden City, N.Y.: Doubleday & Co., 1968.

BIBLIOGRAPHY

Beard, Charles A., and Beard, Mary R. *America in Midpassage.* New York: Macmillan Co., 1939.

Benfield, Raydene James. *Elk City, Kansas: Then and Now.* N.p.: Midwestern Litho, 1964.

Bernardo, C. Joseph, and Bacon, Eugene H. *American Military Policy: Its Development since 1775.* Harrisburg, Pa.: Military Service Publishing Co., 1961.

Bracke, William B. *Wheat Country.* New York: Duell, Sloan & Pearce, 1950.

Bright, John D., ed. *Kansas: The First Century.* Vol. 2. New York: Lewis Historical Publishing, 1956.

Bryant, Keith L., Jr. *Alfalfa Bill Murray.* Norman: University of Oklahoma Press, 1968.

Burns., James M. *Roosevelt: The Lion and the Fox.* New York: Harcourt, Brace, & World, Inc., 1956.

Carson, Gerald. *The Roguish World of Doctor Brinkley.* New York: Holt, Rinehart & Winston, 1960.

Cherne, Leo M. *Adjusting Your Business to War.* New York: Tax Research Institute of America, Inc., 1939.

Coles, Harry L., ed. *Total War and Cold War: Problems in Civilian Control of the Military.* Columbus: Ohio State University Press, 1962.

Conn, Stetson, and Fairchild, Byron. *The Framework of Hemisphere Defense.* Washington: U.S. Government Printing Office, 1960.

Craven, Wesley Frank, and Cate, James Lea, eds. *The Army Air Forces in World War II.* Vol. 6, *Men and Planes.* Chicago: University of Chicago Press, 1955.

Democratic State Handbook (1932). Salina, Kans.: Democratic State Committee, n.d.

Divine, Robert. *The Illusion of Neutrality.* Chicago: University of Chicago Press, 1962.

Donahoe, Bernard F. *Private Plans and Public Dangers: The Story of FDR's Third Nomination.* Notre Dame, Ind.: University of Notre Dame Press, 1965.

Duncan, Lew Wallace. *History of Montgomery County, Kansas.* Iola, Kans.: Press of Iola Register, 1903.

Ekirch, Arthur A., Jr. *The Civilian and the Military.* New York: Oxford University Press, 1956.

Eliot, George Fielding. *The Ramparts We Watch: A Study of the Problems of American National Defense.* New York: Reynal & Hitchcock, 1938.

Fairchild, Byron, and Grossman, Jonathan. *The Army and Industrial Manpower.* Washington: U.S. Government Printing Office, 1959.

Federal Writers Project. *Kansas: A Guide to the Sunflower State.* New York: Viking Press, 1939.

Fenno, Richard F., Jr. *The President's Cabinet: An Analysis in the Period from Wilson to Eisenhower.* Cambridge, Mass.: Harvard University Press, 1959.

Flynn, John T. *The Roosevelt Myth.* Garden City, N.Y.: Garden City Publishing Co., 1949.

Freidel, Frank. *Franklin D. Roosevelt.* Vol. 3, *The Triumph.* Boston: Little, Brown & Co., 1956.

Frye, William. *Marshall: Citizen Soldier.* Indianapolis, Ind.: Bobbs-Merrill Co., 1947.

Gerhart, Eugene C. *America's Advocate: Robert H. Jackson.* Indianapolis, Ind.: Bobbs-Merrill Co., 1958.

Greer, Thomas H. *The Development of Air Doctrine in the Army Air Arm, 1917–1941.* U.S. Air Force Historical Studies No. 89. [Maxwell Air Force Base, Ala.]: Air University, 1955.

Hagood, Major General Johnson. *We Can Defend America.* Garden City, N.Y.: Doubleday, Doran & Co., 1937.

Haight, John McVickar, Jr. *American Aid to France, 1938–1940.* New York: Atheneum, 1970.

Holley, Irving B. *Buying Aircraft: Matériel Procurement for the Army Air Forces.* Washington: U.S. Government Printing Office, 1964.

Huntington, Samuel P. *The Soldier and the State: The Theory and Politics of Civil-Military Relations.* Cambridge, Mass.: Belknap Press of Harvard University Press, 1957.

Huston, James A. *The Sinews of War: Army Logistics, 1775–1953.* Washington: U.S. Government Printing Office, 1966.

Jablonski, Edward. *Flying Fortress: The Illustrated Biography of the B-17s and the Men Who Flew Them.* Garden City, N.Y.: Doubleday & Co., 1965.

James, Dorris Clayton. *The Years of MacArthur.* Vol. 1, *1880–1941.* Boston: Houghton Mifflin Co., 1970.

Janeway, Eliot. *The Struggle for Survival: A Chronicle of Economic Mobilization in World War II.* New Haven, Conn.: Yale University Press, 1951.

Jonas, Manfred. *Isolationism in America, 1935–1941.* Ithaca, N.Y.: Cornell University Press, 1966.

Kimball, Warren F. *The Most Unsordid Act: Lend-Lease, 1939–1941.* Baltimore, Md.: Johns Hopkins Press, 1969.

Kreidberg, Marvin A., and Henry, Merton G. *History of Military Mobilization in the United States Army, 1775–1945.* Washington: U.S. Government Printing Office, 1955.

Langer, William L., and Gleason, S. Everett. *The Challenge to Isolation, 1937–1940.* New York: Harper & Brothers, 1952.

Leighton, Richard M., and Coakley, Robert W. *Global Logistics and Strategy, 1940–1943.* Washington: U.S. Government Printing Office, 1955.

BIBLIOGRAPHY

Leuchtenburg, William E. *Franklin D. Roosevelt and the New Deal, 1932–1940.* New York: Harper & Row Publishers, 1963.

Lindbergh, Charles A. *The Wartime Journals of Charles A. Lindbergh.* New York: Harcourt, Brace, Jovanovich, 1970.

Little Bear Tracks: A Book of Pictures, Articles, Records, and Events That Helped to Form Neodesha's 100 Years. Neodesha, Kans.: Neodesha Printing Co., 1971.

Loosbrock, Richard J. *The History of the Kansas Department of the American Legion.* Topeka: Kansas Department of the American Legion, 1968.

Lunt, Richard D. *The High Ministry of Government: The Political Career of Frank Murphy,* Detroit, Mich.: Wayne State University Press, 1965.

McCoy, Donald R. *Landon of Kansas.* Lincoln: University of Nebraska Press, 1966.

Martin, James J. *American Liberalism and World Politics, 1931–1941.* 3 vols. New York: Devin-Adair Co., 1964.

Matloff, Maurice, and Snell, Edwin M. *Strategic Planning for Coalition Warfare, 1941–1942.* Washington: U.S. Government Printing Office, 1953.

May, Ernest R., ed. *The Ultimate Decision: The President As Commander in Chief.* New York: George Braziller, 1960.

Millis, Walter. *Arms and the State: Civil-Military Elements in National Policy.* New York: Twentieth Century Fund, 1958.

Morison, Elting E. *Turmoil and Tradition: A Study of the Life and Times of Henry L. Stimson.* Boston: Houghton Mifflin Co., 1960.

Official Report of the Proceedings of the Democratic National Convention, Held at Chicago, Illinois, July 15th to 18th Inclusive, 1940. N.p., n.d.

Rauch, Basil. *Roosevelt: From Munich to Pearl Harbor.* New York: Creative Age Press, 1950.

Reinhardt, George C., and Kintner, William R. *The Haphazard Years: How America Has Gone to War.* Garden City, N.Y.: Doubleday & Co., 1960.

Salmond, John A. *The Civilian Conservation Corps, 1933–1942: A New Deal Case Study.* Durham, N.C.: Duke University Press, 1967.

Schapsmeier, Edward L., and Schapsmeier, Frederick H. *Henry A. Wallace of Iowa: The Agrarian Years, 1910–1940.* Ames: Iowa State University Press, 1968.

Schlesinger, Arthur M., Jr. *The Coming of the New Deal.* Boston: Houghton Mifflin Co., 1958.

Schruben, Francis W. *Kansas in Turmoil, 1930–1936.* Columbia: University of Missouri Press, 1969.

Smith, Ralph E. *The Army and Economic Mobilization.* Washington: U.S. Government Printing Office, 1959.

BIBLIOGRAPHY

Sobel, Robert. *The Origins of Interventionism: The United States and the Russo-Finnish War.* New York: Bookman Associates, 1960.

Stedman, Murray S. *Exporting Arms: The Federal Arms Exports Administration, 1935–1945.* Morningside Heights, N.Y.: Kings Crown Press, 1947.

Stein, Harold, ed. *American Civil-Military Decisions.* [University, Ala.]: University of Alabama Press, 1963.

Timmons, Bascom N. *Garner of Texas: A Personal History.* New York: Harper & Brothers Publishers, 1948.

————. *Jesse H. Jones: The Man and the Statesman.* New York: Henry Holt & Co., 1956.

Washburn, Charles G. *The Life of John W. Weeks.* Boston: Houghton Mifflin Co., 1928.

Watson, Mark S. *United States Army in World War II: The War Department: Prewar Plans and Preparations.* Washington: U.S. Government Printing Office, 1950.

Weigley, Russell F. *History of the United States Army.* New York: Macmillan Co., 1967.

Wheeler-Nicholson, Malcolm. *Battle Shield of the Republic.* New York: Macmillan Co., 1940.

ARTICLES

"L'Affaire Chemidlin." *New Republic,* 15 February 1939, p. 44–45.

"America Is Arming." *Nation,* 8 April 1936, p. 436.

"Armaments Arguments." *Aviation,* March 1939, pp. 69–70.

"Arms before Men." *Time,* 22 August 1938, pp. 23–25.

"'Army in Being.'" *Time,* 1 January 1940, p. 12.

Bailey, Richard H. "Dr. Brinkley of Kansas." *Nation,* 21 September 1932, pp. 254–55.

Baldwin, Hanson W. "Our New Long Shadow." *Foreign Affairs,* 17 (April 1939):465–76.

"Behind the Arms Program." *Christian Century,* 25 January 1939, pp. 110–12.

Blum, Albert A. "Birth and Death of the M-Day Plan." Pp. 60–96 in *American Civil-Military Decisions,* ed. Harold Stein. [University, Ala.]: University of Alabama Press, 1963.

Buel, Walker S. "The Army under the New Deal." *Literary Digest,* 26 August 1933, pp. 3–4.

Carlson, Avis D. "Drowning in Oil." *Harper's Monthly Magazine,* October 1931, pp. 608–17.

Chenery, William L. "Ask the Men Who Know" (editorial). *Collier's,* 28 January 1939, p. 66.

"Coalition Bomb." *Newsweek,* 1 July 1940, pp. 28–29.

331

Cole, Wayne S. "American Entry into World War II: A Historiographical Appraisal." *Mississippi Valley Historical Review* 43 (March 1957):595–617.

Davenport, Walter. "Gland Time in Kansas." *Collier's*, 16 January 1932, pp. 12–13.

Denis, Leon. "Training for the Next War." *Infantry Journal*, May/June 1936, p. 225.

Elibank, Viscount (Arthur C. Murray). "Franklin Roosevelt: Friend of Britain." *Contemporary Review* 187 (June 1955):362–68.

Emerson, William. "Franklin Roosevelt As Commander-in-Chief in World War II." *Military Affairs* 22 (Winter 1958–1959): 181–207.

Evans, Derro. "The Twilight of Minerva Brinkley." *Dallas Times-Herald Sunday Magazine*, 2 September 1973, pp. 4–8.

Finger, John R. "The Post-Gubernatorial Career of Jonathan M. Davis." *Kansas Historical Quarterly* 33 (Summer 1967):156–71.

Fleeson, Doris. "Story behind Marshall Blast by Woodring." *St. Louis Post-Dispatch*, 4 August 1954.

———. "Washington Views 'Our Vital Interest.' " *Independent Woman* 19 (June 1940):162 and 188.

Flynn, John T. "Other People's Money." *New Republic*, 28 October 1936, p. 350.

———. "The President's Foreign Policy." *New Republic*, 28 September 1938, p. 213.

———. "Will the Armaments Industry Save Us?" *New Republic*, 6 December 1939, p. 193.

Freidrich, Ruth. "The Threadbare Thirties." In *Kansas: The First Century*, Vol. 2, ed. John Bright. New York: Lewis Historical Publishing Co., 1956.

"From Private to Secretary of War." *Recruiting News* 18 (November 1936):9.

Grafton, Samuel. "The New Deal Woos the Army." *American Mercury*, December 1934, pp. 436–37.

Haight, John McVickar, Jr. "Roosevelt As Friend of France." *Foreign Affairs* 44 (April 1966):518–26.

"The High Cost of Peace." *Fortune*, February 1939, pp. 40–47.

"The Home of the Harry Woodrings." *Democratic Digest*, April 1935, pp. 5–6.

Hope, Clifford R., Sr. "Kansas in the 1930's." *Kansas Historical Quarterly* 36 (Spring 1970):1–12.

Hornaday, Mary. "Washington Speed-up." *Independent Woman* 19 (July 1940): 199 and 221.

Ickes, Harold. "My Twelve Years with F.D.R." *Saturday Evening Post*, 5 June to 24 July 1948.

Kelley, Robert K. "On a Historic Kansas Hill a Former Secretary of War Finds Peace and Content." *Kansas City Star*, 20 April 1941.

Lawrence, David. "American Business and Businessmen." *Saturday Evening Post*, 26 July 1930, p. 34.

BIBLIOGRAPHY

Liebling, A. J. "Profiles: Chief of Staff: General Marshall." *New Yorker*, 26 October 1940, pp. 26–35.

McCoy, Donald R. "Alfred M. Landon and the Oil Troubles of 1930–1932." *Kansas Historical Quarterly* 31 (Summer 1965):113–37.

McFarland, Keith. "Secretary of War Harry Woodring: Early Career in Kansas." *Kansas Historical Quarterly* 39 (Summer 1973):206–19.

——. "Teacher Political Power, 1932-Style." *Kansas Teacher*, May 1974, pp. 15–16 and 28–29.

"Millions for Defense?" *Christian Century*, 10 February 1937, pp. 175–77.

Mitchell, Jonathan. "How We Can Help Britain." *New Republic*, 1 July 1940, pp. 10–12.

——. "M-Day Man: Louis A. Johnson." *New Republic*, 22 February 1939, pp. 63–65.

Morgenthau, Henry, Jr. "The Morgenthau Diaries." *Collier's*, pts. 1–6, 27 September to 1 November 1947.

"New War Secretary Pacifist Enemy." *Christian Century*, 14 October 1936, p. 1373.

"Our Gallery of Illustrious: Harry Hines Woodring." *Reserve Officer* 10 (May 1933):31.

"Our Much Discussed Export Policy." *United States Air Services* 23 (June 1938):26.

Pinet, Frank L. Editorial in *Kansas Teacher*, October 1932, pp. 50–51.

"The Policy and Status of the United States Army." *Congressional Digest* 17 (March 1938):71–73.

Popper, David H. "American Defense Policies." *Foreign Policy Reports* 15 (1 May 1939):34–38.

——. "The United States Army in Transition." *Foreign Policy Reports* 16 (1 December 1940):214–28.

Reagan, Michael D. "The Helium Controversy." Pp. 43–59 in *American Civil-Military Decisions*, ed. Harold Stein. [University, Ala.]: University of Alabama Press, 1963.

Richmond, Robert W. "Kansas in the Late 1940s." In *Kansas: The First Century*. Vol. 2, ed. John Bright. New York: Lewis Historical Publishing Co., 1956.

Sageser, A. Bower. "Political Patterns of the 1920's." In *Kansas: The First Century*. Vol. 2, ed. John Bright. New York: Lewis Historical Publishing Co., 1956.

"Scandalous Spats." *Time*, 9 October 1939, pp. 16–17.

"Skeleton for Expanding U.S. Army." *Literary Digest*, 8 August 1936, pp. 24–25.

Templar, George. "The Federal Judiciary of Kansas." *Kansas Historical Quarterly* 37 (Spring 1971):1–14.

Tucker, Ray. "Washington Letter." *Living Age*, December 1939, pp. 380–83.

BIBLIOGRAPHY

"War Board's End." *Newsweek*, 9 October 1939, pp. 31–32.

"The War Department." *Fortune*, January 1941, pp. 38–42.

Ward, Paul W. "The Inexcusable Woodring." *Nation*, 29 April 1936, p. 529.

Washburn, G. "The Pro and Con of the Regular Army Reserve." *Our Army* 11 (March 1939):4–5.

West, Dick. "Cabinet Names? One Man's Memory Bank Now Bankrupt." *Dallas Times-Herald*, 13 December 1972.

"Who Controls Our Armed Forces?" *Events*, April 1938, pp. 282–86.

"Who's in the Army Now?" *Fortune*, September 1935, pp. 39–48.

"Will U.S. Mobilize Its Industrial Might in Time?" *Life*, 17 June 1940, p. 84.

"Woodring: A Militant Kansan Wins Temporary Job in Cabinet." *Newsweek*, 3 October 1936, p. 20.

Woodring, Harry H. "The American Army Stands Ready." *Liberty*, 6 January 1934.

———. "Better Planes, Faster Procurement Foreseen." *Army and Navy Journal*, 22 August 1936.

———. "Our Power for Defense." *National Republic*, December 1934, pp. 1–2.

———. "The Perfect Army." *American Legion Magazine*, April 1940, pp. 20–21 and 46–47.

———. "Supply Preparedness." *Army Ordnance* 17 (March/April 1937):263–65.

Yoshpe, Harry B. "Bernard M. Baruch: Civilian Godfather of the Military M-Day Plan." *Military Affairs* 29 (Spring 1965):1–15.

Index

Docking, George E., 252–54
Doherty, Henry L., 50–53, 57, 68, 73, 269 nn. 77, 82
Donavon, William, 226
Doolittle, Dudley, 22, 26, 62
Douglas Airplane Company, 187. *See also* B-12
Douglas Bomber. *See* B-12
Drum, Hugh A., 89, 134, 151–52

Early, Stephen T.: and Woodring's article in *Liberty*, 88; as candidate for Secretary of War, 103; opposes Woodring appointment, 105, 108, 154, 227, 311 n.70; and Woodring-Johnson feud, 147–48; and Chief of Staff, 163; and Woodring's resignation, 230
Edison, Charles, 165, 196, 213, 226, 228, 244, 308 n.18, 312 n.93
Educational orders, 124, 287 n.33
Eggers, Walter, 68
Eighteenth Amendment, 64
Eighth Corps Area, 101
Eightieth Infantry Division, 146
Eisenhower, Dwight D.: at Camp Colt, 10–11, 12; as presidential candidate, 250–51; elected President, 251; and Woodring-Marshall-McCarthy controversy, 251–52, 256; at Woodring's wedding, 279 n.29
Eisenhower Foundation, 252, 254
Eliot, George Fielding, 119
Elk City, Kansas, 2, 5, 7, 9
Embick, Stanley D., 151
Emporia, Kansas, 27, 77
Emporia Gazette, 43
Enlisted Reserve. *See* Regular Army Reserve
Espionage Act of 1917, 178

Faddis, Charles I., 142, 227, 231
Farley, James A.: and FDR's 1932 campaign, 60, 62–66; and appointment for Woodring, 76, 79, 108; and removal of Woodring, 109; and appointment of Johnson, 144, 148; and Edison, 228; opposes third term for FDR, 238; and Woodring's third-party scheme, 242, 244; mentioned, 78, 153, 239, 246, 255
Faulkner, Roy, 32, 72
Fechner, Robert, 84
Federal Emergency Relief Administration (FERA), 80
Finland, 219

First Army Corps, 121
First Christian Church of Elk City and Neodesha, Kansas, 4, 9, 15
First United States Army, 134
Fish, Hamilton, 191
Fitzpatrick, W. S., 48
Flying Fortress. *See* B-17
Flynn, Edward J., 140
Flynn, John, 105
Foreign Affairs Committee: House of Representatives, 193, 240; Senate, 240
Foreign sales: War Department policy on, 176, 179–81; of helium, 181–82. *See also* Anglo-French Purchasing Commission; France: French Air Missions
Fort Dix, New Jersey, 12
Fort Monmouth, New Jersey, 142
Foulois, Benjamin D., 93–98, 281 nn.58, 61
Fourth Division, 121
France: French Air Missions, 182–94; sale of U.S. aircraft to, 189–90, 211–18; attacked by Germany, 205; declares war on Germany, 209. *See also* Anglo-French Purchasing Commission.
Frankfurter, Felix, 228

G-1 (Personnel), 118, 278 n.15
G-2 (Intelligence), 178, 278 n.15
G-3 (Operations and Training), 278 n.15
G-4 (Supply), 118, 219, 222–23, 278 n.15, 289 n.82
Gallup Poll, 130
Garand rifle, M-1, 119, 136
Garner, Elmer J., 70
Garner, John N., 59, 61, 64–65, 238
Garnett, Leslie C., 91–92
General Headquarters Air Force (GHQAF), 98–99, 161
General Staff, 108, 115, 118, 124, 141, 150–51, 161, 167, 170, 174, 198, 200–202, 278 n.15
George, Walter, 244
Germany: attacks Poland, 157, 192, 197, 209; at Munich, 160; superiority of its air power, 164–65; takes over Austria, 182; Woodring warns, 191; and nonaggression pact with Soviet Union, 195; mentioned, 194
Gettysburg, Pennsylvania, 10–12
Giornale d'Italia, 191
Glass, Carter, 238
Glick, George W., 262 n.8

338

Goat gland operations. *See* Brinkley, Dr. John R.

Grand-jury investigation, 88–93, 101. *See also* Silverman, Joseph H., Jr.

"Grandsons of the Wild Jackass" speech, 60

Greenleaf, Jesse, 74

Griffith, Evan, 253

Hagood, Johnson, 100–101, 283 n.84

Hahn, Mary, 3

Hall, Fred, 254

Hamilton, John D. M., 28, 32

Harding, Warren G., 81, 176

Harter, Dow W., 142, 213

Haucke, Frank, 23–25, 27, 30–32, 34, 264 nn. 45, 47

Hawaii, 112, 125, 136

Hawk 75-A, 184

Hays, Kansas, 253

Hayward, O. T., 7–8

Heckworth, Green, 222

Helium, 181–82, 300 n.31

Helium Act, 181

Helium controversy, 181–82, 194

Helvering, Guy T.: business career and early political career of, 25; as chairman of State Democratic Committee (Kansas), 25, 58, 60, 70; as Woodring's campaign manager, 26, 71, 74; supports state income tax, 27; and political appointments, 34; at Woodring's inauguration, 36; as political adviser, 46; as Kansas State Highway Director, 46–47, 58; relationship with Woodring, 59; and support for Roosevelt's nomination and election, 60–62, 65–66, 271 n.16; and 1932 primary, 68; seeks appointment from Roosevelt, 77; mayor of Salina, Kansas, 263 n.37; appointed U.S. Commissioner of Internal Revenue, 276–77 n.115; mentioned, 78, 247

Hemisphere defense, 113, 218

Henry, Merton, 125

Highway Commission (Kansas), 42–43, 46

Highway Department (Kansas), 43, 47

Highway Director (Kansas), 46, 58

Highway Investigation Bill, and veto of, 42–43

Highways (Kansas), 43, 47

Hill, Lister, 108, 143

Hill, Thurman, 49, 72

Hindenburg, 181, 300

Hinkle, Fred, 248

His Lordship's Kindness (Woodring home) 100

Hitler, Adolf, 87, 99, 105, 127, 130, 133, 142, 160, 164, 182, 189, 195. *See also* Germany

Hodges, George H., 262 n.8

Holland, 205

Holt, Theodore P., 82

Holt-Dern ore-reduction system, 82

Hoover, Herbert, 48–49, 62, 81, 83, 176, 254

Hoover Citizens Commission, 254

Hopkins, Harry L.: and secretaryship of War Department, 105, 108, 153; in FDR's "inner circle," 154; in FDR's cabinet, 156; and rearmament plans, 169; mentioned, 80, 145, 165, 228, 238, 311 n.70

House Appropriations Committee and Subcommittee. *See* Appropriations Committee; Appropriations Subcommittee

House Military Affairs Committee. *See* Military Affairs Committee (House)

Howard Walker School of Fine Art, 86

Howat, Worden, 248

Howe, Louis M., 63–64, 66, 78

Hull, Cordell: his opposition to Industrial Mobilization Plan, 123; and Woodring, 153; and neutrality, 175; and helium sales to Germany, 182; and French Air Missions, 188; and aid to Finland, 219; and release of army surplus, 220; mentioned, 146, 178, 183, 243

Hyde Park, New York, 57, 60, 77, 104

Ickes, Harold L.: opposes Woodring as Secretary of War, 105, 227; feuds with Woodring and tries to oust him, 153–59, 294 n.90; and helium controversy, 181–82; champions Bullitt, 226; mentioned, 80, 108, 145, 238, 255

Immediate Action Measures, 196

Income tax amendment, 26–27, 41, 68, 70, 72, 265–66 n.80

Independence, Kansas, 8

Independent Petroleum Association, 47

Independent Voters League of Kansas, 274 n.81

Industrial Mobilization Plan, 113, 122–24, 172

Initial Protective Force (IPF), 125, 130–31, 136, 202

Inland Waterways Corporation, 82

Interdepartmental Committee for Coordination of Foreign and Domestic Purchases. *See* President's Liaison Committee